GV
865
.C6
A65
1984
cop.1

Alexander, Charles
C.

Ty Cobb

DATE	BORROWER'S NAME	
7-84		

TY COBB

TY COBB

Charles C. Alexander

New York
OXFORD UNIVERSITY PRESS
1984

Library of Congress Cataloging in Publication Data

Alexander, Charles C.
  Ty Cobb.
  Bibliography: p.   *Cop 1*
  Includes index.
  1. Cobb, Tyrus Raymond, 1886–1961.   2. Baseball
players—United States—Biography.   I. Title.
GV865.C6A65   1984   796.357′092′4   [B]   83-17409
ISBN 0-19-503414-7

Printing (last digit):   9 8 7 6 5 4 3 2

Printed in the United States of America

FOR
Stephen B. Oates
Warren F. Kimball
John Kibodeaux, Jr.
Thomas H. Smith

Acknowledgments

The staffs of the National Baseball Library at Cooperstown, New York, the Detroit Public Library, and the Historical Society of Pennsylvania in Philadelphia cordially and efficiently made available materials pertaining to Ty Cobb and his career. Ray Rowland, Librarian, Augusta College, assisted me in locating prospective interviewees, as did staff members of the Royston *News Leader*. Special thanks are due the various people in and around Royston, Augusta, and Cornelia, Georgia, who were willing to share with me their time and their recollections and feelings about Ty Cobb. My efforts to secure information from surviving members of Cobb's immediate family, however, were not successful.

The Ohio University Research Committee provided funding for most of my travel costs during my research on Cobb. Warren F. Kimball, Rutgers University/Newark College, and Stephen B. Oates, University of Massachusetts, both old enough friends to impose upon without apology, again brought their critical acumen to bear on my work and again improved it. Eugene C. Murdock of Marietta College, whose recently published biography of Ban Johnson was a big aid to my own study of Cobb, also generously took time to read my manuscript. His masterful knowledge of baseball history saved me a number of embarrassing errors, while his willingness to loan me his personal microfilm holdings of *Sporting Life* saved me months of waiting out interlibrary loan procedures. Finally, my wife JoAnn and my daughter Rachel were my loving and forbearing companions—as always.

Athens, Ohio   C.C.A.
March 1983

Contents

TY COBB

Prologue

Ty Cobb's name remains one of the most memorable in twentieth-century American history, even though he played his last game of major-league baseball long before most people alive in the United States today were born. When Cobb retired at the end of the 1928 season, after twenty-four years in the American League as player, player-manager, and then just player again, he held forty-three different records for batting, base-stealing, and durability as a year-to-year performer. By now most of his numbers have been surpassed, including his season and career base-stealing totals, long thought to be as untouchable as Babe Ruth's homerun marks were once supposed to be. Cobb's one absolutely secure record would appear to be his incredible lifetime batting average of .367.[1]

Yet if Cobb's overall statistics, in a sport obsessed with statistical nuance, seem less imperial than they once did, his reputation as the greatest all-around ballplayer persists for a generation of baseball writers, lorists, and ordinary lovers of the game who could never have seen him in action. And while very few ball-playing or sports-writing contemporaries survive, the generation that knew Cobb first hand has left behind a vast quantity of recollections that give us a vivid sense of how he played the game. The common sentiment in such recollections is that nobody before or since played as Cobb did. "The greatness of Ty Cobb was something that had to be seen," said George Sisler, the brilliant first baseman who contended against him for more than a decade, "and to see him was to remember him forever." In the "swift decisiveness that marked his coups," wrote a New York *World* editorialist in 1926 (when Cobb was making one of his regular threats to retire), "there was infectious, diabolical humor. Cobb, charging home when he was expected to stop at third, seemed to derive such unholy joy at the havoc he caused; and when the catcher had muffed the ball and the trick had succeeded, we, too, crowed with glee to see mind triumphant over matter."[2]

Taking the extra base by going in with spikes high and upsetting basemen or adroitly hook-sliding around stabbing tag attempts, dropping perfect bunts, slapping and pushing the ball by infielders or driving it by and beyond outfielders, playing with a knife wound in his back or with legs raw from sliding on baked ground, quarrelling and often brawling with both opposing players and teammates, as well as with umpires and people inside and outside ballparks—thus Cobb was remembered and is still imagined. "Cobb had that terrific fire, that unbelievable drive," recalled Raymond "Rube" Bressler, another American League contemporary. "His determination was fantastic. I never saw anybody like him. It was *his* base. It was *his* game. *Everything* was his."[3]

Cobb was not as inherently gifted as some other ballplayers. He lacked the sheer grace of Napoleon Lajoie. He was not a natural hitter like Joe Jackson or Rogers Hornsby, nor was he as fast as Clyde Milan or Fritz Maisel, the only men to top him in stolen bases in any of the years from 1911 through 1917. And of course he had nothing like the hitting power of Babe Ruth or of Jimmy Foxx, his teammate on the Philadelphia Athletics at the end of Cobb's career. Yet no ballplayer ever brought together such an amalgam of carefully nurtured talents. Cobb was relentless in his pursuit of excellence. One observer saw him in the light of the twentieth century's approved canon for success, as "literally a self-made man."[4] He drove himself to become the dominant performer of the period before 1920, when "inside baseball," with its stress on hit-and-run plays, base-stealing, bunting, and tight pitching, was supreme. Even when the emergence of Ruth and the advent of homerun-oriented baseball undermined Cobb's style of play in the twenties, he remained for many the best that had ever been or was likely ever to be.

Cobb's genius as a ballplayer, practically everybody agreed, was in his intelligence. As his longtime outfield mate Sam Crawford put it, "He didn't outhit and he didn't outrun them. He outthought them!" "The charm of Ruth," said another enthusiast, "lies in his eye and arm. The charm of Cobb lay in his head. . . . He was a Br'er Fox of the diamond." Folklorist Tristram Coffin has elaborated on that theme. Whereas Ruth, according to Coffin, was a "prowess hero" à la Beowulf or Hercules, Cobb was a "non-comic trickster." Ruth's success depended on the simple and straightforward if heroic exertion of strength, Cobb's on guile, deception, surprise. Thus while Ruth's performance seemed elemental, Cobb might seem to be "a creature without normal motivation, a ballplayer . . . who goes about his business oblivious to the laws and customs of the society in which he lives." Behaving as most of us would like to were we not bound by convention and our own timidity, Cobb both fascinated people and made them uneasy.[5]

In his remarkable autobiography, published a short time after his death in the summer of 1961, Cobb described himself as having been "a boy with a vying nature." "Baseball is a red-blooded sport for red-blooded men," he argued. "It's no pink tea, and mollycoddles had better stay out. It's . . . a struggle for supremacy, a survival of the fittest."[6] Not long after Cobb came into the American League, the philosopher William James called on young men and women to enter organized social service and thereby discover a modern-day "moral equivalent" of warfare. Cobb found his moral equivalent day in and day out on the ballfield.

Cobb's combative temperament, his fierce determination to be the best, helped make him the first millionaire professional athlete well before his retirement. Yet however useful such traits might be on the ballfield, they won Cobb few friends and made him numerous enemies. People who knew him during and after his playing days generally agreed that he was a difficult, extraordinarily complex man. Nearly all of those who played with and under him found him hard to get along with. Cobb was "real nasty" on the field, said the old American League infielder Jimmy Austin, and he could be just as disagreeable out of uniform. Charley Gehringer, whose first season as a regular was Cobb's last as manager of the Detroit Tigers, thought that Cobb's fierceness on the diamond "took a lot out of him as far as being a human being was concerned. You can't turn that kind of competitive drive on and off. He was the same off the field as he was on; he was always fighting with somebody. He was a holy terror." Cobb had a "persecution complex," Sam Crawford believed. "Trouble was," said Davy Jones, another of Cobb's early teammates on the Tigers, "he had such a rotten disposition that it was damn hard to be his friend." According to the testimony of Jones and many others, Cobb absolutely lacked the ability to laugh at himself. Sportswriter Fred Lieb, an acquaintance of fifty years, never managed to discover any warmth or love in Cobb's makeup. Cobb, two baseball historians have written, "was a perfect illustration of the proposition that greatness and goodness are separable—some would say incompatible—qualities."[7]

Actually Ty Cobb was capable of warmth, compassion, kindness, and substantial generosity. Proud of his own towering achievements, he could also take pride in the achievements of others, even of those like Crawford who never liked him. Over the decades he managed to acquire quite a number of friends, although they were mostly non-baseball people and they had to be willing to take him on his own terms. Most of all, Cobb enjoyed manly comradeship, especially with those who shared his passion for hunting wild game. As a young husband and father, he seems to have loved his family; later on he showed that he could be an affectionate grandfather. He also gained a large measure of satisfaction from the various good works he accomplished with his money toward the end of his life.

Yet for all his wealth and fame, Cobb never achieved contentment. In his long retirement he was restless, often irascible, repeatedly involved in unpleasantries both public and private. Ultimately he became estranged from most of his family and many of the people he had considered his friends. Much of the time in his last years he spent being bitter, resentful, and lonely.

Without question the major shaping force in Cobb's youth was his father, whom he adored and very much wanted to please. That man's bizarre and ghastly death, coming just before the eighteen-year-old Cobb left for the major leagues, seems to have infused in him a determination to vindicate his family's name and justify his father's reluctant consent for him to become a ballplayer. The theme of vindication runs throughout Cobb's playing career and nearly his whole life. He seems never to have got over the compulsion to prove himself, maybe most of all to himself.

This book aims, first, to describe Cobb's career as a ballplayer and to indicate his significance for baseball in a period when that sport was truly the "national pastime." Because so much of what people have written about Cobb, including what he had to say about himself, has been drawn from memory, apocrypha and legend surround the man's career. Old baseball men characteristically like to perform as raconteurs, and as such, they strive more for effect than historical accuracy. In that respect Cobb was a typical ex-ballplayer. However valuable his autobiography and other remembrances might be for helping us understand his feelings and motivations, they are not the surest guide to the events of his life. As a professional historian, I have taken pains to check Cobb's and others' memories against contemporary descriptions and the written record wherever possible. Cobb's achievements as they really happened are sufficiently stunning without elaborations that may be artistically interesting but often are factually dubious.

I have wanted to do more than write a book about baseball and a particular ballplayer. A deeply flawed, fascinating personality, Ty Cobb would be a compelling subject even if he had been something besides a celebrated professional athlete. Cobb may not have been the most complicated man ever to play major-league baseball, but with the possible exception of Ted Williams, he was certainly the most complicated man ever to become a great star. Yet in seeking to understand him, I have not tried to function as a psychoanalyst. Others writing about Cobb have tossed around terms like "paranoid" and "psychotic" as if they had real meaning outside a clinical context. For myself, I confess to never having been persuaded that the application of psychoanalytical theory to the study of history, manifested mainly in what has come to be called "psychobiography," has greatly advanced our understanding of people we can know only historically and therefore only fragmentarily. My efforts to explain Cobb's life have relied on common sense, logic, a broader awareness of the history of his times, and, I would hope, an adequate measure of sympathy and compassion.

I

"Don't Come Home a Failure"

The Narrows was the name local custom had given to a scattered group of farms in a valley in extreme northern Banks County, Georgia. In the 1880s the people at The Narrows, maybe fifty in all, got their mail out of Baldwin, although for almost anything they needed to buy they had to make a slow trip of three or four miles by wagon, buggy, or on horseback over the rutted road into Cornelia in Habersham County. Situated in the upper Georgia piedmont just at the edge of the southernmost extension of the Great Smoky Mountains, The Narrows was the proverbial geographical expression, appearing on no maps of northeastern Georgia. Like most of that region, it was a place where people plowed the red soil and were able to raise cotton, corn, and maybe even some wheat, but nothing in enough quantity to make anybody rich.

The most prosperous family at The Narrows was that of Caleb Chitwood. After coming back from the Civil War, in which he had ended up a captain in the beaten Confederate army, Chitwood had settled there and begun to acquire land. Within a decade or so he owned several hundred acres, mostly planted in cotton. It was no plantation and the Chitwoods were far from wealthy, but they were well enough off to have several tenants working on the place. They lived in a roomy white frame house trimmed in carpentered Gothic, by the side of the narrow road that many years later would become U.S. Highway 123.

"Captain" Chitwood was probably one of the main contributors to the fund raised locally each year for the little school that was located near by. Its principal and only full-time teacher was a newly minted graduate of North Georgia Agricultural College, over at Dahlonega, named William Herschel Cobb. Originally from near Murphy in Cherokee County, North Carolina, up in the mountains just over the state line, W. H. Cobb claimed ancestry going back to early Virginia and kinship to the illustrious Georgia Cobbs. Among other notable men, that family had produced Howell Cobb, speaker of the U.S. House

of Representatives, later governor of Georgia and secretary of the treasury in
the Confederate government, and finally a Confederate major-general, as well
as Thomas Reade Rootes Cobb, admired for his published defenses of slavery
before he helped take Georgia out of the Union and draw up the Confederate
states' constitution. As a brigadier general, T. R. R. Cobb had died for the
Confederacy at the battle of Fredericksburg. Actually, whatever relation W. H.
Cobb's people might have had to the Georgia Cobbs was tenuous; at best they
were what Southerners call "potato-patch kin." Among the North Carolina
Cobbs, though, the belief in a distinguished family lineage was persistent.

If not distinguished, the family of John Cobb, W. H. Cobb's father, was
known and respected around Cherokee County. Like most people in the
mountain regions of the South in the period before secession, John Cobb had
despised equally the all-powerful big planters and the slaves they owned. But
unlike many other highland Southerners, he had been willing to go to war on
the side of the Confederacy once North Carolina left the Union. John Cobb
was a farmer who did well enough after the war to give four sons and two
daughters at least parts of a college education. Although he had little formal
schooling himself, the people on the neighboring hills often sought him out to
arbitrate their disputes and even took to calling him "squire."

"Squire" Cobb was especially proud of his son William Herschel, a tall,
good looking, rather bookish young man. Not content with the rudimentary
higher learning he had received at Dahlonega, W. H. Cobb the schoolteacher
continued to read avidly and widely after he left college, most of all in science
and ancient history. He worked on his speech and manners in the approved
fashion of the late-nineteenth century's self-improvement literature; and he
early developed the dignified, punctilious way that impressed people in the
places where he taught around northeastern Georgia. It seemed natural for
his patrons to call him "Professor."

At The Narrows the twenty-year-old Cobb met and fell in love with Caleb
Chitwood's daughter Amanda. The circumstances of their courtship have evidently not been either recorded or remembered. Amanda Chitwood may well
have been a pupil at Cobb's little school. That was a common enough beginning for rural romances a century ago. In any case, the two were married in
the summer of 1883 at the Chitwood house, after the Captain had reluctantly
consented. He had good reason to be reluctant. His daughter was only twelve
years old.

It is possible that the marriage was not consummated for a year or even
longer. Certainly W. H. and Amanda Cobb took more time to start having
children than was usual in that day. Meanwhile "Professor" Cobb moved from
one shakily financed and irregularly functioning rural school to another. Early
in the spring of 1886 his fifteen-year-old wife became pregnant. That fall she

returned to The Narrows to be with her family and await the birth of her first child.

The child, a boy, was born on December 18, 1886. W. H. Cobb had read about the stubborn resistance of the city of Tyre to the besieging armies of Alexander the Great in the fourth century B.C. Thus he hit on Tyrus as a suitable first name for his son. For no particular reason, the infant was given Raymond for a middle name.

Tyrus Raymond Cobb's parents continued to move around for a number of years. W. H. Cobb was a familiar nineteenth-century American type, the itinerant rural schoolmaster. Commerce in Jackson County and Lavonia and Carnesville in Franklin County were among the stops the Professor and his family made. Meanwhile another son, named John Paul, was born in 1888, and four years later a daughter, Florence Leslie.

Finally, the Cobbs moved to Royston, in the southeastern corner of Franklin County, where the Professor took over another school. Although it was still the same red dirt, the topsoil here was thicker than that further north. The countryside, while less picturesque, offered gentler hills and more expanses of cleared fields. In general it was better farming country, better able to support education. Between five and six hundred people lived at Royston. The town extended only a few blocks in any direction, but it was a real town with citizens who seemed interested in promoting the local school. W. H. Cobb had enough students to be able to divide them into primary, intermediate, and high school levels; and most of the time he had one or two teachers working under his direction, although he himself taught the most advanced pupils. He did well enough to buy a nice two-story house near the center of town and subsequently a 100-acre farm not far outside Royston. By the end of the 1890s, with the agricultural depression that had scourged the southern states for more than a decade finally past, the cotton grown on his farm was nicely supplementing his principal's salary.

By then Professor Cobb had become one of Royston's most respected citizens. He and his family regularly attended the local Baptist church. If Cobb's scientific readings gave him any doubts about the literal accuracy of the scriptural truths he heard reiterated every Sunday, he kept those doubts to himself. Neither in little southern towns nor much of anywhere else in turn-of-the-century America was it a good idea for the school principal to let his patrons get the notion that he might be a "free-thinker." At the same time, recollections of W. H. Cobb give no indication that he was a notably pious man. Probably he was an ordinary church-going Christian, content to let participation in Sunday services generally suffice for his weekly obligations to his Maker. Certainly there is no evidence of an especially rigorous religious upbringing in what his older son remembered or would have to say about his own beliefs.

If religious and moral skepticism was not welcome in places like Royston, it was even less advisable to question the prevailing racial consensus. The 1890s and the early twentieth century were the bleakest years that American black people had seen since the war brought them their nominal freedom. Across the American South racial extremism was in sway. Besides perpetrating uncounted acts of violence against black people, militant white supremacists mounted successful campaigns in every southern legislature to undermine constitutional guarantees of black voting rights and to mandate rigid separation of the races in virtually all aspects of social life, from seating accommodations on railways to burial plots in cemeteries. It was a period when the governor of Georgia, Hoke Smith, could propose in all seriousness that the federal government forget about the Fourteenth and Fifteenth amendments and let Georgia rule its blacks as Washington ruled its Indian wards, "placing around them restrictions entirely different from those applied to other men."[1]

Meanwhile the rest of the nation was content to write off Reconstruction—that half-hearted postwar experiment in citizenship for blacks—and let the southern states, where the overwhelming majority of black people lived, deal with "the Negro problem" as they saw fit. The most respected scientific and scholarly opinion of the day reinforced popular racial prejudices, confirmed white people, north and south, in their assumption that blacks, if not unregenerately inferior, were at least so backward that it would take decades and maybe centuries before they could reach the standards of white civilization.

All of which is not to say that Royston, Georgia, was seething with negrophobia in those years. Like most communities in the South, Royston escaped the grisly spectacle of lynching and other major episodes of racial violence. Franklin County was well to the north of the Georgia black belt, where racial tensions were highest; fewer than a fourth of the county's residents were black people. To be sure, Franklin County's blacks were subject to the same array of legal and extralegal restrictions on status and conduct under which blacks lived everywhere in the South. They could not vote, run for public office, or go to school with white people. They were expected to behave themselves and remain "humble," work for what whites wanted to pay them, and do whatever they were told to do. Above all, they were not to get "uppity." But as long as they remembered their "place," then relations between the races could go along fairly smoothly.

At the same time that white southerners and white Americans in general were carrying out their "capitulation to racism," the South's Lost Cause became a matter for almost incessant veneration in the states of the former Confederacy. Throughout the region, in sermons, books, memorial addresses, in the activities of the United Confederate Veterans and the United Daughters of the Confederacy, and in many other ways, the memory of the sacred Cause was kept alive for people of all ages. By the end of the nineteenth century the

Lost Cause had become "a functioning civil religion," one whose adherents looked back to the glories of the Old South and the righteous War for Southern Independence at the same time that they were swept along in the commercial-industrial enthusiasms of the bustling New South.[2] Whatever its contradictions, the religion of the Lost Cause was a potent factor operating on the developing outlook of a youngster growing up in Georgia as the century turned.

For Professor Cobb, his young wife, and their three offspring, the times were comfortable enough and seemed to hold considerable promise. The white men of Royston chose Cobb to be their mayor. Soon he had enough capital to start a small weekly newspaper called the Royston *Record*, which he edited and mostly wrote. With his popular base at Royston and with the numerous acquaintances he had made in teaching stints around the area, Cobb was even able to win election to the state senate. His absorbing concern during the legislative sessions in Atlanta was education. He was in the forefront of the successful push to establish tax-supported county school systems. And when the new state school law went into effect, he was easily elected Franklin County's first school commissioner.

Convinced that education was the key to both social progress and personal advancement, W. H. Cobb kept after his children to get as much as they could from the schooling available at Royston and then look forward to college. He had particularly high hopes for Tyrus, obviously an intelligent boy who might very well become a lawyer or a physician. Yet while he did capably in arithmetic and grammar and even won a couple of prizes in school oratory contests, the boy would not apply himself the way he should, seemed distracted by too many things outside school.

Tyrus Cobb also gave signs of being stubborn, high strung, and quick tempered. In the fifth grade he beat up a fat boy for missing a word in the class spelling bee and thereby giving victory to the girls' team. Not that young Cobb was normally so scrupulous in his own spelling. It was just that the kid had flubbed the boys' chance to win because he hadn't worked hard enough. Joe Cunningham, who lived next door to Tyrus and was his best boyhood friend, sensed that there was something in him that made him different from the other town boys. "You saw it the moment you set eyes on him," Cunningham said many years later. "He just seemed to think quicker and run faster. He was always driving and pushing, even in grade school."[3]

Besides spelling bees, that drive and push found expression in footraces, rock-throwing, tree-climbing, and various other demonstrations of boyish physical prowess. Once young Cobb insisted on walking a tightrope stretched across the street in the center of town. Clearly, he was something of a showoff, but he was also a born competitor, obsessed with winning. "I . . . saw no point in losing, if I could win," was the simple way, as an old man, he expressed what he had felt even as a boy.[4]

Eventually it was baseball that became the main outlet for the boy's competitive energies. As was true in small towns throughout the country, the principal manifestation of Royston's collective existence took place at local baseball games. From the 1890s up to the 1920s baseball was far and away the most popular form of athletic competition in America, and going to baseball games was one of the leading forms of entertainment and recreation. On Saturday afternoons all summer, a big percentage of the white townspeople and even some local blacks (carefully kept off to one side) turned out to see the local aggregation compete against some nearby community's team. They called it town or semipro baseball, because sometimes the team members split a few dollars contributed by their followers. Although such baseball was the source for most of the talent that eventually made it into the major leagues, the older boys and younger men who played for the town teams knew how remote the possibility was that any of them would ever be "discovered" by a professional scout. Mostly they played for the fun of it.

Royston went in for baseball in a bigger way than most places its size. Besides the Royston Reds in their flaming flannels, there was also an organized team for younger boys called the Rompers. A righthanded thrower and lefthanded batter, Tyrus played for the Rompers until he was about fourteen. One Saturday the Reds found themselves without a shortstop for a game with Commerce. Pressed into service, the frail-looking boy handled eight chances without an error and, by holding his hands apart so he could get better leverage on the big bat he had to swing, managed to slap three hits through and over the infield.

Soon after that Bob McCreary, who managed and caught for the Reds, clerked in the local bank, and was the son of one of the town's physicians, talked Tyrus's father into letting the boy go with the team to Elberton, some twenty miles south on a spur of the Southern Railroad, in the heart of the peach country. As a brother in the Masonic Order, McCreary promised Professor Cobb that he would look out for Tyrus, make sure he behaved himself. At Elberton, Tyrus again got three hits, the last one driving in the winning run. Later on that summer, playing center field, he saved a win over Harmony Grove with a diving catch. For that the Royston people showered the field with coins and Tyrus picked up ten or eleven dollars, the first money he ever made playing baseball. And he experienced what it was like to be cheered by a crowd. "Once an athlete feels the peculiar thrill that goes with victory and public praise," he said sixty years later in reminiscing about those early exploits, "he's bewitched. He can never get away from it."[5]

By that time Tyrus had already angered his father by trying to trade some of the Professor's books for a new baseball glove he had seen at the local dry goods store. After the Harmony Grove game, though, he no longer had to make do with the old ragged glove he had sewn together himself. He also ordered pamphlets on "how to sprint" and practiced making quick starts for the next base. Baseball had become the focus of his life, and in the summer he played anywhere and as much as he could when he was not having to sit in Baptist Sunday School, work the fields on his father's farm, or listlessly tend to chores around the house in town.

He even played in North Carolina during warm-weather visits to his relatives there. Although the Cobb children evidently saw little of their Chitwood kin, they made regular trips by train up to see their Cobb grandparents. Tyrus grew very close to his "Grandad Johnny," a feisty, imaginative little man who captivated him with tales of bear-hunting in the mountains and also taught him the finer points of 'coon and 'possum hunting. His grandmother healed his cuts, scrapes, and bites and kept his digestive track cleaned out with an array of mountain remedies, and his Aunt Norah often drove him in her buggy into Murphy or Andrews so he could find some boys to get up a ballgame. Tyrus seems to have had his happiest boyhood times with the North Carolina Cobbs, going there not only in summertime but sometimes during the midwinter school recess as well.

He was there early in January 1902 when he received a letter from his father. In later years he would carry that letter on his person and eventually have it printed. Writing under the letterhead of the Franklin County board of education and signing himself "Yours affectionately, W. H. Cobb," his father commented on the two inches of snow that had just fallen at Royston. He was glad that Tyrus was up in "that picturesque and romantic country" where there was "solitude enough to give nature a chance to be heard in the soul." To see "God's handiwork among those everlasting hills," to hear "the grand oratorios of the winds" and "the rush of her living leaping waters"—all that was a vital part of the education he wanted his son to have. To be truly educated was not just to "master the printed page"; it was also "to catch the message of star, rock, flower, bird, painting and symphony," to have "eyes that really see" and "ears that really hear and an imagination that can construct the perfect from fragment." "Be good and dutiful," he went on, "conquer your anger and wild passions. . . ." Be guided by "the better angel of your nature," not "the demon that lurks in all human blood and [is] ready and anxious and restless to arise and to reign."[6]

"My overwhelming need was to prove myself as a man," wrote Tyrus Cobb many years later about his feelings in his adolescence. Clearly, proving himself meant winning and keeping the approval of the imposing man he called not "Pa" or "Papa" but "Father." For all his rhapsodizings about the education of the soul through contact with nature, W. H. Cobb expected his ballplaying son to master lots of printed pages. Yet the boy simply could not share the ambitions his father had for him. Tyrus was supposed to go to college and eventually enter law or medicine. He might even attend the U.S. Military

Academy and embark on a career as an army officer. But he had to settle down and apply himself, even though the boy was convinced that he "could never match my celebrated father for brains." It was not easy being Professor Cobb's son. Too much was expected of him at school and in the town. Both his scholarship and his conduct were supposed to be exemplary—and neither was. "I felt guilty," he remembered, "that some great, vaulting ambition hadn't seized me beyond handling hard hoppers and line drives."[7]

Tyrus dutifully went with his father to Carnesville, the county seat, so he could meet Colonel W. R. Little, one of the area's foremost lawyers, and browse in the Colonel's law library. But he found the reading to be "dry as hell" and decided right then that the law was not for him.[8] Maybe medicine. He began accompanying Doctor Moss on his travels around the southern part of the county. On one occasion he assisted Moss in removing a bullet from a young black whom a white boy had shot in the stomach. Tyrus administered the chloroform and, at Moss's direction, felt around inside the youth to see if he could find the bullet. When he found nothing, Moss declared that the slug must have missed the intestine and sewed the patient up. Somehow he survived. Tyrus, his hand covered with gore, had discovered that the sight of blood and exposed tissue hardly bothered him at all. Conceivably he could become a surgeon. But try as he might, he simply could not work up much enthusiasm for a life in medicine.

About that time Tyrus had occasion to see plenty of his own blood when he accidentally shot himself in the left shoulder with his .22 rifle. After he got the bleeding stopped, W. H. Cobb jumped on a train with his son and took him the seventy-five miles into Atlanta to see a battery of physicians presumed to be more knowledgeable than the country doctors at home. Although they lacked X-ray equipment, the Atlanta doctors were able to determine that the bullet had apparently bounced off Tyrus's clavicle without breaking any bone and then lodged somewhere in the vicinity. Unable to locate the bullet, they sewed up the boy's shoulder and wished him well. The wound healed nicely and the small slug remained inside Tyrus Cobb's shoulder for the rest of his life.

Being shot seems to have interfered not at all with young Cobb's ripening baseball career. Armed with his own bats made, with help from Joe Cunningham, of prime ash in the same toolshed where Joe's father built coffins for local deceased citizens, Tyrus became the star player on the Royston Reds. Having grown to about 5'10" and 150 wiry-muscled pounds by the time he was sixteen or seventeen, he played both infield and outfield, ran the bases with abandon, and hit whistling line drives. In March 1902 a trip into Atlanta and out to Piedmont Park, where the American League Cleveland Broncos were doing their spring training, heightened his baseball passions. Befriended by Bill Bradley, Cleveland's hard-hitting third baseman, Tyrus took pictures of the players with his little box camera and generally reveled in his first encounter with real professional ballplayers, and big leaguers at that.

Back home, as he later put it, "my father held me down, withholding acceptance of me as the man I yearned to be." School no longer held much interest for the youth, and inasmuch as Professor Cobb thought baseball a waste of time, Tyrus could find no way to please this man who awed, intimidated, and frustrated him, but whom he nonetheless loved deeply. No doubt W. H. Cobb also loved his son, but he seems to have been the kind of person who carefully guarded his emotions and, even with his own wife and children, found it hard to show affection. Sparse with his praise, he was quick and sharp with his criticism. It seemed to Tyrus that try as he might, "I couldn't reach him."[9]

In the spring of 1903 the youth finally did reach his father, for maybe the only time in his life. He threw himself into putting in the cotton crop, plowing and seeding from dawn to nightfall, sweating alongside the black hired hand. As the tender plants began to grow, he discovered a new warmth and intimacy with his father, who started talking with him about their crop, about work mules, about the competition American cotton-producers were increasingly meeting from foreign-grown cotton, about whether they should sell or wait for prices to rise. Tyrus was so enthused by it all that he got a job with a local cotton factor and learned how the cotton was ginned, baled, graded, and moved to market. Everything he learned he discussed with his father, who was pleased that at least his son showed a good head for business. Tyrus Cobb would later think back on 1903 as "a great year in my life," the time when "Professor Cobb 'bought' me as his son. . . ."[10]

Yet despite the new closeness with his son, W. H. Cobb had not changed his mind about the folly of baseball. Tyrus felt guilty about taking a few dollars for playing for a team over in South Carolina, because if word got around that he'd played for money, he would be ineligible for college athletics—if he went to college. For Tyrus that was still an open question. Early in 1904, however, he took a step that was bound to decide the issue once and for all. Despite the surge of love he had for his father, "I still felt that I was being held in some sort of bondage. So I decided I would become a ballplayer and get away."[11]

A local athlete named Van Bagwell had had a tryout in 1903 with Nashville in the Southern League but had not made the team. That winter he told young Cobb that he believed Tyrus had the talent to make it in professional ball. That helped the boy get up his courage secretly to write letters to each of the teams in the South Atlantic ("Sally") League, which had just been formed over the winter as a Class C circuit with franchises in six cities in Georgia, South Carolina, and Florida. He included a little information about himself and asked for a tryout. One reply came back, from Con Strouthers, manager and part-owner of the Augusta Tourists, saying that Cobb could come to spring training if he wished but that he would have to pay his own expenses. A couple of days later a contract arrived specifying a salary of $50 a month—if Tyrus made the team.

Dazzled as he was by the contract and the prospect of a professional career, Tyrus dreaded having to tell his father that he was leaving, and that he needed money for traveling and living expenses until he got his first check. First he revealed his plans to his mother. Amanda Cobb—a kindly enough mother, it seems, but not a major factor in the boy's life—told him to go ahead if he had to, and kept the matter to herself. Tyrus waited to confront his father until the night before he had to report at Augusta. Professor Cobb, whose hopes for the boy had swelled over the past year, responded with a stern lecture that went on for hours. Tyrus, he argued, was at a critical point in his life; what he did now might determine his whole future. He stood a good chance to end up " a mere muscle-worker." Baseball was filled with no-accounts who drank and gambled and ran after lewd women. The boy could not argue, only keep saying, "I just have to go." [12]

At last the man gave up, opened his rolltop desk, and sat down to write out six checks for $15 each, which he gave to his son with the admonition for him to "get it out of your system." [13] Early the next morning Tyrus Cobb, age seventeen, stepped aboard a Southern Railroad car for the journey south to Augusta. Although the trip was only about eighty-five miles by rail, it took nearly all day because Tyrus had to change trains at Elberton and again just across the Savannah River at Calhoun Falls, South Carolina. It was late afternoon by the time he got into Augusta on the Charleston and Western North Carolina.

Augusta, Georgia, in 1904 was a thriving little city of something more than 40,000 inhabitants. Proud of its wide downtown streets, its new trolley line, and its attractive neighborhoods, Augusta was an important nexus of the cotton trade and increasingly noted for textile and iron and steel manufacture. Besides Atlanta, it was the biggest place Cobb had ever been.

The next day Cobb donned his red Royston uniform and took the field at neat little Warren Park, home of the new Tourists. He amazed and amused manager Strouthers and the other players by cutting in front of fielders for ground balls and flies to the outfield, making wild dashes from base to base, and generally going against the accepted procedures of the workouts and intrasquad games. He stood around hoping somebody would let him up to the plate for a few swings, but rarely did the other men, nearly all older than he was and most of them with professional experience, give him a chance to hit. When the Augusta team played the Detroit Tigers of the American League, also training at Augusta, Cobb watched from the bench. Nor did he get into any of the other exhibition games.

When the season started all the Augusta infield positions were occupied by veterans. Strouthers's first baseman was being stubborn about signing his contract, so the manager had to shift his center fielder to first. Inasmuch as there were only fourteen or fifteen men still with the team, Strouthers had no choice but to put the young recruit from Royston in center field on opening day, April 26, 1904, at Warren Park against Columbia. Hitting in seventh place in the lineup, Cobb responded with a single and double in four times up against a pitcher named George Engel and scored two runs. Engel helped himself out with a homerun, and Columbia won the game 8–7.[14]

It was an impressive debut, or so Cobb thought. As it turned out, it was a moment of glory and nothing more. After he went hitless the next day, Strouthers called him into his office and told him that his first baseman had just signed, his center fielder could go back to his position, and he could no longer use Cobb. What the boy had dreaded but had not let himself believe could happen had happened. Now he faced the prospect of going back home to his disapproving father and acknowledging that he had been right, that baseball wasn't really a practicable career, only something he'd had to get out of his system.

Confused and depressed, Cobb wandered back to the little hotel where he had a room. There Thad Hayes, a pitcher from Alabama who had also just got his release, told him about a semipro team over at Anniston, Alabama, being managed by Hayes's friend. That team needed a pitcher and maybe an outfielder as well; Cobb should come along with him to Anniston.

Released outright by Augusta, the boy was thus a free agent who could play wherever he wished. Still, he felt compelled to talk over the matter with his father. At the local telephone office he was astonished and overjoyed when W. H. Cobb told him to take the job at Anniston. But whatever happened, "Don't come home a failure." "In giving me his blessing, his sanction of my quest for success in my hour of defeat, my father put more determination in me than he ever knew. I had the shivers when I hung up." So Cobb described his feelings when he recalled that moment more than a half a century later.[15]

Cobb and Hayes used most of the little money they had left in getting to their new team. Anniston, a smoky mill-town in northeastern Alabama, was a member of a loosely organized outfit called the Tennessee-Alabama League. The league was not officially recognized by professional baseball's ruling National Commission and thus was not part of what was called Organized Baseball. Yet even as an "outlaw league," it was considerably above the level of competition Cobb had known with the Royston Reds.

Playing two or three times a week in towns around northern Alabama and southern Tennessee, Cobb soon was the league's leading batter, according to the rough statistics the various teams kept. Although he may not have been greatly affected by Baptist Sunday School back in Royston, he did intend to live rigorously by one Biblical injunction: Put not thy light under a bushel. Playing for Anniston was fun, and at $65 a month plus free room and board, he was doing a lot better financially than if he had managed to stay with Augusta. Sooner or later, though, he had to get back into Organized Baseball.

Grantland Rice, the sports editor of the Atlanta *Journal*, began receiving regular communications from Alabama attesting to the sensational exploits of the young outfielder Cobb. Written in a variety of cursive styles and signed with names like "Jones," "Brown," and "Smith," the letters and postcards continued to come until Rice finally wrote in his column that "over in Alabama there's a young fellow named Cobb who seems to be showing an unusual amount of talent."[16] Not until many years later, when Cobb told him about it, did Rice learn that it was really Cobb who had sent all those notices touting his ballplaying talents. Nor did Cobb himself learn until after his father's death that W. H. Cobb had clipped Rice's column and carried it around to show his friends in Royston and Atlanta.

After about three months with Anniston, Cobb received a telegram from the Augusta club inviting him to rejoin the team. By that time the Tennessee-Alabama League was about ready to collapse anyway. In Augusta, Con Strouthers had sold his interest in the club and resigned as manager, giving way to catcher Andy Roth. Cobb first made sure that Strouthers, for whom he had vowed never to play again, was really gone, then hustled back to the Tourists. He reappeared in the lineup on August 9, again against Columbia. His return to the Sally League proved less than triumphal. Playing all the outfield positions at one time or another, Cobb appeared in thirty-five games during the remainder of the season and finished with an uninspiring .237 batting average, thirty-third among some 50 to 55 regular players in a league that had only one .300 hitter.

Back in Royston for the offseason, Cobb could bask in the adulation of his friends. His father remained unimpressed, even when Cobb banked the $200 he had saved and showed no signs of having lost his virtue during the summer away from home. Again it was necessary for him to work hard at the Cobb farm, this time sowing the winter wheat crop, before his father warmed up and was again willing to offer praise for something he had done.

Otherwise Cobb tramped the woods, sometimes hunting but mostly just staying outdoors as much as he could, and wondered about his future. It was just possible that he might not be good enough to go very far in baseball. He gave some thought to enrolling at the University of Georgia to start the long years of study that would lead to his becoming a surgeon. That would please his father. Over the winter, though, he got an inquiry from Andy Roth about whether he planned to play for Augusta again in 1905. The eighteen-year-old veteran of less than a third of a season in Organized Baseball wrote back saying that he had to have $90 a month. Remarkably, Roth and President John

B. Carter agreed to Cobb's terms, and the youth prepared to give baseball another try.

Cobb had grown another inch and put on a few more pounds since the previous spring, and he was faster than ever. More determined, too. In 1905 the Detroit Tigers again trained at Augusta, having agreed with the Augusta owners to return in exchange for first claim on whatever players Detroit liked on the local team. When Bill Armour, the new manager of the Tigers, showed up at Warren Park for the first time, second baseman Herman "Germany" Schaefer greeted him with an account of the wild antics of a kid on the Augusta team named Cobb. According to Schaefer, Cobb wanted to steal a base on every pitch, tried to take two bases on singles, even tried to go from first to third base on bunts. "He's the craziest ballplayer I ever saw," said Schaefer.[17]

Yet the Tigers soon began to take the kid seriously. In the two exhibition games Augusta played with Detroit, Cobb rapped a single off Bill Donovan, one of the Tigers' aces, another off Jesse Stovall, and a single and triple off Eddie Cicotte, a Detroit semipro star the Tigers had signed and subsequently decided to leave with Augusta.

Cobb started the season as the lead-off hitter and regular left fielder for Augusta. His hitting was mediocre in the early going, and his erratic base-running and outfield play dismayed his manager. He also got on Roth's nerves by complaining that the team lacked discipline, that it was, in the baseball parlance of the day, a "joy club." Cobb himself soon "fell into the spirit of things. I was fast losing my ambition to go higher in the game."[18] At one point Roth wanted to sell his troublesome young outfielder to Charleston for a token $25, but the owners thought otherwise and Cobb stayed.

By mid-July the Tourists had lost fifteen of their last twenty games and were drifting in fourth place in the six-team league. Not that they lacked talent. Besides Cobb, the Augusta roster included three other future major leaguers: Cicotte, who pitched two no-hit games that year; Nap Rucker from Crabapple, Georgia, who roomed with Cobb on the road and pitched a no-hitter of his own; and infielder Clyde Engle. But it was not a good ball club. Roth finally turned over the team to outfielder and team captain George Leidy, although Roth stayed on as first-string catcher.

Soon after Leidy took over, Cobb, in a game at Savannah with his team leading 2–0, took his position in the outfield eating a bag of popcorn or peanuts (accounts vary). As he munched away, a fly ball soared in his direction. Trying to hold onto his snack at the same time that he pursued the ball, Cobb missed making the catch and a run scored. Although Augusta went on to win the game, manager Leidy was not amused by Cobb's gaffe. What followed that night was a scene that might well have been lifted from one of the period's books of boys' fiction, wherein a well-meaning but irresponsible lad is straightened out by the wise counsel of an older man—father, minister, employer, or whatever. In this case it was George Leidy.

A journeyman minor leaguer whose main ambition now was to have a few successful years as a manager, Leidy asked Cobb to ride with him on the trolley line out to a local amusement park. As they rode and later as they strolled around the park, Leidy talked quietly but earnestly, telling Cobb that he had to stop fooling around, that he had a lot of ability and a great future in baseball if he worked hard to make the most of his talents. He went on to describe life in the big leagues—traveling in comfortable Pullman cars, staying in fine hotels in big cities, eating good food, wearing expensive clothes, gaining fame and success. On other nights as well—while they ate together, took in vaudeville shows, or just sat on hotel porches—Leidy continued to boost Cobb's confidence and determination. Completely won over, Cobb promised henceforth to become the best ballplayer he could possibly be.

In the mornings at the ballpark Leidy worked with Cobb, teaching him the intricacies of the hit and run, the delayed steal, hitting to the opposite field, and above all the art of bunting. Hour after hour Leidy threw to him and Cobb bunted at an old sweater placed to either side of homeplate. He worked on sacrifice bunts, on drag bunts, on faking bunts and slapping the ball past third basemen. And in the games in the afternoons, Leidy let Cobb do what he wanted at bat and on the base paths, confident that with what he had learned, the kid would usually do the right thing.

Within a short time Cobb had become the outstanding player in the Sally League. His team continued to flounder, but at the end of July the baseball tabloid *Sporting Life* could report that "Cyrus Cobb" was the first in the league that season to make 100 base hits. The club's owners raised his salary to $125 a month. Meanwhile scouts from Detroit and other big league teams as well as Indianapolis of the American Association turned up regularly at Augusta's games. Henry "Heinie" Youngman from the Tigers sat on the bench with Cobb one day and questioned him about his background. The Macon first baseman told him he had heard Cobb was about to go up. Now it seemed only a matter of time until Cobb could notify his father that he had made it into the big time and was on his way to the kind of rewards and recognition his father had envisioned for him in more traditional endeavors. For a few days during a home stand he happily hosted his seventeen-year-old brother Paul, a good semipro ballplayer himself, who had come to watch Cobb in action.

Early on the morning of August 9, 1905—"the blackest of days," he later termed it—Cobb received a telegram in Augusta from Royston. His father had been killed in some kind of shooting incident. Cobb agonized through the slow, zigzag train trip back to Royston. Tired, bewildered, desolated, he arrived to hear a story of unbelievable horror. His mother, they told him, had shot his father.[19]

What he probably was not told—at least not to his face—was that for some time it had been common gossip in Royston that Professor Cobb's pretty wife had taken a lover. The gossip must eventually have got around to W. H. Cobb. On Tuesday evening, August 8, he had told his wife he was going out to the farm for a couple of days, hitched his horse to his buggy, and left the house. Paul and Florence were staying with friends. Later that night Amanda Cobb went upstairs to the room over the front porch she shared with her husband, locked the windows (even though the temperature had been in the nineties that day and it was still warm and humid), and went to bed. A little later W. H. Cobb was seen alone on foot in town. Shortly after midnight Amanda Cobb was awakened by a noise on the porch roof. A figure she could not make out was struggling to raise one of the windows to her bedroom. Grabbing the loaded double-barreled shotgun that always stood in a corner of the room, she pointed it toward the window and fired once. After what witnesses later described as a considerable interval, she fired again. Approaching the shattered window, she peered into the darkness to find her husband lying in a widening pool of blood.

At the Cunningham house next door, Joe Cunningham heard the blasts and ran over to see what had happened. There he found, as he described it to his daughter many years later, "the worst thing I ever saw." [20] Although Professor Cobb was still breathing, he had a gaping hole in his abdomen and one of the shotgun blasts had literally blown his brains out. The young man ran to get Dr. H. F. McCreary, who pronounced W. H. Cobb dead at 1:30 a.m. He found a revolver in Cobb's coat pocket.

The next day a coroner's jury heard Amanda Cobb give her account of the shooting and others testify about what they had heard and seen. By the end of the day the coroner's jury had ordered Amanda Cobb's arrest on a charge of voluntary manslaughter. W. H. Cobb's funeral was held on August 11 at the Cobb house, where people crowded in and overflowed the front yard and into the street. He was buried at the local cemetery in a coffin built by Joe Cunningham's father, with the Professor's Masonic brothers officiating at the gravesite. The day after that the county sheriff arrested Amanda Cobb, and the local justice of the peace set her bond at $7000. She was quickly able to post the ten percent of the bond necessary to keep herself from having to spend any time in jail. By the end of the month a grand jury sitting at Carnesville had returned an indictment against her. Her trial was to take place that fall.

Tyrus Cobb left no account of what he felt and did in Royston during that dreadful time. He did spend four days after the funeral with his mother, brother, and sister. That he was able to get himself together in fairly short order and resume his baseball duties suggests a great deal about the young man's will, concentration, and above all his continuing drive to confirm his father's trust. Now, though, it was also a matter of upholding the family's reputation at a time when scandal and suspicion hung over it. The best way to do that was to achieve such success as a ballplayer that people would have to respect the Cobb name and especially his father's memory.

Cobb rejoined his team on Wednesday, August 16, at Augusta, where the previous week the local newspaper had tactfully reported his father's death. Against the Charleston Sea Gulls he made two hits in the first game of a doubleheader but went hitless in the second game. By that time George Leidy was out as manager of the Tourists and Andy Roth was in again. Whoever managed Augusta no longer much concerned Cobb, though, because three days after he got back he received formal notification from Charles D. Carr, now club president, that he had been sold to the Detroit Tigers and was to report to that team by the end of the month.

By August the second-division Tigers were plagued by an accumulation of disabling injuries and down to three outfielders, one of whom, the veteran Duff Cooley, was hobbling on one good leg. Club secretary Frank J. Navin and Manager Bill Armour had to pick up somebody to help the team finish out the season, and the club's finances would not permit the purchase of a player from the upper minor leagues. So Augusta, at the bottom of the minors and where Detroit already had an option to buy whichever player it wanted, was the logical place to turn. Good reports had reached Detroit on infielder Clyde Engle, who could also help out in the outfield. But Bill Byron, a native Detroiter umpiring in the Sally League (en route to a notable career in the National League), told Heinie Youngman that Cobb had greater promise. In Detroit, Bill Donovan, whom Cobb had impressed in spring training, told Armour basically the same thing. So for $700—the price agreed to in the spring for the player Detroit chose, plus $200 thrown in because he was being taken before the season was over—Cobb, still four months short of his nineteenth birthday, became a big leaguer. "I only thought," he later said, "Father won't know it."[21]

Cobb played his last game for Augusta on August 25 before a fine Friday crowd of about 1400, against league-leading Macon. His solid hitting and dashing style on the bases and afield had captivated the local "bugs," as baseball fans were called in those days; and when he came to bat in the bottom of the first inning, a group of them met him at homeplate with a bouquet of flowers and a gold watch. He stammered his thanks, shook hands all around, waved to the crowd, finally got into the batter's box, and struck out. Subsequently he singled twice, stole a base, and threw out a runner as the Tourists took another defeat, 5–0. Cobb's final-game performance gave him more than forty stolen bases (third in the league) and, with the Sally League season ending in a few days, ensured him the batting championship at .326. Taking chances in the field, however, had been costly. His thirteen errors gave him the lowest fielding average among outfielders appearing in more than a hundred games.

As would often be the case in his baseball career, Cobb both won the admiration of the paying customers and left a sour taste in the mouths of the club management. Just before he left Augusta, he groused to local sportswriters that he should have got part of his purchase price and that in fact he'd been ill treated all season, being kept at the bottom of the salary scale on the team. Whether or not his complaints were justified, one could well understand his ill temper. Although his big-league adventure awaited him in Detroit, he still had to go by Royston on his way north and, however briefly, again be a part of the mess at home.

Cobb was on his way to Detroit in earnest by Saturday night, the 26th, traveling at the Augusta club's expense. The trip of some 700 miles should have taken about thirty hours, but Cobb missed his connections in Atlanta and Cincinnati. Exhausted and bedraggled, he finally arrived about 10:30 p.m. on Tuesday after being en route from Augusta for something like four days. Carrying his Augusta uniform roll, a small grip, his little Spalding fielder's glove, and three bats in a cloth bag, he alighted from the train at the Michigan Central terminal in Detroit and looked around at "what for me was an unknown land."[22] Nobody was there to meet him. Hiring a horse-drawn cab, he had the driver take him to a cheap hotel that turned out to contain a burlesque house as well, near the Tiger ballpark. There he paid $10 in advance for a week's worth of room and board.

Meanwhile notices about his purchase had appeared on the sports pages of the Detroit papers, giving sketchy facts about his background and indicating that his arrival was imminent. On August 27 the Detroit *Free Press* printed a photograph of Cobb in street clothes. It showed a thin-faced young man with a slightly hooked nose, somewhat jugged ears, small but intense blue-gray eyes, and a full head of finely textured, reddish-blond hair parted in the middle. Three days later Joe S. Jackson, chief baseball writer for the *Free Press*, remarked that all those on the Detroit team who had observed Cobb in the spring had been impressed by his speed, and that Bill Byron thought he was one of the fastest men leaving the batter's box he'd ever seen. Noting that Cobb had led the Sally League in hitting, Jackson added, "He won't pile up anything like that in this league. . . . If he gets away with a .275 mark he will be satisfying everybody."[23] That same day Tyrus Raymond Cobb played in his first game in the major leagues. There would be 3,032 more.

II

The World He Entered

The world of major-league baseball that Cobb entered in 1905 was much like what baseball fans would know seventy-five years later. The game itself would undergo fewer changes in its rules and regulations than any other leading spectator sport. A late-twentieth-century fan who by some feat of magic found himself sitting in a ballpark in 1905 would easily understand and relate to virtually everything happening on the playing field. Yet if that fan followed the day-to-day performances of players and teams, paid attention to such matters as equipment, field conditions, and umpiring, and familiarized himself with the sport's organization and financial structure and its general ambience, then he would discover striking differences between early century baseball and the sport and business as they later developed. Those differences are sufficient to make the years roughly 1900 to 1920 a distinct era in baseball history, one in which baseball had clearly changed from what it had been earlier but lacked major features associated with the sport from the 1920s on.

Major-league baseball's geography and demography were relatively compact in 1905. Each league consisted of eight teams, with eleven of the sixteen teams located in five metropolitan areas. Only Detroit, Cleveland, and Washington in the American League, and Cincinnati and Pittsburgh in the National, were one-team cities. During a half-century of remarkable stability (1903–53), the sixteen franchises remained intact. Throughout that period (and until 1958), the westernmost city in the majors was St. Louis, and travel from city to city by railway continued to be practicable and efficient.

After 1903 (and until 1961) both leagues played 154-game seasons, with each team meeting each of its adversaries twenty-two times, eleven at home, eleven away. Often disturbed by the weather, the symmetry in that arrangement also had to take into account the fact that in the early years of the century baseball games and a variety of other entertainments were strictly prohibited on Sunday under state laws and local ordinances in seven of the eleven

major-league cities. When Cobb broke in, Sunday baseball was legal only in
Chicago, St. Louis, and Cincinnati, and it was common practice for teams
playing in the east to make a one-day hop back to a western city for a Sunday
game. In the early years of the century the Tigers even played a few Sunday
games in Columbus, Ohio. Despite the gradual lifting of the Sunday bans,
Sabbatarianism proved persistent. It was not until 1919 that Sunday ball was
legal in New York, not until the late twenties in Massachusetts and the early
thirties in Pennsylvania.

The owners of the early 1900s assumed that they ought to be able to run
their franchises like baronial fiefs. At least that was the view in the National
League, which since its formation in 1876 had featured weak presidents and
fiercely independent club executives. The American League, on the other hand,
operated under the autocratic regime of Byron Bancroft "Ban" Johnson, who
had started out as an Ohio newspaperman and gone on almost singlehandedly
to create the American League as a rival to the National. Johnson administered his outfit with what seemed like smooth efficiency compared with the
squabbling that went on in the Senior Circuit. After the American League assumed major-league status in 1901, the vain, imperious Johnson dominated
not only its operations but also baseball's governing body. The National Commission was a three-man board in which the presidents of the two leagues plus
chairman August "Garry" Herrmann, president of the Cincinnati club, nomi-
nally shared authority. But with the support of his good friend Herrmann,
Johnson nearly always had his way on matters affecting baseball as a whole.

Within the American League, Frank Navin, secretary and subsequently
president of the Detroit ball club, was one of Johnson's most consistent back-
ers. As player and later as player-manager, Cobb would repeatedly clash with
Navin and would have more than his share of run-ins with Johnson. Two of
the stronger wills and bigger egos in baseball history confronted each other
when Cobb and Johnson were at odds.

One of the problems that Navin, Herrmann, and the other club executives
had to worry about was the threat of fire in their wooden ballparks. That threat
was heightened when they tried to accommodate the big crowds that showed
up most commonly on Saturday afternoons, and on Sundays as well where games
could be held. In 1905 the top seating capacity of any ballpark in the major
leagues was only about 18,000. Pennant-contending clubs frequently had
overflows of thousands of people; in fact the usual way of figuring a park's capacity was to include the estimated number that could sit and stand behind
ropes around the outfield, down the foul lines, and even behind homeplate,
supposedly without disrupting play. Lacking the capital or willingness to pay
for sizable increases in seating, owners favored keeping outfield fences set far
away from homeplate, at least from right-center field around to left-center, so
they could continue to sell as many 25¢ standing-room tickets as possible after

all the seats had been taken. In 1907 Navin had the fences at Detroit's Bennett Park set back still farther to take care of the crowds anticipated for a big series with the Philadelphia Athletics. Such practices helped make possible steady increases in total major-league attendance—from some 3.5 million in 1902 to 4.5 million the next year and to more than five million for each of the next five years.

To control the behavior of the "bugs," owners made arrangements for regular police to be on duty or hired special police, but of course the ultimate responsibility for keeping crowds from interfering with the game itself rested with the umpires. That was often literally a frightening task. Spectator rowdiness was still a characteristic feature of baseball in the early 1900s, as it had been for decades. Not only were beer and sometimes wine sold inside the parks but those beverages—as well as soft drinks—were sold in glasses and bottles that made handy projectiles.

Riots and near-riots were fairly common occurrences. Only a week before Cobb arrived in Detroit, for example, umpire Jack Sheridan forfeited a game to Washington when, enraged that he had allowed the visitors a run on an interference call in the eleventh inning, the crowd of about 1200 Detroit partisans stormed the veteran official and forced him to take refuge in the clubhouse in center field. On opening day 1907 an overflow crowd of 17,000 swarmed the old wooden Polo Grounds in New York, got out of control late in the game, and caused umpire Bill Klem to declare a forfeit to the Philadelphia Phillies. In August of that same year a teenage spectator in St Louis threw a pop bottle at Billy Evans, a fine young umpire serving his second year in the American League, and gave him a severe concussion. Evans was unconscious for several hours and barely escaped with his life.

If umpiring in professional baseball had always been a hard way to make a living, then it should be added that the umpires' circumstances had improved some since the 1880s and 1890s. That was especially true in the American League, where Ban Johnson personally hired his game officials, generally paid them more than their National League counterparts, and vigorously backed up their authority with fines and suspensions for abusive players and managers.

Even so, the overall quality of umpiring when Cobb broke into the major leagues and for some time thereafter was well below what fans would later take for granted. The umpires' frequently dubious and sometimes outrageous calls explain much of the chronic unruliness of participants and spectators. There were no umpiring schools; umpires learned their trade on the job in the minors, and some had yet to master it when they got to the big time. Then, too, a handful of them had to share all the umpiring chores. As late as 1908 each major league had only six umpires. Inasmuch as it was the practice to keep

one man in reserve, then on a full day of four games per league, three umpires in each league would have to work their games alone.

No matter how shrewd and skilled that one man might be, he could not
possibly be in good position for all or even most of the plays. The procedure
was for a lone umpire to remain back of homeplate until a runner got on first
base, then take his position behind the pitcher to call balls and strikes. If the
runner advanced to second or third, he went behind the catcher again, on the
principle that it was best to be there for a possible play at the plate. The hardest play to call, Billy Evans thought, was a double steal attempt, which necessitated trying to watch the action at two bases simultaneously. Despite its
obvious insufficiency, league and club officials were long content with mostly
one-umpire baseball. Not until 1909, moreover, were they willing to have more
than two umpires work World Series games.[1]

In one respect, however, the early century umpires did an excellent job.
To enable as many people as possible to get to the ballpark after work, clubs
waited until 3:00 or 3:30 to start single games. The umpires had to keep the
players hustling, especially in the spring and late summer, to get games finished before dusk. Their efforts, together with the tendency of managers in
that era to make less use of relief pitchers and pinch hitters and in general not
to overmanage, kept the length of most nine-inning games well under two hours.

In those days it would have been hard for managers to do much manipu-
lating of pinch hitters and pitchers anyway, because they had fewer players to
manipulate than would be the case within ten years or so. In 1905 major-league
rosters averaged fifteen to seventeen men from the May cutdown deadline until
September, when expanded squads were permitted so minor leaguers could
be tried out. Thus for most of the season a team would carry four outfielders,
four or five infielders, two catchers, and only five or six pitchers. Obviously
when a pitcher started a game he was expected to go the distance. Even the
non-starting pitchers on a team were not relievers per se, but rather second
liners brought in when a game seemed lost.

Yet by the early 1900s those small pitching staffs were the dominant ele-
ment in the game of baseball. In 1893 a strong surge of batting had followed
the lengthening of the distance between pitcher and homeplate to 60'6", and
in the century's first years the temporary dilution of talent accompanying the
emergence of a second major league caused a milder hitting outbreak. Before
long, though, the pitchers regained the upper hand they would continue to
hold until the 1920s. In the year Cobb came into the American League, for
example, the pennant-winning Philadelphia Athletics topped the league with
617 runs scored, and the second-place Chicago White Sox allowed opponents
only 443 runs. The composite earned-run average for American League pitchers was 2.64. In 1905 a total of 219 shutouts and nearly 2000 complete games

were pitched in the two major leagues. Seventeen pitchers won at least twenty games; Christy Mathewson in the National League won thirty-two. American League teams had a composite batting average of .241; National Leaguers .255. And the sixteen teams hit a grand total of 337 homeruns, most of them inside-the-park blows.

Two basic factors explain the pitchers' dominance in that period: the ball in use and an almost complete absence of restrictions on what they could do with it. The Spalding Sporting Goods Company enjoyed a monopoly on balls supplied to the major leagues (although the balls were manufactured under different labels). Under their stitched horsehide covers, the Spalding balls had solid rubber cores around which woolen yarn was wound. Because the yarn was not wound as tightly as it would be possible to do later on and because the rubber core was not as resilient as the cork-rubber center introduced in 1911, the early century balls simply did not carry well. Moreover, the parsimonious owners of the period insisted that as few balls as possible be used, so that only when one was hit out of the park or otherwise rendered unusable was a new ball put into play. One of the main duties of the attendants or police stationed around the park was to retrieve foul balls from spectators and return them to the field. Bill Klem recalled that when he began umpiring in the National League in 1905, the home team supplied him with three new balls at the start of each game. If they became lost or damaged beyond any possible use, then he got one more ball, not necessarily a new one. "So strange things happened once the local ball club got one run in front," said Klem. "Out would come old discolored balls."[2]

Besides the natural abrasions and discolorations balls acquired by being knocked and thrown around, pitchers wreaked their own ingenious havoc. One widely favored method was to "load up" the ball with the superabundance of saliva produced by chewing tobacco, licorice, or slippery elm. Introduced around 1903, the spit ball quickly became a standard and perfectly legal part of many pitchers' repertoires. Others preferred to scuff the ball against their belt buckles, rub it with an emery board, or even, in the case of Clark Griffith when he was pitcher-manager for the Chicago and New York American Leaguers, pound it against their spikes. Although deliberate mutilation was supposed to be illegal, umpires rarely did anything about such assaults on the horsehide.

Fundamentally a pitchers' game, early century baseball thus became a matter of scrambling to get a few runs by any means and then relying on tight pitching to hold the lead. Moving runners into scoring position—by a stolen base, a well-placed bunt, or a properly executed hit-and-run play—became the preeminent consideration in offensive strategy. Batters stood close to the plate, choked up several inches on their heavy, thick-handled bats, and tried to hit the ball not to the fences but between the fielders. "I hit 'em where they ain't," said little Willie Keeler, the game's finest batter at the turn of the century, thereby giving baseball one of its most enduring axioms.

Besides being skilled at bunting and working the hit-and-run, good ball-players were also supposed to be able to run well—to take an extra base on a hit to the outfield or steal a base in almost any situation. Although Cobb be-came the most spectacular base-runner of them all, base-stealing was a central feature of the game long before he came on the scene. Between 1903 and 1914, total stolen bases in the two major leagues averaged close to 3000 a year. Part of the explanation for the frequency with which runners were able to steal was that many pitchers never developed much expertise at holding runners on base. A bigger factor, though, was that catchers characteristically took their posi-tions a foot or two farther back of the plate than they would a couple of de-cades later. Although the shallower crouch they used probably helped them get off a throw somewhat quicker than the low-squatting receivers of a later period, the slightly greater distance they had to throw, particularly to second base, would give runners an edge they no longer had once catchers moved forward a little, as they had done by the 1920s.

Of course one could hardly blame the oldtime catchers for positioning themselves a bit farther from the bat, inasmuch as the masks and chest pads they wore were less effective than those developed later and their knees and shins lacked any protection at all. One of the more astonishing facts about baseball in the early part of this century is that catchers were able to endure foul tips and hard-sliding runners without shin guards. As early as 1905 catcher J. J. "Nig" Clarke in the American League had the idea of wearing soccer guards underneath his uniform socks, but not until opening day, 1907, in New York (the same game Bill Klem ordered forfeited because the crowd was out of con-trol) did Roger Bresnahan of the Giants introduce shin guards. Bresnahan's white "cricket leg guards," a New York writer thought, "were rather pictur-esque, in spite of their clumsiness."[3] For several more years, however, most veteran catchers resisted Bresnahan's much-needed innovation.

If catching equipment was primitive by later standards, that of infielders and outfielders was equally so. Therein lies the major reason for the numer-ous errors that show up in early century boxscores and season statistics. Field-ers' gloves were flimsy little devices that did little more than absorb the ball's impact until a player could trap it with his bare hand. Sometimes a man made a spectacular one-handed catch; more often the ball popped out of or off his glove. Scorekeepers were not notably lenient in that period, so that a ball a fielder actually got in his glove but failed to hold usually went down as an error. Bad throws, which were also frequent, often resulted from the slipper-iness or partially mutilated character of the ball. Infield and outfield condi-tions provide a third reason for the high number of errors in Cobb's day, especially during his early years in the majors. Unlike the well-manicured and contoured playing fields of a later generation, even big-league fields early in the century characteristically had rocks, ridges, and holes that often produced strange bounces. Over the years a gradual reduction in errors accompanied improvements in gloves and playing surfaces and, after 1920, curbs on ball-tampering. Throughout Cobb's career, however, fielding remained more problematical then it became in later decades.

Although it offered few homeruns or high-scoring contests, the closely played, tightly pitched game of the early 1900s was enormously popular everywhere in the United States and delivered profits to most major-league franchises. Not yet though to the Detroit Baseball and Amusement Company. The federal census of 1900 put the population of Detroit at a little under 286,000. The only smaller city in the majors was Washington. Ban Johnson had reluctantly kept Detroit when he reorganized and upgraded his American League in 1901, and little had happened since then to convince him that the city would consistently support big-league baseball. Three second-division finishes in a row before 1905 and a mediocre showing through most of that season thoroughly soured many Detroiters on the Tigers. For 1905 Detroit ended up last in attendance in the American League with 193,364 and outdrew only the dreary Boston National Leaguers. Detroit offered "big league baseball to bush league crowds," complained a local sportswriter that summer, while a visiting Boston scribe predicted that if any further shifting of franchises took place, "it is a clinch bet that Detroit will be wiped off the major league map."[4]

The owner and president of the Detroit ball club was William H. Yawkey, a young multimillionaire and a considerable playboy, who spent much of his time in New York and left the running of the franchise to Frank Navin, the tight-fisted club secretary. Tall and corpulent, almost totally bald although he was only in his mid-thirties, Navin was a colorless, taciturn man who viewed the world impassively behind his horn-rimmed spectacles. His appearance and manner prompted some of the Tiger ballplayers to call him "the Chinaman"—behind his back.

Navin pinched as many pennies as he could, with the result that he had one of the lowest payrolls in the big leagues. To be sure, nobody anywhere was drawing down a huge amount of money. In 1906 Bobby Wallace, the veteran shortstop of the St. Louis Browns, was the highest-salaried player in the majors at $6500 annually. Navin, though, seems to been exceptionally zealous in holding down costs. He was convinced, for example, that Sam Crawford, his top player, was worth no more than $2700 for 1905, and he urged Crawford to accept his "very liberal offer" and "treat the Club right." At the same time manager Bill Armour wrote outfielder Matty McIntyre that all the other Detroit players "seem to realize that the club has been a losing proposition for a number of years, and are willing to accept a reasonable reduction." To

Bobby Lowe, a utility infielder-outfielder nearing the end of a long and frequently illustrious career, Navin maintained that $1800 for 1905 was "the very best we will do." That sum, incidentally, was also as much as Navin paid himself for four years.[5]

Navin may or may not have realized it, but the Tiger franchise was potentially one of the best in the majors. Detroit was in the midst of a boom that by 1910 would push its population to some 466,000, a rate of growth exceeded only by Atlanta among major American cities. The country's thirteenth biggest city in 1900, Detroit would be its ninth biggest ten years later. Detroit's economic base, built on inland shipping, especially of lumber and iron ore from northern Michigan, and on the manufacture of railroad cars and wheels, stoves, shoes, pharmaceuticals, and tobacco products, took on a potent new ingredient in the early 1900s—automobiles.

Possessing readily available local capital and an abundance of inventors and engineers who also turned out to be first-rate businessmen, the area around Detroit had become by 1910 the automotive center of the United States. Within a few months after Cobb came to Detroit, the Ford Motor Company got so far behind in filling orders at its Highland Park plant that for a while it had to stop taking them. Like the other auto manufacturers in and around Detroit, Henry Ford had chronic labor shortages. In 1908, after several years of experimenting with cars of various sizes and prices, Ford inaugurated production on the Model T, which he marketed for as little as $825, within the reach of millions of middle-income Americans. The next year William C. Durant organized Buick, Oldsmobile, Cadillac, and various other automakers into General Motors, with a capitalization of $10 million and stock that sold for $24 a share.

Tyrus Cobb, awakening in Detroit on the morning of August 30, 1905, could not have known much about the dynamic forces at work in the city he had finally reached the previous night. Nor had he had a chance to learn much about the people of the place that would be his part-time home for the next twenty-one years. Donning his one change of underwear, a fresh shirt and collar, and the rumpled suit he had worn for days on his way north, he had his breakfast and went out onto Detroit's wide cedar-block streets. As he walked he was surrounded by the din of factory and locomotive whistles, clanging trolley bells, clattering wagons, carts, and buggies, peddlers' cries, occasional chugging automobiles. He must have been surprised by the variety of accents he heard. Instead of the soft, slurry southern speech he was used to, everywhere there was the nasal burr of the upper Middle West, the brogue of Irishmen, the guttural sounds of German. It was a city in which one-third of the population was foreign-born, mostly people from the British Isles, Germany, and Canada. Three-fourths of Detroit's inhabitants had at least one foreign-born parent.

On the other hand, the new arrival from Georgia would have seen few black people, certainly not the huge numbers of blacks one encountered in Atlanta and in Augusta and the other deep South towns where he had played. According to the 1900 census, only about 5000 blacks—less than 2 percent of the population—lived in Detroit. The great tide of black immigration, drawn north mainly by the lure of jobs in the expanding auto plants, would not hit the area until after 1910.

Bennett Park, where the Tigers played, was located in the Eighth Ward, an area called Corktown because the Irish population was concentrated there. The park was named after Charley Bennett, the star catcher for Detroit's champions in the old National League in the late 1880s, who had lost a leg in a train accident. Early in the afternoon Cobb found himself at the ballpark, bounded by Michigan, Trumbull, and National avenues and a planing mill that fronted on Cherry Street. It was a rickety little place even by the standards of the wooden facilities of the time. The smallest park in the major leagues, it could seat about 8500 in a long grandstand running down the third-base line, a lower and shorter pavilion extending about two-thirds of the way from homeplate toward the right-field corner, and long, shallow bleachers in right-field. Standing just outside the left-center-field fence on the planing mill property were jerry-built "wildcat bleachers," in which people could sit for 5¢ to 15¢, depending on the importance of the game being played. The playing field left much to be desired. The park had been built just a few years earlier over a cobblestone surface left over from the time when the place had been a haymarket. Cobblestones still poked through the dirt and grass here and there and, as Cobb would soon discover, were responsible for frequent bad-bounce base hits.

Bennett Park nonetheless looked huge and palatial to the rookie up from the Sally League. A groundskeeper pointed out the little clubhouse in the far corner of center field. The Tiger dressing room was the only one in the place inasmuch as at Bennett Park, as at all the other major-league parks at the time, no dressing facilities existed for visiting teams. Visitors put on their uniforms at their hotels and, following a practice that club executives thought offered good advertising for that day's game, rode in open horse-drawn buses through the streets to the ballparks. They returned the same way. It never seemed to bother anyone except the visiting players that along the route unruly "bugs" jeered and sometimes hurled vegetables or rocks at them.

Cobb introduced himself to Bill Armour, a small, dapper man in his mid-forties with a full mustache who managed in street clothes, including a sporty straw boater. Armour gave him his contract to sign. Although it called for a season's salary of $1500, Cobb would get paid for only the last month of the season. Then he he got into his uniform, white flannels with black stockings and white cap with black bill and trim. He turned up the black uniform collar (and would continue to wear it that way, in hot weather and cold, until a decade later when the Tigers became the last team in the big leagues to abandon collars). Proudly rubbing the black gothic "D" on his left shirtfront, Cobb thought the uniform "the most beautiful thing I'd ever seen."[6]

In the dressing room and on the field the accents were again unfamiliar. Most of the men Cobb had played with down south had been from that region. On this team, he learned, he was the only southerner and indeed one of the few in the big leagues at that early date. With a few exceptions his teammates were from the Northeast and Middle West. Maybe two-thirds of them were of Irish ancestry, and Roman Catholics at that. As a southerner he had had little contact with Catholics; as a boy raised in the southern Baptist faith he shared a long Reformationist Protestant tradition of suspicion if not outright hostility toward the Church of Rome, whether or not that bias was an active part of his thinking. Even though they were all native-born Americans and all ballplayers, Cobb's background—and of course his youth—immediately made him an oddity on the club.

Before the game that afternoon, Armour sat with Cobb on the open bench (as yet there were no dugouts at Bennett Park) and inquired about his ballplaying down south. The manager told him that he was down to two healthy outfielders before Cobb arrived and that he was going to start him in center field against Clark Griffith's New York Highlanders. The pitcher he would face would be Jack Chesbro, a rugged spitballer who had won a herculean forty-one games the previous year and was having another good season in 1905.[7] Armour tried to reassure his eighteen-year-old recruit that all he had to do was just stay calm and play his usual game; this was the big leagues, but he could do the job.

Cobb hit fifth in the lineup. With about 1200 people in the stands that Wednesday, the Tigers got something going on Chesbro in the bottom half of the first inning. Left-fielder Matty McIntyre led off with a double, and Christian "Pinky" Lindsay, the Tiger first baseman, singled him home. Lindsay went to second on a sacrifice bunt by Germany Schaefer and took third on Sam Crawford's tap back to Chesbro. While Crawford was up, Cobb drew some attention to himself on deck by swinging three bats at once, a practice he had started back in semipro ball to make the bat he hit with feel lighter. To his teammates, though, it must have looked like showing off.

Cobb positioned himself at the plate in a shallow crouch, with his feet about a foot apart, knees slightly bent, the bat held well away from his body, and with his hands about three inches apart. Yet if he still gripped the bat the same way he had at fourteen, playing for the first time with the big boys, he had long since taken to sliding either of his hands up or down as the pitch came in, and then whipping his bat—34 inches long and weighing 38 to 40 ounches—with either a slightly or fully choked grip. And whip it he did. After missing Chesbro's high first pitch and taking a curve strike, he hit a waist-high fast ball into the gap in left-center field and beat center-fielder Frank Hahn's throw to second base as Lindsay trotted home.

That was the only hit Cobb got that day, although he walked the next time up and was out on the tailend of a double steal attempt. He also handled two fly balls unerringly in center field. Throughout the game, which the Tigers won 5–3 behind stout George Mullin, Cobb watched the others closely. He learned what big-league caliber play was really like. "I'd never dreamed that men could field and hit so wonderfully," he recalled. "Such speed, class, style, speedy maneuvering, lightning thinking! . . . And they went at it with a red-eyed determination I couldn't believe."[8] Schaefer knocked over Norman "Kid" Elberfeld when the grizzled Highlander shortstop tried to block Shaefer on the base path, while rookie Frank Delahanty of New York ended the season for himself by tearing ankle tendons sliding into third. Bill Coughlan, Detroit's third baseman and captain, remonstrated so violently with Francis "Silk" O'Loughlin, the lone umpire, that O'Loughlin thumbed him out of the game. Cobb understood that he had reached a level where the competitors were older, smarter, tougher, and more skilled than anything he had known.

The next day Cobb was again in center field, flanked by McIntyre in left and Crawford in right. He got two singles in four times up off Jack Powell of New York, as good-natured Bill Donovan shut out the Highlanders 5-0. Kid Elberfeld officially welcomed Cobb to the big time after his first hit. Trying for a steal of second base, Cobb undertook a head-first slide, only to have catcher John "Red" Kleinow's throw beat him for the second day in a row. As he tagged the rookie, Elberfeld stuck his knee in Cobb's neck and ground his face in the dirt. With a scraped and dirty nose, Cobb got off the field as fast as he could. Armour and several of the Tigers kidded him about what was then considered a bush-league slide, and after that Cobb rarely went into a base head first.

Cobb had no part in the scoring in that game. In fact in the seventh inning he again demonstrated what a raw rookie he was when, trying to score on a single to center field, he ran through the hold-up sign given by Coughlan at third and was thrown out by several feet. The mild-mannered Armour and the veterans on the team could only shake their heads.

After he joined the ball club, Cobb started all forty-one games that remained on the Tiger schedule. Inasmuch as he hit only .240 (36 for 150), he could hardly have been the catalyst behind the Tigers' surge in the last month of the season. Yet surge they did, winning twenty-seven of their last forty-one games to move from sixth place and edge Boston for third.

Cobb's play was uneven. Sometimes he was brilliant, sometimes bumbling, sometimes foolhardy. In the second game of a Labor Day doubleheader against the pennant-contending Chicago White Sox before some 7500, the biggest crowd in Detroit since opening day, Cobb killed a rally by making a one-handed, over-the-shoulder catch in center on John "Jiggs" Donohue's drive. Later he threw out Donohue as he tried to go from first to third on a single. Returning to the bench, Cobb heard his first sustained ovation in the major leagues and had to doff his cap to the crowd several times.

Then the next day, in the nightcap of another doubleheader that saw the Tigers sweep the White Sox and badly damage their pennant hopes, Cobb infuriated McIntyre and almost cost his team the game when he cut in front of the left fielder and caused him to drop a fly ball. In Washington a couple of weeks later Cobb—"yet a nubbin," as a local sportswriter termed him—dropped three flies in two games, and Armour had him switch positions with McIntyre.[9]

Against Cleveland at Bennett Park, though, Cobb won a game in the ninth inning from Addie Joss, one of the finest pitchers in baseball until meningitis took his life in 1911. The rookie got an infield single (his second hit off Joss), was sacrificed to second, and dashed all the way home on McIntyre's bounder, which the second baseman knocked down. Cobb slid past Nig Clarke's tag to give the Tigers an even won-lost record for the first time since early in the season. His first homerun in the majors came nine days later at Washington. In the opener of a Saturday doubleheader loss, Cobb dropped a fly ball into the right-field corner and, as the ball bounded away from "Honest John" Anderson, circled the bases behind Schaefer and Crawford.

Raw and unpredictable though he might be, Cobb impressed those who watched him play. Paul Bruske of the Detroit *Times*, who wrote a weekly report on the Tigers for the tabloid *Sporting Life*, described him as "an infant prodigy" and "a sensational fielder and thrower." In view of the youth's heavy family responsibilities since his father's death, Bruske thought it "really wonderful that he is able to keep his gait at all." B. F. Wright, the *Sporting News's* Detroit correspondent, had "a half-formed belief that he will be a hummer," even though "at present he is a bit too fast for the good of the team. He is not content to catch the flys that go to his territory, but wants to get those that go to left and right."[10]

Detroit ended the season at Cleveland on October 7, with Mullin winning his twenty-second game, 7–1. Cobb finished on a high note, singling twice off Bill Bernhard in four at bats. He showed he was learning how to play in the big leagues when he slammed into tiny Bill Barbeau at second base and enabled Crawford to score as the ball dribbled into the outfield. That win gave the Tigers third place, their best finish since 1901.

Cobb's play occasionally exasperated the rest of the Tigers, but in 1905 he encountered little overt hostility from the team, except from McIntyre, who apparently disliked him almost from the beginning. Bill Donovan was fairly friendly, and Bobby Lowe and his wife had him to dinner. In later years Cobb said that when he first broke in, manager Armour "appeared to take a friendly interest in my progress and he helped me a lot."[11] Mostly, though, his team-mates just ignored him, which was the usual practice with rookies. None of them seems to have known or cared much about his family's ordeal down in Georgia. The full extent of the trouble, specifically that Amanda Cobb would have to stand trial for killing her husband, apparently was not known in Detroit at that time.

After the Tigers closed the season in Cleveland, Navin and President Yawkey gave a supper for the team to celebrate its strong finish. Yawkey presented a diamond-studded emblem to Armour and predicted an even better season in 1906. Plenty of champagne was on hand, and inasmuch as only Donovan and catcher Lou Drill were reported to have turned their glasses down, it is likely that Cobb tasted his first champagne on that occasion. The world was rapidly widening for the boy who, by his own account, neither cursed, drank liquor, nor used tobacco when he came to Detroit.

Cobb picked up $60 to $70 from two games the Tigers played with Detroit-area semipro teams right after they got back from Cleveland. It was common practice to stage such games, with the players dividing the proceeds among themselves and at least making enough to pay expenses home. By October 10 Cobb was on his way back south. He was a boy with five weeks of experience in the big leagues, with some proud and some embarrassing memories, and ahead of him a struggle to make the team next spring. He would have to start contributing substantially to his mother's and sister's support, although his brother Paul could be expected to take care of himself. Cobb's biggest worry, though, was whether his mother would be able to keep from going to prison.

III

"The Most Miserable and Humiliating Experience"

The offseason months in 1905–06 must have been a bad time for the young ballplayer and just about everybody else connected with the family of the late William Herschel Cobb. As soon as he arrived at Royston, Tyrus Cobb learned that his mother's trial, originally scheduled to be held that fall in the superior court for the Western Circuit of Georgia, had been postponed until the next term of the court the following spring because no circuit judge was available. Amanda Cobb's attorneys, of whom she had hired no fewer than five, would have plenty of time to prepare her defense, but the delay in hearing the case would mean protracted and heavy costs.

Cobb's baseball outlook was highly uncertain. His showing with the Tigers had been mediocre at best. Besides hitting only .240, he had managed but two stolen bases and fielded erratically. The Tigers had released Duff Cooley, but Bill Armour had made it clear that the popular Jimmy Barrett, who had badly injured his knee early in the season, would again be the regular center-fielder if his knee held up the next spring. Then, too, the Tigers had bought another fast outfielder named Davy Jones, who had earlier played with Chicago in the National League and in 1905 had hit .348 in the tough American Association. If Barrett came back, or even if he didn't, either Cobb, Jones, or Matty McIntyre would have to sit on the bench. Reporter Paul Bruske might think that Cobb had made such a hit with the Detroit crowds that "there will be an awful howl if he is allowed to go."[1] As he passed his nineteenth birthday, however, Cobb understood that the club might end up with no place for him.

In January, Cobb received his contract for 1906 and was cheered by Armour's accompanying letter. According to Armour, the salary specified, $1500, was $300 more than he and Cobb had talked about before Cobb left for home. The manager and Frank Navin had discussed Cobb's prospects, Armour explained, and had "decided to do our part to make everything satisfactory to you." Armour hoped Cobb would be able to get his family affairs tended to so he could concentrate on baseball. He cautioned Cobb not to think about quitting the game. That would be "very foolish" because "you have a bright future in front of you if I am any judge of a ballplayer."[2]

Later, after receiving Cobb's signed contract, Armour wrote to urge him to report on time at Augusta, where the Tigers would again do their spring training, "as there are a few points in the game I am anxious for you to get next to." Still later he wrote that he was glad to hear Cobb had been working on his bunting, "as you will find that it will be a lot of good to you." What Armour did not say was that over the winter various teams had contacted Navin about buying Cobb, including Toronto in the Eastern League. To Ed Barrow, the new manager at Toronto, Navin reported that the Tigers had decided "to keep Cobb at least until Barrett comes along."[3]

To bring in a little extra money and maybe also to get away from the house that was still too full of memories of his father, Cobb took a job coaching the team at the prep school the University of Georgia operated at Stone Mountain, east of Atlanta. Armour had earlier said no when Cobb asked whether he could do some coaching before spring training, but Cobb went ahead anyway and moved over to Stone Mountain late in February. When Armour and twelve team members came through Atlanta en route from Detroit to Augusta, Cobb met them at the train station and, on the plea of the school principal, got Armour's consent to stay with the prep schoolers a couple of more days before reporting at Augusta.

On March 9 Cobb checked into the Albion Hotel, the Tigers' headquarters at Augusta, and soon was in uniform and working out at Warren Park. Despite his worries over family and career, his appetite had not suffered over the winter. He had grown another inch and gained fifteen or twenty pounds. At 6 feet and 170 pounds, he was now one of the biggest men on the team. Yet he was already in superb condition and just as fast as he had been when the Tigers looked him over a year earlier. So noted the Detroit writers, who in their dispatches back home still usually referred to him as "Tyrus Cobb." But now they sometimes called him "Ty," as did Armour and a few of his teammates. Joe H. Jackson of the *Free Press* even provided a nickname that would stay with him from that time on—"the Georgia Peach."[4]

As it turned out, Cobb was going to need not just his strength and size but as much mental toughness as he could possibly marshal to endure the agonies that awaited him. What began in Augusta that spring and continued throughout the season of 1906 and on into the next year amounted to "the most miserable and humiliating experience I've ever been through."[5]

Cobb became convinced at the time and remained so for the rest of his life that a clique on the ball club, led by Matty McIntyre, had undertaken to drive him off the team. Cobb attributed the harassment visited on him by McIntyre and his pals to their determination to secure McIntyre's starting berth in the outfield and keep Cobb out of the lineup. In his mid-twenties and starting his fourth year in the American League, the stocky, dark-featured, curly-haired McIntyre had a good arm and covered a lot of ground but was only a fair hitter. Although Jimmy Barrett's knee would not heal and the Tigers soon sold him to Cincinnati, McIntyre, Davy Jones, and Cobb remained in competition for two positions, the other outfield post being conceded to Sam Crawford. McIntyre and his roommate, lefthander Ed Killian (who had matched George Mullin's twenty-two wins in 1905), had no use for Cobb and evidently believed Jones was a sounder ballplayer anyway than the unpredictable Georgian. Crawford and various others on the team also seem to have developed a dislike for Cobb, and either joined in the harassment or looked on approvingly.

Yet it is hard to tell whether the animosity, petty cruelty, and eventual ostracism Cobb experienced in 1906 represented a deliberate effort to get rid of him or simply the usual treatment given rookies, magnified and intensified because of the way Cobb reacted to that treatment. Certainly it was the custom in that day to give newcomers something of a hard time. Most took it, patiently if not good naturedly, and the hazing was soon over. "We weren't cannibals or heathens," Crawford said many years later. "We were all ballplayers together, trying to get along." Cobb, thought Crawford, "came up with an antagonistic attitude, which in his mind turned any little razzing into a life-or-death struggle. He always figured everybody was ganging up on him. He came up from the South, you know, and he was still fighting the Civil War. As far as he was concerned, we were all damn Yankees before he even met us."[6]

Cobb, to be sure, was an extraordinarily sensitive, highstrung, and headstrong young man. Raised to be serious and intense in his purposes, he had a great deal to prove—to the father he had lost, to relatives and friends who wondered why he didn't stay at home and fulfill his new responsibilities as head of the family, to those back in Royston who still whispered about the circumstances of his father's death, to the people in Augusta who had cheered him last year but had doubts whether he could stick in the big leagues, to his Detroit teammates who'd laughed at his rawness and misplays the previous season, to just about everybody, it seemed. On top of everything else, his mother's trial was coming up. Her attorneys were confident that she would be acquitted, but how could anybody be certain what a jury might do?

With all that on his mind that March, the last thing Cobb needed was the kind of abuse that began not long after he reported for spring training. He may as well have been starting out with Augusta two years earlier for all the batting practice the "regulars" allowed him to take. He found it difficult to get into the one bathroom on the floor occupied by the team at the hotel, because

McIntyre and Killian and others they egged on repeatedly locked him out and kept him waiting, chilled and livid, wrapped in a towel or bedsheet. When he finished his dinner, usually eaten alone, and went to retrieve the hat he had hung on a rack, he found the crown ripped out. As he sat in a Pullman car on the team's exhibition-game jaunts, he would be hit on the back of the head by soggy wadded-up newspapers. Finally he found his precious ash bats, turned on Joe Cunningham's father's lathe, all sawed in two.

Cobb cursed his tormentors, using words his father had told him only ignorant and uncouth men would use. They were all a bunch of cowardly Yankees, he stormed, not men enough to stand up and fight him. Manager Armour simply ignored what was happening, apparently on the assumption that it was better for his players to work things out among themselves. Bill Donovan gave Cobb some encouragement, and Davy Jones, an articulate law school graduate from Wisconsin and subsequently a licensed pharmacist, sometimes sat and talked with him on the train rides, trying to understand this short-tempered, suspicious young southerner. Jones soon discovered that Cobb had little sense of humor about anything, least of all about himself. Lonely, bitter, no longer trusting anybody, Cobb started carrying a pistol and sleeping with it close at hand. "I was just a mild-mannered Sunday School boy," he said many years later about that period. "But those oldtimers turned me into a snarling wildcat."[7]

After Crawford ended a mild holdout, signed for $3000, and reported in mid-March, the Detroit sportswriters all assumed that Jones would play center field while Cobb, at least for the time being, would be the extra outfielder. Armour had him on the bench for the first exhibition game against the Brooklyn Superbas, but the next day he played center field, led off with a triple off the Superbas' Mal Eason, later bunted safely, and scored two runs. At Charleston, however, he was twice thrown out at home by the Sally League team's rookie center fielder.

Late on Friday afternoon, March 30, after a game with Augusta at Warren Park, Cobb boarded the train for Lavonia, where his mother's trial had begun a couple of hours earlier. Although Carnesville was the Franklin County seat, the work under way there on a new courthouse had necessitated holding the trial at Lavonia in the northeastern part of the county. Cobb left Augusta with the understanding that he would rejoin the team next week at Birmingham.

The trial must have been an odd one. The testimony for the defense consisted wholly of Amanda Cobb's recounting how she had been awakened by the noise of someone trying to get into her bedroom through the window and, terrified, had fired the shotgun to protect herself and her home. Solicitor General S. J. Tribble, leading the state's four-man prosecution team, questioned her closely and at great length about the interval between the two shotgun blasts and other ambiguities but apparently stayed away from the issue of infidelity. Cobb made his way through the crowd jammed into the courtroom and took a seat near the front just as the cross-examination was ending.

At eight the next morning the defense and prosecution summations got under way. Late that afternoon the case went to the jury, and after about an hour of deliberation, the all-male jurors returned a verdict of not guilty on the charge of voluntary manslaughter. Cobb went to the local telegraph office and wired Armour in Augusta about the outcome of the trial, reaffirming his intention to be back with the team shortly. At least that ordeal was out of the way; in the eyes of the law his family's name was again free of suspicion.

After spending a few days with his mother and sister in Royston and then accompanying his brother on the train to Atlanta, where freshman Paul was playing baseball for Georgia Tech and sometimes attending classes, Cobb caught up with the Tigers at Birmingham. Once again he showed his peculiar ability to concentrate on his game and shut out everything else, getting three hits against the local Southern League team. In two subsequent games in Cincinnati, he hit and ran the bases well and clinched his place on the team, though not as a starter.

As if he had not had enough troubles so far that spring, now Cobb developed an acute case of tonsilitis. Afraid to tell Armour lest he give the manager an excuse to get rid of him, Cobb suffered on the way north to Cincinnati and then through the games he played there. By the time the team stopped in Toledo for a couple of more exhibition dates, he was running a pretty high fever and had to go directly to bed. Swallowing had become so painful that he was trying to live on bread and milk. The next morning, with genial Germany Schaefer accompanying him, he found the hotel physician. Without anesthetic, proper surgical equipment, or much of anything else, the man went ahead anyway, cheerfully cutting away at Cobb's grossly swollen tonsils. Periodically, when the hemorrhaging in his throat threatened to suffocate him, Cobb would ask to be let up to rest a while. Exhausted and semi-conscious, he leaned on Schaefer to get back to his room so he could collapse. The next morning, though, he was in the physician's chair for more unanesthetized cutting and bleeding. A gory third session took place the morning after that, following which Cobb caught a train to Columbus, where he played seven innings and got a hit as the Tigers beat the American Association team. With the resiliency of a youth in prime health, he soon recovered from the butchery visited on him in that hotel in Toledo. About a year later he learned that the physician had been committed to an asylum for the insane.

When the Tigers opened the 1906 American League season at Bennett Park before a record Detroit crowd of nearly 14,000, Davy Jones was in center field and Cobb was on the bench. There he stayed until the Tigers' fifth game on April 21, when he finished the day at Chicago in right field after Crawford hurt his leg. The next day he again played for Crawford at St. Louis in the Browns' home opener, going hitless but scoring a run and executing a neat sacrifice bunt. Inasmuch as Crawford proved unable to do much more than limp to the plate for pinch-hitting assignments for the next week or so, Cobb stayed in right, trying with a fierce intensity to make the most of his break. Overanxious and still deficient in important areas of his game, he did the wrong thing too often to suit Armour. After he booted a ground single and let in a run at St. Louis, the stylish manager had Crawford hit for him, the first of three times Cobb would give way to pinch hitters that year. The next day, before rain stopped an eight-inning tie with Cleveland, Cobb had his first two-hit game of the year, off Addie Joss, but also got mixed up with Jones on Joss's fly and let it fall for a double.

Cobb continued to hit, though, and so frequently that, when Crawford was ready to play again, Armour put Cobb in center and benched Jones. The Georgian was plainly weak against lefthanders, but he slammed righthanders as well as anybody in the league. All those hours working with George Leidy back in Augusta the previous summer were paying off in various ways, most of all in making Cobb the best bunter on the Tiger ball club and maybe the best hit-and-run batter as well. Armour moved him up to the lead-off spot in the batting order to take advantage of his speed. By mid-May B. F. Wright was describing Cobb as "a beardless boy of 20 [sic] who is making good with a rush," while *Sporting Life*'s weekly American League notes termed him "the most timely hitter of the Detroit club." After he made a running, juggling, over-the-head catch to save a game at the Huntington Avenue Grounds in Boston and then won it with a two-run double in the ninth, the *Free Press*'s reporter announced that the "boy baseballist" had won his job as a regular.[8]

At bat, his problems with lefthanders continued. On Memorial Day, before a good crowd at Bennett Park, Chicago's Guy "Doc" White, a fine curve-balling lefty as well as a licensed dentist, struck out Cobb three straight times. Armour finally sent up catcher Fred Payne to hit for Cobb. On and off the field, moreover, his troubles with McIntyre and other teammates persisted. The two outfielders refused to get together on flies hit into left-center, so that several balls dropped in for needless base hits. Armour first tried benching Cobb, but with the youngster leading the team in hitting, that obviously was not sound strategy. He then put Cobb in left and benched McIntyre, finally suspending him for a few games for "indifferent work."

Armour was tired of the feuding on the ball club, mainly that between Cobb and McIntyre and "McIntyre's bosom friend," Ed Killian. According to B. F. Wright in the *Sporting News*, McIntyre had "owned up that he hated Cobb and wouldn't play with him." With Cobb on base, McIntyre made little effort to hit the ball. An opposing team's catcher told Wright that on one such occasion McIntyre had said to him, "You don't suppose I'm going to help that

————————do you?" At the same time, commented Wright, "Cobb is young and aggressive, and doubtless wears a large hat." McIntyre announced to Armour that he wanted to be traded; Armour's reply was that he would play for Detroit or nobody.[9]

Cobb had no real friends on the ball club. Edgar Willett, a handsome and promising rookie pitcher from Virginia, moved in with him for a while at the little hotel where he had lived the previous year. According to Cobb, "the high-living McIntyre crowd" told Willett that either he had to stop being friendly with Cobb or he was "finished." Cobb tried to talk his fellow southerner into staying, arguing that McIntyre and friends only wanted to "make a beer-drinker out of you, like them." But Willett moved out and Cobb was again by himself.[10]

In Detroit and on road trips, Cobb roomed alone, mostly ate alone, and found ways to kill time alone before and after games. He spent many hours wandering through museums and art galleries, browsing in public libraries, and seeing the historic sights in the various American League cities, particularly Boston, New York, and Washington. Raised around books and by a father whose education, if sketchy, was still far better than that of most people in his day, Cobb naturally found reading one way to occupy himself. Biographies and histories and popularly written books on science were his favorite fare. He early developed a fascination with the lives of Julius Caesar and Napoleon, indomitable figures who had imposed their will on the events of their times, and with the fading pseudoscience of phrenology, which taught that the contours of the skull provided the key to understanding a person's character and the degree of his intelligence.

A salary of $1500, drawn from the beginning of May until the middle of October, allowed for little lavish indulgence, especially since part of it had to be sent home every two-week pay period. Still, Detroit and the cities the team traveled to offered an abundant variety of inexpensive restaurants and places where one could find entertainment. The well-brought-up young man generally stayed away from saloons and pool halls. On Sundays, though, there were band concerts at lovely Belle Isle Park in the Detroit River and at night the attraction of a dozen professional theaters where one could see everything from Shakespeare to tawdry melodrama, as well as vaudeville acts ranging from the four Cohans (featuring young George M.) to the breath-taking escape tricks of Harry Houdini. A local cigar-store owner gave Cobb passes to the concerts at the Detroit Opera House, and there the boy from the Georgia hills first heard Beethoven, Brahms, Tchaikovsky, Chopin. Cobb even took ballroom dancing lessons, thereby putting still more distance between himself and his Baptist upbringing.

But most of all he spent his off-the-field time thinking baseball. On long walks and alone in his room, he plotted, calculated, and connived ways to make himself a better ballplayer. Cobb realized that he had to charge balls hit to him on the ground and not wait for them to reach him, that he could get greater momentum behind his throws if he ran up to catch flies instead of camping directly under them. It occurred to him that by watching a third baseman's eyes as he prepared to take a throw from the outfield and twisting his own body accordingly, he could get in the path of the ball, deflect it with his back, and maybe come all the way home. If, on a bunt fielded by the third baseman, that infielder couldn't get back to cover the base and the shortstop was slow coming over, then he could probably go from first to third on the bunt. If he waited until an outfielder raised his arm to throw to one base, he might be able to make it to another bag before the outfielder could straighten himself out and throw where Cobb was going. In general, if he could make the fielders throw the ball, the advantage became his. As the baserunner he was on the attack; he had the initiative; they were the ones likely to make a mistake.

He also figured out how to hit lefthanders. Finally he understood that his basic mistake had been in standing in the middle of the batter's box, so that he had insufficient time to gauge a lefthander's curve as it broke. By standing on the back line of the box, he would give himself a fraction of a second longer to get his bat in motion, and by closing his stance and shortening his swing, he could punch hits into left field.

It worked, not right away in every case but eventually with practically all lefties. Although he never "owned" Doc White, he did hit the part-time dentist for a respectable .278 average in the twenty-six games he played against him over eight years. Against Eddie Plank, the Philadelphia Athletics' great lefty, Cobb hit nearly .300 in thirty-three career confrontations, and he topped .300 in twelve appearances against the brilliant madcap, George Edward "Rube" Waddell. Later on Dutch Leonard and Babe Ruth of Boston yielded hits to Cobb at .375 and .326 rates, respectively.

Over the first half of 1906 the Tigers stayed well above .500, even though tensions remained high on the club. Germany Schaefer's zany antics, such as appearing at second base in a rain slicker during a drizzle at Cleveland and sliding into every base after he pinch hit a homerun out of the park at Chicago, did little to mitigate an assortment of hostilities. Besides the unabating feud between Cobb and McIntyre and Killian, Killian had grievances against the Detroit management for not paying him enough and against his teammates for poor support in the field and at bat. Early in August he came to Bennett Park drunk, took a bat and partially wrecked the clubhouse, and got himself fined and left behind when the team went east. By that time the Tigers had sold reserve catcher Jack Warner, a source of dissension all year. Meanwhile Sam Crawford, a solid all-around ballplayer but nonetheless something of a prima donna, also carried a grudge over his salary. Crawford was one of several on the team who thought they knew more about how to run things than Bill Armour did.

Finally it all became too much for Cobb. The ostracism and abuse that still went on and the strain of his desperate drive to make good steadily wore away at the nineteen-year-old. Late in June his batting average was around .350, close to the best in the league. By mid-July, though, he had slipped to .319 and appeared distracted and confused. Cobb made no mention in his auto-biography of any kind of serious illness in 1906, nor has anyone else taken much note of his protracted absence from the lineup. Yet what happened to him that summer was very serious indeed. A close reading of contemporary press coverage suggests that Cobb suffered some kind of emotional and phys-ical collapse. The official explanation Armour gave on July 18, when he an-nounced in Boston that he had ordered Cobb back to Detroit for a rest, was that his player had "stomach trouble." Nine days later the *Free Press*'s Joe H. Jackson reported that Cobb was at a "sanitarium" in Detroit "and probably wll be there for some time." When the Tigers returned home a few days later, Cobb was able to sit in the grandstand and watch them beat league-leading Philadelphia, but Jackson predicted that "it will be several weeks before he is right." A week or so after that Cobb underwent surgery. The reason for the operation was never reported, but it may have been to remove an ulcer.[11]

With Cobb disabled, with other injuries and illnesses accumulating, and with the pitching shaky, the Tigers had slumped to sixth place by mid-August. It must have seemed that the fates had conspired against the team when, on their return from Washington at the end of the month, their train collided with a freight near Buffalo. Other than bruises, no additional injuries resulted from players being thrown out of their Pullman berths. The roster was so thin, however, that Frank Navin hired forty-six-year-old Sam Thompson, like Char-ley Bennett a mainstay on the champion Detroit team of the late eighties, to play a few games in right field when the Tigers were at home. Doubtless Na-vin also hoped the old favorite's comeback might bolster the badly sagging attendance at Bennett Park.

Meanwhile Cobb rested, recuperated, and regained his mental and phys-ical equilibrium. On August 30 he was fit enough to play with the semipro Cadillacs of Detroit against a local team at Oxford, Michigan, and make three hits. When the Tigers hopped to St. Louis for a Sunday game on September 3, he went with them. That day he made his first appearance since July 18, before only about 300 people at Sportsman's Park. The game was ended by rain after seven innings with the Browns ahead 1–0. Playing center field and hitting fourth, Cobb got a single off Barney Pelty and stole a base, but he also misplayed a wind-blown fly ball into a homerun for the Browns' Charley Hemphill. It was not an encouraging return.

He was soon back in form, though. Three days later Chicago's legendary

"hitless wonders," on their way to a pennant with a team batting average of
.230, uncharacteristically smashed the Tigers at Bennett, 13–5. In that game
Cobb doubled and stole third on catcher Billy Sullivan, and later singled in a
run and took second after daring Sullivan to throw there when he fielded the
peg home. It was a good thing Cobb was back, because for that game the rid-
dled Tigers had to play two reserve infielders, a pitcher in left, and a catcher
in right.

Up to the end of the season Cobb pleased the spectators and at least sub-
dued his critics by playing flashy and generally successful baseball. In a home
win over Washington he went from first to third on Schaefer's bunt and scored
on a roller to the shortstop. Late in the game he almost scored from second
on Schaefer's infield out, the first baseman's throw home barely beating him
on a close call by the flamboyant Tim Hurst. The revived Tigers went on to
win eight more games in a row (including complete-game wins in a doubleheader by George Mullin) before losing to the fading Athletics. In the three
games with Philadelphia at Bennett, however, Cobb ran almost at will on
catchers Ossie Schreckengost and Mike Powers. And at Cleveland, where the
Tigers eliminated the Blues (as they were now called) from the pennant race,
Cobb followed Crawford's walk with a line drive into the right-field bleachers
off Bob Rhoads for his second homer in the big leagues and his only one in
1906.

For Cobb and just about everybody connected with the Tigers, however,
the season ended unhappily. McIntyre had missed games now and then because of assorted minor ailments as well as his brief suspension in June, but
after Cobb became ill he was in left field on a regular basis. His playing had
improved with Cobb absent and with Davy Jones in center (until a hernia ended
Jones's season). After Cobb came back, though, McIntyre again began to let
down. He and Cobb glared at each other when either took a fly in left-center,
and they continued to strike sparks on the bench and in the clubhouse.

On the next-to-last day of the season, October 6, Detroit lost a doubleheader at St. Louis. In the seventh inning of the first game, with a man on
base, the Browns' George Stone, about to finish as the league's batting champion, singled sharply by shortstop Charley O'Leary. Both McIntyre and Cobb
made as if to go after the ball; then both stopped, stood in their tracks, and
yelled at each other as what should have been a single rolled to the flagpole
and Stone circled the bases for a two-run homer. Nobody was more exasperated than Ed Siever, the Tiger pitcher. Besides being, by Cobb's account,
"one of the anti-Cobb ring,"[12] Siever was a capable lefthander who had endured similar outfield shenanigans much of the year. Back in the dugout he
roundly cursed Cobb, who challenged him to fight right there. But Siever insisted he had a game to finish. After the game they again had words until
teammates intervened.

That evening, in the Planter Hotel dining room, Siever renewed the quarrel; but Cobb, according to others there at the time, just walked away. A little later, as the team prepared to catch a train for Chicago, Cobb went to the cigar counter to indulge another of the vices he had acquired since coming to the big leagues. When Siever again came up, Bill Donovan stepped between him and Cobb. Then Siever went over to a corner of the lobby and began talking with McIntyre and a few other players. Cobb was standing near by against a column trying to overhear them when Siever came around the column, yelled a curse, and swung a left. Cobb blocked the punch and floored him with a right to the jaw. Besides hitting Siever in the face several more times, Cobb, said various witnesses, also kicked his enemy in the head.[13] At Donovan's urging, Cobb left the hotel and walked to the railroad station. On the way to Chicago he sat warily alone until bedtime; in his Pullman berth he lay awake with a loaded pistol.

Siever, pretty badly beaten up, was not in uniform for the season-ending game at Chicago the next day. Ed Killian, restored to good graces, stopped the champion White Sox 6–1, as some 10,000 Chicago rooters cheered the Tigers for sweeping three games from New York late in September and thereby putting their team in the lead. Cobb did nothing in five times at bat against rookie Lou Fiene. Before and after the game various Detroit players told newsmen that they blamed Cobb for not going after Stone's hit in St. Louis, inasmuch as Cobb was closer to the ball than McIntyre.

"I was sick at heart and disillusioned," Cobb later described his feelings at the close of the 1906 season. "I'd dreamed of becoming part of the Detroit organization, and all I'd known, so far, was jealousy and persecution."[14] It had been a strange, bitter year, full of anxiety and strife that had driven him to the breaking point and beyond. The wounds would never fully heal, nor would he be willing for them to. Next spring he would have to face the same men with whom he had warred since the previous spring.

It had been a dreary season for the Detroit baseball club, which had finished a distant sixth at 71–78, twenty-one games out of first place. Only 170,376 people had paid to see the games at Bennett Park, a drop of some 23,000 from 1905. The Detroit franchise, never strong, was on more uncertain ground than ever.

Yet Cobb's own record for 1906 provided comfort. According to the official statistics released by Ban Johnson's Chicago office, he appeared in ninety-six games and finished with a batting average of .320, which placed him fifth among American League regulars and thirty-five points above Sam Crawford, the next highest hitter on the Tigers.[15] He scored forty-five runs and stole twenty-two bases, most of them during the last month of the season.

Cobb had established himself as a major-league ballplayer, had proved himself to his teammates (however grudgingly some of them might admit it),

to the people of Detroit, to those in Royston and Augusta as well. He had
shown that he would not be intimidated by catchers like Cleveland's Nig Clarke,
who liked to throw a handful of dirt on his shoes as a pitch came in, or others
like the Browns' Jack O'Connor, who put his hand up behind Cobb's neck and
called for his pitcher to throw the ball there. Most of all, Cobb had gone a
long way toward vindicating the confidence his father had shown in letting
him become a ballplayer. Whatever else had happened, he would not be going
home a failure.

And there was reason to hope that next year would be a better one for him
and for the Detroit team as a whole. Frank Navin had let Bill Armour go and
had hired as the new manager Hughey Jennings, a flaming-haired, freckled-
faced infielder who had starred with the great Baltimore Oriole teams in the
National League in the nineties. Player-manager of Baltimore in the Eastern
League since 1903, Jennings had the same reputation for being a fiery, hard-
driving competitor that manager John McGraw of the National League New
York Giants and all the other old Orioles had. Maybe Jennings could make
the Tigers into a real team, give them the spark they had so sadly lacked in
1906. Maybe he could take players with obvious talent and make them winners. Cobb packed his bags and "headed for the Georgia homeland with far
more confidence than I'd had fourteen months earlier." [16]

IV

A Pennant for Detroit

Back in Royston that fall, Cobb hunted wild turkey and other game as often as he could spare the time away from family business, especially that having to do with the farm. "Cobb is a genuine crank on out-door life," wrote Paul Bruske, "and is an expert camp cook as well as hunter." Cobb could tramp the hills and slog through the marshes feeling reasonably secure about his future with the Detroit club. Obviously Frank Navin as well as Hughey Jennings were convinced of his ability and intended to treat him decently. Before he left for home, he had seen Navin and signed his contract for next year. In reward for Cobb's interrupted but frequently scintillating season in 1906, Navin upped the young outfielder's salary 62 percent, to $2400. Yet Cobb would not get his first check until four months of 1907 had passed, and over the winter he found that he needed money to pay for labor and seed for spring plowing and cotton-planting. Early in 1907 he asked Navin to lend him $300 at interest. Though unwilling to "establish a precedent for the other players," the ever-cautious Navin did advance Cobb $300 on his next year's salary.[1]

That winter was an unusually mild one in the South, and in January and February, Cobb played occasional semipro games in and around Augusta for a few extra dollars. Meanwhile the baseball press carried predictions that Matty McIntyre would be traded in the interest of achieving peace on the Detroit team. It seemed obvious that either McIntyre or Cobb had to go, and Cobb had made himself very popular with the Detroit rooters. From Royston, Cobb let it be known that he intended to give his best on the field in 1907 and wanted to reconcile with McIntyre, but that McIntyre would have to take the initiative. The trouble, as Joe H. Jackson noted, was that while plenty of others on the team held hard feelings against Cobb, McIntyre was the only one who openly expressed his hatred. Meanwhile in Florida, where he was playing semipro ball, McIntyre reiterated that he wanted to be traded. He'd report to the Tigers for spring training, he said, but under the circumstances he couldn't give his best.

Cobb himself reported on March 12 at Augusta, where the Tigers were training for the fourth year in a row. That night he and Hughey Jennings had an hour-long conference, the first time they had talked. Hugh Ambrose Jennings was one of many baseball people who had come out of the Pennsylvania coal mines. Besides having a fine career with the old Orioles, Brooklyn, and the Philadelphia Phillies, Jennings had attended St. Bonaventure College and later entered Cornell University law school. Although he never graduated, he learned enough law at Cornell to gain admission to the Maryland and Pennsylvania bars and then go into practice in the offseason in his native Scranton. Because he had been under a player's contract while managing in the Eastern League and because Baltimore owner Ned Hanlon wanted $5000 for him, Frank Navin simply drafted him as a player for the $1000 draft price and named him Tiger manager. Jennings was a tough, buoyant little man, which was a good thing because he was seemingly disaster prone. Almost killed when hit in the head by a pitch in 1897, he managed a few years later to dive into an empty swimming pool at Cornell and again fracture his skull. Still later, after coming to the Tigers, he was critically injured and a companion was killed when his automobile went off an ice-covered bridge near Scranton.

In their talk at the hotel Jennings tried to give Cobb some fatherly advice about holding his temper and putting the team's welfare before his own feelings. On the field he knew that there was not much he could tell Cobb, who was, as the Detroit *News*'s H. G. Salsinger put it, "immersed in his own style." When Cobb wondered to Salsinger why Jennings paid no attention to him during the workouts and Salsinger passed Cobb's concern along to the manager, Jennings told Cobb he was on his own at bat and on the bases. As Cobb phrased it a few years later, Jennings "allowed [me] to seek my own salvation in my own way."[2]

Yet Cobb's troubles on the club were far from ended. When the team arrived at Warren Park on the afternoon of March 16, Cobb was approached by the local groundskeeper, a black man nicknamed "Bungy" whom he had known for three years. Cobb thought the groundskeeper had been drinking. In any case, the man stuck out his hand and for some unexplained reason called Cobb "Carrie." Cobb's response was to push the man's hand away and, when he again came close, to slap him and chase him toward the clubhouse behind the third-base bleachers. The groundskeeper's wife ran out of the clubhouse, which she had been cleaning, and began yelling at Cobb, who grabbed her and began to choke her.

At that point catcher Charley Schmidt intervened and stopped Cobb from going any further. Schmidt, a burly ex-coal miner from Arkansas who had once fought a short exhibition match against heavyweight boxing contender Jack

Johnson, had come up the previous year with Davy Jones. One of the strong-est men in baseball, Schmidt sometimes amused himself by pounding nails into wood with his fist or lying on the floor and having his teammates try fu-tilely to pick him up. Though a southerner himself, he had strong feelings against hurting women, black or white, and proceeded to tell the Georgian as much. "Whoever does a thing like that is a coward," Schmidt said, to which Cobb answered slowly, "I don't see as it interests you."[3] Schmidt then hit Cobb with a glancing right; Cobb came back with a similarly ineffectual blow; and the two grappled until separated by other Tigers. The players berated Cobb and generally sided with the popular and usually good-natured catcher, while Jennings hopped around, furious with everyone but most of all with Cobb, whom he thought he had straightened out.

That night Jennings wired Macon, where the Cleveland team was training. He offered a deal to Napoleon "Larry" Lajoie, the brilliant second baseman who had just missed winning the batting championship in 1906, his first year as Cleveland manager. Jennings wanted to make a straight trade, Cobb for outfielder Elmer Flick. Flick had led the league himself in 1905, had hit even better last year, but was now at odds with Lajoie and had not yet signed his contract. Meanwhile Cobb told the reporters, "I'm in the right and so long as I know that fact I don't care what's done or said."[4]

The next day Jennings announced that Lajoie, convinced Cobb was a troublemaker, wouldn't trade. Under no circumstances, added Jennings, would Cobb be sold; if he couldn't be traded for a first-rate ballplayer, then Cobb would stay with Detroit. Three days later Flick signed with Cleveland. An offer from New York manager Clark Griffith (whose team was training at At-lanta) of Frank Delahanty, an outfielder who had hit only .238 in part-time duty in 1906, didn't strike Jennings as a serious proposition. In later years both Cobb and Frank Farrell, owner of the Highlanders, often had occasion to ponder how matters might have turned out if Cobb had relocated in the most lucrative and best-publicized baseball market in the country. Within six months, moreover, Larry Lajoie must have come to realize that not taking Cobb had probably cost his team the pennant that year.

Four days after the fight with Schmidt, Cobb played left field in the Ti-gers' first exhibition game, against Augusta. Although he tripled, stole a base, and scored three times, he still impressed onlookers as being listless. Cobb complained that he had no friends on the team and said he wanted to play elsewhere. In Columbia, South Carolina, he cornered Jennings and de-manded to be traded, sold, or released outright. The manager maintained that he was still talking to New York about Cobb. The next day, in Macon, Jen-nings said that Griffith still had offered nothing acceptable and that the ne-gotiations with New York were off. President Charles Somers of Cleveland told the press that while he'd like to have Cobb, he wouldn't dare try to carry him on his team. Whether he liked it or not, Cobb seemed stuck with Detroit.

At Columbia, Cobb got Jennings's permission to leave the team so he could return to Royston to pick up his mother and sister, who would then accompany him as the Tigers began their meandering journey toward Detroit. Whatever questions he may have had about the circumstances of his father's death, Cobb had never given any indication that he questioned his mother's integrity. Although he rarely mentioned her to acquaintances over the years and referred to her only three times in his autobiography, his relationship with Amanda Cobb seems to have been warm and affectionate enough, though not extraordinarily so. Cobb's mother and his sister would live with Cobb in Detroit throughout the 1907 season. Paul Cobb, playing again that spring for Georgia Tech, also later came north for a tryout with Kalamazoo in the Southern Michigan League. (Released after about a half season there, he ended the year playing semipro ball in California.)

Tyrus Cobb and his mother and sister met the Tigers in Atlanta, in time for Cobb to hit a homerun against the local Southern League outfit. Then it was on to Meridian, Mississippi, and, as it happened, a rematch with Charley Schmidt.

An article had appeared in an Atlanta newspaper suggesting that Cobb could whip Schmidt or anybody else on the Detroit club. Although the Georgian denied responsibility for the piece, Schmidt thought his pride was at stake and demanded satisfaction. Long afterward, Cobb maintained that while he was making his way onto the field at Meridian, Schmidt caught him off-guard with a punch. Contemporary accounts held that the two fought only after agreeing to observe Marquis of Queensberry amenities. Everybody agreed, then and later, that the big catcher gave Cobb a thorough beating, breaking his nose and causing both eyes to swell nearly shut. After one round Cobb had had enough. He forgot about the game with the Cotton States leaguers and returned to the hotel, where his mother and sister cleaned him up and cared for his wounds. He was in no shape to play next day at Meridian or the day after that at Vicksburg. He finally reappeared in uniform for a game at Little Rock, singling and subsequently stealing home against a befuddled Southern League pitcher.

By the time the Tigers backtracked to Birmingham for still another exhibition date, the Detroit writers traveling with them had managed to convince themselves that the second Cobb-Schmidt fracas had "cleared the air," as honest manly showdowns were always supposed to do. The whole atmosphere on the team had improved, they thought, and Cobb was "now in better than at any time since he joined the Detroit club." Cobb, said Jennings, was "too good a hitter to let get away, when a little diplomacy will get the boys together"—

which to the wider-read members of the press might have suggested a rather
Clausewitzian notion of diplomacy. Jennings's problem, as Paul Bruske stated
it, was somehow to save for his club "Tyrus Cobb, brilliant fielder, batsman
and base runner, but with a personality that baffles his teammates."[5]

To Hughey Jennings's undying credit as a manager, he hit upon a worka-
ble solution to his outfield problems. Favoring Matty McIntyre (who finally
signed his contract two days into the season) over Davy Jones, Jennings decided to put Cobb in right field and shift Sam Crawford to center. Crawford
was no gazelle, and he had his own unhappiness with Cobb. In his autobiography Cobb remembered still another bat-sawing incident in the 1907 season
and blamed Crawford for instigating that particular petty vandalism. Yet if
prideful and sometimes arrogant, Crawford was also generally a professional,
a man ultimately willing to subordinate personal feelings to team considera-
tions. Thus the blond, broad-shouldered native of Wahoo, Nebraska, moved
to center field, separating Cobb in right from McIntyre in left. It was a solution elegant in its simplicity.

With that outfield alignment and with Cobb hitting in fourth place behind
Crawford, the Tigers opened the 1907 season on a cold gray day at Bennett
Park before a crowd of 6,322 with a 2–0 win over Cleveland, reliable George
Mullin outpitching spit-baller Glenn Liebhardt. Cobb began the year auspi-
ciously with two hits, a stolen base, and two runs scored. In the eighth inning
he executed the first of many demoralizing ventures that year against American League fielders, when he smashed a single past Lajoie at second base,
stole second, continued to third when Nig Clarke's throw skidded by Lajoie,
and came home when center fielder Flick's backup throw got by third base.
After the opener, though, Cobb was bothered by a cold for some time and
played sluggishly. He was hitting only .247 after nineteen games.

Meanwhile Hughey Jennings's antics on the coaching lines hyped players
and rooters and helped make him one of the most memorable managers in
baseball history. Unlike the natty and reserved Bill Armour, who had remained on the bench in street clothes, Jennings coached in uniform at first or
third, stamping his feet, clawing up handfuls of grass, and yelling his ear-split-
ting "Eee-yah." About two-thirds of the way through that season his voice gave
out and he resorted to blowing a whistle to convey his signals to the Tigers.
The umpires and Ban Johnson objected to the whistle, and when Jennings
refused to give it up, Johnson suspended him for two weeks. He came back
sans whistle but with voice restored.

If Tyrus Cobb—or "Ty," as he was now almost invariably called—would
never be entirely reconciled with his early teammates, at least under Jennings
the lingering animosities among the Detroit players no longer interfered with
their play. As far as Cobb's situation was concerned, it helped when McIntyre

broke his ankle sliding into second early in May and was out for the year. Davy Jones took over left field and the lead-off position and went on to have a solid season. Even with McIntyre gone, Jennings kept Cobb in right.

And there, on the bases, and eventually at bat, Cobb's performance in 1907 was consistently spectacular. By early June he had pushed his average well above .300. Crawford was also hitting well, and the team was battling with Chicago and Cleveland for the league lead. Five weeks later Cobb became the first player in either league that season to make one hundred hits, a feat that brought a contingent of Bennett Park (Detroit) rooters rushing onto the field to give him a diamond-studded watch fob. He hit lefthanders that year at a .378 clip, although he still usually had trouble with Chicago's Nick Altrock, whose clowning on and off the field never interfered with his pitching prowess.

If Cobb's base-running was often, as one observer described it, "daring to the point of dementia," it was also successful more times than not.[6] He left everybody stunned at Hilltop Park in New York when he crossed up Highlander first-baseman Hal Chase, who, though only in his third big-league season, was already widely regarded as the most skilled man ever to play the position. After taking a throw at first with a runner advancing to third, Chase liked to snap the ball over to the third baseman and, if not catch the runner off, at least drive him back to the bag. On June 11, in the ninth inning with the Tigers way ahead, Cobb doubled and, instead of stopping at third on Claude Rossman's bunt, roared around the base and came home as Chase, first intending to throw behind Cobb and then trying to stop his motion and peg home, sent the ball flying over third-baseman George Moriarty's head. It was maybe the graceful Chase's most embarrassing moment on the diamond in fifteen years in the majors. Later in the season Cobb similarly embarrassed Moriarty, tearing home and scoring when Moriarty held the ball, unable to decide what to do with it.

Again and again Cobb acted on his theory that the advantage was his when he made fielders throw the ball, and on his passionate conviction that the base paths and bases belonged to him. As an example, in a lopsided victory over Cleveland at Bennett late in June, he tripled to the scoreboard in left-center to drive in Crawford and kept going around third as third-baseman Bill Bradley relayed the throw home. Catcher Harry Bemis had the ball waiting, but Cobb, with a head-first lunge, got a shoulder into Bemis, knocked him over, and made him drop the ball. Enraged, Bemis grabbed the ball and pounded the prostrate Cobb on the head with it until pulled away by Jones and umpire Silk O'Loughlin. Jennings shoved Cobb toward the bench as O'Loughlin threw Bemis out of the game. Subsequently Cobb beat out a bunt, doubled in another run, and stole third.

One stratagem Cobb made almost uniquely his own. Over the winter the club had purchased first-baseman Claude Rossman from Cleveland for $2500. Slow-footed, cantankerous, and with a penchant for erratic throws that would ultimately send him back to the minors, the lanky Rossman was nonethless a reliable hitter and an outstanding sacrifice bunter, better at that particular maneuver even than Cobb. Hitting in front of Rossman, Cobb early learned to take advantage of Rossman's bunting skills. Confident that Rossman would be able to drop the ball where the third baseman had to come in for it, Cobb would flash the bunt sign, take off from first with the pitcher's motion, and head for third as the third baseman fielded the ball, threw to first, and then scrambled back to cover his base. Most of the time he slid in safely. Cobb and Rossman repeatedly executed that play until Rossman left the Tigers in 1909. Cobb would continue to go from first to third on bunts (as well as other infield outs) for years after that, but the play was never so consistently effective as when he worked it with Rossman.

In a period before statisticians gave runs batted in crucial significance, Cobb considered his main value offensively to be a matter of getting on base and scoring runs. On June 29, against Cleveland, he scored four runs for the first time in his career (in the same game in which Harry Bemis tried to beat him senseless with the ball). Characteristically, Cobb's scoring was involved with his ability to steal bases. On July 16 he made his first steal of home in the majors, off Philadelphia's Rube Waddell. Two days later, against Washington, he first stole three bases in a game, and on October 2 he had four steals, again versus Washington.

Meanwhile his fielding, often shaky in 1905 and 1906, improved steadily and sometimes was sensational. Playing a shallow right field, he had thirty assists, more than in any other year he was in the majors. While most came on runners thrown out at second, third, or home, several times Cobb doubled runners off bases, and on a few occasions he threw out slow-moving opponents at first after fielding one-bounce liners.

On August 2 Detroit beat Washington a doubleheader at American League Park in the capital and took the league lead for the first time that year. The major significance of the date, however, turned out to be that it marked the major-league debut of a gangly nineteen-year-old pitcher with remarkably long arms, brought up directly from Idaho semipro ball, named Walter Johnson. In facing Johnson that day, Cobb later said, "I encountered the most threatening sight I ever saw on a ball field." As the rookie righthander took his windup and came around with an easy sidearm motion, Cobb barely saw the ball. "The thing just hissed with danger," he thought. Not only was Johnson by far the fastest pitcher Cobb had ever met; he soon demonstrated that he had nearly pin-point control, most extraordinary in a raw rookie. His first time at bat, Cobb was able to lay down a bunt that the awkward newcomer could not field. Then he went from first to third on Rossman's bunt single and scored on a fly ball. After Washington tied the game in the sixth inning, Crawford hit to the scoreboard in distant left field for a homerun. Meanwhile Cobb threw out a runner at home and another at first. Johnson left for a pinch hitter in the ninth after giving up seven hits and striking out three, with the score 3–1, Detroit. That inning Cobb misplayed a single into a two-base error and let in a run, but Washington's rally fell a run short. Although Walter Johnson took the loss in his first major-league appearance, Cobb and the rest of the Tigers "knew we'd met the most powerful arm ever turned loose in a ball park."[7]

Cobb later claimed that because of his knowledge of phrenology, he could read Johnson's features and tell that he was kindly and even tempered, and thus could take advantage of him by crowding the plate. Johnson, afraid of hitting somebody with his deadly fastball, would not drive Cobb back as other pitchers did. Whether or not that was the secret of his success, Cobb did hit Johnson consistently over the twenty-one years the two faced each other. In sixty-seven games, far more than Cobb played against any other pitcher, Cobb compiled a .335 average.

By mid-August Chicago and Cleveland were gradually slipping back in the pennant race, but Connie Mack's Philadelphia Athletics had come on to battle Detroit for first. After losing two of three games at Philadelphia, the Tigers still led by half a game when they came home for another three games with the Athletics. It was a new experience to be greeted by hundreds of partisans at the railroad station and cheered by others gathered on street corners as the team rode a trolley into the business district. An exultant William Yawkey had his tailor fit each man on the team with a new suit of clothes.

On August 12, with Yawkey and Navin having bought the planing mill property behind center field and moved the fences back to accommodate more standees, some 11,500 turned out at Bennett Park to see the Athletics batter Killian and Siever and win 7–3 behind Waddell. Cobb singled and doubled in the losing effort and made one of his now-typical dashes from first to third on a Rossman bunt, knocking down shortstop Simon Nicholls on his way. The next day Eddie Plank struck out Cobb three times and handled the other Tigers easily as well, 3–0. The Tigers got back to within half a game of first in the series finale, knocking out Waddell and winning 9–2 behind Donovan. Cobb had three singles and a double, scored all the way from second on Jimmy Dygert's wild pitch, and doubled a runner off first after taking a liner.

Detroit then lost two straight to New York before trouncing the Highlanders 13–6 in front of 9,635 in the first Sunday game ever played at Bennett Park. Detroit's mayor and police chief as well as Wayne County sheriff James D. Burns, himself a former owner of the Tigers, all cheerfully acquiesced in this flouting of state and city Sabbath laws. It was a game in which the Tigers ran the bases freely, Germany Schaefer even scoring from second on a bunt by Cobb.

Detroit and Philadelphia stayed at the top of the league for the next month, with the White Sox and the Naps (as Cleveland's rooters had now dubbed Napoleon Lajoie's team) always within striking distance. Cobb played furiously and seemingly without regard for personal well-being. His sliding scrapes became open, running sores that agonized him whenever he hit sun-baked and -hardened infield ground. He finally had to seek medical attention in Cleveland—and never forgave Frank Navin for refusing to pay the bill.

On that same stay in Cleveland, Cobb leaped the ropes holding back an overflow crowd in right to make a catch, landed on a broken pop bottle, and badly cut his right hand. After getting the hand wrapped, he stayed in the game but later tore it open sliding. At St. Louis, hitting with bandaged hand, he got only three hits in five games, two of which were a doubleheader loss that again knocked Detroit out of first. When a pop bottle hurled by a spectator knocked umpire Billy Evans unconscious in that series, baseball writers in various cities called for a ban on bottles inside ballparks, a plea that would go unanswered for several more decades.

On Monday, September 10, his hand infected by now, Cobb missed his first game of the year, at Chicago. He was back in the lineup the next day, though, removing the bandage and then getting two hits, driving in two runs, stealing two bases, and scoring twice, one time when he came all the way around from first on a single, in a 9–1 Tiger victory.

When Cobb's hell-bent style drew charges from people like Horace S. Fogel of the Philadelphia *Bulletin* that he was a dirty player, his defenders came back that he only played the game hard and to win. In September, B. F. Wright, in his regular column from Detroit for the *Sporting News,* insisted that not once during the year had an umpire "heard the sound of his voice in protest," and that now Cobb was "highly esteemed by all his team associates." Said Ed Killian, one of his former tormentors, "Let Ty get on first and all he's got to do is keep running. The other fellows don't know what to do with the ball." Though not quite ready to put local patriotism aside, the respected New York writer Joe Vila was willing to call Cobb "the best all-around ball-player in the country today, barring Hal Chase." And by late in the season Cobb's notoriety had become such that he had made his first commercial endorsement, of Coca-Cola, a product with which he was to have a long and exceedingly lucrative association.[8]

At the end of September what the New York *Times* called "the greatest struggle in the history of baseball" had entered its final week.[9] On Friday, September 27, the Tigers, leading by only eight percentage points, opened a decisive three-game series in Philadelphia. Though giving up thirteen hits, Bill Donovan won the series opener 5–4 over Eddie Plank. Back in Detroit hundreds of people stood in the rain before outdoor scoreboards that provided running accounts of the contest off the wire services. The Saturday game was rained out, so a sellout crowd had to go home to wait through Sunday—when baseball was illegal everywhere in Pennsylvania—for a doubleheader on Monday.

That day more than 24,000 bought tickets to get into Columbia Park, so named because it was located at Twenty-ninth Street and Columbia Avenue. The park had seats for about 15,000, so the surplus ticket-holders crowded up against the foul lines, ringed the outfield, and even sat atop the fences. Although the arrangements were hardly optimum for two games that would probably determine the pennant, the congested, confused scene at Columbia Park on September 30, 1907, was a common enough one in those days.

The first game of the doubleheader turned out to be the only one played. After seventeen innings, with the teams tied at 9–9, it was too dark to continue. The game was an epic encounter, the one singled out by Cobb as the most thrilling he ever played in. Donovan, with two days' rest, started against the little spit-baller Jimmy Dygert.

The Athletics hit Donovan freely in the early innings and led 7–1 after six. Much of the damage resulted from a fly ball near the crowd dropped by Davy Jones, who thereby brought down upon himself the wrath of his keyed-up teammates when he got back to the bench. In the second inning Connie Mack sent in Rube Waddell to relieve Dygert after Dygert made two errors to let in a run. The fun-loving, beer-guzzling Waddell, one of the supremely talented men ever to take the mound, fired his fast ball past the Tigers for four more innings.

In the top of the seventh, however, the Tigers got four runs in a rally highlighted by Crawford's two-run, ground-rule double into the outfield overflow. Philadelphia scored another in the bottom half of the inning; the Tigers matched that in the eighth to make the score 8–6. Then Crawford opened the ninth by singling. Cobb rose to the occasion, lifting the lefthander's second pitch, a curve ball, over the right field fence and into Twenty-ninth Street to tie the game. Cobb's fourth and next-to-last homerun of the year knocked Waddell out of the game and, according to legend, caused the dignified Mack to fall off the Athletics' bench and into a pile of bats. Eddie Plank took over from the battered Rube and retired the side.

Donovan grew stronger the longer he pitched. The Tigers went ahead in the top of the tenth, and although Philadelphia again tied the score in the bottom of the inning, neither pitcher was in trouble after that. Not until the bottom of the fourteenth, when first-baseman Harry Davis of the Athletics hit a fly into center field. Crawford moved back to the roped-in crowd and got ready to make the catch, only to have one policeman on duty jump in front of him and another jostle his arm and make him drop the ball. Jennings, Crawford, and the rest of the Tigers stormed around the umpires (two were on duty) and demanded an interference call. Plate umpire O'Loughlin deferred to Tom Connolly, working the bases, who ruled Davis out on interference. The milling and arguing went on for many minutes, during which first Donovan and then Rossman traded pushes and punches with Waddell (now in street clothes) and utility infielder Monte Cross. Still another policeman arrested Rossmann and took him out of the park.

Finally the crowd was pushed back, the players resumed their positions (with Killian going to first for Detroit), and Donovan pitched to Danny Murphy, who hit a clean single that would easily have scored Davis from second with the winning run. Donovan got out of the inning unscathed, however, and the game went on scorelessly until the people in the grandstand could barely see the outfielders and the umpires called it after seventeen. As one observer said, "players and spectators alike were simply exhausted by the terrific nervous strain."[10] All told, Cobb had a single, a double, and a homerun in eight times up, as well as a stolen base and two runs scored.

The win and tie in Philadelphia left the Tigers with too much of a lead for Mack's team to overcome. Detroit went to Washington and swept four games, in one of which Cobb stole four bases. He had thirteen hits in eighteen at bats against Washington before he collapsed near homeplate during a rundown in the last game. Third-baseman Jim Delahanty first dropped the ball in the chase and then retrieved it and tagged Cobb as he lay two yards from home, too exhausted to get up or even crawl. It had been a long season—and a tough way to make $2400.

The next day the Athletics, after winning twice from Cleveland, lost to Walter Johnson in ten innings at Washington. Meanwhile at St. Louis about 12,000 people turned out on a Saturday to watch the Tigers give Detroit its first major-league championship since the 1887 pennant won by Sam Thompson, Charley Bennett, et al. in the old National League. After Ed Siever beat the Browns 10–2, with Cobb leading the attack by tripling in Jones and later hitting one over the trees beyond the right-field fence, again with Jones aboard, the St. Louis fans surrounded the Tigers and cheered them to their horse-drawn bus.

On Sunday, as Cobb and various other regulars sat out a meaningless doubleheader loss to the Browns, thousands took to the streets in and around Detroit to celebrate. Besides cavorting in old baseball uniforms and a variety of other regalia, quite a few Detroiters painted black tiger stripes on yellowish dogs and paraded with the unhappy canines. That night festive bonfires lighted up Detroit as well as neighboring towns like Highland Park, River Rouge, and Hamtramck.

The sixth-place Tigers of 1906 won the 1907 pennant with a record of 92–58 to 88–57 for Philadelphia. Four sturdy pitchers accounted for all but four of the wins: Donovan, 26; Killian, 24; Mullin, 21; and Siever, 17. At the age of twenty years and ten months, Cobb became the youngest man ever to win a big-league batting championship.[11] His final-game hits gave him 212 for the year and pushed his average to .350. Crawford was batting runnerup at .323, his best showing since 1903. Cobb's five homeruns were second to Harry Davis's eight, and while statisticians paid little attention to runs batted in during that period, it would interest later generations that Cobb led the league with 116. He also led in stolen bases with 49 and was third, behind Crawford and Jones, in runs scored. The Detroit team batting average, .266, was a high one for those years and topped both major leagues.

At season's end Paul Bruske, writing from Detroit in *Sporting Life*, got carried away and declared that Cobb had "won his battle" over the hostility of his teammates, who now mainly credited him with the club's success and would take his loss "as a genuine calamity and a personal bereavement as well."[12] In fact Cobb remained basically a loner, edgy and uneasy around his teammates, as generally they still were around him. In none of the photographs from that period in his life is he caught smiling. Moreover, if one puts any stock in the theory of body language, then there may be some significance in the way Cobb looks in the 1907 Detroit team picture. Whereas on either side of him, third-baseman Bill Coughlan and utility man Jerry Downs sit with legs apart and with knees and hands touching the shoulders of, respectively, Hughey Jennings and reserve catcher Jimmy Archer, Cobb sits with legs together and extended, with elbows tucked against his body, and with hands gripping his glove—as if trying not to touch or be touched.

As has often been the case following a torrid pennant race, the World Series of 1907 was something of an anticlimax. Against the Chicago Cubs the tired Tigers were simply overmatched, just as the whole National League had been in 1906 and 1907. In the Cubs of first-baseman-manager Frank Chance, Cobb and his teammates came up against one of the great outfits in baseball history. It was a team that had won an all-time major-league record 116 games in 1906 before, astonishingly, losing to the crosstown White Sox four games to two in the Series. In 1907 the Cubs won 107 and finished seventeen games in front of second-place Pittsburgh. With five strong pitchers and a staff earned run average of 1.73, the Cubs also had clutch hitting and a tight defense, featuring the brilliant catching of Johnny Kling and the fabled double-play combination of shortstop Joe Tinker and second-baseman Johnny Evers.

On October 8, in the Series opener, 24,337 packed and slightly overflowed the Cubs' West Side Grounds at Polk and Lincoln (later Wolcott) streets. It was the biggest crowd in Series history up to that time. As Cobb approached the plate for his first at bat, umpire Hank O'Day stopped play so a representative of a St. Louis jewelry company could present an ornate diamond-studded medal, the prize the company had put up for the batting champion in each league. Cobb then grounded meekly to Frank Chance. After that Bill Donovan battled the Cubs' Orval Overall and Ed Reulbach to a twelve-inning 3–3 tie, made possible when Charley Schmidt's passed ball on a called third strike let in the tying run in the ninth. Cobb went hitless and had a sacrifice bunt in four times up.

A four-game rout by the Cubs followed. Chicago baserunners had stolen at will in the first-game tie off Schmidt, who was trying to catch with a broken bone in his throwing hand. In the next four games they continued to run with little hindrance from Schmidt, Fred Payne, and finally Jimmy Archer, and ended up with a total of eighteen steals for the Series. Afterward Johnny Evers thought that the inability of Detroit's pitchers to keep runners from taking big leads had been the main factor in the Cubs' base-running carnival.

Overall, Reulbach, lefty Jake Pfiester, and Mordecai Brown held the Tigers to an average of less than a run in each of the four games that counted; Detroit's team batting average for the whole Series was a little above .200. Pfiester outpitched Mullin in the second game, also at Chicago, 3–1. At Detroit on October 10, Reulbach overcame Siever and Killian 4–1; the next day, also at Detroit, Overall did the same to Mullin, 6–1; and on the 12th only 7,370 people showed up at Bennett Park to see Brown end it by shutting out the Tigers 2–0, with Mullin pitching well but taking his third loss.

Yet even after that the Detroit rooters went into the streets again to celebrate the fact that their team had made it into a World Series. Their post-game enthusiasm failed to impress I. F. Sanborn of the Chicago *Tribune*, who believed that the poor attendance in Detroit proved that "a city of that size will not stand for a loser." Sanborn expected "the disappearance of Detroit from the major-league map within a few years."[13]

Cobb managed four hits in twenty official at bats over the five games. He had a single off Pfiester in game two, another single off Reulbach in game three, and a triple into the crowd in center field off Overall to score Schaefer in game four. In the finale he stretched a liner to right-center into a double off Brown but then was cut down trying to steal third by the strong-armed Kling. "The wonderful Ty Cobb," wrote Joe Vila, "dwindled from a world beater to a lame amateur."[14]

The money they made from getting into the Series did a lot to assuage the chastened spirits of Cobb and the other Tigers. Helping to swell their shares was the fact that the owners had agreed beforehand to count receipts from any tie games in figuring the players' pot. Jennings and nineteen Tiger players (including McIntyre) split nearly $22,000 allocated by the National Commission, plus $15,000, the clubowners' share, which President Yawkey generously decided his team ought to have. Thus each Tiger came out with $1,946, which in Cobb's case was only $454 less than his whole season's pay that year. It was quite a dividend for a twenty-year-old only two years from the lowest minors, enough to pay off whatever remaining debts the family may have had, with quite a bit left over for extras.

Well might Yawkey and also Frank Navin be generous, because the Tigers' home attendance had soared to nearly 300,000. Although that was still seventh in the American League, more only than last-place Washington, it was enough to give the Detroit club a substantial surplus. Navin took his share of the profits, about $50,000, and paid back what Yawkey had lent him the previous year to buy a half-interest in the franchise. Over the winter, moreover, Yawkey stepped down as president in favor of Navin, although until his death in 1919 Yawkey would continue to be a major stockholder in the club.

At a goodbye banquet given for the team by Yawkey at the Hotel Cadillac, B. F. Wright paraphrased Ernest R. Thayer's famous poem with something called "Ty Cobb at the Bat," before Cobb was awarded his batting-title medal a second time. The young Georgian responded with appropriate modesty, saying that he deserved no more credit than anybody else on the team.

Then the next day he went to Chicago with most of the other Tigers to begin a series of exhibition games with the Cubs there and at various places near Chicago, with the players to split all the receipts. Hampered by bad weather, the World Series opponents drew poorly. After appearing in only two games and picking up about $100, Cobb headed for Royston with his mother and sister. At home his admirers were waiting with a handsome gold pocket watch for the local boy who had indubitably made good. The perquisites of fame were starting to come fast.

V

Two More Pennants and October Disappointments

Cobb left Detroit with more money than he had ever had, but he intended to make a lot more. The New York *American* was right on target in describing him as having acquired, "above all, a superbly insolent confidence in himself."[1] Cobb was good and he was perfectly aware of that fact. He also understood that within two seasons his rabid way of playing the game had made him probably the top gate attraction in the American League. That offseason he made up his mind that he would never again simply accept what his club was willing to give him, as he had done for the previous two years.

There was also a new reason for Cobb to want to put himself on solid ground financially. Not long before his twenty-first birthday, he wrote the Detroit *Times*'s Paul Bruske a "peppery message" reporting his engagement to a young lady from Augusta named, it later became known, Charlie Marion Lombard.[2] She was the daughter of Roswell Lombard, a well-to-do Augusta businessman who owned a downtown theater, an interest in his brother George's iron and steel works, and various other properties in and around Augusta. He also owned an estate called "The Oaks" out in the country south of the city.

Even though the Lombards belonged to the Methodist Episcopal Church, South, they sent their daughter to nearby St. Mary's convent to be educated. She may have met Cobb as early as 1905 when he was playing for Augusta and she was only fourteen. Cobb began courting her seriously over the winter of 1906–07. He probably had to work at breaking down the common prejudice among genteel folk against ballplayers and theater people. Whatever difficulties he may have encountered were evidently overcome by late 1907. Cobb and Charlie Lombard intended to marry during the coming year, although he told acquaintances that it would not be that spring. Possibly her parents insisted that they wait at least until after the girl's seventeenth birthday.

Early in the new year Frank Navin sent Cobb his 1908 contract, which provided for a flat $3000. Alluding to the economic downturn that had hit the country the previous year, Navin maintained that "the prospects are not very bright for next year" and that "the increase is as large as possible." Cobb sent the document right back unsigned, then made public his own terms: a three-year contract at $5000 per year, personal exemption from the rule whereby a club could release a ballplayer outright with only ten days' notice, and compensation in full in case he were incapacitated through sickness or injury. If he didn't get his terms, said Cobb, then he might play with the powerful Logan Squares semipro team in Chicago or maybe sign with a new professional league called the Union Association just then being formed. The owners had had it all their way, he complained, and "they continue to oppress ball players." He was only "contending for what I consider my rights . . . after two years of good ball at a low salary."[3]

The war of words that ensued was the first of two major salary battles Cobb and Navin would have. Of course the confrontation came more than sixty-five years before the advent of free agency and arbitration procedures in baseball. In Cobb's time players were absolutely bound to their clubs by the reserve clause. If they objected to the terms offered them, their only recourse was to hold out, in which case they might be traded, released, or eventually, if they still refused to sign, ostracized within Organized Baseball. Cobb knew full well the power baseball "law" gave Navin, knew the chance he was taking with his future in the game. At one point, he later claimed, he and his family were so fed up with the whole acrimonious process that he seriously thought about quitting baseball and going to college with the goal of entering law or medicine, as his father had wanted him to do.

Cobb and Navin issued threats and counter-threats, claims and counter-claims. Navin declared that McIntyre (healthy again), Jones, and Crawford would still be the best outfield in the league. Besides, "To allow [Cobb] to bluff us into giving his case different treatment would be to court a hold-up on the part of every other player." Crawford had already signed for $4000 and practically all the other Tigers had settled amicably. Why couldn't Cobb? Generally the Detroit press backed Navin, reasoning that Cobb had done well financially for one so young and should be satisfied with as much pay as many ten-year veterans were getting. Cobb's salary demand, said Hughey Jennings, was "absurd on its face." His teammates Germany Schaefer and Charley O'Leary, in their touring vaudeville act, suggested the sentiments of many baseball followers in Detroit and elsewhere with one of their dreadful puns: "Why does Tyrus Cobb Tyrus?"[4]

At home the Augusta *Chronicle* solidly backed Cobb. When in mid-March the Georgian accepted Navin's invitation to come to Detroit for some man-to-man talk about his contract, *Chronicle* sports editor Thomas Hamilton warned of a doublecross. "The Lord help him up North," prayed Hamilton.[5] Actually

Cobb, wary as he had become and stubborn as he had always been, was quite capable of taking care of himself.

On March 20, Cobb and Navin met inconclusively for three hours. "It isn't a question of principle with me," he told the press afterward. "I want the money." He also admitted, though, that he was "crazy to play ball."[6] That afternoon he received visits from George P. Codd, who until recently had been Detroit's mayor, and Fielding H. Yost, the renowned football coach at the University of Michigan, both of whom urged him to try once more with Navin. That he did after dinner, this time dropping his special-clause demands and finally agreeing to a one-year contract at $4000, with a bonus of $800 to be paid if he hit .300 again. Cobb announced that he was satisfied and would shortly report to Little Rock, Arkansas, for spring training with the Tigers, but only after he had tended to his affairs in Georgia.

Cobb left Royston on March 24 and, after detouring to Augusta to see his fiancée and then up into North Carolina for a visit with his Cobb grandparents, finally headed for the Tiger training camp. This time his mother and sister would make the trip to Detroit on their own. As in 1907, they would live with Cobb at an apartment in a fashionable residential section out on Woodward Avenue, where, among other new effects, he installed a player piano. He had also bought his first automobile, a sporty Chalmers two-seater, and begun to indulge a taste for expensive clothes and good cigars.

Meanwhile Paul Cobb, back from California, prepared to join the Joplin, Missouri, team in the Class C Western Association. Built along the same lines as his older brother but an inch or so shorter and a righthanded hitter as well as thrower, Paul Cobb would enjoy a good season in 1908 at Joplin and later Enid, Oklahoma. In a league dominated by tough pitching, he would hit a respectable .273, with ten homers and thirty-four stolen bases, and would be drafted by the St. Louis Browns.

When he got to Little Rock at the end of March, Ty Cobb again aired his unhappiness with a system under which a ballplayer, even if he had good years, "hasn't the chance of a rabbit unless public opinion is with him. . . . The league has him just where it wants him and it isn't going to pay him any more money than it has to." What ought to be done, he said, was to limit the term of the reserve clause to five years, after which a player would be absolutely free to go with whatever club offered him the most.[7] To the poorly paid sportswriters who patiently took down and reported Cobb's pronouncements, such an idea must have seemed interesting but hopelessly unrealistic. The suddenly affluent young man might be a wizard on the playing field, but he would be better off leaving the business of baseball to the baseball businessmen.

As Cobb would demonstrate annually for many years, reporting late for spring training was no handicap to a man who stayed in shape year round, whether he was twenty-one or forty-one. Three days after arriving at Little Rock, he played against the city's Southern League team, banged out two hits, and stole a base. It was in that game that he got his first look at a young center fielder from Texas who would hit .350 with Little Rock that year, come up to Boston at season's end, and go on to become Cobb's chief rival for all-around stardom in the American League. His name was Tris Speaker.

Although Cobb soon caught a cold at Little Rock and had to go to bed, he was in fine form by April 14, when Detroit opened the season at South Side Park in Chicago before nearly 20,000. Besides singling twice off Doc White, he drove Nick Altrock's curve into the right-field bleachers and received a shower of gifts from Chicago merchants for hitting the year's first homerun. With five errors behind Siever and Willett, however, the Tigers lost 15–5. Three days later they opened at home in Bennett Park, which, after a refurbishing and enlargement directed by Navin over the winter, now seated some 10,500. Navin's official attendance count that day was 14,051, a new Detroit record. Cobb was three for six and drove in two runs in another loss, 9–3, to Cleveland in twelve innings.

Unlike the previous spring, Cobb got off to an excellent start in 1908. By mid-May he was hitting .365, and on his second trip to Chicago the local rooters presented him with a silver loving cup for being the most popular visiting player. On May 2 he passed a personal landmark when, after being called out by Silk O'Loughlin trying to stretch a triple into a homerun against the White Sox at Bennett, he protested so obstreperously that O'Loughlin threw him out of the game, his first ejection in the big leagues.

The team, by contrast, started poorly, losing nine of its first twelve games. But then the Tigers got hot on their initial eastern trip, won nine straight, and came back home to move into first with a Memorial Day doubleheader sweep of the White Sox. After that they again slumped somewhat, but by mid-summer Detroit was locked in a four-way battle for the pennant with Cleveland, Chicago, and the surprising St. Louis Browns, for whom Rube Waddell, sold by Connie Mack in the offseason, was having his last good year.

Despite his contract demands and the fact that after only two full seasons in the league he was making more money than anybody on the club except Crawford and possibly Donovan, Cobb appeared to be getting along with the other Tigers better than at any time since he came up in 1905. Paul Bruske proclaimed Cobb to be "a grown man now, accepted at his own rating by all his mates," a person who "actually accepts advice."[8] If Cobb's relationships with his teammates never became comradely, at least by the 1908 season his worst days were behind him.

Even Cobb and McIntyre, once again the team's regular left fielder and lead-off man, were able to be around each other without bristling, although

Jennings wisely kept Crawford playing between them. Long afterward Cobb maintained that at the time of McIntyre's death in 1920, he had still never once shaken his hand. According to a contemporary account, however, Cobb and McIntyre shook hands and pledged to put aside their two-year quarrel as the team waited on the Detroit station platform for the train to Chicago on the night of June 27. The precipitant in bringing them together supposedly had been Cobb's ejection by Tom Connolly that afternoon after he ran up from the bench to protest a strike Connolly had just called on McIntyre.

Better feelings between Cobb and the rest of the team hardly dampened his fiery spirits on the field. He later claimed that it was not until 1908 that "I felt for the first time the positive conviction that baseball was the career for me."[9] Sure of his own abilities, increasingly aware of the weaknesses of his adversaries, he played with a fierceness that must often have seemed demonic to those who had to contend against him. Fully cognizant of the reputation he was making for himself, Cobb was willing for the image to outgrow the reality. It served his purposes, for example, if opposing basemen really believed that he regularly sharpened his spikes. That particular allegation stemmed from an episode in New York in 1908 when a couple of Tiger benchwarmers, deciding they would try to scare or at least confuse the Highlanders, sat on the bench filing their spikes as the New York players trooped by on their way to the field. By the time various local sportswriters got through, they had Cobb himself doing the sinister work with mouth twisted and eyes ablaze. That yarn became the most durable item in the vast amount of Cobbian folklore accumulating over the decades. At least as far as his public statements were concerned, Cobb let it stand until well after his retirement.

The reality of Ty Cobb, though, was fearsome enough. Insisting that the base paths and bases were his, he often came in hard and with spikes high, and over the years he cut numerous opponents. Cobb deliberately undertook to become what a later generation of sports jargonists would call an "intimidator." His reputation for ruthlessness, combined with his speed and lightning-quick perception, forced opposing players into numerous mistakes and generally gave him an edge that he exploited relentlessly. And if crowds in opponents' ballparks became menacing, as they did in Boston in mid-July when Cobb got tangled up with shortstop Heinie Wagner after he was caught stealing at second, he seemed to thrive on their hostility. In that particular game Cobb singled twice, tripled, and, after his mixup with Wagner, iced a 6–3 Detroit win in ten innings with a homerun into deep right-center field. As he dusted himself off and trotted back to the Tiger bench, Cobb showed his contempt for the angry Bostonians by gesturing for them to sit down and shut up.

Cobb also remained quick tempered with people off the field who crossed him, especially if they happened to be black. Sprinkled along through Cobb's years in baseball were a variety of incidents in which he took violent offense at some black person's behavior. The fracas with the Augusta groundskeeper and his wife during spring training in 1907 was only the first such incident. In simplest terms, Cobb was what, fifty years later, people would freely call a racist. Which is to say that he believed blacks to be fundamentally different from and inferior to whites, and thus necessarily suited to a subservient role in a society that must be dominated by whites. Although most non-southern whites probably felt basically the same way, that belief was most prevalent among white people in the southern states, where the overwhelming majority of blacks still lived and where fear of racial change was most acute. Yet if the doctrine of white supremacy was nearly universal within the white South, obviously the degree of intensity with which it was held would vary from person to person. Cobb's racial feelings appear to have been quite strong indeed. He had pleasant recollections of a black maid who had looked after the Cobb children at their home in Royston, and he was capable of acts of kindness toward particular black persons. But he had no patience whatever with blacks who were insolent, fractious, unsubmissive—in a word, "uppity." In the somewhat less-constrained racial climate of Detroit and the other northern cities where Cobb played, he repeatedly had to deal with blacks who withheld the automatic deference a white man was accustomed to in the South.

An episode in Detroit early in June 1908 would be of no great consequence except that it illustrates the problem Cobb often had. Leaving the Hotel Ponchartrain and starting to cross Woodward Avenue, he stepped into some asphalt just put down by city workers. A black laborer named Fred Collins yelled angrily for him to get out of the area. Cobb took offense and, after an exchange of words, knocked Collins down, then continued on his way. On a Monday morning two days later Cobb had to appear in municipal court, before Judge Edward Jeffries, on an assault-and-battery charge brought by Collins. Claiming that "the negro" had insulted and provoked him, Cobb pleaded not guilty. Jeffries found that Cobb had assaulted Collins, then suspended his sentence and thereby won Cobb's long-lasting friendship. Under the threat of a civil suit, however, Cobb ended up paying Collins $75.

Regardless of his off-the-field difficulties, Cobb continued to play without letup and continued to win the adulation of the crowds at Bennett Park and elsewhere. He had one of his most remarkable games against Boston on July 30, at home before a fine weekday turnout of 4500. Besides making three hits in four times up off forty-one-year-old Cy Young (who had already won more games than anybody else ever would), Cobb scored from second on Rossman's infield hit, threw out Boston catcher Lou Criger on a one-hop liner to right, and even registered a putout at second base when he took part in a rundown play. At the end of July he was hitting .334, had appeared in every game so far, and was relying on trainer Harry Tuthill to care for bruises and sores that "have often made the boy's limbs and body look mottled."[10] The

Tigers, by taking nineteen of twenty-five games on the road earlier that month, had broken out of the pack of contenders, although that proved short lived.

Soon thereafter Cobb demonstrated that he had already reached a place in his profession where he could do virtually as he pleased. On August 2, before a Sunday crowd of 8,638 at Bennett, the Tigers lost to Boston 8–4, with Eddie Cicotte, Cobb's teammate at Augusta in 1905 and a Detroit boy making his debut in his hometown, getting the win. The next morning Cobb caught a train south to get married.

Cobb had arranged his wedding date without consulting anybody in the Detroit management. In the middle of a hot pennant race, with Detroit in first place by only one game over St. Louis, Cobb just left. Hughey Jennings, when informed of Cobb's plans a couple of days earlier, could do nothing but acquiesce in what Cobb intended to do whether or not his manager approved. For Paul Bruske, Cobb's action was just "one of those characteristic idiosyncrasies for which the player is noted . . . but what can you do about it? The player is there with the goods on the diamond." [11]

Cobb went to his wedding by way of Royston, where he picked up A. C. Ginn, his uncle (on the Chitwood side) from Banks County. Finally pulling into Augusta on the Charleston and Western Carolina railroad on Thursday morning, August 6, Cobb and Ginn rushed to a friend's roominghouse and hurriedly changed clothes. After a hectic nine-mile, twenty-five-minute automobile trip south to the Lombard estate, Cobb, Ginn, and the Reverend Thomas Walker of Augusta, who was to perform the ceremony, arrived one minute before the wedding was to begin at high noon.

In a ceremony "marked by that simplicity which is the key-note of excellence," as the local society news reporter described it, Cobb, age twenty-one, and Charlie Marion Lombard, barely seventeen, were married in the parlor of The Oaks before about twenty-five guests. [12] There followed a luncheon, visiting with friends that afternoon, and a wedding banquet that evening at the Hotel Genesta in Augusta. Shortly before midnight they boarded their Pullman car to begin the long journey back to Detroit and the pennant race.

Cobb and his bride missed their connection the next day in Cincinnati and finally got into Detroit late Saturday afternoon. On Sunday the 9th, when he came onto the field at Bennett Park, the applause of eight thousand Detroiters showed that they held no hard feelings about his having left the team. He struck out his first time up, but then singled, tripled, and stole a base in a 5–2 win over Washington, with Ed Summers, the Tigers' knuckle-balling rookie lefthander, picking up another victory. Meanwhile Charlie Lombard Cobb sat in the grandstand, surrounded by rooters straining for a good look at their favorite's bride. Those who got close enough saw a rather pretty, dark-haired young woman, already a bit plump and destined to get considerably more so, but with piercing hazel eyes that were her most attractive feature.

If she was taken aback by the swarm of staring people, she must have suspected that it was something she'd have to get used to.

When the Tigers left Detroit on August 13 to begin another eastern tour, Charlie Cobb went with her husband and saw the sights in the great cities Cobb had toured by himself in previous years. At Washington he got Jennings's consent to pass up an exhibition game scheduled at Newark so he and Charlie could remain an extra day in the capital. But if the trip east served well as a honeymoon, it was not such a pleasant trip for the ball club, which went into a slump that could have been disastrous had not the other western teams also played poorly in the east. Cobb did little of consequence on the trip and lost about twenty points on his batting average. *Sporting Life*'s weekly league notes offered a bit of delicate sexual innuendo, to the effect that since his marriage Cobb had been striking out more than he ever had and not running the bases with his customary zeal. Subsequently Jennings declared that never again would he permit a player to marry in midseason.

Early in September the Tigers torpedoed the Browns' pennant hopes. After two straight losses at St. Louis, Donovan outlasted Waddell 6–4 in front of 26,652, a record-breaking horde that jammed itself around the playing field and onto the grandstand roof and the fence tops at Sportsman's Park. Cobb, besides getting three hits, ended the game by darting into the crowd to take Roy Hartzell's long fly. The teams then went to Detroit, where the Tigers swept a morning-afternoon Labor Day doubleheader before a combined attendance of nearly 29,000.

The team got a lift in mid-September when diminutive Owen "Donie" Bush, a slick-fielding shortstop, came up from Indianapolis to take over from Charley O'Leary. Bush had as much fire as Cobb, was a lot easier to get along with, and quickly stabilized an infield that had been shaky all season. He would remain as the Tigers' regular shortstop for the next twelve years.

When Heinie Wagner's homer beat the Tigers at Bennett on September 21, Detroit dropped from first place for the first time in more than two months. Larry Lajoie's Cleveland club went into the lead, with Detroit and Chicago right behind. The Tigers regained the top less than a week later, when Donovan and then Killian beat Philadelphia. On October 2, while Detroit came from behind to beat the Browns 7–6 at Bennett, with Cobb scoring the winning run on Rossman's double, the White Sox' Ed Walsh struck out fifteen at Cleveland but lost 1–0, because Addie Joss threw a perfect game. The heroics of the big spit-baller, however, kept Chicago in contention. The next day he came right back to beat the Naps 3–2; and after Doc White outpitched Killian at Chicago on Sunday, October 4, Walsh then beat the Tigers 6–1 on Monday, thereby completing his third game in four days and winning his second. It was Walsh's fortieth victory in 1908. Meanwhile Bill Dineen of St. Louis beat Cleveland, so that at day's end Detroit led by half a game over both the White Sox and Naps, with one game to play.

Doc White tried to win it for Chicago the next day but was cuffed around by the Tigers in the early innings and gave way to Walsh, who finally had a bad day of his own and left in favor of Frank Smith. Benefiting from five White Sox errors, Detroit ran up a 7–0 lead. More than 27,000 sitters and standees at South Side Park watched morosely as Donovan held their worthies to two hits and no runs. Although his hitting had been inconsistent over the last part of the season, Cobb was up to the challenge this day, tripling in two runs in the first inning, later singling twice and driving in another run, and harassing Walsh into a wild pickoff throw past first that scored Crawford. Crawford himself had three singles and a double; McIntyre had three hits and scored three times.

Cleveland, by beating St. Louis, finished in second place, half a game behind Detroit and one game ahead of Chicago. It was the closest three-team race in major-league history. The Tigers won because they ended up playing only 153 of their games, while Cleveland played its full 154. Rules later adopted in both leagues would have required the Tigers to make up their missing game and, if they lost and thereby finished tied with Cleveland, forced a playoff. In 1908, though, there was no such provision; neither the Cleveland management, Ban Johnson, nor anybody else could alter the race's freakish ending.

Several thousand people, led by Mayor William B. Thompson, met the Tigers at the Michigan Central station in Detroit. Following speeches and brass-band renditions, the players got into a line of automobiles and, trailed by the band and the crowd, went to the Ponchartrain, "where a jubilee was held in the lobby."[13] Thompson and Detroit's other civic boosters could be proud that the city had finally shown big-league attendance figures to go with its championship team. That year 436,199 had paid to get into Bennett Park, a total topped only at Chicago and St. Louis. Frank Navin obviously had a money-making enterprise on his hands.

Cobb's statistics were less impressive than in 1907, but then the same could be said of most hitters in both leagues. More than ever, 1908 was a pitchers' year, with American League moundsmen holding the opposition to an average of 2.38 runs per nine innings and their National League counterparts recording an all-time-low aggregate E.R.A of 2.34. Francis C. Richter, editor of *Sporting Life* and of the authoritative annual American League guide, was so alarmed by the batting decline that he advocated prohibiting the use of gloves by outfielders in the belief that the gloves in use "enable the veriest dub to face a cannon shot."[14]

At .324 Cobb still hit well enough to win his second batting title in a row. He knocked in 101 runs, the only American Leaguer to pass the hundred mark, and also led in hits with 188. But he was well down the list in runs scored (88) and bases stolen (39). In fact it was Matty McIntyre, having his best year in the majors thus far, who led in runs, with Crawford and Schaefer behind him. Crawford topped the league with only seven homeruns.

The Tiger pitching load was a little more evenly distributed than in 1907. Donovan, hampered by chronic rheumatism, won 19; Mullin, considerably less effective than he had been in recent years, was 16-14; and Edgar Willett and Ed Killian won 15 and 12, respectively. Ed Summers, a tall lefthander up from Indianapolis, where he had developed an effective knuckle ball, led the staff with a 24-12 record and a brilliant 1.64 E.R.A.

Instead of running away from everybody else in the National League as they had in the preceding two years, the Chicago Cubs were forced into a one-game playoff for the championship with John McGraw's New York Giants. The play-off came about because two weeks earlier Giant rookie Fred Merkle had committed a legendary blunder in failing to touch second base as he ran from first while a base hit scored what should have been the winning run against the Cubs. In the mob scene that followed at the old wooden Polo Grounds, the umpires finally ruled the game a tie. When the two teams ended the season with identical records, a one-game playoff was necessary. On October 7 at New York, Mordecai Brown, who had lost part of his right index finger in a boyhood accident and thereby gained the nickname "Three Finger," broke his curve off that finger with sufficient expertise to beat the Giants' great Christy Mathewson 4–2 and send the Cubs into the World Series for the third straight year.

The Chicago team arrived in Detroit two days later and checked in at the Hotel Tuller to await the start of the Series at Bennett Park on Saturday afternoon, October 10. Manager Frank Chance could hardly even whisper as a consequence of having been struck in the throat by a Giants partisan at the end of the game in New York. Yet if the Tigers were no more weary than the Cubs this time around, they were about to find that they were still overmatched.

About 11,000 showed up for the opening game, far fewer than were needed to fill the temporary bleachers Navin had had erected around the outfield. At the same time, he had ordered the rigging of huge sheets of canvas in front of the thicket of wildcat bleachers that had burgeoned outside the left-field fence toward the end of the season. The canvas flapped violently in the wind and light rain that marred the game. The dreary weather might have been an omen for the whole Series.

Leading 6–5 going into the ninth inning, Summers, who had relieved Killian in the third, gave up six consecutive singles and lost it 10–6. Cobb had a good day, singling over Harry Steinfeldt's head at third to drive in McIntyre with the Tigers' first run, singling again in the seventh and subsequently scoring on an infield out, reaching first on a bunt in the eighth when Chance dropped catcher Kling's throw, and then coming all the way home on Rossman's hit and Solly Hofmann's bad throw from center field past Steinfeldt. That run had given Detroit its ephemeral lead.

In game two, on Sunday in Chicago, the Cubs again rallied late, breaking a scoreless tie with six runs in the eighth off Donovan for a 6–1 victory. With his wife watching, Cobb had only one hit, a single in the ninth to drive in Detroit's only run. Then on Monday the Tigers finally won one from the Cubs, knocking around Jake Pfiester for eight runs in as many innings at Chicago while Mullin held the Cubs to three. It was Cobb's best outing in a World Series. He had three singles and a double and two runs batted in in five at bats. In the top of the ninth, with the Tigers well ahead and following his fourth hit, he took his lead off Ed Reulbach, yelled into Johnny Kling that he was going on the next pitch, and proceeded to do just that, knocking over Joe Tinker as he slid in safely. Then he yelled to everybody that he was going to third and stole that base as Kling threw low. When Rossman drew a walk and, in a well-tried Tiger maneuver, rounded first and started trotting toward second, Cobb bolted for home, only to be caught off base by Reulbach's throw and tagged out by third-baseman Steinfeldt. It was a fine show for the Chicago fans, done with Cobb's characteristic brashness.

That was the high point for Cobb and the rest of the Detroit team. On the 14th, back at Detroit, Three-Finger Brown shut out the Tigers 3–0 on four hits, holding Cobb hitless. Cobb struck out once, and Brown got a critical forceout at third on his attempted sacrifice bunt in the fourth inning. Nearly 13,000 turned out for that game, but the next day the smallest crowd in World Series history, 6,210, bothered to come to Bennett Park to see Orval Overall close it out with another shutout, a 2–0 three-hitter. Donovan, like Summers the previous day, pitched well but in vain. Cobb managed only a walk in the four times he came to bat.

Once more it was a case of a good ball club losing to a truly great one. Again the Tigers' hitting had been anemic—a .203 team batting average. And again the Cubs had run pretty much when they wanted to on Detroit's pitchers and catchers, this time stealing fourteen bases. Chance alone accounted for five steals. Cobb's showing in the first three games gave him far and away the best hitting record among the Tigers, a .368 average. Yet Brown and Overall had shut him down in the last two games and thus made the Series another disappointing one in terms of his personal performance.

The poor attendance at Detroit, especially in the final game, held the Detroit players' shares down to $871 apiece; this time, with Navin fully in charge of the club's business affairs, the owners' share of the profits stayed with the owners. The players generously included Donie Bush for a full share, even though he had come up too late to be eligible for the World Series. Out of his own pocket Jennings bought each man a new suit of clothes.

Then, after an appreciation banquet at the Ponchartrain on Saturday night, all the Tigers went back to Chicago for an exhibition game with the world's champions at West Side Park, all proceeds going to the players as in 1907. About 6,600 came out to see not only the game but pre-game sprint events pitting Cobb against the fastest Cubs. Cobb won all three events, dropping a bunt and reaching first in 3.5 seconds, circling the bases in 13.75 seconds, and doing the 100-yard dash in 10.25. Two days later, before some 6000 at Terre Haute, Indiana, the teams were again on display. Each Tiger and Cub gathered about $1100 from the two games.

After that Cobb and his wife, mother, and sister returned to Royston for the winter. But Cobb again exhibited the chronic hyperactivity and inability to stay in one place that characterized his behavior throughout his adult life. The day after he got home, he was at the Atlanta fairgrounds to watch some automobile races and appear at a baseball game between two local nines. The day after that he took a train to New York to participate in a motor caravan from that city to Winston, North Carolina, to promote the national "good roads" movement that had grown up with the rapid spread of automobile ownership. All through the Shenandoah valley, people stood along the roadsides and country lanes to get a look at the caravan and especially Cobb, a fellow southerner who had gone north and become a famous ballplayer. The trip was slow going but fun; at Roanoke, Virginia, after Cobb and associates had covered ninety-two miles that day from Staunton, the local citizens would not be satisfied until the Georgian had made a short speech.

Then Cobb and his wife were off to New Orleans so Cobb could make a few hundred dollars playing in a weekend semipro league. There Cobb indulged one of his fondest notions—that he was good enough to play anywhere on the field, even pitch. Most of the time he played first base, but he liked to work out at all the infield positions and in one game took the mound for the final four innings and gave up only one hit. Over the years Cobb would continue to tinker around with pitching, although he never showed more than a fair fast ball, a modest curve, and reasonably good control.

Predictably, Frank Navin did not like to read about Cobb's pitching experiments. It was all right if Cobb picked up a little extra money playing winter ball, Navin wrote, but as for the pitching, "I wish I had hold of you. I would put your arm in a sling, where you would not be able to use it." Navin also cautioned Cobb about taking chances on the bases in offseason games. "If you take care of yourself," Navin counseled, "you should get enough out [of baseball] to be independently well off, when you are through." [15]

The Cobbs had been in New Orleans about two weeks when Cobb got into another altercation, this one with the manager of the Southern Athletic Club over Cobb's fee for refereeing a Saturday-night boxing card. Cobb made it no farther than the first prelim, when he let one little boxer beat another so badly that the crowd demanded he stop the fight. When he still let the carnage go on, police had to climb into the ring and end it. The club manager immediately fired Cobb, who at first angrily demanded his full fee. After his wife came down with a stomach disorder, Cobb settled for a lesser payment and took her back to Georgia.

By January 1909 Cobb had signed and returned his contract for the coming season. Unlike the acrimonious campaign for a big raise he had carried on a year earlier, this time he quietly accepted Navin's offer of a renewal of his 1908 contract on exactly the same terms. What seems likely is that Cobb, at age twenty-two, knew that he had not yet reached his full potential and was willing to stand pat in expectation of having his biggest season yet, thereby establishing an undeniable claim on Navin's treasury.

The Tigers trained at San Antonio, Texas, in 1909, staying at the Hotel Menger, across the street from the historic Alamo. Cobb arrived on March 16, about two weeks after most of the other players. He explained that he had been delayed by having to go to Hazelhurst in southern Georgia to supervise the construction of some low-rent houses on land he had bought. Charlie remained at The Oaks. Her stomach ailment had bothered her all winter, but she would join Cobb later on the team's way north. Amanda Cobb and Florence stayed back at Royston.

At San Antonio, Cobb quickly renewed acquaintances with George Leidy, his mentor at Augusta and now the manager–first baseman of the San Antonio Broncos in the Texas League. The Georgian weighed 183 pounds when he reported and had finally reached his full height, a fraction of an inch over six feet. Although in his twenties he characteristically lost ten pounds or so during the course of a season, he was still a substantially bigger man than most ballplayers of the period. The day after his arrival, against San Antonio, he demonstrated that he was in top condition when he singled twice, stole two bases, and scored twice. He was in good spirits, too, apparently on friendly terms with his teammates. Later, at Dallas, he was reported to have taken a spin with Crawford, Summers, and Bush in a new Apperson motor car owned by a Dallas baseball enthusiast, who drove so recklessly that Crawford, the oldest and maybe wisest of the group, finally made him slow down.

Cobb's only public complaint that spring had to do with his brother's baseball fortunes. The St. Louis Browns had drafted Paul Cobb from Joplin after the 1908 season, but manager Jimmy McAleer never notified him to report for spring training. Ty Cobb thought his brother hadn't been treated fairly by the Browns, although there was nothing he could do about it but advise Paul to stay at Royston and wait. That spring was as close as Paul Cobb ever got to the major leagues. Released by the Browns, he caught on with an Eastern League team. For the next seven years he bounced from one minor league to another, finally quitting baseball in 1916 to re-enter Georgia Tech. After serving in the army during the First World War, he eventually went into the real estate business in Florida.

When the Tigers got to Dallas early in April for a couple of exhibition dates with the local Texas Leaguers, Ty Cobb found another reason for playing extra hard against the Browns. Over the winter Boston had sold thirteen-year veteran Lou Criger, a good catcher but a puny hitter, to St. Louis, at the same time that Cy Young, Criger's longtime battery mate, went to Cleveland. Just as the Browns left Dallas (their spring training site) and the Tigers came in, the local newspapers quoted Criger as bragging that Cobb had never given him much trouble and that "I've got his 'goat,' and I've got the rest of that Tiger bunch, too." Criger went on to say that in past seasons, when Cobb got up after dodging close pitches called by Criger, "the fight was all out of him."[16]

Before Criger could get out of Dallas, Cobb hunted him up to promise that he would steal on Criger the first time he got on base against the Browns that year. That he did, when the Browns came into Bennett Park on April 30. It would make a good story if Cobb had actually run wild on Criger everytime Detroit and St. Louis met for the rest of the season, as Cobb later claimed in his autobiography. Yet besides Cobb's confusion in chronology, so that he had Criger in 1909 still catching Cy Young for Boston, the fact is that Criger generally held his own against Cobb and the rest of the Tigers on the few occasions when he played against Detroit that year. Cobb never successively stole second, third, and home on Criger, as he maintained. On May 1 he did clearly show up the veteran catcher by taking second after hitting into a fielder's choice, as Criger held the ball at homeplate; and toward the end of the season he stole second and third in succession on Criger. But on June 24 Criger pegged him out twice in a row, and later that day Criger took Cobb's spikes on his unguarded shins to tag out the Georgian as he tried to score from third on a grounder to shortstop Bobby Wallace. Criger stamped the pain off, stuck a gauze pad on his wound, and stayed in.

That particular game, which the Tigers won 2–1, with Mullin outpitching Bill Dineen, pushed Detroit's record to 38–19. Sparked by Crawford's robust hitting, by the flashy play of Bush at shortstop, and by the steady work of George Moriarty, a new third baseman obtained from New York who specialized in stealing home, the Tigers had surged into a five-and-one-half game lead over Philadelphia.

Cobb's hitting was lackluster for the first few weeks of the season. At one point he was in such a bad slump that he bought a new automobile, an elegant Owen touring car, to help take his mind off his troubles at bat. But as he always did, he soon began to hit profusely. By early June he was well above .300 and adding to his average with almost every game.

If not yet satisfied with his own performance (which he never completely was), Cobb at least now claimed to be content in his relations with his manager and teammates. In an interview in May with a St. Louis sportswriter, he praised Hughey Jennings as "a wonder" who had overcome the Tigers' cliquism, largely through the strategy of assigning feuding players to adjoining hotel rooms on road trips so that, especially in sharing bathroom facilities, they had to learn to get along. To that same end, Jennings had made certain players take opposite Pullman berths. In such fashion Jennings had created a situation wherein "all the boys are working like one big family." [17]

In the same interview Cobb denounced as "an injustice" and "infamous" charges made by various players and writers around the league that he intentionally tried to spike people. He had cut a few men, he admitted, most recently Cleveland's Bill Bradley, his teenage hero, whom he had spiked getting back to third on a pickoff attempt. Catcher Nig Clarke had wanted to fight him over that spiking, but Bradley had said, as Cobb quoted him, "Ty, old boy, it wasn't your fault." "Put me right, bo!" Cobb demanded of the press. "I don't mind the bleachers roasting me, but put me right, will you?" While he was "no man's friend" on the ballfield, "After the game is over, it's different." [18]

Of course Cobb held plenty of grudges when he left the playing field. He freely accepted challenges from other players (such as Criger's) and every day seemed to be challenging himself, striving to show everybody how good he could possibly be. Usually he succeeded in what he tried, but like all players, both stars and journeymen, he had his embarrassemnts.

Maybe the worst such occasion was May 11, 1909, when more than 10,000 nearly filled the stands at Bennett Park for the ceremonies accompanying the hoisting of last year's American League pennant. The Tigers battered New York that day 16–5, with Cobb doubling twice, driving in two runs, and making it safely home from second on one of Rossman's expert bunts. In the seventh inning, though, he started home from second again on Rossman's roller to the pitcher, ran right past Crawford at third, and, as an amused Hal Chase just held the ball at first and watched, crossed homeplate and was called out for passing another runner. After several moments of bewildered silence, the Detroit fans gave Cobb the kind of razzing he had never heard at home. The next day, though, he more than atoned for his blunder. Playing with a fury in another lopsided victory over New York, he singled three times and tripled to drive in three runs. He also scored twice, one time by stealing second, continuing to third on catcher Kleinow's wild throw, and coming home when shortstop Jimmy Austin retrieved the ball and threw past Kid Elberfeld at third.

If Cobb had any lingering doubts about his already being a famous man, they should have been banished on the Tigers' second trip into Washington in mid-June. Edwin Denby, U. S. Representative from the Detroit district, escorted the team to visit first Joseph G. Cannon, the aging, autocratic speaker of the House of Representatives, and then over to the White House to meet President William Howard Taft. Cannon knew little about baseball or particular ballplayers, but Taft ebulliently greeted each Tiger and showed considerable knowledge of the game and particularly the sorry fortunes of the Washington team. Grasping Cobb's hand and alluding to his own fondness for playing golf at Augusta, the President said, "I believe you and I are fellow citizens of Augusta, Mr. Cobb." The born-and-bred Georgia Democrat replied that he was glad to be Taft's fellow Augustan, and the Republican Chief Executive joked, "The only difference is that down there they think you're a bigger man than I am." [19]

A dramatist might have drawn the scene more appropriately with Cobb meeting Theodore Roosevelt, the strong-willed exponent of the strenuous, red-blooded life, rather than Roosevelt's obese, easy-going successor. Yet Cobb and Taft hit it off quite well. Over the next few years they would occasionally play golf together at Augusta and become rather well acquainted.

Cobb's hitting picked up still more in July, when the Tigers found themselves increasingly pressed not only by Connie Mack's Athletics but by a resurgent Boston team sparked by Tris Speaker, the marvelous rookie center fielder. In the second game of a rain-splattered doubleheader at Washington, Cobb had his first two-homerun game, slashing one of Charley Smith's pitches past Jack Lelivelt in right field for one and later lifting a drive to deepest center field and coming around through Jennings's holdup sign to barely beat the throw home. The day after that, however, Cobb went hitless in an eighteen-inning scoreless tie, with Summers going the distance for Detroit and thereby, many baseball men later felt, ruining his pitching arm. [20] By striking out with the bases loaded to end the fifteenth inning, Cobb embarrassed the afternoon Detroit *Journal*, which had just published an extra edition proclaiming Detroit the winner on Cobb's base hit!

Cobb's overall play almost justified such blind faith. On July 22, at Bennett Park, he again achieved a personal first. After driving in Bush with a single off Boston's Harry Wolter, he proceeded to outrun catcher Pat Donahue's throws to second and third and, after McIntyre walked, to come home on a double steal, beating second-baseman Amby McConnell's throw back to Donahue.

Hampered by Donovan's sore shoulder, Mullin's fatigue (after he had won his first twelve starts), Crawford's game leg, Cobb's stone-bruised foot, and an assortment of injuries to McIntyre, the Tigers on August 14 yielded first place to the Athletics, the first time they had been out of the lead all season. Meanwhile Jennings, thoroughly dissatisfied with his infield, had undertaken to rebuild it at the same time that he tried to keep his team in contention for a third straight pennant. First the Tiger manager traded the popular but badly slumping Schaefer to tailend Washington for Jim Delahanty, a good hitter, a capable second baseman, and one of five Delahanty brothers to play in the majors. After experimenting with Moriarty at first base, Jennings then put him back on third and dealt the wild-throwing and chronically discontented Rossman to St. Louis for Tom Jones, a stolid veteran who was not much at bat but a steady fielder. The play of the newcomers was not spectacular, but at least the infield of Tom Jones, Delahanty, Bush, and Moriarty reduced the errors on a team that had been second in the league in miscues the previous year.

Late in August the Athletics came into Bennett Park for a three-game series, leading the Tigers by one game. The opener provided the occasion for one of the biggest controversies in which Cobb was ever involved, "one thing," he said more than fifty years later, "that's always stuck in my craw."[21] It was a strange game for Cobb from the outset. In the bottom of the first he coaxed a walk from Harry Krause, Mack's fine rookie lefthander, after taking a pitch while Davy Jones was thrown out at third, an apparent mixup in signs. Cobb promptly stole second on catcher Paddy Livingstone. As Crawford was taking a fourth ball, Cobb unaccountably took off for third. Livingstone's throw to third-baseman Frank Baker had him easily. When Cobb hook-slid to his left, Baker reached over the bag and tagged him with the ball in his bare hand. Cobb's right foot grazed Baker's forearm and opened a small cut. Baker and the rest of the Athletics stormed around the umpires (there were now two for each game), claiming that Cobb should be ejected for deliberately spiking the third baseman. Less than mortally wounded, Baker had a bandage wrapped around his arm and remained in the game.

Cobb stoked his foes' ire later in the game when he doubled in a run and upset Eddie Collins, Philadelphia's outstanding young second baseman, as he slid in. Another run scored while Collins tried to regain his bearings. When it was over, the Tigers had won 7–6 to tie for the lead.

The next day Donovan beat Eddie Plank 4–3 before another big weekday crowd, with Cobb getting two hits and a run batted in. On the 26th Detroit made it a sweep, Mullin shutting out the Athletics 6–0 for his twenty-second win. Crawford and Cobb, having switched places in the batting order (with Crawford now in cleanup), each had two hits; and Cobb again bedeviled Collins, this time scoring when he drew the second baseman's wild throw home.

In the aftermath of the Baker spiking, Connie Mack lost his composure for one of the few times in his life. Calling Cobb the dirtiest player in baseball history, he threatened to take up the issue of Cobb's tactics with the American League owners. President Ban Johnson, exhibiting his frequent impetuosity, warned that Cobb "must stop this sort of playing or he will have quit the game."[22] The next day, though, Johnson backtracked, acknowledging that if Cobb had violated any rules at Detroit, the umpires would have handled the matter then and there. Still later, after examining a photograph by William Kuenzel of the Detroit *News* that showed Baker to be off the base and reaching across to tag Cobb, Johnson announced that Cobb had been within his rights on the play.

Meanwhile spokesmen in Detroit leaped to Cobb's defense. Joe S. Jackson of the *Free Press* suggested that "soft-fleshed darlings" like Baker should follow the rugged example of Kid Elberfeld, who blocked his base, took the spikes, and grinned and bore his pain. Jennings called Mack "a squealer," although he admitted that Cobb was "a bit overzealous at times." Even infielder Bob Unglaub of Washington spoke up for the Georgian, who, according to Unglaub, went only for the bag. "He's playing his style of game," added Unglaub; "he goes at everything in the same manner, and he hates to lose."[23]

The Tigers won fifteen of sixteen games on the same home stand during which they swept the Athletics. Cobb, as was so often the case throughout his long career, seemed to derive energy from adversity and criticism. He hit .640 on the home stand and averaged a stolen base per game. By the time the Tigers left for Cleveland on September 2, they had built leads of five games over Philadelphia and seven and a half over Boston.

The Cobb-Baker affair was still boiling when Cobb got into a more serious escapade in Cleveland. On Friday night, September 3, after a rain-terminated tie at League Park, Cobb went to the theater with some of his teammates. Afterward he had supper with Vaughn Glaser, the play's producer-director, whom he had met a year or so earlier in Detroit. When Cobb returned to the Hotel Euclid about 2:00 and started up to his room, he got into an argument with the black elevator operator, whom he later described as "insolent." Apparently Cobb slapped the man, at which point George Stansfield, the hotel's black night watchman, intervened. Cobb and Stansfield began shouting at each other, and Stansfield struck Cobb with his nightstick. They struggled and fell to the floor, where Cobb managed to get a knife from his pocket and slashed at Stansfield. The watchman threw Cobb off, made it to his feet, pulled his pistol, and knocked Cobb to his knees with another blow from the nightstick. Other hotel employees then came between the two. Holding his head, Cobb finally made his way to his room.

The next afternoon Cleveland's Cy Falkenburg and Cy Young beat Mullin and Donovan in a doubleheader to cut the Tigers' lead to three games. Cobb showed up with head and cheek bandaged, got three hits off Falkenburg, but was held hitless by the venerable Young. Meanwhile the manager of the Euclid finally got around to notifying the police about the previous night's disturbance. By the time two detectives arrived at League Park to talk to Cobb, the second game was over and he and the rest of the team were already at Union Depot, about to board their train for St. Louis.

Although the Detroit papers played down the Cleveland fracas, the press elsewhere carried fairly extensive reports. The New York *Age*, a black weekly, recalled last year's run-in with the black street worker in Detroit and commented that Cobb had "once more come into the limelight for ruffianism."[24] A couple of days after the fight Stansfield, reportedly suffering from head, shoulder, and hand wounds and too weak to leave his bed, had his attorney swear out a warrant for Cobb's arrest on a charge of "cutting with intent to kill."[25] At the same time, Stansfield filed a civil suit against Cobb for $5000 in damages. The word from Cleveland was that a detective would soon be coming to Detroit to serve the arrest warrant.

Frank Navin and the ballclub's attorneys quickly started working to extricate Cobb from the Cleveland imbroglio. Over long distance Navin talked Stansfield's employers at the Hotel Euclid into getting him to drop the criminal charges against Cobb. Meanwhile Edward S. Burke, the club's legal representative, came to Cleveland, had a conference with Stansfield and his lawyer, and arranged a settlement whereby the club agreed to pay Stansfield's medical expenses plus an amount of cash, described by Jake Mintz, the Cleveland detective in charge of the case, as "a pitiful sum, so small I would be ashamed to tell you." Even though Stansfield had dropped his charges, Mintz added, the Cleveland police intended to pursue the warrant on their own. Whenever Cobb crossed into Ohio, Mintz intended to "lay for his train and drag him off. It will cost him a pretty penny to fight the case."[26]

It was bad enough to be facing arrest in Cleveland without having to worry about being shot down by a murderous Philadelphian. Yet that was exactly what was threatened in a dozen notes Cobb had received by the time the Tigers came into Philadelphia on September 15, leading the Athletics by four games, to start a climactic four-game series. Kept going largely by the vitriolic columns of the *Bulletin's* Horace Fogel, anti-Cobb feeling still ran high over the Baker spiking the previous month.

When Eddie Plank took the mound on Thursday afternoon, the 16th, an overflow crowd of 24,710 had jammed into the Athletics' new ballpark, occupied since the beginning of that season. Named after club president Benjamin Shibe and located at Twenty-second Street and Lehigh Avenue, it was the first of its kind, an all steel-and-concrete structure intended to maximize customer comfort and convenience. Not part of the paying crowd at Shibe Park that day were hundreds of policemen who surrounded the Tiger bench, roamed the stands and park environs, and most of all hovered behind a jittery Cobb in rightfield.

As it happened, the only serious work they had to do was keep Danny Murphy and Davy Jones from coming to blows after they exchanged insults near the Tigers dugout before the game. At one point Cobb jumped about two feet off the ground when a motor car backfired outside the park. Otherwise nothing of note took place except good baseball, with Plank outpitching Summers 2–1. Cobb went hitless in four times up and, perhaps understandably distracted, struck out with the bases loaded in the fourth inning.

That evening Cobb left the Hotel Aldine for his customary after-dinner walk and cigar, only to be confronted by a crowd of surly Philadelphians who looked about ready to lynch him. Like the heroes in the western dime novels of those years, he walked right into the crowd, which parted mutteringly and let him go on his way.

The next day, his concentration and fervor back to normal, Cobb had two bunt singles and a sacrifice fly off Harry Krause. Scoring late, the Tigers won it 5–3 for Mullin and restored their four-game margin. When Cobb stole third, Baker shook his hand to signify that by-gones were by-gones. The crowd cheered Cobb when he dived into the roped-off area in the right-field corner to take Harry Davis's foul fly, and again when he returned next inning with five dollars for a man whose straw hat he had crushed in making the catch. And when the game ended, a number of Athletics rooters shook his hand and clapped him on the back.

On Saturday and Monday, first Charles "Chief" Bender and then again Eddie Plank shut down the Tiger batters, 2–0 and 4–3. The Saturday crowd was everywhere, even massed atop the concrete outfield walls and on the roofs of row houses outside the park. The Philadelphia management claimed that 35,000 saw the game, the biggest gathering in baseball history. Another huge turnout on Monday pushed the four-game attendance close to 120,000.

On both days the Philadelphia partisans continued to cheer Cobb, even though he spiked shortstop Jack Barry going into second early in Monday's game. As he left the field to get his leg stitched up, Barry gestured to the fans to indicate that the spiking had been accidental. Almost as if he missed the crowd's hostility, Cobb managed only a single on Saturday and another on Monday.

Although they won only one of four at Philadelphia, Cobb and company left town still two games up. The two teams battled evenly for the next week. Then on September 29 the Tigers clinched a tie for the pennant with a doubleheader victory over Boston, mainly on the heroics of Killian, who went the distance in both games, and Cobb, who had five hits in seven at bats. Detroit backed into a third straight league championship at Boston the next day. Although Mullin failed in a bid for his thirtieth win, Chicago's Jim Scott and Bill Burns beat the Athletics in a doubleheader to put Detroit up by four games with only three to play. Jennings then sent Cobb and seven other mainstays back to Detroit to rest up. Three days later the Detroit substitutes ended the season by beating Chicago for the team's ninety-eighth win, the most in American League history up to then. The Athletics finished three-and-a-half games behind.

With three singles and a double in his last appearance of the regular season, Detroit's next-to-last game, Cobb finished with an average of .377, thirty-one points higher than runnerup Eddie Collins. With the title went a huge silver loving cup given to the top batter in the major leagues by George "Honey Boy" Evans, a well-known songwriter and blackface comedian of the period. Cobb also led the league in hits (216), runs (116), stolen bases (76), runs batted in (107), homeruns (9), and total bases (296). No American Leaguer had ever stolen that many times; only once had any player stolen as many in the major leagues. It was the finest all-around year anybody had enjoyed up to then.

In the National League that year the mighty Cubs won 104 games, but the Pittsburgh Pirates, led by their great shortstop John "Honus" Wagner, were even mightier, ending with a 110–42 record. In mid-season the Pirates had moved into the second of the steel-and-concrete parks that over the next several years would replace the old wooden facilities in the major league cities. Later named Forbes Field, the Pittsburgh park seated just short of 30,000 with standing room for several thousand more in a big outfield. It, Shibe Park, and Chicago's Comiskey Park, where the White Sox would debut in 1910, were the original showplaces of the early twentieth-century baseball boom.

The World Series got under way in the Pittsburgh park on October 7. Cobb arrived by an out-of-the-way route. While the rest of the team came through Cleveland on the Lake Shore railroad, he and his wife traveled across Ontario to Buffalo and then south to Pittsburgh on the Michigan Central and Pennsylvania lines, so that Cobb could avoid being arrested in Cleveland, where the authorities had secured an indictment for felonious assault in the Stansfield matter. For the rest of his Series travels Cobb had to continue to bypass Ohio.

Before game one there was as much betting on how Cobb and Wagner would do comparatively as there was on the outcome of the Series itself. While the Pirates took batting practice and Cobb talked near the Tiger dugout with his wife and with his mother, who had come up from Georgia for the Series, the stocky, amazingly bow-legged Wagner came over and introduced himself. A primitive motion-picture camera recorded Cobb and the popular "Dutchman," who had just led his league in batting for the seventh time, as they chatted amiably, discovered that they used similar hands-apart, sliding grips on the bat, and agreed that Wagner would join Cobb for some bird-hunting in Georgia during the offseason.

Wagner then proceeded to outperform Cobb in almost every category. Although the Tigers put up their best fight so far in a World Series, taking player-manager Fred Clarke's Pirates the full seven games, Cobb's showing was almost as disappointing as in 1907. In the seven games he was only six for twenty-six, an average of .231. Half of his hits, though, were doubles. He also stole two bases.

One of those steals came in game one, when just under thirty thousand watched righthander Charles "Babe" Adams, in his first full year in the majors, beat Mullin 4–1. Cobb walked and scored the Tigers' only run in the first inning, and later got on via a fielder's choice and hook-slid safely into second as Wagner one-handedly fielded catcher George Gibson's low throw and made a swooping tag. In the seventh little Tommy Leach made a running catch of Cobb's drive in deep right-center with two Tigers on base to end the last Detroit threat.

The next day a couple of thousand more people saw the Tigers pound Howie Camnitz and Vic Willis for seven runs while Donovan held the Pirates to two. After walking in the third inning and taking third when Jim Delahanty drove home Davy Jones and Bush, Cobb had his biggest moment of the Series. As Willis went into his windmill windup for his first pitch, Cobb dashed home and slid by Gibson for a clean steal. Later he grounded a single over second.

The two teams combined for twenty hits in game three, played before Detroit's biggest Series crowd thus far, 18,277. Nick Maddox survived six Tiger runs; Summers, Willett, and Ralph Works yielded eight to Pittsburgh. Cobb singled in Davy Jones in a four-run seventh inning, made a tumbling catch of John "Dots" Miller's liner in the sixth, and in the bottom of that inning doubled into the overflow in right to send in Davy Jones again in a two-run rally that fell short.

Cobb had only one hit in each of the next two games. With the Detroit temperatures in the low thirties, Mullin tossed a four-hit shutout in the fourth game, besting Al "Lefty" Leifield and Charles "Deacon" Phillippe 5–0. Cobb's double in the third brought home Davy Jones and Bush, but twice Gibson grabbed his bunts and threw him out. Back in Pittsburgh on October 12, Adams allowed the Tigers six hits (including three by Crawford and a homer by Jones), while the Pirates knocked Summers around for an 8–4 victory to take the Series lead. Cobb's offensive contribution was a line single in the sixth, followed by Crawford's run-scoring double.[27]

In game six only 10,535 chilled fans were on hand in Detroit to see Mullin scatter eight hits and even the Series in a thrilling 5–4 game. Tom Jones had to leave after a collision with Bill Abstein at first, and Schmidt and Moriarty were spiked tagging out runners to kill the Pirates' rally in the ninth. Cobb's liner past Abstein, which rolled into the crowd for a double to score Davy Jones in the sixth, was his only hit, one of ten the Tigers got off Willis, Camnitz, and Phillippe.

Adams's six-hit shutout at Detroit on Saturday the 16th sent the Tigers to another World Series defeat. Donovan left after three innings and two runs that resulted mainly from his wildness; Mullin, with little left after winning twenty-nine regular season games and going the distance in his two Series starts, yielded the remaining six runs. Adams got Cobb to fly out twice and tap back to him in his other two times up. In better weather, 17,562 disappointed fans sat in the Bennett Park stands and stood around the outfield.

The crowds at the seven games set a new Series attendance record and put $1,273.50 in each Tiger's pocket. That and the fact that they had pushed the Pirates to the limit provided some consolation for a unique three straight Series defeats. Again Detroit's catchers, this time Schmidt and Oscar Stanage, had been unable to stop National League baserunners. Pittsburgh stole fourteen bases, with Wagner alone taking six to go with his .333 Series batting average. Weak catching, the inability to hit at critical times, and the unheralded, unanticipated pitching prowess of Babe Adams (who had only twelve wins during the season) pretty much decided the outcome.

Celebrational banquets following Tiger World Series defeats were becoming rather monotonous. Nonetheless, some 250 well-to-do Detroiters turned out at the Ponchartrain to cheer the three-time losers. The banqueters made up a collection of $64 for Ulysses Harrison, a diminutive young black man whom the team had taken on in mid-season as its batboy—or "mascot," to use the term then current. Designated custodian of Harrison's purse, Cobb paternally promised to take the man (inevitably nicknamed "Rastus") back south with him and give him a job around an Augusta automobile dealership Cobb had bought.

There was still that messy business in Cleveland to tend to. On October 20, Cobb, accompanied by Frank Navin and attorneys Burke and R. E. McKisson, former mayor of Cleveland, appeared in common pleas court and pleaded not guilty to the indictment for felonious assault on George Stansfield. Trial was set for November, with Cobb released under a $500 bond.

Back in Detroit, Cobb put his wife on a train for Augusta and prepared to leave for New York. He was scheduled to drive an expensive Chalmers "30" in another good-roads promotional trip, this one terminating at Augusta. Before he left town, Navin arranged for him to come by the Bennett Park office and, for the benefit of the press, smile agreeably, sign a blank contract, shake hands with Navin, and then catch his train, ostensibly happy to trust his boss to do right by him. Actually they had come to terms well before the signing tableau, and with surprising amiability.

Navin could afford to be generous. That year his team had pulled close to half a million people into the cramped Detroit ballpark. Only the Athletics and Highlanders, both located in huge metropolitan areas, had drawn more in the American League. The uncertain Detroit franchise of a few years earlier had turned into one of the most profitable in baseball. So Navin was willing to settle with Cobb for a three-year contract at $9000 per year. Only Honus Wagner, a thirteen-year veteran who had been a top star long before Cobb began playing pro ball, would be making more money in 1910.

After the drive south from New York, an excursion again accompanied by receptions and speech-making, Cobb spent a few days around Royston and in Augusta getting his dealership launched. Then it was back to Cleveland, where Navin's attorneys had plea-bargained the charge against Cobb down to assault and battery. On November 22, Cobb pleaded guilty to the lesser charge and was fined $100 and costs. When he said that he didn't have that much money with him, the judge let him leave the court with the promise to pay the fine on the Tigers' first visit to Cleveland during the 1910 season.

Well-married, famous, on his way to being rich, and with his legal troubles cleared up, Cobb could smile plenty for photographers now. He doubtless looked forward to appearing in more World Series. As things turned out, though, the 1909 team was the last pennant-winner he would ever play on. For the next nineteen years he would be a member of also-rans; only once during that long span would he come really close to another Series. Yet in those years he would amass the most remarkable set of individual statistics in the history of the game. And he would remain a singular personality, frequently surrounded by the acrimony and strife that seemed necessary byproducts of his vying nature.

VI

"The Greatest Player of All Time"

While Cobb spent most of the offseason near his wife, who was expecting their first child, Matty McIntyre led a patched-together group of Tigers to Cuba for a series with two local teams. A year earlier the Cincinnati Reds had dropped the majority of the games they had played in Cuba, and with a squad that lacked not only Cobb but Crawford, Donovan, Summers, and Delahanty and soon would lose Bush because of an injury, McIntyre should have expected a tough time. Of the twelve games played against the all-Cuban Almendares team and the Havana Reds, who had added several outstanding black professionals from the United States, the Detroit aggregation won only four. Clearly the best Cuban baseball was already comparable to the best played by *los gringos*, although for decades North American commentators, even those who saw firsthand how good the Cubans were, continued to downgrade the caliber of play in that country and other parts of Hispanic America.

Meanwhile Cobb threw himself into both recreation and business affairs with the same zeal that he typically brought to the baseball field. At the posh new Augusta Country Club he tried golf, immediately liked the game, and began to play it resolutely. That November he had a short visit with President Taft, down for a little winter golfing at Augusta himself, who called Cobb "the most popular Georgian" and had him pose for the photographers with Major Archie Butt, Taft's military aide and a native Georgian.

Cobb also did a fair amount of offseason hunting, especially on George Stallings's property near Haddocks in central Georgia, where Honus Wagner also dropped in for some bird-shooting in January. Stallings, an Augusta native, had managed Philadelphia in the old twelve-team National League, guided Detroit in 1901 (the first season in which the American League had operated on a par with the National), and then managed in the minors until Frank Farrell hired him to lead the New York American Leaguers, whom he had brought in fifth in 1909. Dark-featured, hot-tempered, known for outbursts of stunning profanity on the bench, Stallings had done well outside baseball. Stallings's place was what northern writers often mistakenly termed the Cobb farm at Royston: an authentic plantation, a 4000-acre domain on which as many as fifty black people produced cotton.

Cobb's business ventures took up most of his time that winter. His automobile dealership in Augusta evidently got off to a good start. Ulysses Harrison, the team mascot to whom Cobb had given a job, returned to Detroit early in February with the report that in his first month Cobb had sold about ten motor cars. On a tract of land at Toccoa in Habersham County, not far from his birthplace, Cobb and his business partners built another group of dwellings for black renters, similar to what they had already done at Hazelhurst in the southern part of the state. As Cobb had sketched the plan the previous spring to a St. Louis sportswriter, "this nigger property down home," dubbed "Booker T. Washington Heights," consisted of a dozen houses constructed at a cost of $200 each and renting for $2 to $3.50 a week. "There's money in it," Cobb was convinced.[1]

Tyrus Raymond Cobb, Jr., was born on January 30 at The Oaks, the Lombard estate south of Augusta. "New right fielder," Cobb wired the Detroit sports editors. "Nine pound boy. Everybody well and happy."[2] By the time the baby was ten weeks old, his father was bragging that he was a lefthanded hitter, had the biggest chest development of any baby in the country, and could already support himself on his own legs if held upright.

Frank Navin congratulated "Friend Cobb" on his son's arrival and extended his wishes that "the young man will prove to be as good a man as his father." He added that he had received a bill for $1200 from the Cleveland law firm that had represented Cobb in the Stansfield case. "I promised you I would see you through in the matter," wrote Navin, "and therefor I paid the same without any parley." He hoped that "it will prove a good lesson to you." Cobb doubtless had that particular favor in mind when, in a letter to the Detroit papers late in March, he declared that Navin "has shown me he is my friend" and "our relations could not be better."[3]

By that time Cobb was engaged in his usual procrastination about going to spring training, which in 1910 was again far away at San Antonio. At his dealership he looked up from fixing something on one of his motor cars and told reporters that his only reason for not being at San Antonio was "these four autos you see on the floor." He had to get back his $4000 investment and couldn't see why he "should pass up a chance to make this extra money just for the sake of going clear to Texas for training." Besides, he had been working out daily with the local Sally League team and sometimes playing against the Boston National Leaguers, also training at Augusta. Navin wanted him to join the team by April 1, "in justice to the club."[4] The club president and everybody else realized that Cobb's presence would make substantial difference in the exhibition game receipts, on which the club depended to help pay spring-training costs. Still Cobb delayed.

The fact was that he despised just about everything having to do with spring training—from the cheap hotels and unpredictable food, to the monotony of morning-afternoon workouts, to the rattling train trips to out-of-the-way places for games on skinned and pot-holed ballfields. Unlike others on his team, Cobb had no close pals whom he looked forward to seeing again after a winter's separation. It was just a dull, lonely routine, and a totally unnecessary one for a man who prided himself on always staying in shape. So year after year, while Navin, Hughey Jennings, and his teammates grumbled about his absences, Cobb took advantage of his star status and stayed away as long as possible.

That spring of 1910, though, he did work unusually hard off the field, so much so that thereafter he left the running of the auto dealership to others before eventually selling out. Looking tired and rundown, he finally left Augusta on April 3. After stopping off at Royston to visit his mother and sister, he joined the Tiger regulars at Evansville, Indiana, in time for an exhibition game.

Although Cobb hardly needed to be told that he was a top star, such reassurances now came from all quarters and in superlatives hitherto not even applied to Lajoie or Wagner. The previous fall, for example, Jimmy McAleer, moving from managership of the St. Louis Browns over to the Washington team for 1910, hailed Cobb as "the wonder of the base ball world" and "the greatest piece of base ball machinery that ever stepped on the diamond." Yet while McAleer's praise was nice, more attention-getting was what Charles Comiskey, owner of the Chicago White Sox, said in a nationally syndicated newspaper piece that spring. After forty years in the game as player, manager, and club executive, Comiskey spoke authoritatively in baseball circles. Thus when the "old Roman" pronounced Cobb "the greatest player of all time," it seemed an especially significant accolade. Cobb, said Comiskey, "plays ball with his whole anatomy—his head, his arms, his hands, his legs, his feet." Dedicated and hard-driving, Cobb was also exceptionally intelligent, able to recognize and overcome his own weaknesses as well as exploit those of others. Above all, Cobb was "a student . . . willing to learn something new about baseball everyday of his life."[5]

Cobb had yet to mature as a man; some might say he never did. By the start of his fifth major-league season, however, he had brought his skills as a ballplayer to a state of maturity that might be termed the Essential Cobb. He had already reached that stage in his career where he could do everything on the ballfield he would ever be able to do, and with greater aggregate talents than anybody who had come before him. The Cobb of the years 1910–17 was the Cobb baseball fans would remember most vividly in the decades after his retirement. Cobb's style and temperament were sufficiently dominant in those years that historians would later describe pre-World War I baseball as the "Cobbian" game, as opposed to the "Ruthian" game that came to prevail after the war.

By 1910 Cobb knew the American League inside out. He knew what kind of stuff the established pitchers threw, knew what they would probably throw in given situations, knew how well or how poorly they held runners on base. He hit nearly all of them at least passingly well—righthanders like Ed Walsh, Cy Young, Walter Johnson, Addie Joss, lefties like Eddie Plank, Doc White, the towering Cy Falkenberg. Cobb also knew the catchers—what kind of arms they had, when they would likely call for a pitchout. And he knew just as well the outfielders' arms, how quickly they fielded base hits, and thus when he could go for an extra base on them. Game after game, play after play, Cobb scrutinized the opposition, seeking some new insight into a man's actions on the field, some idiosyncrasy or minor shortcoming he could capitalize on, if not that day then sometime.

As he swung three bats waiting to hit, Cobb would work himself into a state approaching hatred for the pitcher he was about to face. If they watched closely enough, spectators sitting near the field could see him clenching his jaws and gritting his teeth. When he got to the plate, he might try almost anything to upset the pitcher, including defiant exchanges even with such an august personage as Cy Young. He might take his stance, then suddenly jump backward out of the batter's box, or bend over and reach down for a handful of dirt even as the pitcher delivered the ball, seemingly unmindful of the pitch. On one occasion, in 1917, he stood at the plate with his back turned to Eddie Cicotte, talking to Sam Crawford on deck, while the flustered Cicotte threw four straight balls.

In 1913 Walter Johnson remarked that he could never seem to get a strike by Cobb because he just "nips at the ball."[6] Cobb often hit the ball a long way, but even more often he slapped, poked, or bunted it. Besides bunting to get on base, a skill at which nobody surpassed him, Cobb, playing in an era when even the most feared hitters were expected to give themselves up to move runners along, was also usually up near the leaders in sacrifice bunts. Although he bunted successfully on every infielder, he always claimed that third-baseman George "Buck" Weaver of the White Sox was the hardest man to lay one down on.[7]

Like all hitters, Cobb had his slumps. Bunting for hits was one way he worked his way through such periods. He would also take extra batting practice, not trying to hit the ball for distance but just right through the middle of the infield. In that way he soon regained his timing and began to connect as usual. Cobb claimed that it was easier to pull out of a slump playing away from home, "because I like opposition, and I can get myself straightened out with the crowd hooting me for failing to hit."[8] At any rate, never in twenty-three full seasons in the American League did he have a prolonged batting drouth.

Once on base, particularly after a hard sprint, Cobb sometimes held his leg and limped around in an effort to fool the other team into thinking he had hurt himself and would have trouble running. Typically he kicked the bag forward to get the advantage of the couple of inches of play in the strap that held it down. When he took his lead, he would lunge ahead on false starts, wave his arms, yell at the pitcher, and otherwise do everything possible to upset the opposition. While such actions might seem bush league in a later, more sedate time in baseball history, for Cobb they repeatedly proved effective.

Going into a base, Cobb had little regard for the well-being of infielder or catcher. Most of the time, though, he did not ram straight into the base but executed a graceful hook slide, either touching the bag with his toe or grabbing it with his hand as he went by. Either way, he left little for a baseman to tag. If opponents still got spiked, as they often did, then that was just too bad as far as Cobb was concerned. Over and over he argued that "The baserunner has the right of way and the man who blocks it does it as his own peril."[9]

In general, Cobb viewed the baseball field as an arena of harsh, unrelenting combat where he had to "meet trick with trick." "I have observed," he said in 1914, "that baseball is not unlike a war." A decade later he was still insisting "that it is just as sportsmanlike to make the other fellow tremble as to let him make me tremble." Opponents early came to understand that it was in their own best interest not to rile Cobb unnecessarily. "The one thing we didn't want to do was get him mad," recalled Ray Schalk, the scrappy little man who became first-string catcher for the White Sox in 1913 and remained so for the next thirteen years. So when Cobb came on the field, players on the other team would call out, "Hello, Peach! How are you, Peach!" and otherwise behave affably.[10]

Cobb had no use for the idea that once the contest seems safely won it is inadvisable to embarrass or humiliate the opposition. In his thinking there was always a good, practical reason for pouring it on even after his team got way ahead. As he put it in 1921, "if we cannot only beat them, but run wild on them in addition, treat them like a lot of bush leaguers, it is liable to put them up in the air for a week." What Cobb sought, as both player and later as manager, was to work "a general demoralization on the opposition."[11]

Yet for a man who studied everything about the game so closely, worked to refine his every move, took such a "scientific" approach to baseball that it seemed to one interviewer "he had been spending his off-season in the company of intellectuals," Cobb was a remarkably superstitious person.[12] Besides the usual quirks about horseshoes, rabbits' feet, black cats, and the like, he exhibited several idiosyncratic fetishes. During the cake-cutting ceremony at his wedding, for example, he held a black bat he had used in winning the batting championship the previous year. Cobb still carried that bat around with him even though he never hit with it after 1907. When he was in a hitting surge and playing at home, he followed an obsessive daily routine, which included eating the same food, taking the same route to the ballpark, putting on the same uniform sock first, and wearing the same sweatshirt no matter how rank it got. As long as his hot streak continued, he refused to allow his uniform to be cleaned, even though it was usually the dirtiest on the team. After making four hits in a game in 1909, he became furious with trainer Harry Tuthill for moving his shower towel to a different peg from the one on which Cobb had been hanging it.

Such blind beliefs were part of Cobb's complex makeup as he began the 1910 season, one that as usual would be peppered with controversy. It was a flush time for baseball. Some 25,000 swamped little Hilltop Park in Manhattan, at 168th Street and Broadway, when the Yankees (as people had started calling the New York American Leaguers) opened with the Boston team, now nicknamed the Red Sox. At Washington, a record crowd of 12,226 watched William Howard Taft throw out the first ball and thereby establish a presidential custom. At Bennett Park, where another Navin-directed renovation had added about 3000 seats, the crowd still overflowed to see Addie Joss and George Mullin both stagger the route in a 9–7 Cleveland win. A week later the two teams opened Cleveland's home season before about 18,000 in League Park, enlarged and partly rebuilt in steel and concrete during the offseason. Earlier in the year Ohio's governor had signed a bill making Sunday baseball legal everywhere in that state. Michigan's Sabbatarian restrictions remained on the statute books, but state and local authorities continued to ignore the Sunday games now regularly scheduled at Bennett Park.

The Tigers looked as strong as ever early in the season. Manager Jennings finally settled on Davy Jones for his regular left fielder and, with Crawford bothered by a sore leg, shifted him to right and put Cobb in center. With the two men in their natural positions for the first time in three years, the Tiger outfield was at maximum defensive effectiveness. Even when McIntyre replaced Jones from time to time, Cobb stayed in center. Despite Donovan's worsening rheumatism, which kept him from taking the mound until late May, the pitching held up pretty well around Mullin, Willett, and Summers.

For the first two months of the season the Tigers battled for the league lead with Connie Mack's Athletics and a revived New York team, directed by Cobb's friend George Stallings. A three-game sweep of the Athletics followed by three wins in four games against New York highlighted that period. Late in June, however, the tailend St. Louis Browns blunted the Tigers' pennant hopes by taking four of six games at Detroit, and not long after that the Athletics swept a four-game series at Philadelphia and virtually killed their chances. By mid-July the Tigers trailed the accelerating Athletics by ten games. For all practical purposes the race was over. With sturdy pitching from Jack Coombs (who won thirty that year), Eddie Plank, Chief Bender, and Cy Morgan; sparkling infield play from Eddie Collins, Jack Barry, and Frank Baker; and solid hitting from outfielders Danny Murphy and Rube Oldring, Connie Mack's team ended up fourteen-and-a-half games in front of second-place New York and eighteen ahead of Detroit. Cobb always thought the 1910–11 Athletics were the best team he ever saw, not only in terms of talent but because "boy, they were smart."[13]

On July 9 Cobb was hitting .372, the best average he had shown at mid-season. Yet he was still twenty-seven points behind Napoleon Lajoie. The muscular, swarthily handsome Cleveland second baseman, now freed from managerial burdens, was having his best season since 1901, when his .422 set a standard unequaled in either major league for twenty-three years. A new Chalmers "30," donated by Hugh Chalmers, president of the automobile company that bore his name, awaited the year's top hitter in the majors. Although such a prize would excite few people today, the modest financial rewards available to most players in 1910 along with the glamor that had attached to the Chalmers "30" lent unprecedented drama to the batting competition that year.

The prospect of not winning a fourth straight title and also missing out on the Chalmers may have begun to wear on Cobb's nerves a bit. He seemed sulky and petulant during the disastrous July series at Philadelphia; for one game he did not get to Shibe Park until the third inning and generally played below par. At the end of the month, however, he performed with his customary fire in a four-game sweep at Chicago. The finale, on Sunday July 31, inaugurated the White Sox' new ballpark. Six-year-old James T. Farrell saw that game and never forgot Cobb's homerun off Ed Walsh in the fifth inning, a liner that bounced through an iron gate in the left-field corner. Following a bases-loaded homer to the same spot by Chicago's Lee Tannehill the previous inning, Cobb's drive made the difference in a 6–5 victory.[14]

Back at Detroit for a home stand, Cobb turned problem child again. Since late the previous season he and some of his teammates, particularly Donie Bush and Davy Jones, had occasionally bickered over missed signs. At bat, Cobb would flash his own bunt and hit-and-run signals; baserunners were supposed to watch him, not Jennings, to find out what to do. On August 2, in the midst of a ninth-inning rally against Boston, he and Jones got mixed up in a hit-and-run situation; Cobb looked at Ed Karger's pitch as Jones took off and was thrown out by Bill Carrigan. That ended the rally and sent the Tigers to another defeat. Afterward Cobb and Jones quarreled in the clubhouse.

Following an off day, Cobb refused to suit up for the series finale. Grumbling that he wouldn't play again until Jennings took Jones out of the lineup, he watched from the grandstand as Willett defeated Karger 4–2, with Mc-

Intyre taking his place in center field. When New York came into Bennett Park the next day, Cobb arrived at the clubhouse after everybody else had suited up and started to get into uniform, only to be told by Harry Tuthill that Jennings had said he needn't bother. Again he sat in the stands as, according to one report, his teammates "chuckled with glee."[15] And again the Tigers won without him, battering spit-baller Russell Ford 9–6.

The next day, a Saturday, Cobb had a talk with Navin, acknowledged that he may have been hasty in flaring up at Jones, and announced to Jennings that he was ready to play. This time Jennings went along with him, and that afternoon Cobb contributed two singles, a sacrifice fly, and a stolen base to Mullin's shutout of New York. To appease Cobb, Jennings agreed to drop Bush from second in the batting order down to sixth, so that he would never be on the bases when Cobb was at the plate.

Yet Cobb's dark mood had hardly passed. That same afternoon the left-field bleacherites and people along the third-base foul line rode Cobb from the time he stepped on the field. At one point he started to climb into the stands after a black spectator who had heckled him throughout the game. Police got there just before he reached the man and managed to herd him back to the Tigers' dugout behind third. Wrote the Detroit *Free Press*'s E. A. Batchelor, "Ty is a southerner born and bred, and naturally holds ideas of his own regarding the right of a colored man to abuse him in public." Added Frank Navin, "If [Cobb] were less impetuous, he would be less valuable to the club. . . . He is a youngster, hardly more than a boy, and comes from a section of the country where pride is strong."[16]

The discord on the ball club continued for the remainder of the season. Davy Jones charged that Cobb was more concerned with winning the batting championship again than he was with the team's welfare, and that he often failed to follow through on his own signals if a pitch wasn't to his liking. Jones seemed to have a point, both about Cobb's refusal to swing at questionable pitches with teammates in jeopardy and also the whole matter of individual versus team play.

An exploit at Philadelphia later in August, for example, would have been almost unthinkable on a disciplined ball club like McGraw's Giants or Mack's Athletics. With the Tigers down 7–0 in the ninth inning, Cobb hit a high bounder back of second, kept going around first, and beat Jack Barry's throw to Eddie Collins. When George Moriarty's liner off pitcher Coombs's glove caromed over to Collins and when Collins then threw to first for the sure out, Cobb shot around third and barely beat Harry Davis's throw from first to homeplate. It was all quite sensational, even breath-taking, but also foolhardy and bound to feed his teammates' resentments. It turned out to be futile as well, because Coombs then retired Bush to end the game.

Such cavortings delighted the crowds, though, as did the tight American

League batting race. By the first part of September, Lajoie had tailed off to .372 and led Cobb by only eight points. At that juncture Cobb began to have trouble with his vision and stayed in Detroit when the Tigers went to Cleveland for four games. When the two teams returned to Bennett Park, Cobb was in the grandstand wearing smoked glasses. Although examination by an opthalmologist (or "oculist," as such physicians were then called) showed that Cobb was near-sighted in his right eye, the problem turned out to be an inflammation of the optic nerves in the other eye. The ailment was real enough, but Cleveland sportswriters, still angry about Cobb's spiking of Bill Bradley the previous year, derided him for not going head-to-head against Lajoie.

His eye trouble cleared up, Cobb was back in the lineup by September 20. Playing at home before his wife and eight-month-old son Ty, Jr., who had come up from Augusta in August, he was awarded a homer in the opener of a doubleheader with Washington when his line drive rolled under the turnstile gate in right-center. He passed Lajoie with five for six in two games against New York, where Hal Chase's Machiavellian intrigues had got Stallings fired in favor of Chase. After going four for seven on October 6–7 at Chicago, Cobb, confident that he held a safe lead, passed up the final two games there and left in his automobile for Philadelphia, where the Athletics were to play a series of tune-up games with a team of selected American Leaguers while they waited out another week before the National League season ended. Cobb, scoffed the Cleveland *Plain Dealer*, was "suffering from that peculiar disease, 'congealed condition of the pedal extremities,' known to card players as 'cold feet'." [17]

To catch Cobb, Lajoie needed a hit nearly every time he came up in a season-closing doubleheader at St. Louis on Sunday, October 9. At the end of that bizarre day he had eight hits in nine times at bat and, according to most unofficial calculations, had edged Cobb for the batting championship. What happened was that the Browns, or at least most of them, out of their hatred for Cobb and their liking for the good-dispositioned Lajoie, undertook to fix it so "the Frenchman" would win the Chalmers.

Before the game, Browns' manager Jack O'Connor instructed John "Red" Corriden, a young third baseman who had come up toward the end of the season, to play on the outfield grass behind third to avoid injury from one of Lajoie's vicious line drives. The gullible rookie did just that—all day long. In his first time up Lajoie clouted a legitimate triple over the head of Hub Northen, another rookie, in center field. The next time at bat, though, he bunted toward shortstop Bobby Wallace, who fielded the ball slowly and threw too late to get Lajoie, and the time after that he bunted to third, where Corriden was so far back that he had no chance for a play.

From then on Lajoie bunted to Corriden, six more times. On all but one, a fielder's choice, he made easy base hits, so that he ended with eight for nine. Determined that Lajoie should have a perfect day, Browns' coach Harry Howell first went to the press section to inquire about the scoring on the fielder's choice and then sent over the batboy with a note offering scorer E. V. Parrish a suit of clothes if he changed his ruling. Parrish refused. At the end of the second game (won, incidentally, by Cleveland to give the teams a split), many of the 10,000 or so St. Louis fans on hand poured onto the field to congratulate the popular Frenchman.

The odor hanging over Sportsman's Park was foul indeed. The next day, when all five St. Louis sportswriters at the scene charged the Browns with giving Lajoie hits, O'Connor lamely answered that Lajoie "outguessed us. We figured he did not have the nerve to bunt every time [after tripling]." Said Lajoie, dissatisfied because he had been scored only eight for nine, "I fooled them right along." Red Corriden could only plead, "I wasn't going to get killed playing in on Lajoie."[18] That afternoon Lajoie received a congratulatory telegram from eight of Cobb's teammates.

Ban Johnson's handling of the smelly affair was masterfully politic. After he and Garry Herrmann, National Commission chairman, both issued announcements that there would be no more prizes awarded for batting leadership alone, Johnson had Robert McRoy, his secretary and keeper of the American League's official statistics, hurriedly calculate the season averages. On October 15, less than a week after the St. Louis fiasco, Johnson declared Cobb the batting titlist with an average of .384944 to Lajoie's .384084, at the same time that he affirmed the legitimacy of Lajoie's eight-hit day. "I am simply delighted, delighted, delighted," enthused Cobb in Philadelphia when he heard the news. Maintaining that the competition with Lajoie "was of a most friendly character," he tactfully refused to say anything critical about the St. Louis games. He was just "glad everything has turned out as it did" and "tickled to death."[19]

Shortly thereafter Hugh Chalmers, coupling generosity with promotional acumen, announced that his company would give a Chalmers "30" to Cobb and to Lajoie too. That was done at the opening game of the World Series between the Athletics and Cubs at Shibe Park. Meanwhile owner Robert Lee Hedges of the Browns fired both O'Connor and Howell. Ban Johnson used his vast influence to ensure that neither man found a job with a team in Organized Baseball, although Howell eventually did some umpiring in the minors. Of the whole affair St. Louis *Post-Dispatch* sports editor John E. Wray wrote, "It's a soiled page—let's turn it over for good."[20]

Playing with such stars as Tris Speaker, Clyde Milan, Walter Johnson, and Ed Walsh in three of the five tune-up games with the Athletics, Cobb earned several hundred dollars out of the all-stars' share of the gate receipts, plus a gold watch and diamond stickpin given by the Philadelphia club to each of the players. He stayed over in Philadelphia for the first two games of the Series to make a little more money providing his observations to the Detroit *Free Press*. Cobb then passed up the rest of the Series and, with his wife and infant son, embarked on an arduous journey from Philadelphia to Augusta in the new Chalmers.

Before he left though, he, along with Jennings, Crawford, Donovan, and several others, heard that the investment of their 1909 Series money in a copper-mining venture at Bisbee, Arizona, had just paid off lavishly. The stock they had bought at $3 a share was now worth $1000 a share. Cobb had also put about $1000 into cotton futures on the Tigers' last trip into New York; now he sold for a profit of $7500. Along about that time, moreover, he bought a big block of stock in United Motors, soon to be absorbed into General Motors, at a few dollars a share. Cobb had spent years listening and learning in the heady atmosphere of the Hotel Ponchartrain bar and other favorite gathering places for Detroit's business elite, but he had lacked the capital to follow up on the tips that came his way. Now, having money to invest and a growing number of informative business acquaintances, especially in the burgeoning auto industry, Cobb began to accumulate the stock that would constitute the major portion of his fortune.

If Cobb's financial circumstances improved steadily, his relations with teammates were at their lowest point since the spring of 1907. Cobb was on the outs not only with Davy Jones, Bush, and again McIntyre but now as well with Crawford, who had come to Bush's defense when Cobb criticized the little shortstop's play. Shortly before the end of the season, Crawford publicly complained that the trouble with the Tigers in 1910 had been "too much Cobb." Jennings, Crawford said, let Cobb do about as he pleased. That included not only skipping morning practices and sometimes showing up late for games but also playing mainly for his own statistics. Paul Bruske agreed that "Ty made his season a personal one." With his star now on speaking terms with only a few of the other Tigers, "Hughie Jennings has a problem to solve before next season rolls around."[21]

Within baseball circles that fall, rumors circulated frequently that Cobb would be traded. While Cobb traveled about in his new Chalmers and tried some auto-racing at the Atlanta and Savannah speedways, Frank Navin maintained that "the effect of the alleged dissension" on the team had been exaggerated. "So long as I retain any connection with the Detroit baseball club," he added, "Ty Cobb will play in this city."[22] Regardless of how the other players felt, Navin was not about to trade a man who had just topped the league's hitters for the fourth straight year, led in runs and in slugging average, come in second in homers, runs batted in, hits, and stolen bases, and become the outstanding gate attraction in baseball.

Early in November the alarming news reached Navin that Cobb intended to drive against Nap Rucker, his old Augusta roommate and now a mainstay of Brooklyn's pitching staff, in a ten-mile match race at the Atlanta track. The Tiger president hurriedly got off a wire to Cobb urging him not to go through with the dangerous stunt. Although the match had been heavily promoted in the Atlanta area, Cobb finally heeded Navin's plea and backed out. For three or four more years, though, auto-racing would rank with golf and hunting among Cobb's favorite offseason diversions. What finally scared him off racing, he later said, was the fatal crash of the professional racer Bill McNey at Savannah, only a few days after he and Cobb had hit 105 miles per hour in a test drive on that course.

Also in November 1910, George Mullin led a contingent of Tigers to Cuba for a second series of games with Almendares and the Havana Reds. Billy Evans went along to do the umpiring. Unlike the makeshift group McIntyre had brought down in 1909, Mullin's team included Crawford and all the Tiger starting pitchers, and Cobb had promised to join the team later. Again catcher Bruce Petway and infielders Pete Hill, Grant Johnson, and John Henry Lloyd (sometimes called "the black Lajoie"), who had all played that summer for the powerful Leland Giants of Chicago, were on hand to bolster the Havana team. And again Almendares consisted entirely of native Cubans, or as Bruske termed them, "dusky representatives of the fertile isle." [23]

Lacking enthusiasm for the Cuban venture, Cobb came only because there was money in it. The Tigers had won three, lost three, and tied one against the Cuban teams by the time his boat arrived from Key West on November 26. The next day, before some 15,000 swarming *aficionados* at the Havana stadium, he debuted with two singles and a homerun against pitcher Munoz of Almendares as Mullin shut out the Cubans 4–0. Two days later Gonzales of Havana did the same thing to the Tigers and Willett, 3–0. Cobb went hitless and walked once. When he tried to steal on Petway, the black catcher got the ball to second so quickly that shortstop Lloyd was waiting for Cobb and deftly tagged him out while sidestepping his spikes.

The Tigers perked up considerably after Cobb joined them and finished with a 7–4–1 record. In the last game, against Almendares, they beat right-hander Jose Mendez, a slender, fire-balling, twenty-three-year-old black Cuban who had thrown a shutout early in the series and then battled Summers to a ten-inning tie. Already something of a national idol and well known in North American black baseball as a consequence of a 1909 tour with the Cuban All-Stars, Mendez added to his reputation by holding Cobb to a single and striking him out once, even though the rest of the Tigers hit him well enough to win 6–3.

In the five games he played in Cuba, Cobb had seven hits in nineteen at bats for a .370 average. Crawford hit .360 in twelve games. In their six games against the Tigers, Lloyd hit .500, Johnson .412, and Petway .390—all against frontline major-league pitching. Cobb's competitive instincts should have caused him to speculate on how he would fare season after season against such talent as he had encountered in Cuba—if black ballplayers were ever allowed in his league. Yet according to various accounts, Cobb vowed never again to take the field against blacks. At any rate, he never did.[24]

In 1911 Detroit was to train at Monroe, Louisiana. Cobb was no more anxious to get there than he had been to get to San Antonio the preceding two years. Navin again plaintively pressed him to report with the rest of the players, "as your failure to do so creates a feeling on the club which was brought out in the papers last year." If Cobb got to Monroe on time, tried to achieve harmony on the team, and helped Jennings every way he could, then "I will show you in a very substantial way my appreciation of your efforts."[25]

In mid-March Cobb reported to Jennings at New Orleans, in time for an exhibition game. At least this spring he would not have to contend with Matty McIntyre, who had been sold to the White Sox over the winter.[26] At New Orleans and back at Monroe, Cobb impressed reporters as having slowed down a great deal; one even suggested that while he might become a more powerful hitter, he would never regain his past speed. Unhappy with the spartan accommodations at Monroe and estranged from nearly everybody except the rookies, Cobb got Jennings's consent to train by himself at French Lick, Indiana, a popular resort in the southern part of the state. When he rejoined the club at Evansville a week or so later, he was his usual self on the bases and in the outfield. The startled newsmen with the team discovered that when they had seen him in Louisiana he had been working out with lead weights in his shoes to strengthen his calves and ankles!

By that time Cobb and Davy Jones had smoothed over their differences. When Paul Bruske wrote that Cobb was willing to "eat humble pie" in his feud with Crawford, Navin upbraided Bruske for saying something that "will put him [Cobb] right back on edge again. You know Cobb's disposition as well as I do, and that when he reads an article like that, he is 'up in the air'."[27] At Indianapolis, Navin sought to make peace between Cobb and Crawford and Bush. Bush agreed to try to get along with Cobb, but Crawford refused to be reconciled. Finally, after further diplomacy by Navin, Jennings, and team captain George Moriarty, the two outfielders shook hands on the eve of another season. They would never come to like each other, though.

So, despite the snow flurries that chilled about 5,500 fans on opening day at Bennett, the sun supposedly was shining brightly on Detroit baseball once again. Cobb homered into the left-field bleachers his second time up in that game, off Ed Walsh, and the Tigers went on to win 4–2. They won eleven more in a row, the greatest start any team had made in major-league history. With Cobb and Crawford both pounding the ball and with Del Gainor, a rookie first baseman up from the Central League, hitting around .350 and fielding his position expertly, the Tigers went on to win thirty-one of their first forty games and open up a nine-and-one-half-game lead over the Athletics. They were still playing at a .700 clip in mid-July, despite the loss of Gainor, whose wrist was broken by a Jack Coombs pitch in his twenty-sixth game.

In a season that produced big jumps in scoring and individual and team batting averages in both leagues and much discussion of the apparently livelier, cork-centered ball introduced that year, Cobb's play was frequently awe-inspiring. After he scored from first base on Crawford's single, dashed home from second on a wild pitch, and doubled in two runs at New York, *Sporting Life* estimated his value to his club at $100,000. Late in July he was leading the league at .426. He ran up a forty-game hitting streak, at the time a record for the twentieth century, before Ed Walsh stopped him on July 4. On July 10 he scored from second base on a fly ball against the Athletics and the next day, against the same team, stole second, third, and home on consecutive pitches. Sportswriters covering the Tigers commented that for all his spectacular individual feats, Cobb was playing with a new team spirit, a sole concentration on winning games.

The Cobbs' second child, a daughter whom they named Shirley Marion, was born in Detroit late in June. By then Cobb was talking about making 300 hits in a season and breaking the all-time-high batting average of .492, set by James "Tip" O'Neill with St. Louis in the old major-league American Association back in 1887. Then, troubled by bronchitis and a hacking cough (a symptom that must often have raised the dread specter of tuberculosis in those days), Cobb began to slow down at bat and on the bases. Early in August, *Sporting Life* described him as "in bad shape physically."[28] He finally took himself out of the lineup on the 13th before the second game of a home stand.

The team began to slump, too. Losses on a recent eastern swing had dropped them into second place behind the Athletics. Dissension cropped up among the Tigers again, this time not involving Cobb so much as the unhappiness of various other players with Jennings. Moriarty and Jennings, for example, exchanged angry words over the captain's lack of hustle. Jennings shook up his batting order, putting Cobb in the second spot, but the Athletics continued to extend their lead. On September 26, at Shibe Park, they clinched their second pennant in a row by beating the Tigers, whom they had trailed by twelve games in May, by an 11 to 5 score, with Frank Baker homering twice and doubling twice. Cobb, as well as Crawford and even Jennings, passed up the last two games at St. Louis to get an early start on post-season activities. After losing those two, Detroit ended the season at 89–65, thirteen and a half games out of first place.

Davy Jones told reporters at season's end that Cobb was the only man on the ball club who would still stand up for Jennings. The rest of the players were tired of the manager's sarcasm, his mishandling of pitchers, and his refusal to discipline Cobb. Jennings denied that there was any serious dissension on his team, attributing its fade primarily to Gainor's injury in May.

For a man diagnosed as having inadequate vision in one eye, Cobb had done all right in 1911. His .420 average was the highest he ever attained, twelve points above that of Joe Jackson, Cleveland's slugging young outfielder, who played his first full season that year. Cobb's 248 hits, 147 runs scored, and 144 runs batted in were also career highs for him. Besides also leading the league in doubles, triples, and slugging percentage, he regained the stolen-base title with eighty-three, his most so far. It was one of the finest all-around performances in baseball history. Again the Chalmers Company had an automobile waiting for him, this time for being chosen the Most Valuable Player in the American League by a committee from the Base Ball Writers Association of America.

Sam Crawford also had his best year ever at bat, hitting .378 and driving in 115 runs. Jim Delahanty reached a career-high .339 and drove in 94. In general it was a big year for hitters, with the American League team averages jumping thirty points. The Athletics hit .296 as a club, the Tigers .292. Yet while Philadelphia's pitching remained tough, Detroits's sagged badly. Mullin's 18–10 was the only strong showing on the staff.

After playing another fill-in series with an all-star team that occupied the Athletics while they waited for the National League champion Giants to finish, Cobb again joined the raft of big leaguers whose names appeared on newspaper columns during the World Series. Employed by the Wheeler Syndicate, Cobb worked with Stoney McLinn, a Philadelphia sportswriter, on a daily piece that was syndicated to a dozen or so papers. Cobb always maintained that his material was not ghost-written but was his own, by which he probably meant that he scrutinized and approved what McLinn showed him before it appeared under his name. At that, he would have been doing a great deal more than most of the other hired "analysts" ever did.

Charlie Cobb and the two children remained in Detroit for the 1911–12 offseason, while Cobb embarked on a tour in George Ade's *The College Widow*, a durably popular stage comedy. Cobb had seen the play in Detroit three years earlier, in a production by Vaughn Glaser's company. Unlike a number of baseball notables in that period, Cobb had repeatedly resisted offers of offseason employment on the vaudeville circuit. Glaser, however, finally talked him into making a tour as the star of Ade's play, for a guarantee that was never disclosed but may have been as much as $10,000. So in the lead role as "Billy Bolton," the dashing halfback, Cobb embarked on his theatrical career at Newark, New Jersey, early in November.

Expecting little, the critics were usually generous; some, like the Trenton reviewer who enthused that Cobb "accepted all chances, ran on everything and scored more times than anyone on the team," wrote their dramatic commentary like sports columns. The audiences also expected little but the opportunity to see Cobb in the flesh and in unfamiliar circumstances, and they cheered enthusiastically when he made his entrances and took his bows at curtain call. Although he had no illusions about a future in the theater, Cobb took his role seriously and brought to it his characteristic intensity and determination. Bert Cowan, a bit player in Glaser's company, remembered Cobb as being "exceedingly sharp and quick" and "able to handle his acting chore" respectably.[29]

When the tour reached the southern cities, it became a triumphal procession for Cobb. Arriving with the company at Asheville, North Carolina, wearing an expensive topcoat and fedora and stylishly brandishing a cane, Cobb enjoyed a reception at the Hotel Piedmont and then a banquet after that evening's performance. In Atlanta the Ad Men's Club held the biggest social affair of the tour, a banquet at the Transportation Club attended by seventy-five civic leaders and lasting until 2:00 a.m. There, in Nashville, and elsewhere he played to packed houses. Governor Ben W. Hooper of Tennessee and Dan McGugin, Vanderbilt University's football coach, personally welcomed him. About the only sour note from the South was a critical assessment by Allen G. Johnson, who wrote both sports and theater notices for the Birmingham *News*. Incensed, Cobb fired off an imperious reply to Johnson, enclosing a sheaf of favorable reviews and adding, "I am a better actor than you are, a better sports editor than you are, a better dramatic critic than you are. I make more money than you do, and I know I am a better ball player—so why should inferiors criticise superiors?"[30]

Standing-room-only audiences greeted Cobb when he followed Germany Schaefer's vaudeville act into the Lyceum Theatre in Detroit in mid-December. There, said Ralph Yonker of the Detroit *Times*, the feeling was "that he got away with his lines in excellent shape." But because he "takes everything much in earnest and is anxious to make good at all times," as E. A. Batchelor put it, the strain of nightly performances and matinees on weekends was showing on Cobb. Admitting that he was doing it only for the money, he professed a dislike for acting. It was hard work and hard on his nerves. He had to read for hours after a performance, he complained, before he could fall asleep. Stage success couldn't compare with "the satisfaction of slamming out a nice, clean hit." He had already decided that "I do not like the life and that is all there is to it."[31]

Batchelor's interview with Cobb in his dressing room at the Lyceum, one afternoon during his two-week stand in Detroit, was one of the most revealing he had given up to that time. "It is a wearing, a tearing life," he said of his career in baseball, "but the game is worth the candle." Within four or five years he hoped to be in a position to live comfortably for the rest of his days.

Already he was getting a "big return" on his investments. Cobb also said that he would never play with another team besides the Tigers and would quit when he started slipping, after a last good year. When he first broke in, he admitted, "I thought everybody was fighting me." As a southerner he had considered himself an outsider and had "resented familiarities." Now, though, he was on friendly terms with practically everybody on the team, including "men who took me to task five years ago." As for Jennings's relations with his players, Cobb claimed that only two or three were "sore on him."[32] Jennings, he added, was the most lenient manager in the league—a statement Cobb's teammates would surely have agreed with, at least where Cobb's treatment was concerned.

The College Widow was supposed to tour the eastern theatrical circuit until March. By the time Cobb left Detroit, however, he had already had enough. After appearances in Chicago, Pittsburgh, and New York, Cobb and company closed in Cleveland in mid-January. Declaring "never again," he went home to Detroit. "I believe I was fairly successful for a beginner," he said later. Only once had he forgotten his lines, in Pittsburgh with his wife and children in the audience, when his son yelled "Daddy! Daddy!" at his first entrance.[33] The tour's truncation, not a lack of receipts while it was under way, was doubtless the reason why, according to Cowan, it made little money.

Cobb spent the rest of the winter in Detroit recuperating from the rigors of his ten weeks on the boards. Besides taking up bowling and trying iceboat racing on Lake St. Clair, he studied the history, rites, and rituals of the Masonic Order and, like his father, became a Mason. Cobb also joined Navin, Jennings, and William H. Yawkey in a partnership that bought the Providence club in the International League—an investment that proved one of his least lucrative.

In February the New York *American* paid him for an article in which he offered advice to young men just starting out in baseball. They should dedicate themselves to the game as a profession that could bring big rewards, he admonished. Besides warning against alcoholic beverages and leaving cuts unattended and arguing the sufficiency of two meals a day, breakfast and evening, Cobb also had a few rather eccentric prescriptions. He advised ballplayers to avoid ice water in hot weather and chewing gum, sweet milk, and coffee anytime because they all interfered with one's eyesight.

One of the things that most interested Cobb and many others in Detroit that winter was the construction of a new ballpark for the Tigers. Frank Navin had finally given up on further enlargements to Bennett Park and decided to build a completely new facility, on the same site but reoriented so that homeplate would be where left field had been. Undertaken as soon as the 1911 season was over, demolition of the old park and construction of the new one went forward smoothly through the fall and winter, so that by March the all steel-and-concrete stands were almost finished. The Tigers would open their home season in a park that cost half a million dollars and had seats for about 23,000 people. With covered, single-decked grandstands, covered pavilions, bleachers in right field, and a green concrete wall (kept free of advertisements) in left, it was an attractive and commodious place, a first-class home for the Detroit ball club. Its features included dressing rooms for both home team and visitors, in accordance with Ban Johnson's edict that starting in 1912 all visiting teams must dress on the grounds rather than at their hotels.[34] At Yawkey's insistence, the new park was named Navin Field.

By March the Cobbs were back in Georgia. At Royston, besides seeing Amanda and Florence Cobb, he pitched a shutout for the local nine against Elberton, the first time he had played at his hometown in eight years. This spring he managed to miss Monroe, Louisiana, altogether, joining his club at New Orleans for exhibition games against the Southern League Pelicans before it started north. When the team reached Toledo, the scene of the assault on his tonsils six years earlier, he caught a heavy cold.

Despite a sore throat, cough, and fever, Cobb played all eleven innings in the season opener at Cleveland, going hitless in a 3–2 loss for Mullin to Willie Mitchell. Feeling rotten and in a bad temper, Cobb sought his bed when the Tigers moved on to Chicago. For a couple of years now Navin and Jennings had favored him with a room to himself on the road. Discovering at the Chicago Beach Hotel that the room was next to the Illinois Central railroad tracks, Cobb protested bitterly to the hotel manager and then to Jennings. When told that he could not be shifted that night at the Chicago Beach but that the club would put him up in another hotel, he demanded that the whole team move elsewhere with him. When that was denied, Cobb refused to play the next afternoon at Comiskey Park, then left the team and went back to Detroit.

It was an unhappy beginning to what would be an exceptionally strife-ridden season, even for Cobb, and a poor one for the Detroit ball club. Two days of wet grounds that forced postponement of the gala opening of Navin Field might have been another bad portent. Finally, on Saturday, April 20, a paying crowd of 24,384 plus numerous guests, including Ban Johnson and Garry Herrmann, saw the Tigers inaugurate the new park by beating Cleveland 6–5. Mullin won his own game with a run-scoring single, but before that Cobb, still not feeling his best, thrilled the record throng by singling twice, working back-to-back double steals with Crawford and taking home on the second one, and making two fine catches in center.

The first homerun at Navin Field was Cobb's, a drive into the right-field bleachers on April 25 off the Browns' Earl Hamilton that helped end a four-game Tiger losing streak. Despite Crawford's sturdy presence and Cobb's strong hitting and all-out play on the bases and afield, the team as a whole lacked consistency in any phase of the game. Donovan was finished as a pitcher, as was Summers; Mullin was nearly so; only Willett and Jean Dubuc, a right-hander from Vermont in his first year in the American League, could be relied on. Del Gainor, talented but unlucky, played part of the year before submitting to surgery on his poorly mended wrist. Moriarty was in decline, and Jim Delahanty, Charley O'Leary, and Summers would be let go during the season.

The Tigers were in sixth place with a record of 10–13 when they came into New York for the first time on May 11. An overflow Saturday crowd estimated at 20,000 first applauded Cobb before the game when he received his fourth silver loving cup from little Honey Boy Evans, then berated him when he almost fought with Yankee third-baseman Alvin "Cozy" Dolan after an unsuccessful steal attempt, and finally showered umpire O'Loughlin with bottles and glasses for ejecting manager Harry Wolverton and his pitcher and catcher. Detroit won that raucous encounter, lost on Monday, and then won Tuesday's game. Cobb so far had gone 5–12 in the games at Hilltop Park and had endured steady and harsh razzing from the spectators behind the Detroit bench off third base and down the left-field line.

On Wednesday the 15th, the verbal barrage started as soon as he appeared on the field. One man, wearing an alpaca coat and sitting close to the Tiger bench, was particularly abusive. Named Claude Lueker, he had lost all of one hand and three fingers of the other working as a printing-press operator about a year earlier; now he served as general flunky in the law office of Thomas Foley, former sheriff of New York County. Although Cobb did not know who the man in the alpaca coat was, he recognized him as somebody who had given him a hard time during previous visits to Hilltop Park.

For two innings Cobb and Lueker traded taunts and insults, clearly audible to the writers in the press section back of the plate. According to Cobb's recollection, he did not come in with the rest of the team when New York was retired in the second inning; not due to bat, he remained in the carriage park area in deepest center to avoid further exchanges with his nemesis. At the end of the third he had to come in, but he detoured by the home bench off first to ask Yankee President Farrell to have his park police remove the abusive spectator. Unable to locate Farrell, Cobb returned to the bench, yelling an insult about Lueker's sister as he did. Lueker yelled back, Jennings later told reporters, that Cobb was "a half-nigger."[35]

On the bench Crawford asked Cobb if he intended to take that, whereupon the Georgian vaulted the grandstand railing, reached Lueker about twelve rows up, and first knocked him down and then began kicking and stomping him. Somebody cried out that Lueker had no hands; Cobb shouted back, "I don't care if he has no feet."[36] Meanwhile Crawford and several other Tigers grabbed bats and stood by the railing, daring any of the New York fans to come down. Base umpire O'Loughlin and a park policeman finally pulled Cobb away from the battered Lueker and back to the field. Although umpire-in-chief Harry Westervelt ordered him out of the game then and there, Cobb sat on the bench with his teammates until the middle of the seventh inning, when, to a mixture of cheers and boos, he walked across the field to the clubhouse.

Among those who saw the entire fray was Ban Johnson, in New York on one of his periodic swings around the league. That evening Cobb went to Johnson's hotel room to give his side of the story, then caught a train for Philadelphia with the rest of the team. Johnson waited until he got to Boston the next morning to wire Jennings at the Hotel Aldine that Cobb was indefinitely suspended. Cobb had been the first to use "vicious language," Johnson told newsmen, and there was never any excuse for a player's going into the stands. In Philadelphia, Cobb said that "a great injustice has been done." While acknowledging that the publicity surrounding the New York affair would be "extremely distasteful" to his family, he insisted that he had had no alternative. "When a spectator calls me a 'half-nigger' I think it is about time to fight."[37]

Then began a succession of events unique in baseball history. First of all, to practically everybody's surprise, Cobb's teammates fell into line solidly behind him. After beating the Athletics on Friday with Paddy Baumann taking Cobb's place in center, every one of the Tiger players (except for Donovan and Gainor, who were in Detroit) signed a telegram to Johnson announcing that they would not play again until Cobb was reinstated. Said a gratified Cobb, "We will stick together and win out."[38] The next day, Saturday, May 18, the Tigers, including Cobb, went to Shibe Park, donned their uniforms, and took the field as usual. As soon as they saw Cobb, umpires Bill Dineen and Edward "Bull" Perrine ordered him off. Whereupon the rest of the Tigers followed Cobb to the dressing room and put their street clothes on. It was a full-fledged players' strike, the first ever.

Frank Navin had anticipated such action on the players' part. To avoid having a $1000-per-day fine levied on the Detroit club by the National Commission for not fulfilling its schedule commitments, Navin had instructed Jennings to have some kind of team ready. In turn, Jennings had had coaches Joe Sugden and Jim "Deacon" McGuire hire twelve Philadelphia semipro and college players at $10 each. Wearing the uniforms just left behind by the striking Tigers, that group of young men took the field to play the world's champion Athletics before some 15,000 spectators. With the Tigers watching from the stands and with the forty-one-year-old Sugden playing first and the forty-eight-year-old McGuire catching, the game got under way. Aloysius S. Travers, a seminary student at St. Joseph's College and subsequently a Roman Catholic priest, pitched the whole game against the likes of Eddie Collins, Frank Baker, Rube Oldring, and John "Stuffy" McInnis. Final score: Athletics 24, "Tigers" 2.

Furious when he heard about the farce in Philadelphia, Johnson came to that city on Sunday (when of course there was no baseball) and announced the cancellation of Monday's Tigers-Athletics game. On Monday he met with the Detroit players and threatened them all with banishment from Organized Baseball unless they played at Washington the next day. They finally gave in, primarily because Cobb told them that while he appreciated what they'd done, he couldn't let them jeopardize their careers any further. Johnson fined each of them $100 and fixed Cobb's suspension at ten days and his fine, curiously enough, at only $50. On Tuesday the 22nd Cobb looked on from the grandstand at Washington as Mullin outpitched Walter Johnson 2–0; then he left for Detroit to wait out his suspension.

Thus ended the great Detroit ballplayers' revolt of 1912, the stormiest single episode in the history of the American League up to then. Most working sportswriters tended to side with Cobb, agreeing that spectators' abuse of players had got out of hand and that the slur hurled at him would have provoked almost any white man, especially a sensitive southerner. Editorially though, both daily newspapers and the baseball weeklies *Sporting Life* and *Sporting News* condemned Cobb's action and the subsequent players' strike. The *Sporting News* was particularly hard on Cobb, calling him "a natural insurrectionist . . . pre-disposed to take the law into his own hands," so that it was "time for Caesar to be dealt with."[39]

The Exchange Club of Detroit, on the other hand, adopted a strong resolution in support of Cobb and his teammates. Georgia's entire congressional delegation—two senators and ten representatives—wired Cobb that "As Georgians we commend your action in resisting an uncalled for insult." Mayor Courtland S. Winn of Atlanta praised him for upholding "the principles that have always been taught to Southern manhood," and the city's police commissioner thought that if Cobb hadn't "licked that man as he should, he would have lost the respect of every decent man in the country."[40]

Johnson eventually ruled that Cobb's suspension was retroactive to May 16, so the Georgian was back in the lineup on the 26th to help beat the White Sox at Chicago. Thereafter his play was torrid. In a Fourth of July doubleheader sweep of St. Louis, he went six for seven and stole his way around the bases in the morning game on pitcher George Baumgardner and catcher Paul Krichell. A few days later the Tigers returned to New York for the first time since Cobb's assault on Lueker. With all kinds of rumors of retribution in the air, the local fans warmly applauded his six-for-nine performance in two games. And at Philadelphia in back-to-back doubleheaders later that month, he went fourteen for nineteen, including seven hits in a row, two homers, and twenty-seven total bases. Cobb left Philadelphia hitting around .430 and finished the seventeen-game road trip with thirty-eight hits in seventy-three at bats, an average of .521.

Cobb's heroics failed to inspire his teammates. The Detroit ball club continued to drift in the second division all summer. Players came and went as

Jennings struggled with his lineup. By August, with Bill Donovan having left to become manager at Providence, only Crawford and Mullin were still around from the team Cobb had joined in 1905, and waivers had been asked on Mullin. Jennings got a vote of confidence from Navin when the club president had him sign his 1913 contract, for a salary estimated at $15,000 to $18,000, two months before the season ended. All in all, though, it was a bad year with only a few team highlights—one of which was a 6–4 victory over Boston at Navin Field on September 20 to break the sixteen-game winning streak of Joe Wood, the Red Sox' brilliant young righthander.

One of the unforgettable events of that summer for Cobb took place off the field and had nothing to do with baseball. On the night of August 11, as Cobb was driving to the Detroit station with his wife to catch a train for Syracuse, where the Tigers had an exhibition game with the New York State League team, he was waved down by three men who seemed to need help. As soon as he brought his Chalmers to a stop, the men leaped on the running board and began striking at him. Cobb slid over his wife and out the door on her side and started exchanging punches with all three assailants. One of them pulled a knife and slashed his back. As a streetcar rolled by they ran off, with Cobb in pursuit. He caught one mugger, clubbed him with a big Belgian revolver he usually carried, and then trapped another at the end of an alley. Cobb beat the man senseless with the revolver and left him there. When he boarded the train, a teammate noticed the blood-soaked back of his coat. Trainer Tuthill cleaned and bandaged the knife wound. Cobb got three hits at Syracuse the next day.

Only eleven Tigers were in uniform when the season closed at Navin Field on October 6. Cobb had already left for New York to work again for the Wheeler Syndicate on the Red Sox–Giants World Series. Bobby Veach, a wiry, sharp-hitting Kentuckian up from Indianapolis, took his place in center field. After losing that game to the White Sox, Detroit finished in sixth place at 69–84, thirty-four and one-half games behind Boston. That was by far the worst record any Tiger team had made since Cobb came to Detroit.

Even so, Frank Navin made money that year, largely as a result of the crowds that came to see Cobb play in the other American League cities. That August *Sporting Life* had estimated that Cobb would be personally responsible for putting $30,000 into the Detroit ball club's treasury over the course of the season. Navin had become the only club executive besides Charles Comiskey at Chicago to achieve wealth through the baseball business alone. By 1912 Navin had made as much as $365,000 with the Detroit franchise, which now had an estimated value of $650,000.

If Cobb's play was not enough to lift the team in 1912, neither did the team's pallid performance slow him down much. His .410 average was the second best of his career. Cleveland's Joe Jackson, whom Cobb always regarded as the greatest natural hitter he ever saw, hit .395 and again was runnerup. Because Jackson had not pressed him so closely this year, apparently Cobb had not had to resort to stratagems like the alternating displays of aloofness and friendliness with which, as he later claimed, he had so befuddled the illiterate and gullible South Carolinian that he blew the 1911 batting title. Of the other major offensive categories in 1912, Cobb led only in hits (227) and slugging average (.586). Clyde Milan's 88 stolen bases, a new major-league record, far outdistanced him.

Cobb remained at the top of the baseball world, a celebrity whose name was one of the best known in the country. His expanding business interests now included the substantial amount of stock that went with being a director of the First National Bank of Lavonia, Georgia; part-ownership in the W. B. Jarvis Company, a sporting-goods firm with stores in Detroit and Grand Rapids; and investment in a Detroit auto dealership.

He also agreed to serve as one of the four vice presidents of the Baseball Players' Fraternity, organized in New York right after the World Series. David Fultz, its president and an attorney and former American League player, planned a campaign to get the owners to grant a series of concessions that seem modest enough today but initially struck most magnates as radical. Nearly 300 major and minor leaguers eventually joined the BPF. What Fultz's organization wanted boiled down to curbs on spectator rowdiness, assurances that the owners would live up to the terms of contracts, some modification in the waiver rules, and the owners' agreement to pay players' expenses during spring-training. When the National Commission and the club executives eventually came to realize that the BPF represented no threat to the sacrosanct reserve clause, they conceded most of what the organization wanted. It declined precipitously in the midst of the Federal League struggle in 1914–15, when the players themselves were doing most of the contract-breaking, and was moribund by 1916.

For Cobb the BPF vice presidency was essentially honorary; certainly it did not interfere with his 1912–13 offseason activities. Despite being quoted as saying that he wanted to make his permanent home in Detroit, he resumed his wintering in Georgia, playing much golf at Augusta, driving racing cars, and hunting and trap-shooting at George Stallings's plantation and elsewhere.

When Cobb's name appeared in the news that offseason, however, it was usually in connection with his salary prospects for 1913. His three-year contract at $9000 per year had run out. Having won six straight batting titles, topped .400 two years in a row, and reached a point where many people came to ballparks primarily to see him play, Cobb knew he was worth a lot more than Frank Navin had been paying him. Though already well along toward being a wealthy man, he still needed the additional money—for his growing family's needs, to be sure, but most of all for the sake of his own pride. He was the greatest ballplayer of all time, they said. Now he wanted to be paid more than any ballplayer had ever made, more even than Honus Wagner. He wanted $15,000 a season.

Cobb in 1906, his first full
season in the American
League. (*National Baseball
Hall of Fame and Museum*)

Cobb in spring training at
Warren Park, Augusta,
Georgia, 1906. (*National
Baseball Hall of Fame and
Museum*)

Detroit Tigers, 1907 American League Champions. *From left to right—front row:* Ed Siever (p), Jimmy Archer (c), Hughey Jennings (manager), Charley Schmidt (c), Charley O'Leary (ss); *middle row:* Davy Jones (of), Jerry Downs (2b), Ty Cobb (of), Bill Coughlan (3b), Germany Schaefer (2b-ss), Bumpus Jones (p); *back row:* John Eubank (p), Claude Rossman (1b), Sam Crawford (of), Bill Donovan (p), George Mullin (p), Edgar Willett (p), Fred Payne (c), Ed Killian (p). *(National Baseball Hall of Fame and Museum)*

Detroit Tigers, 1908 American League Champions. *From left to right—front row:* Matty McIntyre (of), Herman Malloy (p), Davy Jones (of), George Suggs (p), Charley Schmidt (c), Red Killefer (2b); *middle row:* Germany Schaefer (2b-ss-3b), Bill Donovan (p), George Winter (p), Frank Navin (president), Hughey Jennings (manager), Bill Coughlan (3b), Charley O'Leary (ss), Ty Cobb, (of); *back row:* Tuthill (trainer), Oscar Stanage (c), Ed Killian (p), Jerry Downs (2b), Ira Thomas (c), Claude Rossman (1b), Ed Summers (p), Edgar Willett (p), George Mullin (p), Sam Crawford (of), George Mullin (p). *(National Baseball Hall of Fame and Museum)*

Cobb sliding safely into third at Bennett Park, Detroit, 1909, with Philadelphia Athletics shortstop Jack Barry covering the bag. *(National Baseball Hall of Fame and Museum)*

Cobb and Honus Wagner chatting before the first game of the 1909 World Series, at Pittsburgh. *(National Baseball Hall of Fame and Museum)*

Cobb at Bennett Park, Detroit, in 1910. *(Detroit News and National Baseball Hall of Fame and Museum)*

Cobb demonstrating his bunting technique at Comiskey Park, Chicago, ca. 1911. *(National Baseball Hall of Fame and Museum)*

Cobb in his 1911 Chalmers "30," his prize for being named Most Valuable Player in the American League for that year. *(National Baseball Hall of Fame and Museum)*

At Hilltop Park, New York, May 11, 1912, Cobb with George "Honey Boy" Evans and Evans's trophy given to the leading batter in the majors for 1911. Four days later Cobb went into the stands after Claude Lueker. *(National Baseball Hall of Fame and Museum)*

Left to right: Cobb, Joe Jackson, and Sam Crawford before a game at Cleveland, 1912. *(National Baseball Hall of Fame and Museum)*

Cobb ending his holdout and signing his contract in Frank Navin's office, April 25, 1913. *(National Baseball Hall of Fame and Museum)*

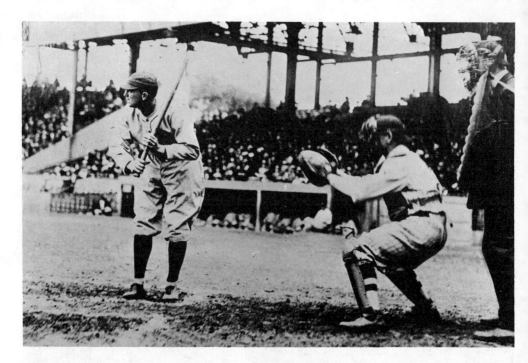

Cobb batting at American League Park (later Griffith Stadium), Washington, D.C., in 1922, his hands-apart grip clearly visible. The catcher is Pat Gharrity. *(National Baseball Hall of Fame and Museum)*

Hughey Jennings and Cobb on the steps of the Detroit City Hall during festivities in honor of Cobb's becoming Tiger manager, February 1, 1921. *(Detroit News and National Baseball Hall of Fame and Museum)*

Cobb at the new Yankee Stadium, 1923. (*National Baseball Hall of Fame and Museum*)

Cobb in 1923. *(Detroit News and National Baseball Hall of Fame and Museum)*

Cobb with William Jennings Bryan at Navin Field, Detroit, in 1924. *(Detroit News and National Baseball Hall of Fame and Museum)*

Left to right: William "Kid" Gleason, Eddie Collins, Cobb, Zack Wheat, and Connie Mack during spring training in 1927 at Fort Myers, Florida. *(National Baseball Hall of Fame and Museum)*

Cobb stealing home at Boston, April 26, 1927, on Tony Welzer of the Red Sox. The catcher is Grover Hartley, the batter Dudley Branom, the umpire Billy Evans. *(National Baseball Hall of Fame and Museum)*

Cobb as a Philadelphia Athletic in 1928, his last year in the majors. (*National Baseball Hall of Fame and Museum*)

Left to right: Charlie, Beverly, Ty, James Howell, and Herschel Cobb, upon their arrival at Honolulu, December 1928, en route home from Japan. *(Wide World Photos and National Baseball Hall of Fame and Museum)*

Avid golfer Cobb in California in the mid-1930s. *(National Baseball Hall of Fame and Museum)*

Cobb and Frances Fairburn
Cass in September 1949,
shortly before their marriage,
posing at her father's summer
home, Point Abino, Ontario.
(*Acme and National Baseball
Hall of Fame and Museum*)

Left to right: Davy Jones, Sam Crawford, and Cobb at the Hall of Fame banquet in Cooperstown, New York, in 1957, when Crawford was inducted into the Hall. (*National Baseball Hall
of Fame and Museum*)

Cobb at Emory University Hospital in Atlanta in December 1959, at the time his cancer was diagnosed. *(Associated Press and National Baseball Hall of Fame and Museum)*

Cobb family mausoleum, Royston, Georgia. *(Photograph by Joyce Crowe)*

Defunct Ty Cobb Memorial (now City Hall, Royston, Georgia). *(Photograph by Joyce Crowe)*

Cobb Memorial Hospital, Royston, Georgia. *(Photograph by Joyce Crowe)*

VII

"Ty Cobb's Most Glorious Years Are Behind Him"

Cobb did not get his $15,000, not for 1913, anyway. But during the first months of that year he mounted a forceful campaign against Frank Navin, who proved equally stubborn and finally even more so. While Bill Armour, now part-owner of the Milwaukee American Association team, volunteered that if he were still managing the Tigers, he'd gladly pay Cobb what he asked, Navin pleaded that his team's poor showing in 1912 had hurt severely at the gate and that he couldn't possibly spare that kind of money. The Detroit president blamed Cobb's demands for the trouble he was having getting Crawford, Dubuc, and others to sign. "It isn't a star that makes a ball club, anyway," he declared. "If a team is winning, the fans will turn out, regardless of the personnel."[1]

By March everybody except Cobb had signed and reported to the new training site at the coastal resort town of Gulfport, Mississippi. There the Tigers stayed at the elegant Great Southern Hotel and began workouts on a diamond at the local fairgrounds. Crawford, after much complaint, took the $5000 Navin offered, the same salary he received in 1912 despite having a .325 year. Cobb's contract came back unsigned, along with news that he had recruited a team of semipro, college, and ex-professional ballplayers—dubbed the All-Georgians— to barnstorm with him that spring while he staged what had become a full-fledged holdout. After three games with the Atlanta Southern League team, Cobb's outfit played the Brooklyn Superbas, training at Augusta, then moved into South Carolina for several encounters with local semipro and college nines. The tour drew well; Cobb both played himself into top condition and took about $1500 out of the profits.

Yet even that venture did not end without the kind of ugly incident that punctuated Cobb's career. At Spartanburg, South Carolina, during a game with Wofford College, a Wofford student with the impeccably southern name of Rutledge Osborne coached at third and traded insults and threats with Cobb, until players from both sides had to keep them from coming to blows. Three days later the two met by chance in Greenville and renewed the quarrel. Osborne, Cobb, and three All-Georgians went to Cobb's hotel room, where, by Osborne's account, Cobb and his men held him on the floor and took turns kicking him. In the version told by one of Cobb's men, Cobb had only given Osborne "a spanking" with his fists. Shortly after the Osborne incident, on April 9, Cobb disbanded his team and returned to Augusta to stay in contact with Detroit.

When the Cobb-less Tigers played at Mobile, Charley Schmidt, first sent to Providence in 1912 and now reduced to catching in the Southern League, acknowledged that Cobb was "individually the greatest ball player who ever stepped on the field." But Schmidt went on to say that he "overdoes the star thing so much that he offsets his ability and is of no more value to the club than an average player." Though maybe not willing to go that far, Navin let newsmen know that he was thoroughly fed up with Cobb's behavior—his various scrapes, especially the one that had precipitated the players' strike the previous year, his absences from spring-training and morning practices, his periodic sulkiness and tardiness in getting to games, in general his presumption of favored status on the ballclub. "He has grown to believe that his greatness precludes his being a subject to club discipline," said Navin. "It has now reached a point where there must be a showdown." Cobb's reply was that Navin had "seen fit to throw mud at me and blacken my name as a ballplayer," adding that the club president was "very nice and pleasant to a fellow" when Cobb had made $2400 and $4500 in pennant-winning years.[2]

So it went through March and most of April, at a considerably higher decibel level than had been the case during Cobb's and Navin's first contract impasse in 1908. When the Tigers began the season (by losing two in a row to St. Louis), Cobb technically went into suspension under National Commission rules. Whereas a few months earlier he had talked about quitting baseball to become a cotton buyer, now he said he was dickering with an auto supply company based at Logansport, Indiana, which had supposedly offered him $15,000 a year to head up its sales operations in Chicago.

Meanwhile political leaders from his home state came to his support, as they had the previous year in the Lueker episode. Although a resolution calling for an investigation of baseball as a trust in violation of the Sherman Act was already before the House Rules Committee, Representative Thomas Hartwick from the Augusta district announced his intention to bring forward such a resolution of his own. U. S. Senator Hoke Smith of Georgia wired Cobb to send him a copy of his last contract, saying "What I understand exists cannot exist legally."[3]

Cobb later believed that such congressional interest in his case was an important factor in causing Navin to soften his position. At any rate, Navin finally took the initiative and invited Cobb to come to Detroit for salary talks.

What ensued was a fairly close replay of 1908. Cobb arrived on the afternoon of April 24. This time his friend Vaughn Glaser, whose acting company was then appearing at the Lyceum, served as go-between, visiting Cobb at the Hotel Ponchartrain as soon as that evening's performance was over and then driving him over to Navin Field the next morning. After all the acrimony, it took only about two hours for ballplayer and club president to come to terms.

Cobb ended up also softening his own position very considerably. He finally signed a one-year contract at $12,000. Inasmuch as Cobb had already missed two weeks of the season, however, Navin prorated his pay for the rest of the year, so that Cobb would actually receive $11,332.55 for 1913. "This is my last holdout," he announced after the photographers had recorded the signing for posterity.[4] That afternoon he visited the Tiger bench, got a warm welcome at least from Jennings, and then watched the team lose to Cleveland, its ninth defeat against five wins. In Washington, Hartwick said that he would no longer push for an antitrust investigation of baseball. The resolution already before the Rules Committee got nowhere that session or thereafter. In the Senate, Hoke Smith quickly lost interest in the issue.

Cobb's 1913 debut came on April 30 against the White Sox at Navin Field. Under temporary reinstatement by the National Commission, he received a two-minute ovation from 6,732 Detroit partisans the first time he came to bat. That day he managed a single to drive in Crawford but also hit back to the pitcher to kill a rally. The Tigers went on to lose again, 6–5 in twelve innings.

In giving Cobb full reinstatement the next day, the National Commission fined him $50 for his holdout, commended the Detroit club for its firm stand against his demands, and threatened to take action to discipline players whose conduct was "detrimental to baseball," meaning Cobb presumably. The *Sporting News* joined baseball's rulers in condemning Cobb, who, said the baseball weekly, "has done more than any other individual to give [baseball's] enemies a chance to make attacks. But what does Cobb care? He is for Cobb. That is the way he plays the game whether it be on the field or in negotiating a contract." He would find the going harder from here on, though, because fans and players alike were down on him. "Ty Cobb's most glorious years are behind him."[5] It was not one of the usually sage St. Louis weekly's more prescient prophecies.

Cobb started slowly, complaining that he had caught a cold when he drove over to Ann Arbor to scout a star pitcher-first baseman for the University of Michigan named George Sisler. After being struck out twice in a row by New York spit-baller Ray Keating, he took himself out of the lineup for a few days. By the middle of May, though, he had caught fire, hitting everybody and running the bases with his customary abandon. Against Boston he yelled to third-baseman Larry Gardner that he was going to bunt, did just that on the next pitch, and beat Gardner's throw. Later in the game he made it to second on a grounder up the middle before Tris Speaker could get the ball back in. On May 18 he stole home on Walter Johnson, his team's only run in a 2–1 loss before a Sunday crowd of 24,466, a new Detroit record. Two days later he repeated the feat on the Athletics' Byron Houck. In the Philadelphia series he had a streak of seven hits in a row before Eddie Plank stopped him. After eighteen games Cobb was hitting .492. Then he was called home from Chicago because his wife was ill.

That would be Cobb's pattern for most of the season: stretches of spirited play interrupted by absences from the lineup for one reason or another. First-baseman Wheeler "Doc" Johnston of Cleveland jammed his knee into Cobb's back during a rundown on June 22 and put him out for several games. Almost as he soon returned, he was spiked by Chicago's Buck Weaver and again sidelined when his knee became badly infected. With his wound still not fully healed, Cobb talked Jennings into playing him at second base on July 12 against the Athletics at Navin Field. In a weird game that featured twenty-nine hits and twenty-two walks, Philadelphia won 16–9. Of Detroit's six errors, Cobb made three (in five chances), thereby proving to E. A. Batchelor "that he is the worst second baseman living or dead." Vaudeville agents, joked Batchelor, would pay Cobb great sums "to play second base on the stage just as he played it on Sat."[6] The next day Cobb returned to center field, but on the 14th he cursed out umpire George Hildebrand and got a one-day suspension from Ban Johnson.

Again Cobb's ball club settled in the second division early on and stayed there all season. Crawford, whatever his contract complaints, was still durable and reliable. He led the league in times at bat in 1913, hitting .317 and, as usual, sending outfielders chasing after more triples than anybody else. But aside from Cobb, Crawford, and Donie Bush, it was a team in transition. Davy Jones had been sold to Chicago during the winter, and Mullin went to Washington on waivers early in the season. Jennings was accumulating another pennant contender in younger players like Bobby Veach, infielder Oscar Vitt, and pitchers Jean Dubuc and George "Hooks" Dauss. In 1913, though, the Tigers were still a lackluster outfit, for the present offering little to the Detroit fans beyond Cobb's dazzlements.

By late July, Cobb, still hitting above .400, now trailed Joe Jackson by ten to twelve points. He had become increasingly restless with the mediocrity that surrounded him at Detroit. In Boston he said he'd be happy to be traded to either the Red Sox, the Yankees, or the Athletics. For the present, however, Boston owner Joseph Lannin was satisfied to have Speaker as his center fielder. New York owner Frank Farrell, according to rumors, wanted Cobb badly; but to Frank Chance, now managing the last-place Yankees, the Georgian was "too much of a trouble-maker."[7] Chance had already had enough of that from Hal Chase, whom he had traded to Chicago earlier in the year. Later Clark Griffith, manager and part-owner at Washington, claimed to have offered Navin $100,000 for Cobb. Navin refused to confirm the offer; sportswriters around the league ridiculed the story on the grounds that (1) no ballplayer was worth that much, (2) Navin would never sell Cobb, and (3) Griffith, handicapped by having the smallest ballpark in the league, would never have that kind of money anyway.

As if to encourage trade talks, in New York, early in August, Cobb had three bad days in a row. He muffed a fly ball to let in two runs in one game, was caught off third after overrunning the bag the next day, and in the third game of the series was thrown out by fifteen feet trying to go first-third on an infield out; later he failed on a delayed-steal attempt.

The season ground on for Cobb, free of untoward happenings off the field except for one harrowing time in Philadelphia late in August, when he was nearly mobbed by hostile street youths outside Shibe Park. After he jumped aboard a passing trolley to escape the yelling crowd, one boy climbed on the trolley's roof and disabled its electrical connection, and only after the conductor reconnected the wire and the motorman left the taunters behind was Cobb able to feel safe.

September brought Cobb's annual drive for the batting title and a corresponding slump on Jackson's part. Cobb took the lead in mid-month, with Ralph Yonker commenting in the *Sporting News* that "The club has been down and out, and Cobb has played for batting averages more than for ball games of late."[8] On September 27 he got six hits in seven times up, including two triples and a double, in a doubleheader sweep at Cleveland. When Jackson went only 2–5, Cobb had his seventh straight batting title sewed up. Again he passed up the season finale to head east for more World Series newspaper duty, this year to cover the Athletics–Giants clash. The Tigers completed the season again in sixth place with a 66–87 record, a little worse than they had done the previous year.

By 1913, batting and slugging averages and runs scored totals were about where they had been before the hitting upsurge of 1911. The pitchers had obviously regained the upper hand. Cobb's .390 was seventeen points better than Jackson's average and twenty-seven better than Speaker's. But his 122 games and 428 times at bat amounted to the least amount of playing time he had seen since 1906. Slugging average, where he trailed Jackson, was the only other offensive category in which he was among the leaders. His 51 steals were his fewest since 1908. Acknowledging that he had slumped in 1913, Cobb attributed his difficulties to being on a sixth-place ballclub and to playing golf during the season. From then on he would fret over whether and to what extent his fondness for golf interfered with his hitting.

With the season over, Cobb and his wife finally moved into a house of their own. Since their marriage in 1908 they had divided their offseason time between his family's place at Royston and hers outside Augusta. Late in November 1913 they moved into a two-story, wooden-frame structure at 2425 William Street in Augusta. Located in what was then a newly developed residential section about three miles north of the business district, the house was architecturally undistinguished but spaciously comfortable, with plenty of room for live-in domestic help. It was well suited to a young couple who already had two children and anticipated having more.

Earlier that month, in Detroit, Frank Navin, at Cobb's request, released a letter from Cobb that referred to their having already agreed on a salary for 1914 while both were in New York for the World Series. In his letter Cobb said that their "understanding" "pleased me immensely." He went on to confess "how foolish I think that I have been to think of leaving Detroit [to] play with some other team. I am entirely satisfied with conditions. . . . I want to be loyal to my club."[9] Although Cobb had not yet signed his contract, to all intents he was committed to the Tigers for the coming year.

Cobb's word, plus an offer of the $15,000 he had not received in 1913, were enough to seal his bond with Navin. The Tiger president had good reason to want to get at least Cobb's oral commitment; agents of the ambitious new Federal League were all about and signing one big-league player after another. Unlike other efforts in recent years to establish a rival major league, this one was well directed by the Chicago manufacturer James Gilmore and well financed by the likes of Charles Weeghman, a Chicago restaurateur; Robert B. Ward, a Brooklyn bakery tycoon; and oil magnate Harry Sinclair. Eventually 172 players with American or National League experience signed contracts with Federal League teams, including such notables as Eddie Plank, Chief Bender, Joe Tinker, Hal Chase, George Stovall, and Ed Reulbach. Detroit was one of the few ball clubs that managed to keep all of its leading players.

That was so because, for all his reluctance to part with a dollar, Navin already had one of the highest-paid teams in the majors. He upped Crawford's and Bush's salaries substantially to keep his ace right fielder and shortstop, and he was willing to come across with the money Cobb had sought a year earlier. In January, Gilmore wired Cobb, who was hunting at Royston, an offer of $15,000 a year for five years and proposed paying the first year's salary in advance. Harry Sinclair added that if the Federal League folded, then he would make Cobb his best-paid oil lease man.

In his autobiography Cobb claimed that Navin had intercepted his mail late in the 1913 season and otherwise behaved underhandedly in an effort to get him tied down before the Federals could talk to him. That version does not square with his effusive letter to Navin in November. It seems likely that the subsequent breakdown of the two men's relationship during Cobb's last years as Tiger manager distorted and colored the Georgian's memory many years later. At any rate, in a wire to E. A. Batchelor on January 18, 1914, Cobb let it be known that he had no intention of signing with the Federals. "I would gain nothing by change," he said.[10] Early in March, when Navin got back to Detroit from New York, Cobb's signed contract specifying $15,000 for 1914 was waiting for him.

It is doubtful that Cobb ever seriously considered jumping to the new league. Apart from his well-founded skepticism about its long-term survivability, Cobb's professional pride worked against his going with a league where he knew the caliber of play had to be below major-league standards. The question on which baseball historians might speculate endlessly, however, is how much the caliber of play in the American and National leagues suffered during the 1914 and 1915 seasons as a consequence of defections to the Federals.

Needing bigger profits to cover the bigger payroll he had had to take on, Navin raised the prices of box seats at the Detroit ballpark to $1.25 and grandstand seats to 75¢–$1, although he kept the 50¢ and 25¢ pavilion and bleacher prices. While the competition from the Federal League, which went head-to-head with the established teams in four major-league cities, caused a general attendance slump in 1914–15, Navin continued to make money. Aside from the lack of a Federal League rival in Detroit and the Tigers' resurgence in those years, Navin benefited from operating in the most economically expansive area in the majors.

On January 5, 1914, Henry Ford proclaimed his new policy of paying workers at his plant five dollars a day for an eight-hour day. Such a mass of job-seekers stormed the plant gates the next morning that mounted policemen and fire hoses had to be used to drive them back. Ford had begun to put into practice his theory that improving workers' buying power meant more customers for his Model Ts. Meanwhile Chevrolet, part of the General Motors combine, began to challenge Ford's supremacy in the inexpensive-car market. By 1917 some 100,000 Chevrolets a year were rolling off the production line.

Cobb's future, as both baseball player and businessman, was intimately tied to the rise of Detroit as the hub of world automobile production in the century's early decades. In his hustle and drive, his ingenuity, his willingness to take chances, in his competitive ruthlessness as well, he often appeared to personify that city in its heroic age, a time when the automobile became central to American life and Cobb became central to American baseball.

The most likely reason for Cobb's delay in signing his contract for 1914 was his habitual aversion to spring-training. Had he signed earlier, he would thereby have bound himself to report to the team at least thirty days before the season opened. As it was, he could stay in Georgia until mid-March, when the Tigers quit Gulfport, and then meet them at New Orleans when they began their exhibition tour.

More new people were with the team this year than ever before, both because Jennings was rebuilding and because the American League had enlarged the May-September roster limit to twenty-five. Among the newcomers were Harry Heilmann, a big outfielder-first baseman purchased from Portland in the Northwest League; George H. Burns, up from the Western League, who would soon take over at first; and Harry Coveleski, a lefthander who had earlier pitched in the National League and then had worked his way back up from the minors. Yet for all the new faces, the Tigers preserved an old-fashioned look in 1914, because on their home uniforms they continued to wear full collars, the only team in the majors that still did.

Paul Bruske remarked on the harmonious atmosphere among the Tigers and thought it was because Cobb had played so much of the exhibition season. The Georgian seemed unusually amiable, befriending rookies and chatting with fans around the hotels. In Jackson, Mississippi, he addressed a joint session of the state legislature, which had originally voted to adjourn to see the Detroit-New Orleans game that afternoon and then voted to hear Cobb when the game was rained out.

The Tigers started the season before more than 21,000 at Navin Field. They recorded a 3–2 win over the St. Louis Browns, now being managed by thirty-three-year-old Branch Rickey, a former Browns catcher and most recently baseball coach at the University of Michigan. Cobb's wild throw home let in the tying run, but in the thirteenth inning he tripled into the roped-off area in right-center and scored the winning run on Bobby Veach's sacrifice fly to center-fielder Burt Shotton.

After that the Tigers stayed at or near the top of the league for two months, contending closely with the world's champion Athletics and a Washington team that, propelled mainly by Walter Johnson's magnificent hurling, had finished second to the Athletics last year. Crawford's bat was especially potent in the first part of the season; Burns also hit well; and Coveleski and Dauss became the new pitching bulwarks. Although Cobb's batting was not up to his own standards, he still kept opposing fielders and catchers in disarray much of the time.

Then on May 18, on the Tigers' first eastern swing, a pitch from right-hander George Foster of Boston hit him in his right side and cracked a rib. Unable to swing a bat or throw, Cobb got Jennings's permission to return with his family to their new home in Augusta to give himself time to heal. Ralph Yonker thought that Cobb's "playing attitude is contagious. Take him out and the pep dies down and the team takes on a sluggish air."[10] The team did slump a little with Cobb sidelined, although it stayed within reach of the league lead.

On June 5, at Detroit, Cobb pinch ran for Veach, stole third, but was caught off base by catcher Sam Agnew of the Browns. He returned to center field the next day, getting two singles as the Tigers beat the Athletics. Meanwhile he announced that he had given up golf for the season; "pasture pool," he was convinced, hampered his hitting.

It was still a three-team race two weeks later, when Cobb once again got into the kind of off-the-field trouble that seemed to follow him around. On a Saturday evening, after a game at Navin Field with Washington, Cobb brought Clark Griffith home with him for dinner. As soon as he arrived, Charlie Cobb told him about quarreling earlier that day with William L. Carpenter, the owner of a butcher shop on Hamilton Avenue, after she tried to return 20¢ worth of fish she had decided was spoiled when her cook prepared it. Cobb immediately called up the butcher, accused him of insulting his wife, and grabbed his revolver and rushed out.

Fingering his weapon, he walked into Carpenter's shop and demanded that Carpenter telephone his wife and apologize. That the butcher quickly did, whereupon Cobb thanked him, patted him on the back, and asked for his bill. Carpenter's assistant, a young black man named Harold Harding, then appeared and began arguing with Cobb, at the same time brandishing a meat cleaver. "Our little affair was practically over when Harding butted in," Cobb said later. "He seemed to want trouble and I was so angry I gave him what he was looking for." [11] While Carpenter called the police, Cobb pulled his pistol, scuffled with Harding, and managed to hit him over the head several times. A patrol wagon finally arrived and hauled Cobb to the Bethune Avenue station, where he discovered that he had fractured his right thumb during the fight. After getting it bandaged, he was put in a cell and kept overnight, then released in the morning when Harding declined to file charges.

The following week, while Navin sighed that "Cobb's greatest fault is his hot temper," the Georgian was again arrested, this time on a charge of disturbing the peace filed against him by Carpenter. [12] In magistrate's court he pleaded guilty and paid a $50 fine. It was either that or face a six-month term in municipal jail.

Disabled again and thoroughly depressed, Cobb renewed his complaints about not being treated well by Navin and again said he'd like to be traded. He even left open the option of signing with a Federal League team. With Cobb out for close to two months, the Tigers finally faded toward the end of July, losing seven straight and tumbling ten games out of first place. By the time he returned for good, on August 7, the team was out of the running, having lost twenty-five of forty-two games during his inactivity. At .342 Cobb was still in contention for batting honors, but he had appeared in only forty-five of Detroit's 102 games.

Then came another furious Cobb charge for the title. On August 27 he trailed Joe Jackson by twenty-one points. A month later he had overtaken Jackson as well as Eddie Collins and Tris Speaker, his other main rivals. Cobb ended the season in style, driving a pitch by Cleveland's Willie Mitchell past center-fielder Harry Leibold to the Navin Field flagpole for a homerun, and two innings later scoring from first when second-baseman Bill Wambsganss let Crawford's bounder get away from him. By winning 11–6, the Tigers finished at 80–73, a half-game behind third-place Washington. Although it was Detroit's first time in the first division in three years, Cobb's long absence, as Jennings sadly put it, "just naturally ruined us."[13]

Despite Cobb's having only 345 official times at bat, Ban Johnson again certified his batting leadership. His final mark was .368. Besides hitting only two homers, he had driven in just fifty-seven runs and stolen twenty-two bases, his fewest since 1906 and an even fifty less than league leader Fritz Maisel of New York. Cobb-haters—of whom there were plenty around the American League—may have noted that so far the *Sporting New*'s 1913 prophecy seemed to be working out.

Still relatively fresh after appearing in only ninety-seven games, Cobb skipped the World Series and earned extra money by playing with a team of major and minor leaguers representing Shelby, Ohio, in a four-entry tournament held in that town the weekend after the season closed. Cobb's two-run double in the seventh inning was the winning margin in Shelby's 7–6 win over Bucyrus for the tournament championship.

Primarily because of the Federal League's challenge, 1914 was a bad year for both of the established majors. American League attendance dropped 21 percent that year and would drop another 12 percent in 1915. Dwindling crowds coupled with the bigger salaries necessitated by the new league's inducements meant that nearly everybody lost money in those years. At Philadelphia, Connie Mack took his losses at the gate, heard talk all season of more desertions to the Federals, and then watched in dismay as his team lost four straight in the World Series to George Stallings' Boston Braves. Tired of it all, he sold Eddie Collins to the White Sox and Jack Barry to the Red Sox in the first in a succession of personnel changes that wrecked his great ballclub and reduced it to a horrendous 42–109 record in 1915.[14]

With an improved team, Frank Navin came out of 1914 in better shape than most of his peers. Able to sign all of the Tiger regulars before they scattered for the offseason, he felt safe from further raids by the Federals. Miles Main, a reserve pitcher, became only the second Tiger (following Edgar Willett) to go over to the "invaders." Among those whose signatures Navin obtained before they left Detroit was Cobb, who was quite pleased when Navin offered to put him under contract for the next three years at $20,000 per annum. In 1914 Cobb's $15,000 had not actually made him the highest-salaried man in the game, because Boston had signed Tris Speaker for two years for an aggregate $33,000. But for 1915 and for several years thereafter, Cobb's pay would be the tops in all baseball.

Back home in Augusta, Cobb said that he intended to retire within four years, in large part because he was weary of "the unenviable notoriety and wounded feelings I have been subjected to," including occasional threats on his life.[15] It was good therapy for his emotional hurts to play a lot of golf at the Augusta Country Club and to hunt quail on Stallings's land with the man who had led the Boston National Leaguers out of last place on July 15 to a pennant and then a sweep of the mighty Athletics.

In that period in his life Cobb seems to have been a reasonably contented family man. He was not only a good provider but an affectionate husband and father, about as attentive to his family's non-material needs as a busy professional athlete with an exceptionally impatient, restless disposition was likely to be. Charlie Cobb stayed out of the limelight as much as possible after she married Cobb, although occasional items about her showed up in the press, attesting, for example, to her horseback-riding skills and her liking for baseball. Late in 1914 *Sporting Life* described her as "a very patient little woman who has her time taken up completely with the two little Cobbs. . . ." Tyrus, Jr., was "a bright, active little fellow with brick-red hair, and large bashful blue eyes," while Shirley was a "blue-eyed tot with flaxen hair."[16] At mealtime, reported the sports weekly, Tyrus, Jr., sat in a highchair at his mother's side, Shirley in another next to her father.

Cobb surprised nearly everybody in the spring of 1915 by arriving at Gulfport on March 20, as trim and ready to play as always, in fine spirits, and packing his golf clubs. It was easier to get in shape now than when he'd been younger, he announced. Wandering down a row of newsmen who sat behind tables and pounded their typewriters at the fairgrounds ballfield, Cobb picked up a copy of Francis Richter's history of baseball, came across a mention of Wagner's eight straight National League batting titles (which he had just tied), and remarked that he wanted to lead the American League for ten years. Amazingly, in view of what he would do that year, he said that he wouldn't concern himself with stolen-base honors anymore because he wanted to avoid injuries.

Once the season was under way, Cobb hit safely in his first ten games and ran the bases with greater frequency, skill, and success than he ever had. With the outfield of Veach, Cobb, and Crawford hitting for a combined average of nearly .500; with Oscar Vitt and Donie Bush solidifying the left side of the infield, rookie Ralph "Pepper" Young doing well at second, and utility-man Marty Kavanaugh filling in capably at first for an ill George Burns; and with Coveleski, Dauss, Dubuc, and newcomer Bernie Boland anchoring the pitching staff, the Tigers shot into the lead and stayed in or near first place week after week. Hughey Jennings clearly had an authentic pennant contender on his hands once again.

Cobb stole bases in clusters, a total of thirteen in eight games, including four in one thirteen-inning encounter with the now usually inept Athletics. In June he stole home five different times for a total of six since the season began. Even in these days "when the fate of empires trembles in the balance," editorialized the New York *Times* in reference to the vast carnage the peoples of Europe had inflicted on each other since the outbreak of war the previous summer, Cobb remained "a personality of national importance." "I don't know what he's gettin'," Ring Lardner had one of his fictional ballplayers say of Cobb, "but whatever it is, it ain't enough. That bunch could get along just as well without him as a train could without an engine."[17]

Cobb's way of playing the game was as combustible as it had always been. If he had few spats with teammates now, he could be as mean as ever to the opposition. In May, during a game with the Red Sox at Navin Field, lefty Hubert "Dutch" Leonard repeatedly threw close to Cobb and finally hit him. The next time up Cobb dragged a bunt between the mound and first. When Leonard took the throw from the first baseman and crossed the bag ahead of Cobb, the vengeful Georgian veered off the baseline, left the ground with spikes flashing, and tore one of Leonard's stockings, although he failed to cut the pitcher's leg. Leonard returned to the mound "deathly pale," according to Bozeman Bulger of the New York *Evening World*. "He never threw another beanball at me," Cobb later claimed.[18]

In 1915 Cobb again struggled with himself over his golf-playing, to which he was now thoroughly addicted. Shooting consistently in the eighties, he played several times a week at Detroit as well as in cities on the road. Ultimately he again convinced himself that golfing interfered with a ballplayer's swing and that he had to quit it during the season. In July he promised to play one more match, with Clark Griffith in Washington, "and then I am through until after the season ends in October."[19]

If golf was really bad for Cobb's hitting, ballplayers around the league must have wondered if they shouldn't take up the game. At the end of July he was still around .400. On the bases E. A. Batchelor described his as "yelling like an Indian, running up and down the line and carrying on generally." In one of the syndicated columns Cobb occasionally did for the Wheeler Syndicate that season, he rebuked non-hustlers. "I would think anyone who is able to get a good salary in baseball would have ambition enough to try to earn it," he said. "Baseball does not demand anything so very onerous of its disciples, and a man who can't work hard for a couple of hours a day and keep himself in condition to do his best makes me tired."[20]

The pennant race turned into a tight three-team battle involving Boston,

Detroit, and the Chicago White Sox, sparked by Eddie Collins, their offseason second-base acquisition from Philadelphia. The Red Sox—bolstered by powerful pitching from Dutch Leonard, righthanders Ernie Shore, George Foster, and Joe Wood (sore-armed but still good in spots), and a husky young lefty who also showed a potent bat, named George Herman "Babe" Ruth— held a slender lead as they came into Detroit for three games late in August. Boston had won fifteen of its last eighteen, Detroit sixteen of nineteen.

Shore beat the Tigers and Coveleski 3–1 in the first game. Cobb tripled off the screen in front of the right-field bleachers in the fifth to drive in Detroit's lone run. Every time he came to bat he complained to umpire Hildebrand that Shore was roughing up the ball with an emery board. After grounding out to shortstop Everett Scott in the eighth, he went to the Red Sox dugout behind third to remonstrate with manager Bill Carrigan about what Shore was throwing. Glaring down on the stocky Carrigan, he shouted "Goddamn you, I'd like to take a punch at you!" "Hit me, hit me!" Carrigan shouted back in Cobb's face. Muttering that the Boston manager just wanted to get him thrown out, Cobb finally retook the field under the urging of Hildebrand and base umpire Silk O'Loughlin.[21]

The Red Sox also won the second game, 2–1 in thirteen innings. Leonard took over from Ruth after the Tigers tied it in the ninth. Boland, pitching in relief of big Bill James, gave up the winning run, with Cobb's double in the last of the thirteenth going for naught because Speaker ran down Crawford's drive in deepest center. Before the series finale on August 26, a delegation of Detroit rooters gave Cobb a bouquet of roses to commemorate his tenth anniversary with the Tigers. The gesture did nothing to mellow him. In the fifth he overslid second trying to steal. Called out, he stormed at O'Loughlin and twice grabbed him by the arm as Ban Johnson looked on from Navin's box. "Francis [O'Loughlin] happened to be in a good humor," wrote Batchelor, "and let him get away with it."[22] The Tigers won in twelve, 7–6. Errors by Cobb and George Burns helped Boston go ahead in the ninth, but Detroit tied it in the bottom of the inning. Cobb opened the Tiger half of the twelfth with a line single, went to second on Crawford's sacrifice, and strolled home on Veach's drive off the left-field wall.

Boston left town leading by three-and-a-half games, a margin the Tigers were never able to close. Crawford, Veach, and Cobb all slumped, with Cobb experiencing an 0–18 drouth, one of the worst of his career. But by sweeping the White Sox in three games at Navin Field, the Tigers squelched that team's pennant prospects. After Labor Day the Tigers left Detroit for the remainder of the year except for two season-ending games at Navin with Cleveland. That was one big factor hampering their pennant drive. Mainly, though, it was tough Red Sox pitching.

Trailing by two and a half, Cobb and company opened a showdown four-game series on September 16 in Fenway Park, the pretty steel-and-concrete facility the Red Sox had occupied since 1912. By that time quite a lot of bad feeling had developed between the two teams, particularly between Cobb and the Boston pitchers, who, so he believed, had been throwing at him for two years. Equipped with tin horns and cowbells and continually singing "Tessie," the ditty with which they had accompanied Boston's victory in the 1903 World Series, 22,000 Red Sox rooters hectored Cobb throughout the first game, won by Detroit 6–1 behind Dauss. Foster and rookie Carl Mays threw at Cobb everytime he came up. After two more close ones in the eighth inning, Cobb slung his bat at Mays and called him a "yellow dog," whereupon Mays nicked him on the wrist with the next pitch. Trotting to first, Cobb dodged several pop bottles. After he caught a fly for the final out, the crowd poured onto the field. Surrounded by what looked like 5000 hostile fans, Cobb, instead of running in like the other players, walked deliberately and fixedly toward the clubhouse passageway entrance inside the hometeam dugout. He was cursed, pelted by paper wads, and grazed by a bottle before two policemen and several Tigers armed with bats got to him and provided an escort to safety. "None of the mongrels in the crowd had the nerve to attack him," wrote Batchelor, "each waiting for somebody else to strike the first blow."[23]

After an off day on Thursday the 17th, Leonard gave up only a homer to Cobb with Vitt on base in the ninth in beating the Tigers 7–2 to restore the Red Sox lead. On Saturday a huge overflow of more than 35,000 saw Shore outduel Coveleski 1–0 in a brilliant twelve-inning performance by both men. Following the mandatory Sabbath rest, Ruth and Foster outpitched Dauss 3–2 to all but kill Detroit's chances for the pennant.

At Philadelphia three days later, Cobb stole his ninetieth base to break what was then thought to be Clyde Milan's record of eighty-nine (actually 88, as established by a subsequent records rectification). About 300 people were there to see it. A week after that, when the Tigers lost to St. Louis despite Cobb's two hits and two steals, the idle Red Sox clinched their fourth American League championship. This year, though, Cobb played out the season so he could pile up as many steals as possible. On October 3 he went two-for-three and stole for the ninety-sixth time in his 156th game (including two ties). By defeating the Cleveland Indians (as they were now called with Lajoie gone), the Tigers won their 100th game, the first time any team had won that many and not earned a pennant. The Red Sox finished with only one more win but with three fewer losses, a difference of two-and-a-half games.

Cobb's ninety-six stolen bases established a record long thought to be unbreakable. It did hold up for forty-seven years, while the thirty-eight times he was thrown out in 1915 proved an even more durable mark, lasting until 1982. He ended the year hitting .369, way ahead of Collins, Speaker, and Jack Fournier of Chicago. Besides also leading in hits (208) and runs (144), he walked

118 times, only one less than Collins. Crawford and Veach tied for runs batted in with 112; Cobb was next at 99. Everything considered, thought H. G. Salsinger, it had been Cobb's finest year.

Everything considered, it had been a good year for the Detroit franchise as well. Navin's profits totaled about $64,000. Joseph Lannin also did well at Boston, and Charles Comiskey, according to *Sporting Life*'s estimates, about broke even at Chicago. For the other American Leaguer owners and for baseball as a whole, however, 1915 was a second-straight bad season.

Cobb did more hunting than usual that fall and winter. An arms manufacturer had recently given him a .35-caliber automatic rifle, and back in July the Shriners of Philadelphia had honored their fellow Mason with a new Fox shotgun. On a six-day expedition into southern Alabama, Cobb reportedly killed two deer and nearly a hundred squirrels. He also spent time with Stallings both at the plantation near Haddocks and at Dover Hall, a 2400-acre estate near Brunswick on the coast. The previous August a group of fifty baseball men, including, besides Cobb and Stallings, Ban Johnson, Frank Navin, and National League president John Tener, had each put up $1000 toward the purchase of the estate, originally conceived as one grand spring-training site for all the major-league teams. That notion proved fanciful, but with a plentitude of deer, wild turkey, quail, duck, and other game, Dover Hall became a favorite retreat for baseball notables over the next decade or so.

Among Cobb's new business ventures was a substantial investment in an apartment project in Augusta. He also continued to pick up tidy sums from a variety of product endorsements. Something called Nuxated Iron, for example, he credited with bringing him back from an early season rundown condition. Not only did he endorse cigars and cigarettes; he also, according to one observer, "smokes more different brands of tobacco than most men ever heard of."[24] Despite his warning a few years earlier that chewing gum was bad for one's vision, he chewed it often himself, if his endorsements were to be believed. Among the other items he praised for public consumption were overcoats, underwear, and suspenders. And of course in exchange for allowing the Hillerich and Bradsby Company to market bats carrying his signature, he got all the made-to-specification Louisville Sluggers he wanted from the company. That arrangement would eventually become almost universally available to major-league ballplayers.

Because a hurricane the previous fall had wrecked the Great Southern Hotel at Gulfport, in 1916 the Tigers shifted their training site to Waxahachie, Texas, a town in the northern part of the state known for its mineral baths and for being the seat of the nation's foremost cotton-producing county. The whole state of Texas was excitable and nervous that spring, because General John J. Pershing had just led 6000 troops into northern Mexico on what turned out to be a quixotic expedition against the marauding guerrilla forces of Pancho

Villa. Meanwhile, on the other side of the Atlantic, French and German soldiers died by the hundreds of thousands in the ghastly stalemate at Verdun.

The little world of baseball, by contrast, was at peace in the spring of 1916. During the winter the Federal League capitalists had given up, as part of a general settlement that enabled Charles Weeghman to buy the Chicago Cubs and Phillip de Catesby Ball, owner of the St. Louis Federals, to buy the Browns. Despite earlier vows by American and National league officials and owners to blacklist everybody who jumped to the new league, all the players who wanted to and were still good enough were permitted to sign with teams in their former leagues. Yet the demise of the Federal League brought a general belt-tightening throughout the majors, both because the owners had regained their power over the players and because the war with the Federals had cost most teams dearly. Thus many players suffered pay cuts, including big stars like Walter Johnson and Joe Jackson. When Joseph Lannin cut Tris Speaker's salary almost in half, the Red Sox center fielder refused to sign, whereupon Lannin sold him to Cleveland for $50,000 and two unproven players.

Of course Cobb, with two years to go on his $20,000 per year contract, was immune to such heavy-handed austerity. He took his time getting to Texas, while the people at Waxahachie and surrounding towns chafed to see him. He did not show up until April 1, by which time the Tigers had broken camp and were in Houston, playing a series with the New York Giants. He explained that business complications, resulting from a big fire at the Augusta apartment complex in which he had invested, had kept him from joining the team earlier.

At Houston, sportswriters and fans talked up a grudge match between Cobb and Benny Kauff, who had led the Federal League in both 1914 and 1915, then had signed with John McGraw's Giants and reportedly bragged that he would outdo Cobb during the coming season. Cobb gave little indication that he either knew or cared much about Kauff one way or the other, although he did pose shaking Kauff's hand and towering over the 5'8" Giant outfielder. In the game that followed, the finale between the two teams, Cobb doubled twice, stole two bases, and made two fine catches. Kauff hit one double but also stumbled around in the outfield.

The 1916 season opened for the Tigers in newly enlarged Comiskey Park, where an estimated 32,000 White Sox rooters watched in astonishment as Harry Coveleski not only shut out their favorites 4–0 but collected two singles, a double, and a triple. Cobb, now hitting third in front of Veach and Crawford, contributed a single and double. Two games later severe colds felled Cobb and Crawford; both missed the home opener on April 21. After being out for two more games, Cobb returned to the lineup. Jennings announced that Crawford's slowness in right field hurt the team and that the thirty-six-year-old veteran of seventeen major-league seasons would no longer play regularly.

Harry Heilmann took over for him, with Crawford now relegated to fill-in and pinch-hitting duties.

When Babe Ruth and Ernie Shore beat them on consecutive days at Boston late in May, the Tigers dropped into seventh place (thanks to eight straight road losses). Cobb's hitting had been mediocre for the first month of the season. In June, though, both Cobb and the team turned their seasons around. On the 18th Coveleski shut out Cleveland at Navin Field to put the Tigers and Indians, for whom Speaker was hitting well about .400, into a first-place tie. Cobb had built his average to around .355 and was way out in front in stolen bases, although he was stealing at a rate considerably below that of 1915.

On the first Sunday in July, in Chicago, Coveleski lost 1–0 in twelve innings to another lefthander, Ewell "Reb" Russell. In the seventh, umpire Bill Nallin called a third strike on Cobb and then ordered both the Georgian and Hughey Jennings out of the game when they protested at length. As he left, Cobb threw his bat high into the air. It landed in the first-base stands back of the Tiger dugout, fortunately in an area recently vacated because a light rain had started. That evening Cobb heard from Ban Johnson's office that he was suspended for three days and fined $25. He returned to Detroit to spend the Fourth of July with his family.

Cobb returned to the lineup on July 6 and got six hits, including a homer, in two lopsided victories over the Athletics. By that time everybody in the league had a shot at the pennant except the miserable Athletics, who lost twenty straight games in July and August and finished at 36–117. Even Washington, ending up in seventh place, would play only one game below .500 baseball in a year of extraordinary balance in the American League.

The Tigers were badly wounded when the Red Sox, who had finally scrambled into the lead, came into Detroit at the end of July and swept four straight. Back in action after jamming a finger on his throwing hand and bruising a knee on a slide into catcher Forrest Cady a week earlier in Boston, Cobb performed weakly at the plate throughout the four games in Detroit. After that, though, he and the rest of the Tigers rallied quickly. By the end of August they were in second place, only two-and-one-half games behind Boston. In the batting race Cobb's .354 was still nearly thirty points behind Speaker, who, with his new ball club, was having his finest year.

On September 12 the Tigers pounded the Indians at Cleveland, 10–2. Besides getting two infield singles, Cobb hit one homer over the right-field wall with Vitt aboard and then drove the ball past Speaker to the bleachers in left-center, chasing in Bush and sliding home under Steve O'Neill's tag. That win, coupled with a Red Sox loss at Washington, moved Detroit to within one-half game of the top. By beating New York behind Dauss two days later, the Tigers achieved a virtual tie with the defending champions.

That was as close as they would get to a pennant. On September 18 they could do nothing against Philadelphia's Elmer Myers, who beat them 2–0 while Ernie Shore was defeating the White Sox. The next day the Red Sox came into Detroit, and again baseball's strongest pitching staff prevailed over an ordinary one. Some 40,000 turned out for three weekday games at Navin Field. Carl Mays beat Dauss 3–1 on Tuesday; Leonard outpitched Howard Ehmke, just up from the New York State League, 4–3 on Wednesday; and in the finale Ruth held the Tigers to two runs while his mates battered various Tiger hurlers for ten. In the midst of a second straight mysterious slump in September, Cobb had only three singles in twelve times up in the three games.

Cobb hit well for the remainder of the season, but that did little for the Tigers' fortunes. Washington eliminated them from contention on September 25 despite Cobb's three hits and three steals. The White Sox slipped into second place ahead of Detroit in the final week of the season, only to see Boston clinch its second straight pennant on October 1. Chicago finished two games behind the Red Sox, Detroit four.

In a season-ending 6–3 victory at St. Louis, Cobb hit two singles and a double to bring his average up to .371, fifteen points behind Speaker but thirty ahead of Joe Jackson, who had been sold to Chicago late the previous season. For the first time since he was nineteen years old, Cobb was not the American League's batting champion. He had simply fallen too far behind Speaker earlier in the season. He did again steal more bases than anybody in either league, 68, and also topped the majors in runs scored with 113. For the sixth time he made more than two hundred hits. Moreover, in eight different games in 1916 he made four or more hits.

His friend H. G. Salsinger of the Detroit *News* believed that despite not winning the batting title, Cobb had worked harder, played more spiritedly, and generally been more valuable to his team than ever before. He had even contributed on the coaching lines, where he took his position when he became too impatient to sit on the bench during the Tigers' turns at bat. "Ty as a coacher was a revelation," Salsinger wrote. "The quick thinking that makes him great at bat and on the bases was demonstrated in directing his teammates, and the qualities he displayed have been stowed away for future reference."[25]

Cobb's pace in the weeks following the end of the season was frantic. First he hurried from St. Louis to Augusta, where the Cobbs' third child, a son they named Roswell Herschel, had been born before he could get home. After a few days with his wife, he was off to New York to pick up his syndicated World Series column at the third game between the Red Sox and the Brooklyn Robins. On Sunday, October 12, after Boston for the second straight year disposed of its National League opponent in five games, most of the Red Sox, headed by Jack Barry, went to New Haven to meet the Colonials, a strong semipro club owned by a twenty-one-year-old entrepreneur named George Weiss. Cobb played first base for Weiss's team, handled eight chances, and got two hits in a game called after nine innings with the score 3–3. The game violated a National Commission rule against post-season play by World Series teams. Ban Johnson subsequently fined ten Red Sox players as well as Cobb $50 each for performing at New Haven. The levy against Cobb still left him with a profit of about $750 on what Weiss had paid him.

From New Haven, Cobb hustled back to New York to become the first professional athlete to star in a commercial motion picture. In fact, he had been in the middle of a screen test in St. Louis when he received word of Roswell Herschel Cobb's birth. The movie was produced by an outfit called the Sunbeam Motion Picture Company, of which Vaughn Glaser was vice president. It was Glaser who had overcome Cobb's fear of making a fool of himself and convinced him that he ought to make a movie. Although he never revealed how much he was paid for doing the picture, it must have been at least as much as he got for his theatrical tour in 1911–12.

Entitled *Somewhere in Georgia* and filmed in about two weeks, the movie was written by Georgian Grantland Rice, now a top sports columnist for the New York *Tribine*. Rice's scenario had Cobb, as a small-town bank clerk and ballplayer in love with the bank president's daughter, being signed by the Detroit Tigers. Homesick, he leaves the Tigers to return to Georgia and his girl, only to be attacked and kidnapped by ruffians hired by his rival, the villainous bank cashier. Finally overcoming his abductors and making his escape, he arrives driving a mule wagon just in time to win a crucial game for the home nine and his sweetheart's hand as well.

It was a pretty dreadful movie, but Cobb again took his work seriously. Director George Ridgewell commented on how studious Cobb was, how he seemed to anticipate instructions. "I've never had to tell him more than once what I wanted done," Ridgewell said.[26] The main problem had to do with Cobb's love scenes with the female lead, played by Elsie MacLeod. Cobb was quite timid, reported Ridgewell, so much so that it had been necessary to direct those scenes with extreme delicacy.

Baseball had boomed again in 1916 with the restoration of stability and with close races in both leagues. American League attendance was up by more than a million over 1915. Frank Navin's profits more than doubled, to $126,000. Of course the principal beneficiary of Navin's prosperity over the past decade, apart from Navin himself, had been Cobb. *Sporting Life* estimated that in 1916 his salary had accounted for fully one-fifth of the Detroit club's total payroll.

In turn, Cobb's baseball salary was only a fraction of what he earned that year. The star of stage, screen, and ballfield celebrated his thirtieth birthday at Augusta that December. His present to himself was an English setter named

Curtis Pierce Proctor, son of a national champion pointer and one of several highest-pedigreed hunting dogs he had acquired. That Christmas the country was still at peace.

President Woodrow Wilson had been re-elected, though narrowly, the previous month largely because he had kept the United States out of war with Imperial Germany. For all his friendship with William Howard Taft, Wilson's Republican predecessor, Cobb had been raised to believe that the Democratic party was the white man's party. Like nearly all white southerners, he backed Wilson not only because he was the Democratic candidate but because, as a native Virginian, he was the first elected southern President since 1850. Late in the previous season, when the Tigers were in New York, Cobb had stopped by the Democratic party's national headquarters to announce for the benefit of assembled newsmen that his biggest wish, next to a pennant for Detroit, was Wilson's re-election.

The United States would not stay at peace much longer. Early in 1917 the German Imperial High Command announced the resumption of unrestricted submarine warfare in the Atlantic, which inevitably meant the loss of American ships and lives. As the Wilson administration broke off diplomatic relations with Germany and moved the country toward war, Tillinghast L'hommedieu Huston, a former army officer who, along with Jacob Ruppert, had bought the New York Yankees from Frank Farrell in 1914, proposed the institution of military drills at all major-league training camps that spring, as well as drill sessions for the teams before each game during the season. Shortly thereafter the American League owners endorsed Huston's idea and voted to ask the army to assign a drill instructor to each training camp. With a war coming, the patriotic magnates sought to provide an example in employee "preparedness" to the rest of the nation. By the time the new season got under way, it would no longer be a question of preparedness but of mobilization to fight a war the Congress, at Wilson's urging, had just declared.

VIII

A World War and a New Era

Inasmuch as in 1916 Cobb had joined the Tigers at Houston in the midst of their spring series with the Giants, he got his first look at Waxahachie, Texas, on March 26, 1917, when he arrived at the team's training headquarters. Cobb had greatly disappointed the citizens of that blackland-prairie town of 6500 by not showing up the previous year before the Tigers left. Now crowds of them came to the ballfield to watch Cobb work out and hung around the hotel to see what he looked like in street clothes. "Every white man in Ellis County has shaken hands with him," reported E. A. Batchelor to his readers back in Detroit, "and the African brother has worshipped from afar."[1]

Besides taking batting and fielding practice, Cobb joined in the spectacle that was a feature of all the big-league camps that spring. In their baseball livery and shouldering bats rather than rifles, the Tigers performed daily military drills in accordance with what the clubowners earlier in the year had agreed to have their players do. An army recruiting sergeant stationed at Fort Worth came over to Waxahachie to serve as drill instructor.

Whereas a year earlier people at Waxahachie and throughout Texas had expected war with Mexico, now they along with Americans everywhere took for granted that it was only a matter of time until the United States went to war with Imperial Germany. They did not have long to wait. On the evening of April 2 President Wilson addressed a joint session of Congress and called for a war to "make the world safe for democracy." Four days later the Congress gave him his war declaration.

Shortly before the nation entered the conflict in Europe, Cobb had plunged into another little war of his own—one of his most-publicized and best-remembered brawls. It happened on March 31 at Dallas, where the Tigers were playing the second game in another exhibition series with the aggressive New York Giants. That morning, a Saturday, Cobb played eighteen holes of golf with Hughey Jennings and his wife and a friend of Jennings. When Cobb showed up only minutes before game time that afternoon, shortstop Art Fletcher and second-baseman Charles "Buck" Herzog, two of the more hard-bitten Giants, immediately started calling him "swell-head," "showoff," and various less genteel designations.

His first time up, Cobb singled off lefthander Ferdie Schupp. Yelling to Herzog that he was coming down, Cobb took off on the first pitch. The catcher's throw got to second well ahead of Cobb, whose spikes ripped Herzog's trousers and cut his leg slightly. The two scuffled and rolled in the dirt while Fletcher ran over to join the fray. Players from both teams and several policemen quickly separated the antagonists. At that point umpire Bill Brennan, trying (with McGraw's help) to get back into the National League after jumping to the Federals, thumbed Cobb out of the game but permitted the two Giants to remain. Prolonged protests by Jennings and the 5500 fans who had filled the Dallas ballpark largely to see Cobb were unavailing.

While Cobb was finishing his dinner that evening at the Oriental Hotel (where both teams were staying), Herzog came over and told Cobb that he wanted to see him in Cobb's room. About a half hour later, after Cobb had cleared away his rugs and furniture, Herzog arrived with infielder Heinie Zimmerman. Out of the group of players gathered in the hall outside his room, Cobb called on Oscar Stanage, the Tigers catcher, to act as his own second. Tiger trainer Harry Tuthill was the agreed-upon choice to referee the Herzog-Cobb match. As Cobb remembered it, he sprinkled water on the floor to make it slippery for Herzog, who was wearing sneakers and also had done some boxing in the army. The two then went at it, with Cobb having a weight advantage of at least twenty-five pounds. Accounts of the fight vary considerably, but all agree that Cobb got the best of the exchange. According to one version, Cobb had Herzog stretched backward over the footpost of the bed and was pummeling him when Tuthill stopped it.

The next morning John McGraw confronted Cobb in the hotel lobby and was so abusive that Cobb told the Giants manager that if McGraw were younger he'd kill him. That afternoon an overflow crowd came to see a renewal of yesterday's violence, only to find Herzog absent because he was in no shape to play and Cobb sitting in the grandstand because he refused to. Cobb announced that he would not take the field again against the Giants, adding that "McGraw is a mucker and always has been and I don't intend to stand for his dirty work."[2]

Cobb traveled with the Tigers to Wichita Falls. There, despite the pleas of a delegation from the local Chamber of Commerce, he again refused to play and then left the Tigers-Giants tour for Cincinnati, where he would continue his workouts with manager Christy Mathewson's Reds. Jennings agreed with Cobb's decision; anyway, he told reporters, he wouldn't have allowed Cobb to play again against the "three anarchists" on the New York infield—Herzog,

Fletcher, and Zimmerman. Cobb was "too valuable a piece of property to be brawling around with men that have less to risk."[3]

Punctuated by a fight between Fletcher and Tiger rookie third-baseman Bob Jones and by a ball-and-bat-throwing incident between pitcher Willie Mitchell and Zimmerman, the tour wound northward through sandstorms and snow flurries, finally ending at Kansas City. It had been a most uncommon exhibition series. Before leaving Kansas City, McGraw and the entire Giants team sent Cobb a wire: "It's safe to rejoin your club now. We've left."[4] That he did on April 9, when the Tigers got to Toledo for a game with that city's American Association entry.

On April 11, for the first time in baseball history, a season opened with the country at war. Besides the customary flag-raisings and patriotic airs, military drills by the players also marked the 1917 openings. At Detroit nearly 26,000 people saw Cleveland's Stanley Coveleski, righthanded younger brother of the Tigers' Harry, survive a barrage of doubles into the outfield overflow, including a pair by Cobb, to beat Detroit 6–4. Cobb played right field, as he had in the exhibition season, as Jennings experimented with Harry Heilmann in center. The Detroit manager soon put Cobb back where he could range over as much as possible of the territory left uncovered by the heavy-footed Heilmann and Bobby Veach in left.

The season proceeded amid mounting apprehension on the part of baseball officials and owners. As it turned out, the war affected baseball relatively little in 1917. The Congress did not get around to voting a conscription law until May 18, and it would take months for the draft system to become fully operational. Very few professional ballplayers volunteered for military service before the season was over; nearly all waited to find out their draft classifications. Although neither major league produced a close pennant race, attendance held up fairly well at about five million, and most teams showed at least a modest profit.

Mainly on the strength of the crowds they drew at Navin Field early in the season, the Tigers returned a profit of about $50,000 to Frank Navin and the other stockholders—about one-half of the surplus for 1916. That spring Detroit seemed wild over baseball, as evidenced by the 15,000 who sat in freezing temperatures and snow flurries on Sunday, April 15, to see their team drop its third game in four outings, to the White Sox. The Tigers never were able to overcome their sorry start that year. By May 25 they were in last place with a record of 11–20. Detroit led the American League in team batting average (.259), but inconsistent pitching now that Harry Coveleski's arm had gone dead and an infield that proved particularly inept when it came to double plays kept the Tigers from rising above mediocrity. Two doubleheader losses to Chicago in late June and early July cooled them off at a time when they seemed about to make a run for the pennant.

Cobb, by contrast, started well and got better as the season progressed. In a fourteen-game eastern swing in May and June, he made twenty-eight hits in fifty-three times up. When he came into New York's Polo Grounds, where the Yankees had played for the past four years (since the rebuilding of the Giants' ballpark following a fire), the hostile crowds let him know that they remembered his fight with Herzog. As he usually did in such circumstances, Cobb responded by playing a little harder and better, going nine for seventeen in the four games at the Polo Grounds, including two singles, a double, and two triples in the nightcap of a Registration Day doubleheader that drew a record Yankee turnout.

Just before the New York series, Cobb had begun a hitting streak that eventually reached thirty-five consecutive games before the White Sox stopped him on July 6. The high point of the streak came at St. Louis in back-to-back doubleheaders with the Browns on June 30–July 1. After singling and doubling in the opener on the 30th (which Detroit lost), he tripled and then belted a grand-slam, opposite-field homerun over the left-field bleachers in game two— the longest hit anybody could remember seeing in St. Louis, longer even than Babe Ruth's to the same area the previous season. Cobb's homer, wrote a local sports columnist, prompted "the most spontaneous and prolonged applause that has ever greeted an alien enemy athlete." After the Tigers won 5–3, the St. Louis fans went home "fully convinced of the fact baseball will be a bum game with Tyrus retired."[5] The next day, in another split, Cobb was five for nine and put on a show for the crowd of 13,000, repeatedly calling for the ball to examine it when at bat, kidding the umpires, and even listening in on a conference between the Browns' battery mates.

In mid-August, with the Tigers in fourth place but going nowhere else, Cobb had to leave the lineup for the first time all year with a leg that was sore and badly scraped from sliding. Even out of a game, though, he remained a factor in it. He delighted fans with his vociferous coaching at either first or third. On one occasion, against Washington at Navin Field, he prompted a big controversy by grabbing George Burns when Burns hesitated at third and shoving him halfway home to score the winning run. The Senators, led by manager Clark Griffith, demanded that umpire Hildebrand rule interference and declare Burns out, but Hildebrand remained unconvinced that Cobb's highly physical guidance had been pertinent to Burns's run.

Cobb returned to the lineup for good on August 22, with a double in a victory over New York. By that time he was batting around .385 and was far ahead of Cleveland's Tris Speaker and St. Louis's George Sisler. (In 1917 Sisler came into his own as a hitter after joining the Browns out of college as a pitcher–first baseman.) As in other years, though, Cobb seemed to play with greater enthusiasm than most of his teammates. As part of a seven-game losing streak early in September, the Tigers dropped two straight doubleheaders to the first-place White Sox. To H. G. Salsinger the team did not seem to care where it placed.

Before the Tigers left home to finish the season in the east, Sam Crawford pinch hit in a game against Cleveland, grounded out, and departed for California, where he now lived. Only his sixty-first appearance of the season, it was his last in a major-league uniform. His three-year contract with Detroit (at $7500 a year) would expire at season's end, and Frank Navin was not interested in keeping the thirty-seven-year-old veteran of nineteen campaigns in the majors. Crawford went home with $1200 from the receipts of a late-August testimonial game as well as a lifetime batting average of .309, 1,525 runs batted in, an insurmountable 312 career triples, and an evident lack of concern for being only thirty-six hits shy of three thousand. At the time he also held the major-league record for consecutive games played at 472, although Eddie Collins would surpass that early the next year. Despite having gained only a fifth-grade education in Wahoo, Nebraska, Crawford was an intelligent and inquisitive man who took pride in his elegant penmanship and subsequently developed a fondness for the writings of Balzac and the nineteenth-century philosopher Robert G. Ingersoll. A durable and dependable professional, he had bulwarked the Tiger ball club from the time he joined it in 1903 after jumping from the National League. It had been both his fortune and his fate to spend his best years playing in the shadow of the great Cobb.[6]

The day after Crawford's last game, Cobb broke out of a 1–21 slump with three hits aginst Cleveland in the Tigers' final home appearance of 1917. His bat stayed hot during the next two weeks in the east, where Detroit ended the season by losing a doubleheader to the once-proud Athletics, mired in the cellar for the third straight year. At 78–75, the Tigers finished in fourth place, more than twenty games behind the pennant-winning White Sox and nine and a half behind third-place Cleveland. The team's major accomplishment had been to take twelve of twenty-one games from the two-time world's champion Red Sox, of which nine wins were shutouts by an otherwise undistinguished group of pitchers.

Cobb recaptured hitting homors with an average of .383, thirty points above Sisler and Speaker. His fifty-five steals again led the majors, and he also topped American Leaguers in base hits (225), doubles (44), triples (24), total bases (336), and slugging percentage (.571). He trailed teammates Bobby Veach by one in runs batted in (102) and Donie Bush by five in runs scored (107). In virtually every respect it had been another outstanding year for Cobb, one that left little indication that the thirty-year-old Georgian had lost anything at bat, afoot, or afield. Moreover, once the season got under way and the Herzog fracas was behind him, Cobb had stayed out of trouble and seemed to enjoy himself more than in any previous season.

In 1917 Cobb turned down another $1000 fee from the Wheeler Syndicate to work the White Sox–Giants World Series, and hurried back to Augusta. Recently he had obtained a distributorship for Bevo soft drinks in the Augusta area. The St. Louis-based maker of the beverage had reportedly guaranteed Cobb $10,000 for handling it over the next year. With the sale of liquor illegal everywhere in Georgia, Cobb figured to do well selling Bevo to the two big army encampments situated near Augusta. Salsinger, who was about as close to Cobb as any sportswriter ever got, estimated that his personal income for the year would exceed $50,000.

After getting the soft-drink distributorship launched, Cobb left for a long-planned hunting trip into northern Canada. Accompanying him were Matt Hinkel, a Cleveland boxing promoter, Tiger pitcher Willie Mitchell, and Fred Hall, a Detroit businessman. Deep in the woods of upper Ontario they left their train to be greeted by Jack Miner, their guide. Cobb had become acquainted with Miner earlier in the year after reading in outdoor magazines about Miner's work in wildfowl conservation and the bird sanctuary he operated in western Ontario near Kingsville, about twenty-five miles from Detroit. Cobb also befriended Manly Miner, Jack Miner's twenty-year-old son, and often had young Miner as his guest in Cobb's personal box at Navin Field. Despite his ardent conservationism, Jack Miner was quite amenable to showing those who wanted to shoot big game the places it would most likely be found. On this particular trip he guided Cobb's party to an area where Cobb was able to shoot two caribou, while Mitchell and Hall got one each.

Over the next few years Jack Miner and Cobb would become close friends. In the 1920s Ty Cobb, Jr., spent three summers at the Miner sanctuary and farm, and Charlie Cobb and her children often came there for church parties. When the Cobbs' fourth child was being born in 1919, the older children stayed with the Miner family. "Jack Miner was closer to nature's wonder than any man I ever knew," Cobb said in his autobiography. "Just to know him was one of the finest things that happened to me . . . away from baseball."[7]

While Cobb was traipsing the Canadian wilderness, Sam Crawford out in California was venting his long-accumulating resentments against the Detroit ball club and especially Hughey Jennings and Ty Cobb. To reporters in San Francisco and Los Angeles he complained that in 1917 Cobb had really run the team, that it was Cobb and not Jennings who had determined that Heilmann would permanently displace Crawford in right field rather than play first base, the position Heilmann preferred. Heilmann, according to Crawford, resented Cobb's influence over Jennings, as did Bobby Veach. In past years, moreover, "I saw a number of men sent from the team because of Cobb's dislike for them" (meaning presumably Matty McIntyre and Davy Jones). On his testimonial day at Navin Field late the previous summer, Crawford added, Cobb and Jennings had remained in the dugout while the rest of the team crowded around homeplate to wish him well. In general Cobb had been "a disorganizing influence" on the Tigers.[8]

Crawford's well-publicized complaints helped spark new rumors that Cobb would be traded. When Navin was observed in a tête-à-tête with Miller Huggins, the new Yankee manager, at the midwinter baseball meetings in New York, reporters speculated that Detroit would swap Cobb to the New York team for some much-needed pitching. Back in Detroit, however, Navin reiterated what he had often said in the past: ". . . Cobb will never be sold, traded or released."[9] Meanwhile Cobb had signed and returned his 1918 contract, a one-year pact calling for $20,000, the same salary he had drawn in 1915–17.

It looked for a time that winter as if Cobb might not be with the Tigers next season after all. In June, at the time of the national draft sign-up, Cobb had registered by mail with his Augusta board, the ninth man to do so in that city. With a wife and three small children, he had requested division-two classification; but because he had neglected to complete the part of his questionnaire having to do with dependents, the Augusta officials had promptly put him in division one, making him liable for immediate conscription. By the time he got the misunderstanding straightened out, the army's provost general had already ordered the exemption of men with dependents, and Secretary of War Newton D. Baker had recommended against the drafting of men who had turned thirty-one since registration. Qualifying on both counts, Cobb ended up in division two, although he said he was ready to go "when the government needs me."[10]

Fearing the effects of conscription, the government's takeover of the railroads, and a host of other wartime imponderables but lacking any better plan, the owners in both leagues voted to proceed with a full 154-game schedule for 1918. They also agreed to distribute receipts from the first four games of the World Series among the first-division clubs in each league. It proved an inopportune time to inaugurate such a practice, inasmuch as the Series, pitting the Boston Red Sox and the Chicago Cubs, would be poorly attended. That was indicative of the overall attendance picture that year. Lengthened workdays, a general dislocation of the work force by war production and military manpower demands, and deterioration in the quality of play as many ballplayers volunteered, were drafted, or sought jobs in essential employments, all helped produce the smallest aggregate turnout since early in the century. Major-league attendance barely exceeded three million in 1918. The Detroit franchise lost some $30,000.

For the third and last time the Tigers trained at Waxahachie. Bill Donovan, fired as Yankee manager after his team came in sixth the previous season, was taken on as pitching coach by his old ball club. Donovan, together with

Donie Bush and of course Jennings, would be Cobb's only remaining personal links with Detroit's pennant-winning teams. If Jennings would just leave the pitchers alone, Salsinger thought, then Donovan might be able to help the team's lackluster mound corps. In truth, whatever other merits as a manager the feisty redhead may have had, his knowledge of pitchers and pitching seldom rose above the level of sandlot clichés. With sturdy men like Donovan, Mullin, Killian, and Summers, who usually just needed to be given the ball, Jennings had won three straight pennants. Since those fond days, however, Tiger pitching had been perennially problematical.

Cobb again passed up the delights of Waxahachie and reported at Dallas in time for an exhibition game at the end of March. Fulfilling the pledge Navin and Jennings had given the Cincinnati Reds in arranging a spring tour with the National Leaguers, Cobb played in all the games between the Tigers and Reds, of which Detroit won eleven of thirteen. The Tigers also batted above .500 against Reds pitchers and looked generally imposing. That lusty performance only served as another reminder that pre-season wins and losses usually have no bearing at all on what a ball club will do once the season gets under way.

After losing twenty-seven of their first forty games, the Tigers found themselves in last place at the end of May. Suffering from the cold he usually caught on the trip north in the spring, Cobb missed three of the team's first four games and started poorly. He had finally pushed his average to the vicinity of .300 when, on May 25, he made a shoestring catch in a game at Washington and fell heavily on his right shoulder. Although he stayed in the game and managed to steal a base after Walter Johnson walked him his next time up, he finally left in the sixth inning in severe pain. Unable to throw, Cobb could only pinch hit over the next nine games (in one of which, at Boston, he made the final out in Dutch Leonard's no-hitter).

Cobb returned to the lineup on June 5, playing a couple of games at first base to test his arm before moving back to center. Up to then he had stolen only six bases. The team, meanwhile, continued to flounder, not leaving last place to Philadelphia, the accustomed inhabitants, until June 18. With one player after another either departing for military service or for shipyard, munitions, or some other kind of work that provided a deferment, Jennings struggled with his lineup but had little success with any of the numerous combinations he tried that year. Attendance at Navin Field dwindled throughout the season; by June, Salsinger was writing that the Tigers no longer seemed to care about winning and that the weekday turnouts were the smallest since Detroit became part of the American League.

However lethargic and disorganized the team as a whole may have been during that strange wartime season, Cobb played as hard as ever, motivated by an undiminished pride in his own performance. On June 30 he was 7–9 and stole a base in each half of a doubleheader as the Tigers swept the Indians before the year's biggest crowd in Cleveland. (That evening, in another part of the same city, federal agents arrested the Socialist leader Eugene V. Debs for violating the wartime Espionage Act in advocating resistance to the draft.) Four days later Cobb went 5–6 in a twelve-inning loss at Chicago, and four days after that he stole home twice in a game at Philadelphia, on pitcher Scott Perry and catcher Cy Perkins. After getting his first homer of the year on July 13 at Washington, a drive over Howard Shanks's head in center field, Cobb was hitting .378. The team stayed out of last place by the margin of one game.

Later that month Cobb hurt his left shoulder at New York, first on a slide and then on a swing, and missed six more games. Returning in the sixth inning against the Yankees at Detroit, he hit towering Elmer "Slim" Love's first pitch down the left-field line for a double to drive home Bobby Jones and Veach, then tripled in Veach in the eighth. By then he had a lead of 25 to 30 points in the batting race over Philadelphia's George Burns, whom Jennings had given up on and Navin had sold over the winter.

It was about that time of the season that Cobb had Manly Miner bring Jack Miner over for a game. As the ferry from Windsor pulled up on the Detroit side of the river, the Miners found Cobb gesticulating to two policemen and denouncing a customs official who, in pushing the crowd back from dockside, had caused Cobb to fall over backwards. "I am a Mason and the customs official is a brother Mason," they heard Cobb say, "but be damned if he's going to push me around when I'm here meeting guests." Still in a rage, Cobb got into his Oldsmobile with the Miners and started to drive off, only to stop and jump out, cursing the customs man and threatening to go back and "lick the sonufabitch." At the urging of the policemen, who knew both Cobb and Jack Miner and impressed on Cobb that he was "embarrassing Mr. Miner," Cobb finally got back behind the wheel and drove his guests from the scene.[11] That was the first of a number of times that Manly Miner would chance to witness an explosion of the famous Cobb temper.

Given the kind of man Cobb was, such an incident could have happened almost anyplace and anytime. That particular August, however, he may have been a bit more tightly wound than usual. He had decided on a course of action that had nothing to do with baseball, one that might profoundly affect his life, even be the cause of his death. When the Tigers were in Washington at the start of their next eastern swing, Cobb went to the War Department and applied for a commission in the Chemical Warfare Service. He also took his army physical examination. About a week and a half later, in New York, he received notification that his application had been approved, that he was now a captain in the CWS, and that he was to report for duty by October 1.

Like most other Americans and especially southerners, Cobb had enthusiastically supported President Wilson's decision to take the country into the

European war. Imbued with a great deal of old-fashioned patriotism, Cobb had never questioned the necessity for American participation or the rightness of the American cause. Though initially obtaining a deferment, he had simply come to believe that he had an obligation to serve. Typically, he chose the most risky but also most glamorous branch of the armed forces next to the Air Service.

On Saturday, August 24, between games of a Tigers-Yankees doubleheader at the Polo Grounds, Cobb stood on the roof of the visitors' dugout behind third base and, along with Jennings, made a plea for the fans to purchase U. S. Savings Stamps to help finance the war effort. He'd just bought $250 worth, he said. By October, he went on, he would be on his way to France. Whatever happened, he didn't expect to return to baseball. As he waved his cap, some 12,000 Yankee partisans roundly cheered him.

Two days later, at Boston, Cobb homered with Bush aboard in a 6–3 victory over the frontrunning Red Sox and Carl Mays, then left for Detroit to settle his personal affairs. He rejoined the team at Cleveland on the 30th, in time to go hitless in a doubleheader defeat. But then at St. Louis he made nine hits in three games, during the last of which, on September 1, he and George Sisler pitched against each other for a couple of innings.

On September 2, Labor Day, the baseball season came to its earliest conclusion ever. Operating under the pressure of Secretary of War Baker's "work or fight" decree, which restricted activities not contributory to the war effort, baseball's magnates had secured the government's permission to keep the season going through Labor Day and then, as a special concession, to hold the World Series directly thereafter. So like everybody else, the Tigers and White Sox brought things to a close with a Labor Day doubleheader. Cobb was 3–5 in each game, as the Tigers swept the sixth-place defending world's champions but still ended up a dismal seventh themselves, with a record of 55–71. The nightcap was another for-the-fun-of-it game, featuring the forty-two-year-old Donovan as the Tigers' starter and subsequent alternating stints on the mound by Veach and Cobb.

It was an interesting and enjoyable way to end what many feared would be the last baseball season for a long time. Although the U.S.-Allied counteroffensive had already turned the tide of battle in France, the widely held assumption both inside and outside the American government was that the war against Germany would last well into and maybe throughout 1919. Bidding farewell to "Captain Cobb," the St. Louis sports columnist T. C. David wondered whether the great Georgian had closed his career "perhaps for all time."[12]

If so, then Cobb had gone out in high style. In 111 games he hit .382 to Burns's .352 and Sisler's .341, thereby taking his eleventh batting championship in twelve years. His fourteen triples also led the league. He was second (by only one) to Cleveland's Ray Chapman in runs, trailed Burns in total bases, and yielded the slugging leadership to Babe Ruth. (Spending an increasing amount of his time in the outfield, Ruth led both major leagues with eleven homeruns.) Cobb's thirty-four steals were his fewest since 1908 and a clear sign that he was starting to lose his fabled speed. Henceforth his base-path exploits would depend more on craft than quickness.

Cobb relocated his family at the house on William Street in Augusta, said goodbye to his mother and sister at Royston (Paul Cobb was already in uniform), and left for New York to report by October 1, as ordered. Among other athletic notables holding commissions in the Chemical Warfare Service were Christy Mathewson, Branch Rickey, and Percy Haughton, head football coach at Harvard and president of the Boston Braves. Those three were already in France, where Cobb was also to receive his training. After that they would all be assigned as staff officers and technical advisers to various divisions. Late in October, Frank Navin received a postcard from Cobb reporting his unit's safe arrival overseas.

Meanwhile a trainee in the Air Service had sought Cobb's advice on physical conditioning. The ballplayer's written reply, endorsed by the chief of aircraft operations for distribution to the Service's other trainees, prompted considerable publicity in the United States. Again Cobb's opinions combined common sense with folk superstition, some of which doubtless derived from time spent with Grandma Cobb in the Carolina mountains. Cobb advised exercise—a daily mile walk ended with a sprint "to keep your liver clear"—and care for the stomach, "your power plant." One should always play on an empty stomach, said Cobb, and presumably fly on one as well. Once more he cautioned against sweet milk, which "fogs the eyes," as well as coffee at night or before games. One cigar was all right after each meal; cigarettes should be shunned.[13] Unfortunately, like many other men in the First World War, Cobb would find that taking a quick smoke with a cigarette was an increasingly tempting way to use tobacco, an indulgence to which he had long been addicted.

Cobb's advice to the Air Service was about his most substantive contribution to the victory that came unexpectedly within two-and-a-half weeks following his disembarkation. Even that short time, though, was enough for Cobb to have a terrifying experience, one that almost cost him his life. He and the other new CWS officers received no more than a week or so of training at an airfield near Claumont, France. Then they were put in charge of training the enlisted men, "largely . . . hard cases and rejects from other services," as he remembered them. "The theory was that they would listen to well-known sport personalities."[14] The training procedure was to march the recruits into an airtight chamber where, on signal, poison gas would be released. On that signal everybody was supposed to clap his gas mask on his face and wait calmly until the gas dissipated. On one occasion, though, there was some mixup and the gas was already in the chamber before Cobb and Mathewson, the officers in charge, realized it. Eight men inhaled a lethal dosage before somebody got the door open. Cobb breathed a little of the poison but was soon all right. Mathewson, however, took in a big whiff of the deadly vapor, so much that Cobb and many others were later convinced that the gas was the main cause of the tuberculosis that took Mathewson's life seven years later, at the age of forty-five.

Aside from nearly being hit by a fragment from an exploding shell in camp, the gas-chamber episode was Captain Cobb's biggest scare in uniform. After the fighting ended on November 11, he was lucky enough to get on the first troop ship home, the *Leviathan*. He found himself in New York harbor on December 16, two days before his thirty-second birthday. Cobb told the newsmen who greeted him that he intended "to break away from baseball. I'm tired of it. I've had fifteen years of it, and I want to quit while I'm still good." [15]

Then it was back to Georgia for a reunion with family and a delayed and therefore intense period of hunting with what had become a highly valuable assortment of setters and retrievers. His favorite was a Llewellyn setter named Cobb's Hall, given to him by his Detroit friend Fred Hall. In the next few years Cobb found much satisfaction in showing the dog. One year Cobb's Hall came in second in the national championships at Grand Junction, Tennessee.

Early in 1919 the baseball owners again miscalculated. A year earlier they had decided to go ahead with a full schedule of games, only to have the season truncated. Now, anticipating a slower demobilization of the armed forces and reconversion to a peacetime economy than turned out to be the case, they determined on a 140-game schedule. What they did not suspect was that baseball and spectator sports in general were about to enter a new boom era, a time of unprecedented prosperity in which the crowds and revenues of the past would be dwarfed. Helped substantially by a new state law that made possible Sunday ball in New York for the Yankees, Giants, and Brooklyn, attendance would climb back to six million in 1919 despite the trimmed schedule. It was the beginning of a sustained surge that would last for a decade.

Because of the new schedule, the teams gathered for spring training about two weeks later than usual. The Detroit club took over the facilities used by the Yankees the past several years at Macon, Georgia, about a hundred miles southwest of the Cobbs' home at Augusta. Over the winter the Tigers had fired Bill Donovan and brought in Dan Howley, a minor-league manager and former National League catcher, to work with the pitchers. The club had also obtained catcher Eddie Ainsmith from Washington and pitcher Slim Love from the Yankees and traded Oscar Vitt to the Red Sox for outfielder Chick Shorten. The new men would have to contend with the holdovers and rookies for four fewer places on the ball club, inasmuch as both leagues had again cut back the May-September rosters to twenty-one in an effort to minimize anticipated losses in 1919. And because for 140 games the players' contracts specified less money, an unusual amount of straggling and complaining accompanied spring-training that year.

At Augusta, Cobb conducted what might be termed an informal holdout. Now denying that he had ever really wanted to quit baseball, he talked about being a free agent. He argued from the fact that, to avoid paying their players after Labor Day in 1918, the clubs (except for the World Series teams) had officially released everybody on their rosters. At the same time, however, a gentlemen's agreement among the owners prevented any of them from signing players from any club besides their own. So while Cobb was technically correct, in practical terms he would have to sign again with Frank Navin or not play. As incredible as it might seem in a later time, Navin actually wanted Cobb to take a modest cut for 1919. That Cobb would have none of. "Naturally, I feel that my services are worth a certain sum and I wouldn't play for less," he said.[16]

So Cobb stayed home all March, working out some at Warren Park with Clark Griffith's Washington team. As it happened, he was in Augusta when William H. Yawkey, still a major shareholder in the Detroit franchise, suffered a heart attack there en route from New York to Florida. Cobb was among those at the bedside of the generous, high-living multimillionare when he died in a local hospital at the age of forty-three.

By the end of the month Navin had given up trying to trim Cobb's salary, had sent him a contract for another year at $20,000, and had received the signed document in the mail. Cobb appeared in his first game that spring at Rock Hill, South Carolina, one of the many obscure places where the Tigers played George Stallings's Boston Braves on a gruelling tour arranged by Braves general manager Walter Hapgood. In mostly foul weather, the expedition continued through the wilds of the Carolinas, Virginia, and West Virginia before the Tigers mercifully terminated it by splitting away to meet the Reds at Cincinnati.

Rain, snow flurries, and icy winds postponed Detroit's season-opening game, at Navin Field, until April 25. Before only about 8000 spectators, including a couple of thousand convalescent veterans from the local military hospital, the Tigers beat Cleveland 4–2, largely on the strength of Cobb's windblown single and double. Howard Ehmke's strong performance in outpitching Stanley Coveleski prompted Jennings to brag that he had a real pitching staff for the first time in five years, along with the strongest outfield in baseball and improved catching. His team had a good chance at the pennant, he enthused.

In practically every respect 1919 was a better year for the Detroit franchise than the previous two. Jennings did have a respectable ball club again, although that was hardly apparent in the early going. By mid-May the Tigers had won less than a third of their games and remained out of the cellar only because Connie Mack had another miserable outfit at Philadelphia. Late in May, though, they began to play solid baseball, especially after Navin paid the Yankees $15,000 for Dutch Leonard, who had been unable to agree on salary terms at New York following his purchase from Boston. Selling Leonard was one of Red Sox owner Harry Frazee's early steps toward the dismantling of the 1915–16 and 1918 World's champions. The clever lefthander now joined Dauss, Ehmke, and Boland to give Jennings an effective rotation.

Cobb was hitting .377 at the end of May, with five steals in twenty-six games. Later he yielded the batting lead for a time, first to Bobby Veach and then to Joe Jackson, but throughout the summer he continued to pound the ball consistently. He also continued to be, as Salsinger put it, "the busiest man on the team."[17] Whether he was working the coaching lines when not at bat, yelling in exhortations from the outfield, or joking with fans, Cobb remained a constant and conspicuous presence on the ballfield.

Even with Cobb out for thirteen games in June and early July with a boil on his leg, the Tigers improved steadily in the standings. When he returned to the lineup on July 4, they were in fourth place at 31–29. On the 21st they were seven-and-a-half games behind the White Sox, who had taken the league lead from Cleveland and New York, when lefty Herb Pennock of Boston stopped them at Navin Field, 8–0. The next day Babe Ruth, now playing nearly every game in the outfield, hit a ball over the bleachers in right, the longest homer up to then at the Detroit ballpark. It was Ruth's fourteenth of the year, thereby breaking the American League record set by Boston's John "Buck" Freeman in 1903. Meanwhile Cobb punched out three singles and stole a base. Ehmke beat the Red Sox 6–2, in a game that provided a sharp contrast between the older Cobb-style baseball and the Ruth-influenced game that would soon be in sway.

By winning seven straight in the east in the first part of August, the Tigers crept to within four games of first-place Chicago. Then they came home to take two out of three from New York, drawing nearly 50,000 for the weekday games. That was as close to the top as they were to get. The high point of the season, though, may have been the following Sunday, August 17, when 31,000 people overflowed everywhere to see Washington's Walter Johnson outduel Leonard in eleven innings 4–2, despite Cobb's two doubles. Later in the week, when Boston took two out of three games, with Ruth homering four times in the series, the Tigers fell six games off the pace. A doubleheader defeat by Chicago on Labor Day, which ended when Eddie Cicotte struck out Cobb and Veach for his twenty-sixth win, about finished whatever pennant aspirations Detroit fans may still have had.

A couple of days later, during a game with St. Louis at Navin Field, Cobb several times warned an unruly customer behind the Tiger dugout to shut his mouth. At the end of the game the fan came onto the field, challenged Cobb, and got a disabling knee in the groin for his trouble. Later Cobb came out of his shower to tell off several of the man's friends, only to be confronted by them again as he was about to get into an automobile that Navin, worried he might be mobbed, had waiting for him at the ballpark entrance. Enraged by that time, Cobb walked down the block asking every man he came to if he wanted to fight. Finding no takers, he returned to Navin's auto and was driven away. "This ball park is our office," he declared to reporters the next day, "and we are entitled to a certain amount of respect."[18]

The Tigers played poorly on their last eastern trip and found themselves in danger of losing third place to New York. Because for 1919 only the first three teams in each league would share in the World Series money, the difference between third and fourth was about $550, a substantial sum to everybody on the Tiger ball club besides Cobb. On September 26 Detroit made eighteen hits in closing out its home season with a 9–5 victory over Cleveland. (Years later that particular game would be the subject of a bitter controversy involving, among others, Cobb, Tris Speaker, and Dutch Leonard.) At Chicago the Tigers took two out of three from the pennant-winning White Sox but still saw the Yankees, by beating Philadelphia in their last outing, slip into third place by half a game and secure the Series money. Detroit's fourth-place record, 80 wins and 60 losses, left the Tigers eight games out of first.

That was a big improvement over 1918 and a cause for much optimism about next year in Detroit. So was Cobb's performance, which resulted in another hitting title, his twelfth, and again demonstrated for those who might have any doubts that the Georgian's bat was as potent as it had ever been. His .384 average and 191 hits, both tops in the majors, were accomplishments that he "felt unusually pleased about," particularly inasmuch as when he got back from France he had not been sure he wanted to play anymore baseball.[19] Although he stole only twenty-eight bases in 1919, five fewer than Eddie Collins's league-leading total, Cobb had such a successful year otherwise that, at least for the time being, he quit talking about retirement.

Cobb's teammate Bob Veach was batting runnerup at .355 and trailed only Ruth in runs batted in. It was Veach's best year in a number of fine ones in the majors. Overall the Tigers had become a heavy-hitting outfit. Shorten and rookie Ira Flagstead, who divided the time in right field, hit .315 and .331, respectively, so that Detroit's four outfielders averaged a dazzling .346. Moreover, Harry Heilmann, playing first base most of the time that year, batted .320 and was well on his way to becoming one of baseball's greatest right-handed hitters.

Of course the biggest story of the season was Babe Ruth. His twenty-nine homeruns startled the baseball world. Nobody had ever hit that many; nobody since 1900 had come close. Distances, moreover, seemed not to matter to Ruth. His homers were commonly great soaring drives, the likes of which fans at Fenway Park and around the American League had never seen. After four years as the outstanding lefthanded pitcher in the league, the twenty-four-year-old Ruth had given the game another dimension. "Ruth was such a sensation last season," proclaimed the New York *Times,* "that he supplanted the great Ty Cobb as baseball's greatest attraction. . . ."[20] Fully as much of a sensation as Ruth's 1919 performance was his sale to the New York Yankees on January 3, 1920, for an unheard-of $125,000.

A fourth-place finish had saved Hughey Jennings his job, despite continuing complaints from some men on the team about his interference with Howley's work with the pitchers, about his sarcasm with players who were not doing well, about Cobb's influence on him. So, in November, Jennings signed for another year, his fourteenth at Detroit. Shortly thereafter Cobb, who had repeatedly denied gossip that he wanted to manage the team, agreed with Navin on $20,000 for 1920. Even though he had not had a raise since 1914, he remained the best-paid player in baseball. He had continued to do well off the field, too, especially in the fall of 1919, when he took advantage of the sky-high market for American cotton overseas to sell his futures for a profit of $155,000. Like all good investors, Cobb had sensed the right time to move. A year later cotton prices and futures plummeted.

Over the winter Cobb did his usual amount of hunting, although he stayed relatively close to home because the Cobbs had a new baby girl, named Beverly, born in Detroit near the end of the previous season. Charlie Cobb was slow in recovering from her fourth childbirth. Like others inside baseball that offseason, Cobb was aware of rumors that there had been something phony about the recent World Series, in which a fine White Sox team had lost five of eight games to the Cincinnati Reds, generally considered an inferior ball club. Yet at the time Cobb assumed that the White Sox simply had been overconfident. Neither he nor most other people suspected that seven members of the Chicago team had been on the payroll of gamblers.

By 1920 a new baseball era was at hand not only in terms of the sport's drawing power, which would carry major-league attendance past the nine million mark that season. Ruth's homeruns had signaled the coming of a new way of playing the game, featuring the steady decline of bunting, base-stealing, and the other arts of pitcher-dominated baseball and the ascendancy of hitters and especially long-ball hitters. Contemporary observers believed and baseball historians have agreed ever since that after the war something happened to the baseballs manufactured by the Spalding Company. The company's explanation was that while the design of the ball changed not at all, Spalding had put into use a higher-grade of woolen yarn from Australia that wound tighter. Whatever the reason, by 1920 the balls were carrying a lot farther.

The consensus within and without baseball was that the "dead" ball of past years had gone out in favor of a new "lively" ball.

Then, too, early in 1920, after years of discussion, the National Commission finally barred the spit ball and other forms of ball-tampering except for seventeen established pitchers in the two leagues, who would still be allowed to doctor the object until they had finished their careers. Adopted at least as much to reduce errors by fielders mishandling slippery and mutilated balls as to boost hitting, the ban on the wide assortment of "trick pitches" did much to tip the game's delicate balance of skills in favor of the hitters. So did the increasing tendency of affluent owners to let spectators keep balls hit into the stands instead of having attendants or park police retrieve them and throw them back on the field. Clean, new, easier-to-see baseballs meant another edge for hitters.

Changes in the ball itself, in what pitchers could do to it, and in what happened to it when it left the field of play—combined with the willingness of more and more players to try to emulate Ruth's long-distance prowess—produced a proliferation of homeruns and substantial increments in runs scored from 1920 on. Using 1917, the last previous 154-game season, as a base, one discovers an 86 percent increase in homers in 1920, a 176 percent increase in 1921, and a 211 percent gain in 1922. Total runs scored grew by 35 percent, 1917–22. The combined earned run average for both leagues swelled from 2.68 to 4.60 over the same period.

By the spring of 1920 Cobb must have been at least vaguely aware that a profound transition was under way in the game he played for a living. Basically, though, he would continue to play as he always had, stressing precision over power, guile over muscle. Yet instead of going all out all the time, as he had ten or twelve years earlier, now he was more inclined to pick his spots and generally to control his movements on the ball field more carefully than he had in the past.

That spring Cobb also picked where he wanted to play—or rather decided that he would not play with the Tigers and Braves on another of Walter Hapgood's cow-pasture pilgrimages. The Tigers could train in the cold and wet at Macon and then hop through Georgia and the Carolinas and on to points north without him; and the local people could protest his absence all they wanted to. He worked out regularly, again with Washington at the Augusta ball park, played golf, and finally met the team at Indianapolis on April 10, only four days before the season opened.

That opening took place at Comiskey Park in Chicago. An offseason filled with dark hints about a fix in the World Series had not diminished the enthusiasm of the White Sox rooters. Claud "Lefty" Williams, who had lost three games in the Series, gave up only four hits in eleven innings, two of them by

Cobb, in beating Hooks Dauss and the Tigers 3–2. After rainouts the next two days, Cicotte, loser of the other two Series games, shut them out 4–0 on five hits, with Cobb again collecting two.

It was a bad start to what quickly became a wretched year. The 1920 Tigers, though talented and relatively young, were the worst ball club Cobb ever played on after coming into the American League. They began by losing their first thirteen games. It was the third week in June before the hapless Athletics finally fell past them into last place. In seventh they stayed, finishing with a pallid 61–93 record. Jennings bickered with his players all season, especially with his pitchers and with Harry Heilmann. Dutch Leonard, demanding to be traded, quit the club in mid-September and went home to his big fruit farm near Fresno, California. A few days later Jennings suspended Heilmann for not hustling. Cobb seemed about the only man on the team who still got along with the little manager.

By then, according to what Cobb related in his autobiography, Jennings had become a heavy drinker, "pathetically tired, ineffective, and with the old grin faded."[21] During evenings on the road, when Cobb kept Jennings company in a hotel room, the old Oriole would go over his troubles with the team and end by insisting that he was quitting and wanted Cobb to take over for him. Despite Cobb's continuing and and sometimes vehement denials, speculation that the Georgian would follow the example of Tris Speaker, who had assumed the helm at Cleveland, grew steadily as the season progressed.

Cobb's start in 1920 was almost as bad as the team's. After seventeen games he was barely hitting 200. He was still way below his usual standards when the Tigers, at 7–21, moved into the Polo Grounds on May 24 to meet the Yankees for the first time since Ruth had come to New York. With Ruth ahead of his 1919 pace in homers, sportswriters and fans naturally focused on the comparative performances of the big Yankee and Cobb. It was not much of a contest that time around. In the series opener Cobb singled and later scored for Ehmke as the tall righthander beat New York 5–1, Ruth accounting for the only Yankee hits with a triple and single. The next day Ruth's upper-deck homer with a man aboard in the first inning started the Yankees on the way to a 4–3 win; Cobb went hitless. And in the finale Ruth's eighth homer of the year, into the area of the lower right-field stands already called "Ruthville," propelled his team to a 4–1 victory, with Cobb again drawing the collar. In the season's first encounter between "the supermen of baseball," enthused the New York *Times* reporter, "Cobb was in eclipse for the first time since he began to show his remarkable ability [here]. Ruth has stolen all of Cobb's thunder."[22]

Cobb's hitting picked up on the rest of the road trip; by early June he was finally above .300 and had an eleven-game streak going. But on June 6, at Chicago, he collided with Ira Flagstead in right-center, twisted his left leg as he fell, and had to be helped off the field. X-rays showed that he had torn the ligaments in his knee. It was the worst injury in Cobb's whole career. On crutches, he returned with his family to Augusta, where he not only got conventional medical attention but also tried out some of his grandmother's home remedies.

After being out for twenty-seven games, he limped to the plate at the Polo Grounds on July 8 to hit for part-time first-baseman Herb Ellison, with the score tied in the top of the ninth. Acknowledging the applause of some 20,000 weekday fans, he stepped in and poked a single to right to score Veach. He insisted on staying in to run and subsequently got hit by a pickoff throw at second, enabling Heilmann to score what proved to be the winning run. The next day he was on the coaching lines, but the day after that he played the whole game, singled twice, and drove in two runs. Ruth hit his twenty-sixth homer and chased Cobb back to the center-field fence for another drive as the Yankees won 7–6. Cobb homered himself the next day, sending a pitch from Carl Mays into the right-field upper deck near the foul line, and also touched Mays for a single; but again New York came out the winner 6–5.

At Boston on July 14 he hurt his knee again going after a ball. Despite being carried from the field, he played the next game, singling twice, doubling, and scoring from first on Veach's double for the winning run in the tenth inning. He wrenched the unhealed knee still again on the 17th at Washington, and a few days later he gave up trying to play and returned to Detroit for more treatment.

The knee held up after he came back on the 31st to double in a run against Washington at Navin Field. A few days later, when the Yankees arrived to break all local attendance marks for four games, Cobb was not yet in top form, although he managed eight hits in the series. On the bases he was noticeably slower. In game three, after being thrown out at the plate trying to score from first with two down on Shorten's bloop double, he pulled up at third on Heilmann's two-bagger. "In his speedy days, Ty would have gone home on a tap like that," commented the New York *Times* correspondent.[23]

Ruth hit three homers in the first two games to bring his year's total to forty-one. The Detroit fans, wrote Salsinger, gave Ruth "the welcome due a conquering hero. He got the applause, the shrieking adoration of the multitude, in Cobb's own city. Cobb, standing aside, could feel deeply how fickle the adoration of the sport-loving public is. He saw before him a new king acclaimed. . . ." Real students of the game preferred Cobb, acknowledged New York manager Miller Huggins. Those were the people "who could fully understand and appreciate his finesse." Ruth, on the other hand, was for everybody. "They all flock to him," said Huggins, because nowadays the American public "likes the fellow who carries the wallop."[24]

Mainly because of Ruth's wallops, the Yankees were making a strong bid for their first pennant. They were in close contention with both Cleveland and Chicago when Speaker's Indians came into the Polo Grounds for a double-header on August 16. Speedy Ray Chapman, the Cleveland shortstop and the most popular man on his ball club, led off the first game against righthander Carl Mays, who specialized in high-and-tight pitches from a three-quarter underhand or "submarine" delivery. By that time Mays had built a considerable reputation as a mean pitcher, a man who actually liked to throw at people's heads. His first pitch struck Chapman squarely in the left temple, shattering his skull. Chapman died following surgery early the next morning.

The first and only on-field fatality in major-league history, Chapman's death triggered angry protests against Mays not only from the sorrowing Indians but from teams and individual players around the league. In Boston the Red Sox, several of whom were still upset with Mays for jumping the team the previous year, held a common clubhouse meeting with the Tigers. The two teams agreed that some kind of official action ought to be taken against Mays but that Speaker ought to be consulted first. That was as far as any prospective anti-Mays movement ever got. Ban Johnson rashly predicted that Mays would never pitch again, although he acknowledged that he could not "conscientiously attempt to make any trouble for Mr. Mays."[25] In fact Johnson's careful investigation absolved Mays, and the pitcher returned to the mound after only one week's layoff. Among the Indians there was some talk about not playing New York if Mays pitched, but after burying their teammate they resumed their ultimately successful pennant drive, during which they faced Mays again without incident.

In New York, instead of anti-Mays feeling, a strong tide of sentiment against Cobb developed. From New York a reporter for United Press called Cobb in Boston to get his personal reaction to the fatal beaning of Chapman. Presumably Cobb had been present at the Red Sox–Tigers meeting, although there is no way of knowing whether he had anything to say. At any rate, he always insisted that he had refused to make any comment to the press about the incident, inasmuch as he hadn't seen it. In New York, however, several newspapers reported that Cobb had declared Mays should be barred from baseball, thereby inflaming Yankee fans.

Anti-Cobb feeling was running high when the Tigers arrived in New York to begin a four-game set on August 21. Cobb was in bed at the Hotel Ansonia with a heavy cold and a fever when his friend Grantland Rice came by to urge him not to play. Determined to deny the angry New Yorkers any excuse for thinking him a coward, Cobb got out of his bed, went up to the Polo Grounds, got into his uniform, and emerged through the gate in right field to take batting practice. At that nearly 30,000 fans, who had arrived early for the purpose of greeting Cobb when he showed, bombarded him with such verbal abuse as he had rarely heard in sixteen stormy seasons in the league. Cobb walked straight across the field to a spot back of homeplate, where he doffed his cap, bowed slightly to the stands, and then gestured toward the press section, indicating that it was the writers who were at fault, not he.

All through the game, which Detroit won 10–3, the crowd stayed on him. In the seventh inning he briefly quieted them by singling, stealing second and taking third on catcher Fred Hofmann's wild throw, and scoring on Veach's single. But the next inning he misplayed Aaron Ward's base hit and let in a run. His real vindication came the next day, before a Sunday capacity crowd of some 36,000. In an 11–9 slugfest, again won by the Tigers, he had five hits in six times up—four singles and a double—and drove in two runs. By the late innings much of the crowd was on his side. The next day he had two hits off Mays, making his first start since the Chapman beaning, but Mays scattered those hits and eight more in shutting out Detroit 10–0. In the last game Cobb was hitless as the Tigers, playing some of their best ball of the year, made it three out of four by beating the pennant contenders 5–3.[26]

Sunday, August 22, in New York was the apex of Cobb's least-impressive season overall since 1906. He played hard the last month and was able to get his average up to around .330, still far behind such men as Sisler, Jackson, Speaker, Collins, and Ruth. Along with the rest of the Detroit ball club, on September 27 he had the distinction of playing against the Chicago White Sox in the last game within Organized Baseball that six of them would ever suit up for. That particular game was a 2–0 shutout by the little lefthander Dickie Kerr. The next morning, following confessions by Eddie Cicotte and Joe Jackson and various other revelations, the Cook County grand jury indicted eight members of the 1919 White Sox for taking bribes to throw the World Series. Club president Charles Comiskey immediately suspended the six men still with the team. At the time his club was in a virtual tie with Cleveland for first place. While the Indians won three of their last five games, what was left of the White Sox sagged two games back. New York finished third, three games behind Cleveland's first-ever league champions. Detroit, in seventh place, was thirty-seven games out of first.

Cobb's final average, in only 112 games and 428 times at bat, was .334. George Sisler became the first man to top .400 since Cobb in 1911, hitting .407 to Speaker's .388. Cobb's sixteen steals were fewer than he had ever made in a full major-league season. As a ballplayer Cobb seemed indeed to be going into eclipse, his still-considerable abilities overshadowed by Ruth's incredible homerun feats (54 that year), by the all-around brilliance of Sisler, by the continuing strong yearly performances of veteran stars who seemed less injury prone, like Collins and Speaker.

Sore knee or not, Cobb went through with his long-made post-season plans. After taking in part of the exciting Cleveland-Brooklyn World Series (an event that by itself did much to redeem baseball's integrity in the wake of what was now almost universally called the Black Sox scandal) and then spending a short time in Georgia, he was on his way out to California. Along with Heilmann, Sisler, and Rogers Hornsby, who had just won his first batting title in the National League, Cobb was to manage a club in a four-team league operating in October and November. Cobb headed the San Francisco team; the others were located at Oakland, Los Angeles, and Vernon, then a Los Angeles suburb. H. G. Salsinger put his pay at close to a $1000 for every game he played in, which would mean that he made about $10,000 out of the California venture, besides getting in some fine duck-hunting. He also was a big hit with the West Coast press, because, said Salsinger, "he can talk and give them something to write about." Interviews with Ruth when he had played on the Coast the previous fall had elicited mostly monosyllables.[27]

On his way west Cobb had received notification of Hughey Jennings's resignation, which he and nearly everybody connected with the Detroit club had long anticipated. In fact Cobb had talked with Frank Navin at the end of the season and had reiterated that he didn't want to manage the team. "I'd worry myself to death," he had reportedly told the club president.[28] Then, according to Cobb's account, Navin called him while he was in California and told him the job was his; all he had to do was say yes. Again Cobb turned him down. In succeeding weeks both Clarence "Pants" Rowland, who had been the White Sox manager when they won the 1917 world's championship and was now a Tigers' scout, and George Stallings, who had recently quit the Boston Braves, were mentioned as candidates for the post. Cobb obviously remained the top choice for Navin and even more so for John Kelsey and Walter Briggs, who the previous spring had paid a half-million dollars for the shares in the Detroit franchise William Yawkey had held at the time of his death. Kelsey and Briggs, both major figures on the Detroit automobile scene, were also both warm friends of Cobb. Briggs, in fact, had frequently accompanied Cobb to listen in on the business talk at the Hotel Ponchartrain back when Cobb was a young ballplayer and Briggs was a coal checker for the Michigan Central railroad.

On his way home early in December, Cobb left the Southern Pacific at New Orleans for still more duck-hunting in the marshlands near the mouth of the Mississippi with Rick Woodward, owner of the Birmingham Southern League team, and several others. At the Roosevelt Hotel in New Orleans he encountered E. A. Batchelor, who had come down to cover the University of Detroit–Tulane University football game. "Batch" urged Cobb to take the manager's job, warning that if he didn't, then Pants Rowland, whom Cobb considered an incompetent fraud, might very well get it and Cobb would have to play for him. When the Georgian wavered, Batchelor called Navin, who was in New York for the American League winter meeting, and arranged for Cobb to meet with him.

On his thirty-fourth birthday, December 18, 1920, Cobb spent nearly four

hours closeted with Navin at the Hotel Vanderbilt. At about two in the afternoon they emerged to announce that Cobb had agreed to manage the Tigers
in 1921 and, at his insistence, had signed only a one-year contract. The amount
of Cobb's salary was not specified; he later revealed that it was $35,000, which
gave him the top salary not only among the ballplayers but, with the exception of John McGraw, among the managers as well. "I am going to rub the
boys the right way," Cobb told the couple of dozen newsmen on hand, "not
to do anything that would tend to discourage them. And when I feel compelled to apply vile names to them to get action, that is the time to clear them
off the club. What I want is a hustling ball club." [29]

Exhausted and battling another bad cold, Cobb finally boarded a train at
Penn Station bound toward Georgia. Nine years earlier, during his stay in
Detroit with *The College Widow*, he had told Batchelor that a star player should
never "be handicapped and burdened by managerial worries or even the cap-
taincy of a team." The main reason he was now willing to go back on that oft-
repeated disclaimer, some commentators were convinced, was his desire to
emulate player-manager Speaker, who had just had one of his finest years at
bat while leading Cleveland to a pennant and victory in the World Series.
Whether that was the reason, whether it was fear of having to play for Rowland, or whatever it was, Cobb had made his decision. "That," he later lamented, "was an error I'll always regret. . . . I wish now I'd never stuck my
neck into the noose that the Tiger management represented." [30]

IX

Boss of the Tigers

"Cobb Mania Seizes Detroit" headlined the *Sporting News* on the eve of Cobb's arrival in the city for the elaborate doings that would commemorate his becoming manager of the Tigers. H. G. Salsinger wrote that he was the popular choice among fans and players alike, and that late the previous season several Tigers had gone to Frank Navin to make a personal plea for Cobb to become their new boss. Just before leaving Augusta on his way to the festivities, Cobb promised to quit after one year if the team finished no higher next season than it had in 1920. Today's ballplayers, he added, were different from those in the old days. Instead of an iron hand, "Encouragement and advice are the best practices in this day and generation."[1] That was not only implicit criticism of Jennings's frequent resort to sarcasm and invective; later on it would also make bitterly ironic reading for some of Cobb's own players.

For now, though, Cobb was at the summit of his life in baseball. When he arrived at the Michigan Central station at 9:00 a.m. on February 1, 1921, a reception committee headed by Mayor John C. Lodge was on hand to greet him. The welcoming party escorted Cobb to the Hotel Statler, where the entire mezzanine had been reserved for him. At noon he went to city hall to receive the keys to the city; after that came a luncheon at the handsome Detroit Athletic Club. That evening, before his testimonial dinner at the Statler, Cobb gave a reception for a couple of hundred people. Then some 600 paid $10 each to go to the dinner itself. After being entertained by a succession of vaudeville acts and a Shriners band, they listened to speeches by Ban Johnson, Congressman Riley Wilson, Hugh Chalmers, and a number of others, including Jennings, who got the biggest ovation of any speaker next to Cobb himself. The new manager lauded his ex-manager, promised that the team would give its best, received a silver loving cup, and sat down to huge applause.

For a year now Detroit, like everywhere else in the United States, had been legally devoid of alcoholic beverages under the Eighteenth Amendment to the Constitution and the national Volstead Act. Because of its location just across the river from Canada, however, the city was one of the wettest places in the country throughout the thirteen years of the prohibition experiment. The liquor had flowed freely all day, especially at Cobb's reception earlier in the evening. Cobb had asked Manly Miner, now almost twenty-four, to come over from Ontario to serve as his official greeter for such distinguished callers as Lodge, Chalmers, former mayor Oscar Marx, and the popular poet Edgar Guest. Cobb, Miner remembered, knew what everybody wanted to drink and so instructed his bartenders. Early the next morning Cobb and Miner got back to Cobb's suite to find thirteen drunken sportswriters who had bribed a bell-boy to let them into the suite, where they had consumed what remained of Cobb's liquor. Cobb, Miner, and various hotel personnel hauled the boozy scribes into a couple of other rooms on the mezzanine; Cobb and his young friend finally got to bed themselves about 3:00. Tired and a little dazed by it all, the new manager said goodbye to Miner the next day and boarded a train for Georgia.

In the interval between the Detroit celebrations and the start of spring training, Cobb may have permitted himself doubts about whether he had done the right thing in taking the Detroit managership. Certainly he did not need the extra money Frank Navin would pay him to manage. If not already a millionaire, he was very close. His highly diversified investments—stocks, bonds, real estate, various business operations—had made him rich, quite apart from his wife's share in the Lombard family's wealth. Scanning the stock listings in his morning newspaper had long been part of his daily routine, and wherever he happened to be, he kept in frequent contact with his brokers. In business as in baseball, commented John Wheeler, head of the Wheeler Syndicate, Cobb's mind was "an intellectual blotter."[2]

In the 1920s Cobb's Coca-Cola stock would prove particularly remunerative. Since his first commercial endorsements for the soft drink in 1908, Cobb had been friends with Robert W. Woodruff, who in 1923 succeeded his father as president of the Atlanta-based business. Woodruff and Cobb were frequent hunting companions, especially at the Woodruff family's plantation in southwestern Georgia. Many people later regretted not getting in on the ground floor with Coca-Cola, as Cobb had done; but maybe none were sorrier than the three sportswriters whom Cobb, relaxing in New York on the evening after he was named Tiger manager, futilely urged to buy Coca-Cola at a little more than twenty dollars a share. Within a few years that stock was worth nine times as much. Cobb himself continued to buy into Coca-Cola, whose operations and profits expanded spectacularly throughout the 1920s, and eventually came to own 20,000 shares.

Without question Cobb had misgivings about being a player-manager. To be sure, in his time Frank Chance with the Cubs, Fred Clarke with the Pir-

ates, Jake Stahl and Bill Carrigan with the Red Sox, and most recently Tris
Speaker with the Indians had all been both championship managers and fully
active players. Later on in the twenties Bucky Harris at Washington, George
Sisler with the Browns, Eddie Collins with the White Sox, Dave Bancroft with
the Boston Braves, and Rogers Hornsby with the St. Louis Cardinals would
join Cobb in the ranks of player-managers. Yet the demands made on a man
to direct a ball club and still look after his own performance at bat and afield
were staggering. Cobb must have wondered what would happen to the towering personal standards he had set and met over the years.

Cobb's assumption of the manager's job followed by little more than a month
the radical restructuring of Organized Baseball's governance precipitated by
the Black Sox revelations late the previous summer. In November 1920 the
major-league clubowners named Kenesaw Mountain Landis, the crusty and
controversial judge for the federal district of northern Illinois, to be commissioner of all baseball. Given virtually dictatorial powers, Landis began an autocratic reign that ended only with his death in 1944. The institution of the
commissioner system, as much as the introduction of the lively ball and the
enormous attendance boom, gave baseball a character distinctly different from
what it had been up to the 1920s.

Making the Tigers into a distinctly different ballclub was what Ty Cobb
intended to do when he arrived at San Antonio, the team's training site, on
March 3, 1921. After joking with the Detroit baseball writers about having to
report earlier than he ever had, Cobb stepped on the trainer's scales and hit
197 pounds, the most he had ever weighed. Over the years he had become a
big man, considerably stronger if also considerably slower than in his early
seasons.

Because the New York Giants and the San Antonio team already occupied
the local Texas League ball grounds, the Tigers had to train at Brackenridge
Park, a municipal facility lacking stands, regular dressing quarters, fences, or
much of anything else except some rough diamonds. There Cobb gathered his
players and announced several changes in spring-training procedures and in
overall direction. There would be no morning practices; the men could sleep
until mid-morning, then eat breakfast and have plenty of time to digest it before going out for a lengthy afternoon workout. Cobb would conduct no in-
door "skull sessions"; the team would work on the field on what needed to be
done in specific situations. And it would practice a great deal on bunting and
the hit-and-run, two maneuvers Cobb cherished and in which Jennings's last
few teams had been plainly deficient. Cobb did not intend to enforce curfews
or otherwise police behavior off the field. On the field, though, he would demand hustle at all times and promised to get rid of any laggards.

Finally, Cobb wanted no friendly conversation on the field and as little
fraternization as possible otherwise between his players and members of other

teams. To Cobb the opposition was the enemy; he wanted his own men to stay in "a combative frame of mind."[3] Even though the Giants were in the same town, Cobb would not consent to exhibition games with them. He warned his players, moreover, that they were not even to cross Alamo Plaza to the hotel where John McGraw's team was staying.

Cobb's refusal to play the Giants irked local fans, but otherwise he seemed to be doing everything right that spring. He threw himself into managing with the same fiery enthusiasm he had always shown as a player. Harry Bullion of the Detroit *Free Press* reported glowingly on his camaraderie with the men in camp. He had become "just like a big brother to the rest of the Tigers," inquiring about their needs, passing out cigars and candy, listening to their yarns. Having transformed the team's outlook "with the gentleness of a kitten," Cobb would become, Bullion was convinced, "an ideal manager." H. G. Salsinger of the Detroit *News* went on about the team's "vim and enthusiasm" and about Cobb's "wonderful personality" and "personal magnetism." "It looks like a Tiger year," bubbled Salsinger.[4] Cobb, fully aware of his weak pitching and porous infield, would only predict a better finish than in 1920.

On the way north from Texas, with the Tigers playing only local minor league teams at various stops, Cobb demonstrated that his left leg was sound again. He was in center field as usual on April 14, when the Tigers debuted under their new manager. Despite drizzle and chill, 23,000 enthusiastic Detroit fans paid their way into Navin Field. They went home happy when Harry Heilmann's drive into the overflow in right-center scored Pep Young in the bottom of the ninth to give Cobb his first win, 6–5 over the reconstructed Chicago White Sox. In the late innings Cobb brought in rookie Harvey "Suds" Sutherland in relief of Dutch Leonard and later used two pinch hitters and a pinch runner. All of his managerial moves worked, and he himself doubled in a run and later scored as the Tigers overcame a four-run deficit. It was a fine beginning, although it left Cobb wondering whether his own play would suffer from his having to direct twenty-five men (the restored roster limit) day in and day out.

The "Cobbmen," as the sportswriters were already euphemizing the Tigers, then dropped four of their next five. After a rain-shortened loss at Chicago, Cobb barely kept his anger under control in the clubhouse. He was "permitting reverses to prey on his mind," Bullion thought, and if he continued to agonize over each game the way he had so far, he would become an old man before his time.[5]

Yet agonize he did, game after game, as well as engage in considerably more manipulation of his personnel than was usual in that period in baseball history. Cobb was a convert to the already widely held belief in the greater effectiveness of most lefthanded hitters against most righthanded pitchers and vice versa. Several times in 1921 and in succeeding years as well he removed his starting pitcher after he had faced only one batter and brought in a pitcher who threw from the opposite side, in an effort to influence the opposing manager to change his original lineup. Cobb also freely platooned his own players. On a couple of occasions early in his first season as manager, he even benched Heilmann, who was in the process of winning the first of his four batting championships. in favor of lefty Chick Shorten.

That was one reason Cobb's relations with his best ballplayer were less than congenial. Another was his determination to keep Heilmann in right field and play rookie Luzerne Atwell "Lu" Blue, a stylish fielder and competent switch hitter, at first base. Then, in Washington in June, Cobb changed his batting order without telling Heilmann, so that the big Californian was batting out of turn in the first inning when he hit a drive into the distant bleachers in left-center with Donie Bush aboard. As Heilmann crossed the plate, umpire Billy Evans called him out and disallowed both runs. Finally, Cobb insisted that Heilmann ride Bobby Veach, who was too good natured and easy going for Cobb, on the theory that if Veach stayed mad he would hustle and hit better. It apparently worked, because Veach batted .338 and drove in 128 runs that year. But when, after the season, Cobb failed to tell Veach about putting Heilmann up to the mischief, Veach and Heilmann became permanently estranged.

Whatever devious stratagems Cobb resorted to, he got results—at least for the first two months of the season. At the end of May the Tigers were three games above .500 and in third place behind Ceveland and New York. The whole pitching staff, anchored around Leonard and Hooks Dauss, was unreliable; righthander Bert Cole, whom Cobb had scouted on the Pacific Coast and touted as an outstanding prospect, proved a particular disappointment. But the Detroit hitters produced runs in sustained barrages. Heilmann, Veach, Blue, Bob Jones, and practically all the regulars as well as the utility men hit well. For all his fears about the effects of managing on his playing, Cobb had a resurgent year, staying around .400 for most of the season and hitting more homeruns—nearly all over the fences—than he ever had.

The clouting of the Detroit team was only part of a general burgeoning of batting statistics that year. Sportswriters reported amazedly on the "epidemic" of homers in both leagues. On June 23, at Philadelphia, the Tigers and the still-tailend Athletics hit eight homers between them, a new record, in a 15–9 Philadelphia win. Cobb might continue to drill his players in how to bunt, hit and run, and run the bases; but among the Tigers, as indeed throughout baseball, Babe Ruth's example was proving far more influential.

In the same years in which Ruth's prodigious homeruns were helping to revolutionize the sport, Cobb's attitude toward the mighty Yankee slugger became increasingly contemptuous. It was more than the natural rivalry of two great stars competing within the same league. It was also the special rivalry of two men who represented radically contrasting approaches to the game. Cobb appears to have grasped early and completely the fundamental threat Ruth posed to his whole set of values, both as to how baseball ought to be played and how successful ballplayers ought to behave. Not only Ruth's playing style but his hedonistic life style were at variance with the dedicated, self-denying code by which, so Cobb had insisted, a man must live to excel and stay on top year after year. Whereas Cobb kept himself in condition the year around, Ruth invariably reported for spring training fat and out of shape. Whereas Cobb looked scrupulously to his rest, Ruth drank and wenched his way from city to city, seemingly unaffected by his gross dissipations. Whereas Cobb was the persistent spartan, Ruth was the unregenerate epicurean. Thus Cobb refused to hide his dislike for the new hero, the man who followed none of the rules but nonetheless performed heroically and with every passing season undermined Cobb's stature as the greatest player ever.

Cobb's harassment of Ruth was steady, systematic, and often vicious. He liked to dwell on the Babe's well-known carelessness with his personal hygiene, commonly asking others around the batting cage when Ruth happened by if they smelled anything. Cobb also liked to call Ruth "nigger," in reference to his dark complexion, round face, and broad nose. Not surprisingly, Cobb and Ruth became not only rivals but enemies as well, men whose mutual animosity generated extraordinary tension whenever their ball clubs met.

In mid-June 1921, for example, Cobb's riding almost caused him to come to blows with Ruth three separate times in a 12–8 New York victory before 32,000 Sunday fans at the Polo Grounds. Ruth hit his nineteenth homer in that game. The next day Ruth not only homered again but started on the mound, held the Tigers to three runs in six innings, and ended up the winning pitcher. In the five-game series with Detroit, Ruth had seven homeruns.

The Tigers lost all five games in New York that trip and went on to lose four more in a streak that put them in the second division. At that juncture Cobb had to make a hurried trip home to be first at the bedside and then the funeral of his beloved grandmother Cobb. He was barely back with the team when, hook-sliding into second base at Cleveland and trying to avoid spiking shortstop Joe Sewell, he spiked himself badly in the left knee, the same one he had damaged the previous season. Requiring five stitches and quickly becoming infected, the knee kept Cobb out of the lineup for a month except for occasional pinch-hitting spots.

Despite getting eight hits in his first eleven at bats following his return to the lineup, Cobb could ignite the Tigers neither by deed nor word. It did not help that early in August he had to leave the team and go back to Georgia again, this time to be with his wife, who on July 23 had prematurely given birth to a baby boy in Detroit. Suffering from severe post-partum complications, Charlie Cobb had gone to Georgia with her children to recuperate. The baby, named James Howell Cobb, remained sickly for some time, as did his mother, whose fifth childbirth was her hardest.

Cobb rejoined the team in New York on August 4, hitting a triple, rocketing a pitch from Bob Shawkey into the upper deck in the right-field corner, and scoring three times in an 8–3 victory. His average remained at .400, while Heilmann's had climbed to .420. Despite its lusty hitting, however, the club remained in the second division and gradually slipped downward through August and September. Salsinger described the Tigers as "a miserable fielding team . . . a team that discounts fairly good pitching by poor and stupid fielding."[6] Late in August, Detroit asked waivers on Donie Bush, a thirteen-year veteran who no longer covered much ground at shortstop. His departure to Washington left Cobb the sole survivor of the 1909 pennant winners.

Cobb was in an increasingly sour mood by the time the Tigers began a road trip that would last nearly to the end of the season. Taking along eleven-year-old Tyrus, Jr., evidently did nothing to improve his spirits. At Boston he bawled out Veach right in front of the whole grandstand after Veach missed homeplate on his slide and was tagged out. A few days later, in New York, he embarrassed Dutch Leonard and necessitated a dubious pitching change when, disgusted because Leonard had failed on two bunt attempts, he sent up Chick Shorten to hit with only one strike left. After Shorten grounded into a forceout, reliever Jim Middleton took over with the Yankees ahead 2–1 in the seventh. Middleton yielded two more runs in what ended up as a 4–2 loss to the league leaders.

At Washington on September 24, Walter Johnson shut down the Tigers 5–1. Still fuming over being called out by umpire George Hildebrand when he tried to steal home in the fourth inning, Cobb went into a rage the next inning after Billy Evans also called him out, this time on an attempted theft of second. Despite Cobb's lengthy fulmination, Evans let him stay in the game. Afterward, though, Cobb went to the umpires' dressing room under the stands and challenged Evans, who was roughly the same size, less than three years older, a recreational boxer, and generally a well-conditioned athlete himself. After agreeing that nothing would be reported to Ban Johnson, the combatants stripped to the waist and went at each other before a small crowd of fans and Detroit and Washington players. Many years later Sammy Barnes, a young infielder just brought up for a trial with the Tigers, described the fight as the bloodiest he ever saw in baseball. While Ty, Jr., watched between players' legs and kept yelling "Come on, daddy," Cobb split Evans's left eyebrow and right cheek. Evans got in a few punches himself before the two wrestled to the ground. Cobb was banging Evans's head into the cinders when a burly groundskeeper pulled him off and ended the fray. After stanching his wounds and showering and getting dressed, Evans came over to the Detroit locker room and shook Cobb's hand.[7]

Despite Evans's pledge, Hildebrand felt that he had no choice but to report the fight to President Johnson. With Johnson's office having taken no action, Evans and Cobb both appeared at Washington the next day, the umpire to cheers, the manager to a round of boos. Cobb got two hits off lefty Tom Zachary but was also thrown out at the plate twice, with the Tigers losing again, 3–2. That night he heard directly from Commissioner Landis's office that he was suspended indefinitely as a player, although he could continue to suit up and manage. Actually Cobb played three straight exhibition games, in Baltimore, Utica, and Buffalo, then sat out the last two games of the season, against St. Louis in Detroit. Lee Fohl's Browns won both games and clinched third place. The Tigers ended up in sixth with a record of 71–82.

Because Heilmann, who had been tailing off for several weeks, managed only one for nine in the final two games, various unofficial statisticians reported that Cobb had edged him out for the American League batting championship. But the official league statistics released two months later by Johnson's office confirmed that Heilmann had won his first title, hitting .394 to Cobb's .389.

Cobb had put in a remarkable year. He had batted close to .400 almost all season; appeared in 128 games despite injuries, family troubles, and finally a suspension; hit twelve homers; driven home 101 runs; stolen twenty-two bases (to George Sisler's league-leading 35); and done all that while managing his team to a ten-and-one-half-game improvement over its 1920 record. Sixth place was still a disappointment; the team had lost too many games, Cobb said in a public statement released to the Detroit press at the end of the season, through its own mistakes. Yet it would become a contender, he promised. For now, he thanked Tiger fans for their patience and generous treatment.

Only Washington and Philadelphia had made more errors in the American League that year; only Chicago and Philadelphia had allowed more runs. In one area, though, Cobb could find considerable satisfaction. Largely through his work with his men in the batting cage, a team that had been sixth in the league in hitting in Jennings's last year led both major leagues in 1921, with an aggregate average of .316. In fact not since the old Orioles of 1897 had any team hit that well. Having persuaded Heilmann in the spring to stand back in the box, put his feet closer together, and hold his hands away from his body, Cobb felt that he could take much of the credit for the husky outfielder's league-leading performance.

While Babe Ruth led the Yankees into their first World Series, where they lost to John McGraw's Giants, Cobb spent a couple of weeks with his family in Augusta and then took off for California to manage again in the four-team California Winter League. His San Francisco team finished last and lost money, as did the whole league in its ten-week season. The Georgian scouted players, appeared in about one game a week, made another $10,000 or so, and got into the national sports news when he was fined $150 by league president Frank Chance for verbally abusing an umpire and using stalling tactics in a game against the Vernon team.

In New York by mid-December for the annual offseason major-league meetings, Cobb said that he expected much from pitchers Herman Pillette and Sylvester Johnson, whom Navin, at his behest, had bought as a package from Portland of the Pacific Coast League for $40,000 and five players. At the time the Tiger manager seemed satisfied that he had secured the best pitching talent available on the coast, although afterward he pilloried Navin for not also buying Ray Kremer, destined to become a mainstay for Pittsburgh during the mid- and late-twenties. Cobb and Navin also sought infield help, notably Everett Scott from Boston and Joe Dugan from Philadelphia. When the Yankees got both men, Detroit had to settle for George Cutshaw, a veteran second baseman obtained on waivers from Pittsburgh, and Emory "Topper" Rigney, a young shortstop bought from the mighty Fort Worth Texas League team.

At Cobb's insistence the Tigers shifted to Augusta for their 1922 spring training. Besides acknowledging that he preferred to live at home while the team trained, Cobb maintained that the area's temperate weather would make for less climatic shock when his men went north. It was also probably more than coincidental that a year earlier Cobb had joined a syndicate of local businessmen in buying the Augusta franchise and ballpark. Obviously Cobb would get something out of the fee the Detroit club paid Augusta for the use of its playing facilities.

The city's Hotel Albion having recently burned, the boss of the Tigers decided to install his players in two fine Greek Revival mansions that stood side by side across the river in North Augusta, South Carolina, Cobb even hired two chefs to prepare the players' meals so he could be certain that they ate properly. Such extraordinarily comfortable surroundings failed to mollify Howard Ehmke, a long, lean curve-baller who had pitched poorly in 1921 and in six seasons with the Tigers had never been able to get along with Cobb. Ehmke now declared his wish to be traded; Cobb replied that Ehmke would stay with Detroit. Meanwhile Dutch Leonard, offered only a $1000 raise, quit the game and went back to his Fresno Valley fruit farm.

Everybody else seemed happy that spring, including Heilmann, who threatened a holdout but finally signed for $12,500, a $5000 raise. Cobb settled on Cutshaw for his second baseman and put Pep Young, mysteriously given to erratic throwing in 1921, on waivers. Among the rookies Cobb especially liked Fred Haney, a scrappy little infielder up from Omaha of the Western League. He saw little, however, in Floyd "Babe" Herman, a stringbean outfielder who would put in several more years in the minors before becoming the darling of the Brooklyn fans.

Cobb's main problem that spring was how to get his team through another gruelling whistle-stop exhibition series arranged by Walter Hapgood, this time with the International League Rochester Broncos. Hapgood, who had become Rochester's general manager when George Stallings went there as manager and part-owner, had again persuaded Frank Navin that good money could be made on such a tour, more than enough to pay for the two teams' spring-training expenses. So, after playing at Augusta, the Detroit and Rochester teams rode the trains to daily stops in places like Anderson and Greenville in South Carolina and Griffin and Americus in Georgia. At the last town Cobb, trying to reach third from first on a single, caught his spikes in a clod as he slid on the lumpy infield and tore ligaments in his right knee and ankle. "The play was a silly one," wrote H. G. Walker, now Detroit correspondent for the *Sporting News*, especially inasmuch as it occurred in the ninth inning with the Tigers ahead 10–1. Cobb's explanation was simply that the local fans had paid their money and were entitled to see him give his best. Yet he added, "I'm getting old and I can no longer pull the stunts I once did. . . . I'm easier to hurt and harder to mend."[8]

Treated by his own physician in Augusta, Cobb had to walk with a cane as the team played its way north. In Cleveland he got more treatment, from a local specialist, and was able to pinch hit in the season opener there, bouncing into a game-ending double play in a 7–4 loss to the Indians.[9] He did not play for the next four games, all of which the Tigers lost, and finally reappeared on April 20 in Detroit's home opener. In four times at bat, Cobb drew a walk, as the Tigers dropped their sixth straight to Cleveland. After that he coached and occasionally pinch hit but did not get into the lineup for good until April 29, against Chicago at Navin Field. Detroit lost that game, too, making their record 4–10. It got really discouraging the next day, when Charley Robertson, the White Sox' rookie righthander, pitched a perfect game and beat Detroit 2–0. All of Cobb's favorite harassments, including numerous demands for the umpires to examine the ball Robertson was using, failed to rattle the young Texan.

In May, though, the ball club righted itself and climbed above .500, where it stayed. Cobb drove his men relentlessly, inspiring by example with his strong hitting, skillful if no longer daring base-running, and incessant hustle. In winning three out of four at New York from the defending league champions, the Tigers impressed a local writer as "a peppery, savage and fierce team which took advantage of every opportunity presented—an apt description of Cobb himself." Cobb was "the busiest manager in six states," a man who "paced up and down the coaching lines like a caged animal, raged at the umpires, yelled at the bench for 'more pep,' turned his head to exchange quips with the crowd and patted his players on the back when they made a good play. He had a hand in everything, did Ty, and he kept the Tigers fighting. . . ."[10]

The Tigers' record for June was 22–4, and by the end of July they were only five games behind the Yankees and the powerful St. Louis Browns, who battled for the lead nearly all season. Cobb's performance on the field suggested that the pressures of managing actually heightened his playing skills. Again his hitting remained around .400 month after month, and for one stretch he took over the league leadership from George Sisler, who was having his finest year. A three-day suspension, imposed by Ban Johnson after Cobb stepped on umpire Frank Wilson's foot during an argument in St. Louis, failed to slow the Georgian. Nor did his troubles with various team members, notably pitchers Carl Holling and Lil Stoner, whom Cobb sent home from Boston after he got tired of their nighttime excursions and ineffective moundwork.

Detroit never climbed higher than third place or closer to the lead than five games in 1922. Heilmann, hitting .356 with twenty-one homers and ninety-two runs batted in, broke his collarbone late in August and was lost for the season. Dauss pitched erratically, and Ehmke as if he did not care; only Pilette, who won nineteen games as a rookie, was a dependable starter.

Cobb's club did make a decisive contribution to the pennant race by knocking the Browns out of first place at Sportsman's Park on September 9. Although the Browns took the remaining three games of the Detroit series and fought the Yankees furiously to the end, the finest American League team in St. Louis history was never able to regain the lead. Sisler sat out the final game of that series, having injured his arm so badly reaching for a throw the previous day that he could scarcely raise it above his waist. Five days later, however, he tied Cobb's 1911 record of hitting in forty consecutive games, and on the 17th his single against the Yankees broke it. Meanwhile Cobb tripled and singled against Washington to give himself another 200-hit season.

The Browns' victory over the White Sox on the last day of the season, which still left them a game behind New York, assured the Tigers, at 79–75, of third place over Cleveland and Chicago—Detroit's best finish since 1916. Yet Cobb's team was still thirteen games behind St. Louis and fourteen behind New York. The Tigers were not yet real contenders, even though they had provided base hits in abundance, again topping .300 as a team, and improved markedly afield with Rigney at shortstop and Cutshaw or Haney at second. The main problem remained Cobb's pitching staff, among the league's wobbliest.

Sisler's .420 was well ahead of Cobb's runnerup batting mark. Exactly what that mark might be became the subject of a controversy that left hard feelings in various quarters. Back on May 15, at the Polo Grounds, rain had just begun in the second inning when Cobb hit a grounder toward shortstop Everett Scott. On an infield that was already muddy from earlier rain, Scott mishandled the ball and Cobb made first safely. At the time each game had an official scorer whose rulings on hits and errors showed up in the final statistics put out by the league offices. For daily boxscores, however, most newspapers relied on the Associated Press. That day Fred Lieb, scoring for the AP, had moved up under the second-deck overhang out of the rain. He scored a hit for Cobb. John Kieran of the New York *Tribune*, the official scorer, remained in the ground-level press section behind homeplate and ruled it an error on Scott. Because Lieb and Kieran failed to consult about the play, the conflict in their scorings went unresolved. As things turned out, whether Cobb had hit .400 depended on that one hit.

When Lieb learned about the discrepancy at the end of the season, he repudiated his ruling and insisted that Kieran's should be determining. But Irwin Howe, the American League's official statistician, accepted Lieb's scoring in the AP records. Thus he certified Cobb as having an average of .401 on 211 hits in 526 at bats. Ban Johnson backed Howe, claiming that his office had been unable to authenticate any ruling besides the AP's.

Lieb and the other members of the New York chapter of the Base Ball Writers Association of America argued all fall that the issue was whether or not the American League was going to accept official scorings, and that Johnson's office had had no authority to disregard Kieran's ruling. In December they condemned Johnson's action as "arbitrary" and "taken without inquiry or investigation," and a few days later, in the BBWAA's annual meeting, the chapter chairmen from the various major-league cities voted to endorse the New York chapter's statement. Johnson replied that writers should "put their house in order before sending me scurrilous and questionable complaints."[11]

By that time Cobb, home in Augusta, had worked up a burning resentment against the New York writers. Not only did he imply prejudice in the matter of the May 15 scoring; he also accused them of taking three hits away from him and adding two times at bat during the last series the Tigers played in New York in 1921. "I have tried to let it pass by," he said, "but since they are raising such a commotion in New York over the disputed hit, let them investigate this matter also." Of course Cobb got no action on his demand and probably expected none. A few days later, in New York for the American League winter meeting, he had apparently cooled down. All he would say was, "In my time I have made too many hits to quibble about one now."[12]

Less than earth-shattering, the argument over Cobb's final 1922 average nonetheless stirred some strong emotions. No love had ever been lost between Cobb and Ban Johnson. Yet in this case, as in the 1909 furor over whether Cobb had deliberately spiked Frank Baker and the one the next year over whether Cobb or Lajoie had won the batting title, Johnson came down resolutely on Cobb's side. In doing so, Johnson damaged his prestige with the BBWAA and especially the New York contingent at a time when he was fighting to preserve his power under the new commissioner system. Meanwhile Cobb's relations with the New York writers, never the best anyway, turned permanently sour.

His third .400 season officially confirmed if somewhat tainted by contro-

versy, Cobb passed his thirty-sixth birthday and then took up his usual win-
tertime routine of hunting and golfing. At a for-men-only club he frequented
on a privately owned lake outside Augusta, he developed an acquaintance with
President Warren G. Harding. There the affable Ohioan relaxed at poker, im-
bibed freely of the liquor that was supposed to have vanished from the land,
and generally behaved as "just one of the boys down there." Cobb liked Harding
and thought him an honest man, but some of the sleazy politicos who accompanied him, Cobb remembered, "were a caution." [13]

Cobb also spent a good portion of his time in long-distance telephone con-
versations with Frank Navin about player changes. They got rid of Howard
Ehmke and Carl Holling, sending the two malcontents along with $25,000 to
Boston for infielder Del Pratt, an eleven-year veteran, and righthander Warren "Rip" Collins, who had won fourteen games for the last-place Red Sox the
previous season. They also bought lefthander Ray Francis from Washington.
Even though Francis had lost eighteen games in 1922, he had impressed Cobb
by, among other things, repeatedly throwing at his head.

March 1923 again brought a gathering of Detroit ballplayers—regulars,
hangers-on, and hopefuls—at Augusta. Again they stayed across the river in
the twin mansions. The most-watched rookie in camp that spring was Henry
"Heinie" Manush, a muscular, lefthand-hitting Alabamian purchased from
Omaha, where he had hit .376 in 1922. Cobb immediately began working with
Manush, urging him to choke up some on the bat, shorten his swing, and hit
the ball where it was pitched instead of trying to pull everything. It was hard
to argue with Cobb's instructions in light of Heilmann's arrival as one of baseball's premier batsmen, Fred Haney's remarkable .356 average in 213 at bats
in his rookie year, and Topper Rigney's .300 as a full-time rookie shortstop.
The Tigers were not a particularly powerful team; their fifty-four homers were
fourth best in the league in 1922. But they had become a collection of smart,
skilled men at the plate. "In all modesty," Cobb said in his autobiography, "I
could teach hitting." [14]

At Rome, Georgia, on one of the many stops Walter Hapgood had again
arranged for the Tigers and Rochester Broncos that spring, Heilmann, Blue,
and pitcher Syl Johnson were all injured. That prompted Cobb to vow publicly that his team had taken its last Hapgood tour. Nonetheless he tried to
make the best of the trip, pleasing the locals at Lindale, Georgia, by pitching
three innings against George Stallings's team.

Back at Augusta, though, Cobb's general unhappiness with the way things
were going erupted against National League umpire Harry Pfirman. Hired by
the St. Louis Cardinals to work their games that spring, Pfirman was on the
bases during the first in a series of Tigers-Cardinals exhibitions starting that
day in Augusta. When Pfirman called him out on a close play at second to end
the sixth inning, Cobb threw dirt in the direction of the umpire and otherwise

behaved so badly that Pfirman ordered him out of the game. Instead Cobb trotted out to his position in center. Plate umpire Harry "Steamboat" Johnson, a colorful veteran of the Southern and many other leagues, who was being paid by the Tigers, went out to remonstrate with Cobb. When he still would not leave, Johnson declared a forfeit to St. Louis. The crowd, the biggest ever at Warren Park, spilled onto the field and jostled the umpires until they reached the safety of the clubhouse. Cobb barged in to tell Johnson that he was fired. That evening, though, the Tiger manager relented, called Johnson while he was preparing to leave for his home in Memphis, and assured him that he could stay on for the rest of the series. The next morning the two teams and the two umpires headed for Chattanooga.

Before the Tigers got to Detroit, Cobb had gone so far as to predict a pennant for his team in 1923. In that city, reported the *Sporting News*, people had gone "simply baseball crazy," thousands of them camping out all night to be in line for tickets to the home opener with the Browns.[15] Ban Johnson had scheduled the opening of the American League season for a week later than usual to provide additional time for expansion work at Navin Field and, more importantly, for the completion of the huge new sports facility the Yankee ownership was having built in the South Bronx. The occupation of Yankee Stadium by Babe Ruth and his teammates late in April marked the close of the great period of privately financed modern ballpark construction that had begun in Philadelphia and Pittsburgh in 1909.

While his ball club was winning four of its first six games, in St. Louis and Cleveland, Cobb demonstrated that this year, maybe more than ever, he had fire in his eyes. Dent McSkimming, a St. Louis writer, remarked on Cobb's inability to conceal his displeasure with his players when they did poorly. Such "public chastisement" as Cobb was given to would not set well with the Tiger veterans, McSkimming predicted. Watching the Tigers take three out of four from the Browns at Detroit, John E. Wray, sports editor of the St. Louis *Post-Dispatch*, was dismayed by Cobb's "bullying, goat-getting, rough-riding stuff" with the umpires and the St. Louis players. There was a difference between aggressiveness and rowdyism, Wray insisted, and Cobb was "approaching dangerously near to rowdyism." The next week Stuart Bell of the Cleveland *Plain Dealer* commented on Cobb's "wicked tongue," which had finally so upset the Indians' Guy Morton that he walked Cobb on four pitches to force in the tying run in a game Detroit won 4–3. And like a growing number of baseball observers around the league, Bell also complained that largely because of Cobb's frequent trips in from center field for conferences with his pitchers, protracted wrangling with the umpires, and other dilatory actions, Tigers games usually consumed more than two hours.[16]

Yet however much the Tigers might drag out their games, the ball club was vastly popular with its fans. A new second deck that stretched from first base around to third gave remodeled Navin Field a seating capacity of about 30,000. Beginning with an opening-day overflow estimated at 36,000, the Tigers repeatedly filled their ballpark that year. Somehow an officially recorded 40,884 got into the place on Sunday, May 13, to see George Dauss beat the Yankees for his sixth straight win.

Next to Ruth and the Yankees, Detroit was also the league's biggest draw away from home. On the Tigers' first visit to Yankee Stadium something like 97,000 New Yorkers saw the four-game set (which the teams split), including a turnout of 52,000 on Sunday, June 16. As was true most of the time that season, throughout the New York series the Tigers battled not only the opposition and the umpires but each other as well. In the finale, for example, Cobb bawled out Bob Jones in full view of everyone after Jones, coaching at third while he nursed a broken hand, kept Del Pratt from coming home on Cobb's double. To a New York writer it was "the same thing . . . that has caused dissension on the team and kept it down in the race."[17]

Indeed the Tigers were down in the race then and remained so for two more months. In 1923 Dauss, in his twelfth year with Detroit, was the only pitcher Cobb could depend on. Dauss won twenty-one games that year; but Pillette, a nineteen-game winner the previous season, lost an equal number, and Colins and Francis, of whom Cobb had expected much, won eight games between them. Both fell from Cobb's favor early in the season for spending too much time enjoying the nightlife in league cities. In September, at Cleveland, Cobb and Francis exchanged angry words and then slaps and punches in the dugout after Cobb took the lefthander out.

With George Sisler missing the entire season following delicate surgery for sinus blockages that had affected his eyesight, the Browns slumped badly. There really was nobody else strong enough to challenge the Yankees, who were already far out in front by mid-summer. It took the Tigers until August to establish themselves in the first division. Cobb's hitting was not what it had been for the past two seasons, and he missed a number of games in June and July because of trouble with his oft-injured knees and then a strained back. Meanwhile rumors surfaced here and there that Bill Donovan, currently managing New Haven in the Eastern League, would succeed Cobb at the end of the season.

Although it was much too late to catch the Yankees, both Cobb and the rest of his club were able to salvage part of the season during its last six weeks. Despite having to play six doubleheaders in six days in September, the Tigers won thirty-three of their last fifty-three games, eleven of their last fourteen. By beating St. Louis 7–6 in the season finale, with Cobb hitting a pair of doubles, they finished at 83–71, edged Cleveland for second place, and thereby secured about $1000 apiece out of the runnerup's World Series share. Yet while the ballclub climbed a notch higher in the standings, it also ended up one game farther from first place, sixteen games behind the Yankees.

In 145 games in 1923, Cobb hit for a .340 average with six homers, 88 runs batted in, and 103 runs scored. He added about twenty points to his average during the team's late-season surge. His four-for-four day at Boston on September 20 put him ahead of Honus Wagner in career base hits, and his 1,741st run, scored on May 25, broke another of Wagner's career marks. Yet for the second straight year the onetime scourge of the base paths could manage only nine stolen bases and again was thrown out on a majority of his attempts. He did flash his old style on October 2, when he stole home—for the first time since 1920—on Paul Castner, a jittery rookie lefthander with the White Sox.

The aggregate earned run average of Cobb's pitchers was 4.09, next to the fattest in the league. And despite his efforts to develop a running ball club, the Tigers, like most other teams beginning in the twenties, depended on hitting prowess, not speed, to get their runs. The whole club stole eighty-seven bases in 1923, nine less than Cobb had stolen by himself eight years earlier. Nor, despite Cobb's rebuilding efforts, had the Tiger infield really become an effective unit. Detroit's 103 double plays were the fewest in either major league that year.

But hit the Tigers could—.300 as a team, one point less than Cleveland. Heilmann's .403 led the league and established his curious pattern of outhitting everybody every other year, in odd-numbered years. Rigney hit .315, Pratt .310, and Bassler .298. Having finally convinced himself early in the season that Veach lacked sufficient determination and hustle (despite successive .338 and .327 seasons), Cobb kept the swarthy Kentuckian on the bench most of the time. In his place he platooned Manush and Bob Fothergill, a rotund, robust hitter up from Rochester. Manush hit .334, his rookie counterpart .315. (In pinch hitting and fill-in assignments, Veach still hit .327.)

The Tigers' strong finish seems to have allayed whatever doubts Frank Navin may have begun to have about Cobb's managerial capabilities. At least Navin had to be happy with the year's attendance, which was close to one million, second only to the Yankees'. Whatever else might be said about Cobb as a manager, his team was making the Detroit franchise one of the three or four richest in baseball. So shortly after the season's end, Navin affirmed that Cobb would be back and signed him for another year, at about $38,000.

After he watched the Yankees finally beat the Giants in the third straight all-New York World Series, Cobb headed west for his second hunting trip into northern Canada. Again his guide was Jack Miner; the party also included Dan Howley, Cobb's former subordinate, who now managed Toronto in the International League. Later that winter Howley spent about a month with Cobb in Georgia, hunting, planning an exhibition tour for the spring between Detroit and Howley's team (which would train at Macon), and generally becoming better and better friends. Howley was one of the few men inside baseball who ever got really close to Cobb.

Over the winter Navin and Cobb tried, without success, to make a deal for an established second baseman. They also agreed to sell Bobby Veach to the Red Sox and Ray Francis to Atlanta in the Southern League, and to release George Cutshaw. Thus they were able to do nothing to strengthen the team, which remained slow on the bases and afield and sorely in need of consistent pitching. Cobb did expect some help from Earl Whitehill, a smart young lefthander brought up from Birmingham late in 1923 in time to get credit for two wins.

Determined to get full concentration on baseball, Cobb confiscated every set of golf clubs his players had in their baggage when they checked into the new Hotel Richmond in Augusta that March. He was still convinced that golf during the season did not mix with baseball, both because golf threw off a ballplayer's swing and took his mind away from his work. The ban on golf made the Georgia Sundays, when the ballpark was closed under state law, even more tedious. Cobb finally relented where his golfing pitchers were concerned.

The newcomer who most caught Cobb's eye that spring was a slender, twenty-year-old infielder from rural Michigan named Charley Gehringer. After the season ended the previous fall, Bobby Veach, playing with a semipro team around the state, had seen the youngster in action and recommended him to Cobb for a tryout. The Detroit manager "took me under his wing right away," Gehringer remembered. "He kept telling me I was going to be tremendous." After watching and working with Gehringer for a week, showing him how to position himself in the box for different kinds of pitchers, how to spray the ball around the field, how to lay down bunts, Cobb had a contract drawn up. While Gehringer got no bonus for signing, "I did get a lot of tips on the stock market from Cobb, which didn't do me any good; I didn't have the money to invest."[18] For 1924 Cobb had Gehringer assigned to London in the Michigan-Ontario League.

When Gehringer first saw Cobb, the Georgian no longer reminded observers of a greyhound, as he had in earlier years. The lean, thin-faced teenager with a full head of hair who had come up in 1905 was now a rather jowly and heavyset, mostly bald man with deep lines around his eyes—a man who might easily have been taken for a successful middle-aged business executive. Yet a magazine journalist who interviewed him at Augusta that spring found him to be still youthfully enthusiastic, as well as a person of firm convictions who expressed his views forthrightly and articulately. Again Cobb urged dedication, sacrifice, and hard work as the requisites for success. "I've always been intensely interested in trying to do what I'm doing better than anybody else," he said. "I try to improve on what I'm engaged in, and to improvise." While he was willing to acknowledge that most ballplayers probably came to spring training in better shape than they used to, he went on to lament the decline of "inside baseball" in favor of the present "power game." But inasmuch as "Baseball, like everything else, travels in cycles," maybe someday the old-style game would come back.[19]

Whatever his regrets and misgivings about the way baseball had changed in his time, the power game was in full sway, and Cobb had to manage basically according to its dictates. The team he fielded in 1924 had major deficiencies, but it became a legitimate contender for the American League pennant, the only such team he was ever to manage.

The Tigers won five of their first six games, starting with Dauss's 4–3 victory over Cleveland at Navin Field before 35,000, many of whom sat in temporary bleachers Navin had ordered installed in right and left fields. Positioning himself second in the batting order behind Lu Blue, Cobb hit at better than .450 for the first few weeks of the season, as did Heilmann. Looking faster than he had in years, Cobb even stole home twice in April: at St. Louis on the 22nd on Bill Bayne, at Detroit on the 27th on Ted Lyons of the White Sox.

As the season progressed, Dauss lost his effectiveness as a starter, and Cobb converted him into one of the game's earliest relief specialists. Rookie Whitehill and a rejuvenated Collins became the strong men of the pitching staff. Lil Stoner, back after winning twenty-seven at Fort Worth, and second-year man Ken Holloway rounded out Cobb's starting rotation. Blue, Pratt, Rigney, and Jones supposedly made up the regular infield, although Haney and rookie Les Burke also played much of the time. Johnny Bassler, a .346 hitter that year, was usually the starting catcher; his backup, Larry Woodall, also hit above .300. Cobb played all but one game and Heilmann missed only two, but in left field Cobb used not only Manush and Fothergill but also Al Wingo, a left-handed hitter bought from Toronto.

Juggling, finagling, exhorting, encouraging, railing, and fuming at his ballclub, Cobb kept it in contention nearly all season. His men had to respect his past and continuing achievements as a ballplayer. Some of them may even have feared him. But apart from Haney and maybe one or two others, they did not find him likeable. The simple fact was that neither age, wealth, fame, nor parenthood had mellowed Cobb. As a manager he was what he had always been as a player—smart, ingenious, hard-driving, ruthless, and overbearing. Long accustomed to his celebrity status, he was charming and graceful on public occasions, as when, at a reception in mid-May in Washington attended by Michigan's two U. S. Senators and thirteen Representatives, he received a set of twenty famous historical biographies to commemorate his twenty seasons in the American League. A few days later in Philadelphia, however, he was "back in old form," as the *Sporting News* put it, punching a black groundskeeper after an argument over use of a Shibe Park telephone.[20] And a few days after that he was at Yankee Stadium hurling ugly epithets at Ruth, jumping around to distract the New York pitchers, and egging on Blue and Haney into fights with Yankees Mike McNally and Wally Pipp.

Plenty of bad feeling remained from that bitterly fought four-game split when the Yankees made their first trip into Detroit in June. After the Tigers won the opener 7–2, with Cobb lashing two triples and a single, the Yankees pounded out a 10–4 win, Ruth hitting his fifteenth homer. The next day the Yankees were ahead 10–6 in the top of the ninth when Bert Cole, in relief of Stoner, threw at Ruth's head. After fouling out, Ruth told Bob Meusel, up next, that he had seen Cobb in center field signal Cole to throw at Meusel as well. Cole's first pitch hit Meusel in the ribs, whereupon the big Yankee out-fielder charged Cole and both benches emptied. Ruth and Cobb headed directly for each other; for a moment it seemed that their long-building feud was about to reach a violent climax. But Miller Huggins and umpire Emmett "Red" Ormsby managed to get between them and prevent any blows from landing. The Detroit fans also poured onto the field, some grabbing field-box chairs and throwing them in the direction of the New York players. Despairing of ever getting the field cleared, umpire-in-chief Billy Evans had police escort the Yankees to their dressing room and then declared a forfeit to New York. It happened to be Friday the 13th.

On Saturday some 40,000 people showed up expecting more trouble. Navin had more than a hundred policemen on hand, some on horseback, to keep the overflow crowd in check. Meusel and Cole had heard from Ban Johnson that they were suspended, Ruth that he was fined $50. Cobb, maybe the *agent provocateur* in the whole affair, went unpunished. It was painful enough, though, for him to have to watch the Yankees take their third game of the series behind Waite Hoyt, 6–2. Those who came to see renewed mob violence had to sit and stand through an exceptionally strife-free game, at least as Tigers-Yankees encounters went.

That left the Tigers at 28–25, in third place behind New York and a Boston team that had surprised everybody so far but would soon sink far into the second division. Washington, in its first year under manager–second-baseman Stanley "Bucky" Harris, was the hot new contender in the second half of the season. The Senators had climbed to third by June 23, the day the Tigers first slipped into the lead. For the next six weeks Detroit, New York, and Washington were never more than a few games apart.

Late in July, after winning twelve of fifteen games in the east and eight straight, the Tigers had become the bookmakers' pennant favorites. They lost the lead briefly, then on August 3, before a Navin Field crowd announced as 42,712 (another new record), Whitehill mastered the Yankees to put Cobb's club back in first by percentage points. They had again yielded first by the time the Yankees left town, but by taking three of four from Boston, they got back on top. In the Boston-series finale Cobb made two hits, scored four runs, and stole four bases, including home. It was his third theft of the plate in 1924.

That game, a 13–7 battering of the Red Sox, might be taken as the pinnacle of Cobb's career as a manager. What happened to the Tigers after that was not so much a collapse as a slow fade. In the east and then at St. Louis and Chicago they won only ten of twenty-five games. A doubleheader defeat by the White Sox on Labor Day left them seven and a half behind Washington, five and a half behind New York. Again Cobb's pitchers failed him. Dutch Leonard's late-season return from the California semipro leagues was not much help in bolstering the staff. The hitting of both Cobb and Heilmann, moreover, fell off in the last half of the season. The loss of Lu Blue for thirty-eight games because of torn knee ligaments hurt badly. Cobb never forgave Frank Navin for refusing to buy Johnny Neun, first baseman for St. Paul in the American Association, to replace Blue while the Tigers were still in the race.

There was some satisfaction for Cobb and the Tigers in spoiling the Yankees' pennant chances by beating them three straight times at Detroit later in September. Cobb also took satisfaction in standing in the coach's box at third during the last game—in which he made three hits—and taunting the Yankees in their dugout near by until Everett Scott and Lou Gehrig, a muscular first baseman just up from the Eastern League, charged out to confront him. Umpire Tom Connolly threw both of them out, while Cobb stood by innocently. And it was nice to win seven games in a row at the end of the year, until a last-day loss to Chicago in the only game Cobb sat out. Thereby the Detroit team finished with a record of 86–68, its best since 1916. Washington's pennant-winners were six games better, the Yankees three.

In 1924, at the age of thirty-seven, Cobb had played more baseball than in any year since 1915. His 625 times at bat were the most plate appearances he ever made in a season. With 211 hits he finished at .338. Cobb's four homers and seventy-four runs batted in were not impressive, but twenty-three stolen bases, his most since 1919, placed him fourth among American Leaguers. As a team the Tigers hit .298, still good enough to lead the league, but they managed only thirty-five homers. Heilmann, who finished far out of the batting race at .346, was the only Tiger to hit as many as ten four-baggers.

Worn down no doubt by the season's rigors, Cobb attended the Washington-New York Giants World Series and then went home. Before a game at the Polo Grounds, he posed shaking one of Ruth's hands while George Sisler, now player-manager of the Browns, shook the other. Cobb and Ruth made their peace on that occasion as they sat together and reviewed their years of combat. From then on they no longer flared at each other on the field; off the field they even began to build something of a friendship.

Cobb hunted and golfed some that winter, particularly with Robert Wood-

ruff. Mostly, though, he took it easy. The major personnel changes he insti-
gated were the releases of Del Pratt, considered too slow around second despite his .301 season, and of Cole and Pillette, pitchers who had once promised
much but of late had delivered little. As for his own future, Cobb said that he
intended to appear in no more than 75 to 100 games in 1925. He would already have cut down on his playing time, he contended, if he'd been able to
find an adequate center-field replacement.

While Cobb's remarks might suggest that he was ready to slow down as a
ballplayer, he was not about to calm down, either in or out of uniform. How
little he had really changed over the years was again evident in a well-publicized altercation he had in the railroad terminal restaurant in Atlanta late in
February.

Accompanied by former Washington manager George McBride, whom the
club had signed as a coach for the coming year, Cobb was on his way home
from Detroit and talks with Navin about spring training plans. Following lunch,
Cobb began arguing with a waitress about the bill. According to one report,
Cobb upbraided the waitress until the cashier, who was also the manager's
wife, got into the dispute and ended up hitting Cobb over the head with a big
glass dish. Hearing the commotion, a policeman ran in, got into a scuffle with
Cobb, and wrestled him to the pavement outside the restaurant. The policeman started to call a patrol wagon but yielded to Cobb's urgings that they take
a taxi to the police station. Cobb's version, substantiated by McBride, omitted
the glass dish and the wrestling match. He did acknowledge disagreeing over
the bill, being told by the cashier that he was no gentleman, and replying,
"that I was as much a gentleman as she was a lady." Cobb also said he had
"politely remonstrated" with the policeman, who had insisted on taking him
in. Everybody agreed that Cobb posted an $11 bond before leaving the police
station "in a towering rage."[21]

Whatever actually happened, it was the kind of silly, unnecessary, ugly
little scene in which Cobb had been involved all too often in his life. At the
age of thirty-eight he was still in many ways the same suspicious, thin-skinned,
quick-tempered kid who had come up from the Sally League in 1905. And he
always would be.

Spring training 1925 at Augusta was relatively uneventful. Dutch Leonard,
presumably back for the whole year, was more impressive on the golf links
than on the mound. Cobb looked over Gehringer again, judged him still not
ripe, and put him in the care of Dan Howley's Toronto club. Cobb would end
up playing Frank O'Rourke, a journeyman infielder used sparingly the previous year, at second most of the time in 1925. Bob Jones gave way to Haney
at third. Having sold Topper Rigney to Boston, a favorite dumping ground,
Cobb would have to rely on rookie Jack Tavener, Rigney's successor at Fort

Worth, to do the job at shortstop. In general his team was getting older and had remedied none of the weaknesses that had characterized it since he took over in 1921.

After dragging for two weeks, Cobb came down with a severe case of flu while the Tigers were playing their way north. Typically, Ruth's collapse en route from Florida—from an intestinal abscess brought on by sustained digestive abuse—completely overshadowed Cobb's illness. He was still too weak to do anything but sit in the dugout when the team opened the season with a 4–3 victory over Chicago. Heinie Manush was in center field. Nearly 36,000 fans turned out in warm sunshine, a rarity for Detroit home openers. More than one million of them had passed through the Navin Field turnstiles in 1924. It looked like another splendid year at the gate for Frank Navin.

On the field, though, the year was another disappointment. After that first win the Tigers lost seven straight, fourteen of their first eighteen, and floundered deep in the second division, in the unaccustomed company of the Ruthless Yankees. Cobb batted for Holloway and drew a walk on April 20, the Tigers' fifth outing and his first, in a game Cleveland eventually won in fifteen innings. He did not put himself in the starting lineup until a week later, against St. Louis at Navin Field, and then in right field. It was May 2 before he resumed his place in center, hitting a double and two singles in another loss.

Then came one of the great hitting sprees in Cobb's career and indeed in baseball history. On May 4, in the opener of a series at St. Louis, Cobb made two hits in still another defeat for the Tigers. During batting practice the next day, Sid Keener, a young reporter with the St. Louis *Star,* entered the Detroit dugout and found Cobb talking with H. G. Salsinger, "his favorite sportswriter," and as usual swinging his three bats. For years, Cobb said to Salsinger and anyone else within earshot, he'd been reading how he got his hits on grounders and bunts and how Ruth socked them out of the park. "I'll show you something today," he promised. "I'm going for home runs for the first time in my career."[22]

What followed was quite astonishing. Against five pitchers in a 14–8 Detroit win, Cobb made six hits in six at bats—two singles, a double, and three homeruns. Two homers, off Joe Bush and Elam Van Gilder, landed in the right-field bleachers; the third cleared the bleachers and landed in the street beyond. Cobb's sixteen total bases set a new American League record. The next day the Tigers again battered Browns pitching, 11–4. Cobb singled and homered two more times, off lefties Dave Danforth and Chester Falk. His first-inning single gave him nine hits in a row. By hitting five homers in two games, he matched what Adrian "Cap" Anson, leader of the old Chicago White Stockings, had done back in 1884. Since then neither Ruth nor anybody else had been able to accomplish that particular feat. The next day, moreover, Cobb's line drive off the right-field wall, driving in O'Rourke in the first inning, missed landing in the bleachers by a foot. All told, he made twelve hits in nineteen times up in the St. Louis series for twenty-nine total bases.

The Sportsman's Park homerun outburst marked no new, power-oriented phase in Cobb's career. He hit seven more homeruns that season and only seventeen over the remainder of his career. He had, though, made his point: There were different ways to play baseball. He still loved the old game, still preferred most of the time just to "nip" at the ball, as Walter Johnson had once described his hitting style. But he could also clout with the musclemen when he chose. It was a question of how the game *ought* to be played.

Despite Cobb's batting heroics, which kept him well above .400 into July, the Detroit slump persisted. When the Yankees, still minus Ruth, came into Navin Field for the first time that year and crushed the locals in the series opener, the New York writer James P. Harrison observed that "The city has soured on the Tigers." The crowd continually hooted at Cobb, especially when Bobby Veach, now with New York but still one of the most popular players in Tiger history, slammed two doubles. And when world's champion Washington came in a few days later, N. W. Baxter, sports editor of the Washington *Post*, commented on "the 'raspberry' chorus" that greeted Cobb every day. Baxter had even heard that some Detroit fans were circulating a petition asking Navin to fire Cobb.[23]

But then Cobb's club, aided greatly by his own strong hitting, got hot and probably saved his job. By the end of June, having recently won nine straight, the Tigers had climbed into fourth place. Cobb, Heilmann, and Wingo, now getting the call most of the time in left field, were all batting around .400. Despite his pre-season talk about playing less, Cobb was in the lineup every game. Even though he collapsed and had to be carried from the field after second-baseman Joe Klugman fell on his leg at Cleveland, he was back the next day. On July 18, however, he drew a five-day suspension from Ban Johnson after rowing with Pants Rowland, now an American League umpire, about a called third strike to Larry Woodall and then renewing the quarrel following the game.

Cobb went into a slump after that and saw his average drop twenty points. Early in August he took himself out, complaining of "a troublesome hip." When Manush, playing in center, hit a single and two doubles in a 3–2 win at Washington, Baxter remarked that "the result of the game gave some point to the oft-heard story that Cobb's refusal to bench himself is one of the principal problems with the present Detroit machine."[24] Cobb had obviously slowed down afield, and his arm was no longer as strong as it had once been. But then none of Detroit's outfielders covered much ground or threw particularly well. Cobb remained convinced that he handled center field better than anybody else he had on the team, yet he was also interested in Manush's development. Beginning in mid-August, he gave way to Manush most of the time and platooned Wingo and Fothergill in left, although he put himself in frequently to pinch hit.

Despite Cobb's unpopularity with many Detroit fans, a group of his well-to-do admirers went forward with plans for festivities to mark his twentieth anniversary with the ball club. Before the game on Saturday, August 29, against Connie Mack's rebuilt Philadelphia team, now serious pennant contenders, Cobb exposed his nearly bald head to a crowd of 30,000 and stood by the gate to the third-base field-boxes. Hundreds of Detroit rooters, among whom were doubtless some who had seen Cobb break in back in 1905, streamed down from the stands to shake his hand and get his autograph on their scorecards. Cobb then singled, doubled, scored twice, and drove in a run in the Tigers' 9–5 victory.

That evening six hundred people toasted Cobb at a banquet held in the new Book Cadillac Hotel. Mack, Billy Evans, and Mayor John T. Smith were among the eulogizers, as well as Ban Johnson, who hailed Cobb as "the greatest player of all time." As gracious as always on such occasions, Cobb minimized his accomplishments, regretted that he hadn't been able to do more. He then received a huge grandfather clock, valued at $1000, as a gift from the city council, and a check from the Detroit Base Ball and Amusement Company for $10,000, which practically everyone in the room understood to be also a gift, bestowed freely by Frank Navin. The $10,000 was no gift at all, Cobb later maintained, only the balance of the salary—$50,000 in all—that Navin had agreed to the previous fall. But since Navin had not wanted to put in writing that he was paying Cobb as much as Ban Johnson was getting as president of the American League, Cobb and Navin had agreed that the extra money would be paid in lump sum at the end of the season. When Navin extolled Cobb and then presented what was really his salary check in advance, "There was a roar of approval from the audience," Cobb recalled. Yet it was a "phony act," one that "soured my stomach" and "detracted from one of the finest evenings of my life. . . ."[25]

Earlier that August, Miller Huggins and Babe Ruth had finally had a showdown over Ruth's lack of self-discipline and arrogant, subversive conduct on the ball club. The little Yankee manager had levied a staggering $5000 fine and sent Ruth home from St. Louis under indefinite suspension. The national sports press roundly condemned "baseball's baby" and contrasted his chronic irresponsibility with Cobb, described by one magazine as "the Admirable Crichton of baseball." Besides Henry Ford, editorialized the New York *Evening Telegram*, Cobb was Detroit's "first citizen," a man who had studiously applied himself and "succeeded so well that he has passed out of the ranks of

baseball into one of the builders of Detroit." The feting of Cobb on his twentieth anniversary, said the New York *Times*, was a tribute to his "strong character," a quality sadly lacking in Ruth.[26]

Detroit's defeat of Philadelphia on Cobb Day was the middle game in a
three-game sweep that kept the Athletics on a losing streak eventually reaching fourteen games. That destroyed their pennant hopes and enabled Washington to take an insurmountable lead en route to its second straight pennant.
Meanwhile the Tigers went on to win ten straight before Garland Buckeye,
Cleveland's 250-pound righthander, hit two homers and pitched a 7–2 win on
September 10.

By sweeping three games at St. Louis to end the season, Cobb's team could
have finished third. Instead it was George Sisler's Browns, with a 4–3 win in
the first of the series, who clinched the third spot. On October 1 Cobb played
the doubleheader that closed the season. In two slugfests won by the Tigers,
Cobb was 6 for 10, including his twelfth homer, and stole two bases to give
himself thirteen for the year. As they had several years earlier, Cobb and Sisler both pitched a little, Sisler holding the Tigers scoreless in the eighth and
Cobb doing the same in the bottom of the inning before umpire Ormsby called
the second game because of darkness. Cobb also "frisked around the outfield,
joking with the bleacherites, and on three occasions lost flies in the sun." All
in all he "enjoyed himself thoroughly," apparently glad that another tough,
frustrating season was behind him.[27]

Cobb's batting in the St. Louis doubleheader pushed his final average up
to .378 for 415 times at bat and 121 games, in a number of which he only
pinch hit. Heilmann, by going 6 for 9 on the final day, beat out Tris Speaker
for his third batting title, .393 to .389. The team finished at 81–73, half a game
behind St. Louis and eight and one-half behind Philadelphia. First place, again
occupied by Bucky Harris's Washington club, was a distant sixteen games away.
Again the Tigers made lots of hits, enough for a .302 team average, and nobody in the league scored as many runs. But Cobb's pitchers were worse than
ever, allowing 4.61 earned runs per nine innings.

At the World Series that October, Cobb made his peace with John Mc-
Graw, as he had with Ruth a year earlier, and watched Walter Johnson struggle vainly to hold back Pittsburgh in game seven. From Pittsburgh, Cobb
headed for Detroit and Windsor to join up with Jack Miner for still another
hunting trip into the Canadian woods. It proved a pretty harrowing experience for both of them when they lost their bearings and had to walk for two
days before they reached the Canadian Pacific tracks. Near Cochrane, Ontario, about two hundred miles south of Hudson's Bay, they loaded Cobb's
moose head, with an antler spread of forty-five inches, into the baggage car
and started for home.

Before he left Detroit on his way back to Georgia, Cobb arranged a deal whereby Fred Haney went to Boston for two minor leaguers, who were then assigned to Fort Worth in exchange for pitcher Augustus "Lefty" Johns. At Augusta he spent a quiet thirty-ninth birthday, golfed and did some more hunting, and also took his dogs to a few field trials. A photograph taken on one such occasion, at Waynesboro, Georgia, shows him wearing a suit with bow tie and contrasting vest, big, western-style hat, and knee-length hiking boots, looking every bit the well-fixed country gentleman.

Which is what he might have become if he had been willing to retire from baseball at that point in his life. For reasons he never made clear, he decided to come back for another year as Tiger manager. And for reasons that are even less fathomable, Frank Navin was willing, just before Cobb left for the World Series, to hand him another contract, this one for a straight $50,000. In retrospect, it would have been better for both men if Cobb had quit after 1925's respectable showing. The club was not likely to do any better next year and might very well do worse. Whatever happened, Cobb would have to put up with what he later described as "the worst ownership any manager ever suffered."[28]

Cobb's and Navin's relations had become outright hostile. Their grievances against each other went way back, maybe as far back as Navin's refusal to pay a medical bill for Cobb in 1907. Cobb later charged that Navin time and time again refused to put out the money to buy critically needed ballplayers. That very winter of 1925–26, according to Cobb, Navin missed a chance to buy Paul Waner, the kind of smart, spray-hitting player Cobb liked, from San Francisco, where Waner had just hit .401. Navin balked at the $45,000 price that Pittsburgh was willing to pay for the future Hall of Famer. Navin even denied Cobb day-to-day expense money, so that the Tiger manager had to cover unanticipated costs, such as a ballplayer's need for a quick loan, out of his own pocket. At the same time, Navin inveterately played the horses, throwing his money away on long shots at the Windsor Jockey Club races. "It got so that I couldn't stand to look at Navin."[29] So Cobb had come to feel about the man who had signed his paychecks for twenty-one years.

If it had become so bad, then why did Cobb return for 1926? Maybe because he wanted to carry through with the development of various younger players, particularly Manush and Gehringer. Maybe because he already was at least partially aware of what he would later come to understand fully: He needed baseball more than it needed him. For whatever reason, Cobb made ready for his sixth season as Tiger manager.

Through no fault of his own, Cobb missed the first two weeks of spring workouts at Augusta. It was the beginning of March before he could be scheduled in for long-needed surgery on his eyes at the renowned Wilmer Eye Clinic, part of the Johns Hopkins University medical complex in Baltimore. A filmy substance medically termed pterygium and commonly called proud flesh had gradually grown over both eyes and clouded his vision. He had had a hard time following the ball the past season, he said, although his .378 batting average hardly indicated as much. The surgery, performed by a team headed by Dr. William H. Wilmer, a fellow Georgian, was completely successful. A week later, when his bandages and stitches were removed and he found his sight cleared, Cobb bolted out of bed intending to head for Georgia, only to be overcome by splitting pain behind his eyes. Obediently he returned to bed and submitted to daily bathings of his eyes in a medicated solution, until he was discharged on March 13. The next day, wearing smoked glasses and with cameramen all over him, he watched his first practice at Augusta and even took a few cuts in the batting cage. In his absence George McBride had been in charge.

By now only Heilmann, Bassler, Blue, Woodall, and Dauss remained from the team Cobb took over in 1921. Dutch Leonard had left the club in a fury the previous September. After winning five games in a row, the lefthander had complained of overwork and a sore pitching arm. Unconvinced, Cobb had left him in to take a 12–4 battering from the Athletics before the home fans on July 14. When Leonard refused to pitch on the subsequent eastern trip, Cobb sent him back to Detroit. Early in September the eleven-year veteran learned that he had been put on waivers. When nobody claimed him, Frank Navin sold his contract to Vernon in the Pacific Coast League. Convinced that Cobb had been determined to drive him out of the big leagues, Leonard refused to report to Vernon and went back to his Fresno Valley farm.

In the spring of 1925 Cobb judged Charley Gehringer at last ready to become the Tigers' regular second baseman. He was also impressed by a lanky lefthander up from Oklahoma City of the Western League named Carl Hubbell, but for the coming year, he decided, Hubbell should pitch at Toronto. Later on it became a familiar baseball yarn that Cobb failed to appreciate Hubbell's potential and released him. In fact Hubbell remained under a Detroit contract at Toronto and was released only after Cobb left the organization. Cobb always insisted that he urged Navin to keep Hubbell until he developed control of his strangely breaking pitch, later dubbed a "screwball." It would be 1928 before Hubbell began the career with the New York Giants that would lead to the Hall of Fame.

Among the people Cobb had played with early in his career, Ed Siever, Matty McIntyre, and Bill Donovan were already dead, Siever and McIntyre from tuberculosis, Donovan having been killed in a train wreck in upstate New York late in 1923. Now Hughey Jennings, a coach under John McGraw since leaving the Tigers, was terminally ill with tuberculosis at a sanitarium in Asheville, North Carolina. When Detroit and Toronto played an exhibition game there late in March, Cobb kept his old manager waiting anxiously all one morning while he busied himself with various matters. He finally got out to see Jennings early in the afternoon. After an hour or so of reminiscences, Jennings was crying when Cobb left for the local ballpark. Less than two years later, at his home in Scranton, Jennings would die at fifty-eight.

"All we can do is hope," Cobb replied when queried about his team's chances for 1926.[30] He knew that he was stuck with an aging, mediocre club, one that could boast of strong hitting and little else. Having appeared in only four exhibition games that spring, Cobb had made up his mind not to play regularly in 1926, even though he could still claim to be an asset to the team. Its 1925 record with him in the regular lineup had been 58-46, without him, 23-27. Fothergill was in center field and Manush in left when the Tigers opened against Cleveland on April 13, before the usual capacity-plus crowd at Navin Field. Cobb lined into a double play pinch hitting late in that game, but it was April 27, following five straight losses, before he put himself in the starting lineup. Against the White Sox he singled, doubled, and tripled, scored twice, drove in four runs, and made a running over-the-shoulder catch to save a run. The Tigers won that one, 8-7.

Meanwhile Cobb also kept Gehringer, his prize rookie, on the bench. The manager did not want to put too much pressure on the young second baseman too soon, explained the Detroit writers. What had actually happened was that Gehringer had angered Cobb during an exhibition game by talking back when Cobb fussed about a lack of pep in the infield. Gehringer finally got into the lineup on April 28 against Chicago, but then only because Frank O'Rourke had the measles. A few days later, at St. Louis, Ken Williams's homer in the ninth inning beat the Tigers 7-6. Earlier in the game Gehringer, playing back on the grass, had been unable to get Williams on a bunt. Afterward, as Gehringer recalled, Cobb "kept me after school, like a teacher would. Just kept me sitting in the clubhouse for an hour after everybody had left the ballpark."[31] Yet the next day Cobb had Gehringer back at second base. There he stayed for the rest of the year, hitting a respectable .277, forming a capable double-play combination with Jack Tavener, and solidifying his hold on the job he would handle quietly but brilliantly for Detroit over the next seventeen years.

Cobb played nearly every day through May and into June despite being bothered by a lame back. At Yankee Stadium he hit two homers and two singles to power the Tigers to a wild 11-10 win before 55,000 Sunday fans, who repeatedly cheered the man at whom they had directed so much vituperation in the past. Cobb's early season hitting was a big factor in keeping the Tigers in the first division. But with Johnny Bassler out for the year with a broken ankle and with his pitchers yielding runs in bunches, Cobb's team was not really capable of contending. So in mid-June he stopped playing regularly, choosing to go most of the time with an outfield of Fothergill, Manush, and Heilmann. Cobb still put himself in the starting lineup now and then, usually in left field instead of "Fatty" Fothergill. He even stole home on July 3 off George Uhle, Cleveland's ace righthander, after having walked, stolen second, and gone to third on an infield out. Cobb was over the plate before Uhle's pitch even got to catcher Luke Sewell's glove.

But as Cobb told Henry P. Edwards, Cleveland *Plain Dealer* sports editor, playing every day and particularly patrolling center field just took too much out of him. Thus he had given way to Manush, who had become a good outfielder besides staying up among the leaders in batting. "The last few years I played, I was just tired, tired, tired," Cobb said long afterward. When the team was on the road, he typically would go back to his hotel after a game, have his dinner sent up, and then settle into bed to read himself to sleep. He would remain in bed until late morning, when he would again eat in his room, then dress and go to the ballpark. At the Cobbs' apartment in Detroit it was not possible for him to get much rest. "People pestered me, day and night," he recalled. "I was always on edge, irritable. . . . I was like a steel spring." Gehringer remembered him as being "awfully touchy. I don't think anybody got along with him."[32]

As the Tigers failed to move up in the standings, the home fans got on Cobb worse than ever. "Ty Cobb has lost his popularity in the city," Edwards wrote from Detroit, "and there are hundreds, yes, even thousands of fans who attend the games at Navin field in hopes of having a chance to boo and jeer their former idol." Probably one reason Cobb played sparingly in the last half of the season was to avoid the deluges of groans and catcalls he provoked whenever he called time and trotted in from center to change pitchers or talk strategy. He used more players and especially more pitchers than any manager in the majors. Cobb's pitcher-switching verged on "managerial hysteria," complained Detroit sportswriter Harry Bullion after watching him remove Stoner, pitching a shutout at Yankee Stadium, because Stoner had walked two men in the eighth inning; then jerk Johns when he gave up one hit in the ninth; and then bring in Wilbur Cooper, a recently acquired National League veteran, who proceeded to yield four runs and lose the game.[33]

Cobb did not help his reputation as a manager or as a man by engaging in a demeaning spat with his old friend Clark Griffith when the Washington president protested to Ban Johnson about Cobb's umpire-baiting, repeated stalling, and generally obnoxious behavior during a late-July series in the capital. In a public letter to Griffith, Cobb called him a "prevaricator and inconsistent," because in his days as New York manager Griffith had carefully taught his players how to stall. Griffith had also encouraged the Washington writers to "get" Cobb, and on other occasions had slandered Connie Mack and Miller Huggins. In general, Griffith was "a very vicious gentleman."[34] "The Old Fox," as baseball men liked to call Griffith, let Cobb's blast go unanswered.

"I guess some of the fans hope it's true," said Cobb when asked about reports that he intended to retire and that Dan Howley would manage the Tigers in 1927. But those were just "rainy day yarns," he added.[35] At the end of August he still had his team solidly in fourth place, six games above .500. From that point, however, the Tigers were only 15–17. They thus failed to take advantage of a late-season slump by the frontrunning Yankees, who were barely able to hold off Tris Speaker's red-hot Cleveland ballclub. With the whole league tightening up, Washington and Chicago slipped past the Tigers, who found themselves still above .500 but in sixth place.

There they finished the season, with a record of 79-75, after sweeping a doubleheader from last-place Boston. By gathering six hits in the two games, Manush beat out Ruth for the hitting title, .378 to .372. Fothergill, ponderous in everything except swinging the bat, pounded out a .367 average in 110 games; and Heilmann, persisting in his up-and-down, odd-and-even-year course, hit for the same figure. In 233 at bats Cobb hit .339. Of the seventy-nine games he appeared in, he started only sixty-one, most of them before July.

It was a strong sixth-place showing, only twelve games behind the champion Yankees, but still sixth place—where the Tigers had been at the end of Cobb's first season as manager. With rumors rife that either Cobb would quit or that Navin would refuse to renew his contract, Cobb skipped the World Series and went home with his family to Augusta. Then he was off to the Grand Teton mountains in Wyoming to hunt bear and moose in a party that included Tris Speaker and big Garland Buckeye, whose Cleveland Indians had just missed the pennant by three games. Altogether the trip consumed about three weeks. During that period the Detroit press, noting that the Tiger front office had already announced a shift from Augusta to San Antonio for next year's spring training, speculated freely on who the next manager would be.

Cobb arrived back in Detroit on Wednesday, November 3. He carried with him a letter of resignation, which he left at Navin's office. Gone before reporters in Detroit could get to him, he talked to the press for the first time between trains in Atlanta. After confirming Navin's announcement of his resignation, Cobb read a statement saying that he had left because "I foresaw I could not win a pennant within the next few years under existing circumstances and I wanted to quit while I am still among the best." It was time to "quit taking chances and that means that it is time for me to get out. I don't want to be one of those men who fade or have to be pushed out." His greatest regret, he went on, was not being able to win a pennant for the Detroit fans, "who have been wonderful to me." As to his plans, he said he intended "to spend the winter with my gun and golf clubs" and "settle down and live with my folks a while." But since he knew nothing but baseball, he thought he might buy "an interest in some club somewhere." Asked how he felt, he answered, "Of course I'm not feeling too good. I love the game. . . . Of course I can still hit 'em. . . . It's just this—I'm tired."[36] With that Cobb and his wife, who had come up from Augusta to meet him, boarded their train for home.

The post-mortems on Cobb's managerial career began immediately in the baseball press. The almost universally held view was that, as the New York *Times* put it, "the same qualities which made him a great player dimmed his record as a manager. Cobb was not made to manage a team." The problem, baseball observers agreed, was that he expected everybody who played for him to have the same passion to excel, the same obsession with winning, that he had always had. He could never understand, wrote E. A. Batchelor, who had helped persuade Cobb to take the job, how any player talented enough to make the big leagues could fail "to make every separate game a challenge."[37]

More than anything else it was a matter of temperament. Cobb wanted to control everything that happened in the game, run it strictly according to his ideas, wrote Sam Greene of the Detroit *News*. "Since many of those ideas were built for Cobb and since there was only one Cobb, they obviously wouldn't work." Instead of cooperation, he got resentment from his players for trying to think for them. H. G. Salsinger, who had watched Cobb for more than twenty years, described him as "a man of many moods" but "never temperate," one who was characteristically "in the heights of optimism or the depths of despair. . . . He lashed into sudden fury over some trivial matter and the fury passed as suddenly." So Cobb's criticism was often unjust and nearly always too harsh. "He left wounds that never healed." Harry Bullion's opinion, that Cobb "couldn't nurse the virtue of tolerance," was echoed many years later by Charley Gehringer: "He was very tough to play for. Very demanding. He was so great himself that he couldn't understand why if he told players how to do certain things, they couldn't do it as well as he did. . . . he got very frustrated with a lot of guys."[38]

Down in Augusta, as he read the commentary of Greene, Bullion, Salsinger, and others, men he had often gone out of his way to cultivate, Cobb must have gritted his teeth and sworn a whole new set of oaths against baseball writers. For all of his achievements as a player, they said over and over, he had been a bust as a manager. Yet if Cobb seethed in retirement, he did seem to be safely retired. At least he did for a few weeks following his resignation. Then the Cleveland management announced that Tris Speaker had also quit as the Indians' manager. That puzzling event led to a succession of disclosures that clouded in scandal the names of both Cobb and Speaker and ultimately set Cobb again on a course of vindication, one that would, he became convinced, compel him to return as an active player.

X

"Is There Any Decency Left on Earth?"

Cobb's departure was plausible enough. A sixth-place finish, slumping attendance at Navin Field in the second half of the season, an antagonistic relationship with the club president, and reports of widespread discontent among the players all added up to a strong case against Cobb's continuing for a seventh year as the Tigers' manager. But the resignation of Tris Speaker, announced on November 29 by president E. S. Barnard of the Cleveland club, made no sense at all. In September, Speaker had led the Indians in a furious charge that came close to overtaking the Yankees. After that exciting and promising season, why would the great "Spoke" walk away from his $35,000 salary for what he described as "a vacation from baseball I expect will last the rest of my life."[1] Speaker's explanation—that after bringing his club back into strong contention, he now felt justified in resigning—sounded pretty lame. Maybe, as some baseball men argued and as Eddie Collins's exit at Chicago and George Sisler's at St. Louis suggested, owners had soured on the idea of having big stars as player-managers.[2] Even so, there seemed more to Speaker's situation than had been made public.

How much more—in Speaker's case as well as Cobb's—began to come out on December 21. That day, at his office in Chicago, Commissioner Landis released a collection of documents consisting of charges made by onetime Detroit pitcher Dutch Leonard that Cobb and Speaker had been part of a conspiracy to fix a game seven years earlier, together with two letters Leonard claimed supported his charges and testimony taken by Landis in the matter. Specifically, Leonard maintained that after pitching and winning a game against Cleveland at Detroit on September 24, 1919, he, Cobb, Speaker, and Joe Wood, the former Boston pitching ace who had hurt his arm and then become a utility outfielder for Cleveland, chanced to meet under the Navin Field grandstand. According to Leonard, Speaker offered that inasmuch as his club had already clinched second place behind Chicago, and Detroit was vying with

New York for third and a slice of the World's Series money, the Tigers didn't have to worry about tomorrow's game with the Indians. They were sure to win, especially with Bernie Boland, known for his mastery of Cleveland, scheduled to pitch. Then, said Leonard, the four agreed that they might as well bet some money on the game. Cobb was to put up $2000, Leonard $1500, and Wood and Speaker $1000 each. Cobb suggested that a park attendant named Fred West would be a good man to place the bets for them. But because Detroit was a 10-7 favorite and because the local bookmakers were unwilling to handle so much money without contacting their bosses in Chicago, West had only managed to get down $600 against the bookmakers' $420, for each of three betting partners, by game time on September 25.

On a cold, windy day Detroit won 9-5. Leonard had already left for home, and Wood sat out the game. Notably free of arguments with the umpires or other delays and featuring, one reporter thought, "good fellowship" among the players, the contest took only an hour and six minutes to play. Elmer Myers, the Cleveland pitcher, held Cobb to a single in five times up but was pounded by the rest of the lineup. Boland lobbed the ball up to Speaker and "gave" him two resounding triples—strange behavior by both Boland and Speaker in a game supposedly fixed for Detroit to win.

In a letter from Augusta, dated October 23, 1919, Cobb wrote "Dear Dutch" that "Wood and myself were considerably disappointed in our business proposition. . . . we completely fell down and of course felt badly over it." Wood would tell him all about it "when we get together." The whole matter had been "quite a responsibility," Cobb said, "and I don't care for it again, I can assure you." Subsequently Wood wrote Leonard, from Cleveland, enclosing a certified check for $1650. That comprised Leonard's $1500 stake plus a third of the money won on the September 25 game, minus $30 paid to West for his services. "Cobb did not get up a cent," Wood added. "He told us that and I believed him." After explaining, as Cobb had, why West had been unable to bet more than $600 for each of them, Wood went on to say that "If we ever get another chance like this we will know enough to try to get down early."[3]

So went Leonard's story, and such was the evidence with which he sought to back it up. At a glance, it all looked pretty damaging. Thomas K. Rice, in the Brooklyn *Daily Eagle*, captured the sentiments of baseball fans everywhere: "Darn the whole mess. It has had the same effect as if a lifeong friend had suddenly died." As more and more facts came out, however, it became apparent that Leonard had plenty of reasons for wanting to defame Cobb and Speaker.

Both men, Leonard was convinced, had helped "railroad" him out of the big leagues. Back in August 1924 Leonard had rejoined the Tigers, having refused to sign his contract for 1922, played semipro ball in California, and then won reinstatement from Commissioner Landis. He had pitched two no-hitters in his years with three world's champion Red Sox teams, had posted an earned run average of 1.01 in 1914 (the lowest in major-league history), and was still considered a capable pitcher. Over the years, though, the lefthander had acquired a reputation as a whiner and a laggard, one who disliked facing tough opponents. That was not the kind of man Cobb wanted on his club, even if, as Leonard claimed, Cobb had talked him into coming back into Organized Baseball.

In the first half of the 1925 season, Leonard later told Damon Runyon of Universal News Service, Cobb had worked him so much that his physician warned that he was in danger of injuring his arm permanently. When he protested to Cobb, the Tiger manager berated him in the clubhouse in front of the other players, shouting "Don't you dare turn bolshevik on me. I'm the boss here." Leonard then took the mound at Detroit against Philadelphia and gave up twelve runs. Cobb refused to take him out and laughed when, as Leonard said he later learned, Connie Mack protested to Cobb, "You're killing that boy." Put on waivers after refusing to pitch on the road trip that followed, Leonard fully expected at least Cleveland to claim him for the $7500 waiver price. But Speaker, his teammate on the 1913–15 Red Sox and his presumed friend, passed over him along with the other major-league managers. Thus Speaker had cooperated in Cobb's scheme to get rid of him.

Late in May 1926 Leonard had come east from California bent on revenge against Cobb and Speaker and recompense from the Detroit baseball club. First he had gone to Ban Johnson's office to tell his story and show his letters, only to be told that Johnson was out. He then went to the hotel where the Washington Senators were staying while they played a series with the White Sox, and showed the letters to Washington manager Bucky Harris and club secretary Edwin Eynon. Eynon dropped in on Johnson at home with the news, whereupon Johnson tried unsuccessfully to locate Leonard. After hurrying to Cleveland to apprise Speaker of what he had heard, the American League president was off to Detroit to see Frank Navin, his friend and faithful supporter in baseball councils. There Johnson learned that Leonard had not only talked to Navin but offered to sell copies of the letters to a local newspaper and even shown them to Harry Heilmann, who in turn had told Cobb. When Johnson found that the elusive Leonard had gone back to Chicago, he returned to his office and finally met with the ex-pitcher.

Realizing that Leonard might go public anytime with his charges, Navin and Johnson decided to buy him off. Henry Killea, the American League's attorney, arranged a deal whereby Leonard surrendered his letters for $20,000, the amount Leonard claimed the Tigers owed him for cutting short his career in the majors. Johnson took custody of the letters and kept quiet about them over the summer. On September 9, however, he brought the Leonard-Cobb-Speaker matter before a secret meeting in Chicago of the American League club presidents, who voted to turn the evidence over to Landis. Johnson then had secret meetings with Cobb and Speaker just before they left on their Wyoming hunting trip. He told the two managers what he knew and insisted that each resign. "He was heartbroken and maintained his innocence," Johnson later said of Cobb's reaction. "I told him that whether guilty or not he was through in the American League." Effectively bluffed, first Cobb and then Speaker resigned when they got back. Whereupon their ball clubs also released them as players.

Meanwhile Landis decided to pursue the matter on his own. When Leonard refused to return to Chicago because, he said, "they bump off people once in a while around there," Landis made the long journey out to Leonard's farm near Sanger, California. There, on October 29, he took Leonard's testimony. A month later the commissioner was supposed to see Cobb and Speaker in his office in Chicago. They had demanded that Leonard make his accusations to their faces and in Landis's presence. When Leonard still would not leave his sanctuary, Landis postponed the meeting. That day the Cleveland management made Speaker's resignation public.

For the next few weeks the two men stewed. Finally they asked Landis for a formal hearing at which they would answer all allegations. They also wanted Joe Wood, baseball coach at Yale University since 1923, and Fred West, still employed at Navin Field, to be present. Landis agreed. On the morning of December 20, Cobb, Speaker, Wood, and West met with Landis in his little office in the People's Bank Building, overlooking Lake Michigan.

Cobb acknowledged to Landis that in writing the letter to Leonard, he had "connected myself with the proposition." But he went on to explain that he had only acted as an intermediary, passing along information from Wood to Leonard at Wood's request. He had also suggested Fred West when Wood asked if he knew anybody who would be willing to place bets. Cobb insisted that he bet nothing on the Detroit-Cleveland game in question. In fact he had put money on only two games in his life, losing $150 on the first two games of the 1919 World Series because those games had actually been fixed for Cincinnati to win. The September 25 game, though, was played squarely, as Cobb's failure to get more than a single and Speaker's two triples indicated. As for the meeting the previous afternoon under the stands, it had simply never happened.

Speaker also denied talking with Leonard, Cobb, and Wood after the game of the 24th or betting anything on the game the next day. In fact he knew nothing about anybody's betting until Leonard's charges came out. He also mentioned his two triples and pointed out that he hadn't even put Wood in the lineup for the game they were supposed to have fixed. Wood then corroborated what both Cobb and Speaker had said. Neither had bet anything; Speaker had known of no bets; the game had been honest. Wood identified the mysterious third party in the split of the winnings as "a friend of mine from Cleveland." West testified that he had put money on the game for Wood without knowing Leonard was involved, and that neither then nor at any other time had he placed bets for Cobb or Speaker.

Cobb and Speaker then demanded that Landis release all the material he had in the case, including what they, Wood, and West had just told him. The next day Landis did just that. When reporters asked what he intended to do now, he replied, "These men being out of baseball, no decision will be made, unless changed conditions in the future require it."

The release of the evidence in the Cobb-Speaker "scandal" prompted a storm of publicity across the nation comparable to what had followed Joe Jackson's and Eddie Cicotte's confessions that they and others had thrown the 1919 World Series. Baseball writers and editorialists analyzed and argued over the charges and denials. Now free to speak out, Cobb plaintively put his case to the public: "Is there any decency left on earth? I am beginning to doubt it. I know there is no gratitude. Here I am, after a lifetime in the game of hard, desperate and honest work forced to stand accused without ever having a chance to face my accuser. It is enough to try one's faith."[4] Out in California, Leonard told Runyon, "I have had my revenge."

Among the many people inside and outside baseball who rallied around the two baseball greats was Billy Evans, who called Leonard "gutless," a man the umpires had no respect for. "It is a crime," declared Evans, "that men of the stature of Ty and Tris should be blackened by a man of this caliber with charges that every baseballer knows to be utterly false."[5] Jack Graney, Charley Jamieson, and Harry Lunte, who had played for Cleveland in the questionable game, as well as Chick Shorten, in right field for Detroit that day, all denied any knowledge of a fix. "It's all the bunk," said Lunte.

In Augusta some five hundred of Cobb's supporters gathered around the flag-draped Confederate monument on Broad Street to cheer him. The dignitaries speaking in Cobb's behalf included Federal Judge William H. Barrett and Mayor William B. White. Cobb himself, facing a banner that read TY IS STILL OUR IDOL AND THE IDOL OF AMERICA, said that he was "sad and happy both on this occasion." Affirming that Speaker was "just as innocent as I," he declared his intention to do whatever was necessary to clear his name. Joe Wood's sworn testimony "exonerated me," he told reporters, "and my letter to Leonard cleared Speaker." "He may have his faults but dishonesty is not one of them," Charlie Cobb joined in. "I know him better than anyone else. He has lived clean and played the game clean."

If Dutch Leonard thought Cobb and Speaker had got together to run him out of baseball, Cobb would go to his grave believing that he had himself been the target of a conspiracy formed by Frank Navin, Ban Johnson, and Kenesaw M. Landis. An interesting theory, but one with more passion than logic behind it. Navin was doubtless telling the truth when he maintained that, well before the season ended, he had made up his mind not to keep Cobb for another year. In fact, he said, he had considered changing managers in 1925, when eleven or twelve Detroit players asked to be traded. He had even sought Heilmann's help in trying to do something about Cobb's deteriorating relations with his players. Cobb had been a failure as a manager, Navin believed, so he had been let go. Besides that, Johnson told newsmen, Leonard had been in possession of sworn statements from five members of the 1925 Tigers, attesting that Cobb had been determined to drive Leonard out of the game. Under the threat of a suit, Navin had had no choice but to settle with Leonard and then get rid of Cobb.

Johnson himself seems to have been convinced that Cobb and Speaker, while not guilty of fixing that game back in 1919, had at least committed serious improprieties. He had just not been satisfied with Cobb's explanation of the letter to Leonard. At the same time, the florid league president was fully willing to concede Cobb's integrity. "I love Ty Cobb," he declared. "I know Ty Cobb's not a crooked ballplayer. We let him go because he had written a peculiar letter about a betting deal that he couldn't explain and because I felt that he violated a position of trust." Speaker was "a different type of fellow," "cute." He had a long history of gambling—on both baseball games and horses—and of letting his players do too much of the same. Actually, Johnson contended, the American League had tried to protect both men's names by keeping the charges against them secret. Consequently he was shocked that Landis would release material in a matter that was supposed to have remained closed. At any rate, the "guilty" had been punished; neither Cobb nor Speaker would ever again play in the American League.

As for Landis, the hard-bitten commissioner had his own game to play. Landis's contest for supremacy with Ban Johnson had been going on ever since he became commissioner and was only incidentally related to the Cobb-Speaker affair. By December 20, when Landis took testimony from Cobb, Speaker, Wood, and West, a considerable number of people within baseball already had heard about Leonard's accusations and had connected them with Cobb's and Speaker's resignations. It was not likely that the messy business could be kept out of the newspapers much longer. At the same time, by releasing all the evidence in his possession, Landis could both embarrass Johnson, who thought he had everything tidied up, and put himself in effective control of the situation. Having just been re-elected to a new seven-year term by the club presidents, who had also upped his salary from $50,000 to $65,000 a year, Landis could afford to bid his time, watch Johnson become steadily less credible and more vulnerable, and eventually decide the fates of Cobb and Speaker on his own.

So nothing decisive happened in the weeks that followed Landis's public disclosure. Baseball men generally agreed that betting on games, usually though not always on one's own team, had been common in the pre-Landis years. "The Washington club went broke one day and won back all they lost the next day," Wood told Landis during the December 20 hearing. John McGraw, who had quietly dropped Hal Chase, a notorious gambler and fixer, from the Giants roster after the 1919 season and then had gone through another fixing scandal in 1924 that ended in the banishment of rookie Jimmy O'Connell, thought the current Cobb-Speaker controversy only demonstrated what happened when opposing players got too friendly.

Meanwhile Cobb and Speaker sought first one and then another means of redress. On December 26 Cobb caught a train in Augusta for Washington. Joined in the capital by Speaker and William H. Boyd, Speaker's highly regarded Cleveland attorney, Cobb sought to use his political connections to put pressure on Organized Baseball. But while Senators William H. Harris of Georgia, Pat Harrison of Mississippi, and other congressional acquaintances of Cobb were suitably indignant about what had happened and sympathetic to the predicament of the two ballplayers, they had to tell them that in light of the U. S. Supreme Court's decision four years earlier in the Federal League case, there was no basis for government action against baseball under the antitrust laws. At the Justice Department they were given the same word.

From Washington the three men traveled to Cleveland. Cobb went on to Detroit in the company of Edward S. Burke, "an admirer and friend," who was the same attorney who had represented the Detroit ball club and Cobb in the Stansfield affair back in 1909. In Detroit, Cobb retained James O. Murfin, a former Michigan circuit court judge, a regent at the University of Michigan, and one of the Motor City's best-known jurists. While Murfin and Joe Wood sat near by, Cobb paced his hotel room and told reporters that he'd been forced to resign, that stories about discontent on his teams had been exaggerated, that most of the Tiger players had sent him telegrams of regret when they heard he'd quit. At home, moreover, the wires, letters, and postcards were piling up from well-wishers across the country. Cobb then left for Augusta, while Wood entrained for New Haven and Yale, where the university authorities were discussing whether they wanted to keep an admitted gambler as their baseball coach. (They shortly decided that they did.)

As if the furor surrounding Cobb and Speaker were not enough to befuddle baseball fans, early in 1927 a new set of sensational allegations pre-empted the sports headlines. Charles "Swede" Risberg had been the regular shortstop on the 1917–20 Chicago White Sox teams. Along with seven other members of the 1919 American League champions, Risberg had been barred from Organized Baseball by Commissioner Landis in the aftermath of the Black Sox scandal. Now Risberg came down to Chicago from the Minnesota dairy farm he managed and, on New Year's Day, read to newsmen an affidavit he had just given to Landis.

In that document Risberg claimed that in 1917 the White Sox had contributed $45 to $50 apiece—$1100 in all—to bribe the Detroit team to "slough off" (throw) consecutive doubleheaders at Chicago on September 2–3. Everybody on the ball club contributed to the pot, said Risberg, even the imperious Eddie Collins. First-baseman Charles "Chick" Gandil collected the money and later traveled from New York to Philadelphia to deliver it to Tiger pitcher Bill James. The White Sox went on to take the pennant. When a reporter interrupted to ask whether Cobb had got any of the money, Risberg replied that he doubted it, adding, "There never was a better or straighter baseball player than Cobb, or Speaker, either, to my way of thinking." Near the end of the 1919 season, Risberg went on, the frontrunning White Sox had "sloughed off" two games to the Tigers, who were trying to finish in third place.

If Dutch Leonard and Swede Risberg were to be believed, the Tigers had received more than a little help from their friends in their unsuccessful pursuit of a portion of the 1919 World Series money. Within a couple of days, moreover, Chick Gandil and Oscar "Happy" Felsch, White Sox center fielder in 1917–20, had supported Risberg's charges in interviews with the press. Gandil and Felsch, though, were also banished "Black Sox." Like Risberg and like Dutch Leonard, too, they were embittered, revengeful men whose word practically everybody was ready to discount.

Commissioner Landis must have felt that he was earning his recently improved salary when he considered what to do about the two messes now on his hands. A crafty procrastinator so far in the Cobb-Speaker affair, he moved rather quickly to dispose of the Risberg matter. On January 5 and 6 Landis held an open hearing on Risberg's accusations in his Chicago office. At one point Irving Vaughn, a local sportswriter, counted seventy people crowded into the little room. The famous stage and screen humorist Will Rogers, jammed against the back wall, was one of them. Chain-smoking cigarettes and sitting to Landis's left, Risberg told his story again. On the 6th, Gandil, just in from Hurley, New Mexico, where he was managing a copper company's semipro team, joined him and again backed up his account.

Thirty-four others who had been with the Chicago and Detroit teams in 1917 also testified. To a man they contradicted what Risberg and Gandil said and agreed on a very different version of what happened. The pot the White Sox players made up, they said, was not in any way a bribe paid to the Tigers for losing but rather a reward or "bonus" given to the Detroit pitchers as well as Oscar Stanage, Detroit's first-string catcher, for beating the Red Sox, Chicago's closest rival that year, in twelve of the twenty-one games Boston and Detroit played, including nine shutouts. That was the money Gandil took from

New York to Philadelphia to give Bill James. Furthermore, the reward was the kind of thing ball clubs frequently did in those days and was common knowledge at the time. "Everybody and his brother knew about that," said little Harry "Nemo" Leibold, then a White Sox outfielder. Bernie Boland, former Detroit pitcher, finished his testimony and then leaned over Risberg and snarled, "You're still a pig," to which Risberg rather unimaginatively responded, "I'm not a pig."

The most dramatic moment in the hearings occurred when Cobb, who had come up from Augusta, was called to testify on the first day. "You could see by the expression on Cobb's face that he was very bitter at Landis," wrote Vaughn. Cobb vigorously denied any knowledge of what Risberg claimed had taken place and went on to declare, "There never has been a baseball game in my life that I played in, that I knew was fixed." When he finished he asked Landis sarcastically, "Want to swear me?" After that he left to catch a train home. As soon as he got back to Augusta, he rushed to the nearest telegraph office and wired Landis to ask every witness whether he knew of Cobb's ever being involved in any crookedness. When Landis obligingly posed the question, every past and present player in the room affirmed Cobb's honesty.

By the time Landis ended the hearings on the afternoon of January 6, it was pretty obvious to everyone who had followed the testimony (copiously reported by the wire services) that Risberg and Gandil—for revenge or for whatever other reason—had simply lied. However ethically dubious the cash "bonus" paid to the Tiger pitchers for beating the Red Sox may have been, that episode had nothing to do with the back-to-back doubleheaders Chicago took from Detroit. That was Landis's verdict, issued on January 12. In a 3000-word opinion he cleared everybody Risberg had accused of taking part in a fix in 1917. The payment to the Detroit pitchers was an act of "impropriety, reprehensible and censurable, but not corrupt."

Speaker and Cobb remained in limbo. It still seemed quite possible that Landis would do nothing, content to let their careers end under a cloud of doubt and suspicion. But then Landis summoned the American League club presidents to an emergency meeting on January 24 to inquire into press reports that the league had additional evidence on Cobb and Speaker it had not given to Landis, and that the two had been blacklisted within the league. By the time the meeting took place, Ban Johnson had publicly admitted being the source of the reports. Chronically afflicted with foot-in-mouth disease, he had finally blustered into an untenable situation.

Before the club presidents, Johnson had to concede that Landis was already in possession of all the evidence in the case that he (Johnson) had ever seen. After Johnson's physician certified that he was suffering from a variety of serious ailments and needed a rest, the assembled baseball executives voted unanimously to give him an indefinite leave of absence. Frank Navin became acting league president. Johnson would be back in time for the 1927 season opening. But in October of that year, in failing health and greatly reduced in power and influence, he would end his twenty-eight-year reign as boss and builder of the American League.

Now Landis could finally break his silence on Cobb and Speaker, who had been serviceable if unwitting pawns in his and Johnson's complicated power game. On January 27, Leslie O'Connor, Landis's secretary, gave out to newsmen copies of a written statement by baseball's "czar." After briefly reviewing Leonard's charges, Landis fully exonerated Cobb and Speaker. "This is the Cobb-Speaker case," Landis concluded. "These players have not been, nor are they now, found guilty of fixing a ball game. By no decent system of justice could such a finding be made."

Landis also announced that he had rescinded the releases given Cobb and Speaker and restored them to the active rosters of the Detroit and Cleveland clubs. That same day, as instructed by Landis, Navin wired Cobb in Augusta that he was free to sign with any American League team and that the Tigers would transfer his contract without cost. Cleveland similarly notified Speaker. By virtually insuring that the two ballplayers would remain in Ban Johnson's league, Landis administered a final embarrassment to the man who had said they would never play in his circuit again.

While Landis's main object in his handling of the Cobb-Speaker case appears to have been to use it to undermine and discredit Johnson, he doubtless intended to clear them anyway, sooner or later. That was not the way Cobb saw the outcome of the painful controversy, though. "The famous Landis 'verdict' was dictated to him by attorneys representing Speaker and myself," he contended near the end of his life. James O. Murfin, "an exalted man, tough," had "*dictated* and *forced* Landis' decision." Otherwise Cobb was ready to "*tear baseball* apart." Edward S. Burke had even been in touch with Charles Evans Huges, recently Secretary of State and before that U. S. Supreme Court justice, who, so Cobb claimed, had agreed for a $100,000 fee to represent Cobb in a suit against Organized Baseball. Even after his exoneration, while he hunted ducks in South Carolina to escape a barrage of public and private felicitations in Augusta, Cobb still pondered legal action. Sometimes he felt "ready to bust it [baseball]," ready to take "my pound of flesh."[6]

Instead of that, he jumped back into baseball with both feet. He'd intended to retire, he told a reporter by telephone from Georgetown, South Carolina. Yet even though he'd "suffered deeply," he'd decided "to go back and have one more big year." Cobb knew that despite his forty years, aching legs, and hefty salary, he was still a marketable commodity. He could still hit and draw people into the park. Right after Cobb's resignation as Tiger manager, John McGraw had wanted to start dickering with him, only to be told by Landis, "Lay off Cobb." Subsequently Jack Dunn, owner of the prosperous

Baltimore International League team, had offered Cobb $25,000 to come play there. After Landis's statement clearing him and Speaker, Cobb later claimed, Clark Griffith at Washington offered him $50,000 "just to show up at his park and appear on the field when I felt like it." Phil Ball, owner of the Browns, and his new manager, Cobb's friend Dan Howley, offered "something around $30,000" and probably a percentage of the gate receipts as well.[7]

Speaker, a year and a half younger than Cobb, was also still marketable. After talking with Miller Huggins and general manager Ed Barrow of the Yankees and then with Connie Mack and Eddie Collins, who had recently signed with the Athletics as player-coach, Speaker decided to take an offer from Clark Griffith. On January 31 he announced that he had signed with Washington for what baseball insiders figured to be about $35,000.

Cobb waited another week. In Augusta he received Connie Mack, who made the long trip down from Philadelphia determined to get him into an Athletics uniform. After eight straight cellar finishes and ten years out of the first division, the sixty-four-year-old manager and part-owner at Philadelphia had built another strong club. His Athletics, featuring outstanding young players like catcher Gordon "Mickey" Cochrane, outfielder Al Simmons, pitcher Bob "Lefty" Grove, and a muscular nineteen-year-old named Jimmy Foxx, for whom Mack had not yet found a regular place, had finished second and third the last two years. The crowds had started coming back to Shibe Park, but the Philadelphia management suffered from not having Sunday home dates—a handicap that cost the club at least a quarter of a million dollars a year.

Mack knew Cobb's presence would mean bigger gate receipts for the Athletics both at home and away; he also hoped the Georgian might be able to help his ball club. Mack offered Cobb either a $40,000 salary, a $25,000 bonus for signing, and another bonus of $10,000 to be paid at the end of the season, as newsmen close to the deal understood it; $70,000 in salary and bonus plus 10 percent of all exhibition game receipts, as Cobb remembered it; or a salary of $80,000 plus a $20,000 bonus if Philadelphia won the World Series, according to Mack's recollection. Whatever the specifics of the arrangement, it came out to a lot of money, enough to make Cobb again the best-paid player in baseball.[8]

Yet Cobb needed a big baseball salary even less in 1927 than he had when he took the Detroit manager's job six years earlier. It would be a matter of pride to come back as the highest-paid player, but Cobb was already rich and destined to get much richer. He signed with Mack because he wanted to play on a winning ball club, because he had come to revere the Athletics' leader, and, most of all, because once more he had something to prove. The integrity of the Cobb name again had been called into question. Coming back in 1927, as he later wrote Mack, was a matter of necessity—of "my vindication to the public."[9]

XI

Vindication

After spending a night and most of the next day in hiding in New York to avoid being hounded by reporters, Cobb took a train to Philadelphia late in the afternoon of February 8. That evening Mack—tall, thin, finely erect, dignified—introduced Cobb at the annual dinner of the Philadelphia chapter of the Base Ball Writers' Association. There Cobb officially announced that he would play for the Athletics in 1927. It would be a great pleasure, he told the seven hundred people in the Hotel Adelphi banquet room, to play for "Mr. Mack" and with Eddie Collins. He only wished he'd come to Philadelphia a few years earlier, "when I probably had more spring in my legs." Interrupted by shouts of "You still have enough left," he went on to promise that "There will be not a day, not an hour nor a minute next summer that I won't be giving the best that's in me." Beaming through the raucous standing ovation that followed, Cobb pondered the "strange twist" of his life: "I'd battled and feuded with the A's and their fans most of my career, needed police protection at Shibe Park and received a good dozen anonymous death-threats there."[1]

The next afternoon Cobb signed his contract at Mack's Shibe Park office and got measured for his first big-league uniform that would not have a "D" on the shirtfront. Since the end of the season, newsmen estimated, Mack had spent something like $250,000 to strengthen his team. Besides Collins and Cobb, thirty-eight-year-old Zack Wheat, an outfield star for eighteen years with Brooklyn in the National League, had also come to the Athletics. Moreover, Mack had paid Jack Dunn at Baltimore a handsome sum for shortstop Joe Boley, who now rejoined Lefty Grove and second-baseman Max Bishop, Boley's teammates on what had been one of the greatest minor-league outfits ever.

Cobb left town promising that he'd be at the Athletics' spring-training camp at Fort Myers, Florida, when it opened on March 1. Experienced baseball people knew better than to take Cobb at his word when it came to spring reporting dates. With Charlie and son Herschel, now ten, he made a leisurely trip down from Augusta in his $6000 Chrysler, stopping off at Sarasota to spend a few days with brother Paul, now a successful realtor, and his mother and sister Florence, who a few years earlier had also moved there. Cobb went on alone to Fort Myers, the southernmost of the major-league training sites, and arrived on Sunday night, March 6. The next day he weighed in at 192½ pounds, got into uniform, and went out to oblige a dozen photographers and newsreel cameramen by posing with just about everybody, including the octogenarian Thomas A. Edison. For the moving-picture crews, Cobb tossed a ball underhand to the famed inventor from about eight feet and almost had his sparse hair parted by Edison's sharp line drive.

On March 9, Cobb appeared in his first game as a Philadelphia Athletic. Charlie and Roswell Herschel Cobb, Amanda and Florence Cobb, and Paul Cobb, his wife, and Paul, Jr., all came down the sixty or so miles from Sarasota to see him in action against the Giants. Cobb played right field, doubled his first time up off Virgil Cheeves, later made a nice catch going back on Bill Terry's drive, and retired after six innings. When Mack, who had wondered how Cobb would respond to instructions, waved his famous scorecard to position his outfielders, Cobb "saluted me as a soldier salutes a general and followed orders." Cobb felt so good physically and about things in general that he was already talking about maybe playing another year beyond this one. "You'll see a new Ty Cobb on the ball field this summer," he told St. Louis sportswriter Sid Keener.[2]

An incident occurred eight days later at St. Petersburg that was all-too reminiscent of the old Cobb. The Athletics were ahead of the Boston Braves 5–0 in the top of the fourth, with Eddie Collins at bat and Cobb on deck. The plate umpire was Frank Wilson, who had worked his way back up to the National League staff after being fired by Ban Johnson a few years earlier. Cobb's frequent adversary in the past, Wilson now suddenly whirled and yelled, "Get out of the park, Cobb; get out of the park!" As Cobb came forward protesting that he had said nothing, Wilson snatched off his mask and, according to Cobb, "said something about beating my head in."[3] At Collins's urging Cobb returned to the bench, where he had a drink of water, fussed with his glove, and then sat on the bench with a soft drink (no doubt a Coke). At that point Wilson turned to the near-capacity crowd and declared the game forfeited to Boston. Emil Fuchs, president of the Braves, and Al Lang, a prominent St. Petersburg businessman and sports promoter, rushed onto the field and hastily arranged for a second game. Cobb refused to participate.

With Mack's approval, Cobb sat out three subsequent Athletics-Braves games that spring because Wilson was umpiring. In one of those encounters, on March 23 at Fort Myers, the Athletics razzed Wilson so hard that he chased every player on the Philadelphia bench, fifteen in all. Cobb watched the spectacle from the stands. A couple of days later the commissioner's office notified him that he would have to pay a $100 fine for his run-in with Wilson at St. Petersburg. In Philadelphia the fans could rest assured that Cobb's presence on the ballfield would generate as much electricity as it always had.

Cobb did play in several other exhibition games against the Giants and minor-league teams before leaving Mack's ball club at Waycross, Georgia, so he could drive to Augusta, drop off his automobile there, and take a train north with his family. Minus Ty, Jr., who was already enrolled in prep school at Princeton, New Jersey, the Cobbs arrived in Philadelphia on April 2 and moved into a house Cobb had leased in Cynwd, an exclusive Philadelphia suburb to the northwest of the city. The next day he debuted before about five thousand of his new home fans in the opener of the annual spring series with the city's woeful National League team. Playing the whole game in rain and sleet, Cobb did nothing at bat, got caught stealing once, and muffed a foul fly. His team won anyway, 5–1.

He played all the way in the remaining four games of the city series, and to bring in a little more money for Mack (and maybe for himself as well), he also went the full nine innings in exhibition games at Baltimore and Newark. By opening day he had again brought himself around to top physical condition. In what was described as "his slow, drawling manner," he told the Knights of Columbus at their luncheon in the Hotel Adelphi that he was "enjoying the happiest days of my baseball career." He would always be grateful to "the team and the city that took me to its heart in my darkest days last winter."[4]

On April 12 the Athletics opened the season in New York. Seventy-two thousand people, according to Ed Barrow, packed Yankee Stadium for what turned out to be a historic occasion. The game itself was nothing extraordinary. The Yankees knocked out Lefty Grove and went on to win 8–3 behind Waite Hoyt. Cobb, batting third and playing in right, received a floral horseshoe from the Georgia Society of New York City and a big ovation when he came up in the first inning, and proceeded to ground out. His one hit of the day was a bunt single in the sixth, after which he took third on Sammy Hale's single and center-fielder Earle Combs's wide throw to third, and scored on Dudley Branom's single. The historic significance of the game had to do with the presence of no fewer than thirteen future Hall of Famers: Mack and Huggins as managers; Cobb, Collins, Wheat, Grove, Al Simmons, Jimmy Foxx, and Mickey Cochrane among the Athletics players; Ruth, Hoyt, Lou Gehrig, and Herb Pennock among the Yankees.

In evaluating the Athletics' prospects, the baseball press tended to dwell on the team's graybeards. Besides Cobb, Collins, and Wheat, Mack had Jack Quinn, a forty-two-year-old righthander who had compiled 180 wins over eighteen seasons in the American, National, and Federal leagues and would last seven more years in the big time. "Connie Mack . . . appears to have an interesting but not highly valuable collection of antiques," wrote the New York

Times's James R. Harrison. "Collins and Cobb are not covering half the ground that they did ten years ago."[5] The key to the team's future, though, was in youngsters like Cochrane, Simmons, Foxx, Grove, Bishop, and Boley, and in veteran but still relatively young players like infielder Jimmy Dykes and out-fielder Edmund "Bing" Miller. Simmons was already an established star, a powerful righthanded hitter who, despite an awkward "foot-in-the-bucket" style, had batted .384 and .343 in the past two seasons. Cobb befriended Simmons, sometimes shared a room with him on the road, and offered batting tips; but not even Cobb would risk tampering with Simmons's way of hitting.

Cobb's new team was a good one, possessing the ingredients for the powerhouse that would win three pennants and two world's championships, 1929–31. In 1927, however, the Athletics and the rest of the league were up against maybe the finest team ever assembled. With Ruth hitting sixty homers to break his own record and Gehrig adding forty-seven and driving in 175 runs, the Yankees piled up 110 victories, won the pennant by eighteen-and-one-half games, and then swept Pittsburgh in the World Series.

Whether or not the Athletics had a realistic chance for the pennant, Cobb intended to go full tilt and leave no doubt that he was really earning the biggest bimonthly paychecks in baseball. At Washington he made seven hits in three games and, in game two, stole home on rookie righthander Alvin Crowder. As Washington sportswriter Shirley Povich described it, "Cobb beat the throw easily, breaking into a broad smile as he bounded to his feet after the slide."[6] That was the highlight of the Athletics' 3–1 win.

Cobb was hitless in the home opener on April 20, an 8–5 victory over New York before a capacity 35,000. But he had two hits the next day (a 13–5 drubbing by the Yankees) and then tripled, singled, and stabbed Combs's drive against the fence in the final game of the series, which Philadelphia won 4–3. Four days later, at Boston, Cobb hit two singles and a double and drove in two runs. With the bases loaded in the seventh, he picked his spot and stole home on pitcher Tony Welzer, hook-sliding around catcher Grover Hartley. He ended the game by tearing in from right to take a line drive and then beat the runner back to first for an unassisted double play. All in all a remarkable game for a forty-year-old.

A week later, at Shibe Park, the Athletics were trailing the Red Sox by a run in the bottom of the eighth when Cobb hit one over the right-field wall into Twentieth Street for an apparent homerun. Referring to an old, rarely used rule, plate umpire Red Ormsby called it a foul ball because it veered foul after leaving the park. Cobb put up something of a protest; Simmons, the on-deck hitter, complained at such length that Ormsby threw him out. Cobb then resumed his position in the batter's box, but just as the pitcher started his motion, he jumped out and back, bumping Ormsby with his shoulder. At that, despite Cobb's insistence that the bump had been accidental, Ormsby also ejected Cobb. When the game ended 3–2 in Boston's favor, fans threw bottles and seat cushions and Ormsby had to leave under police escort.

Upon reading Ormsby's report on the Philadelphia fracas, Ban Johnson, back from his "furlough," quickly notified both Cobb and Simmons that they were under indefinite suspension. Cobb was livid when he found Johnson's wire waiting for him in Cleveland. Although he did not plan to play there anyway because he had pulled a muscle in an exhibition game at Buffalo on the way, he regarded the suspension, levied by the man who had recently tried to ease him out of the league, as more shabby treatment from Johnson. "It's all a mystery to me," he said. "I've stood for a lot of things in the past, but I'm not going to stand for them any longer." Cobb's admirers in Detroit were just as upset, because his suspension interfered with their plans for a big homecoming for the Georgian when the Athletics moved into Navin Field on Tuesday, May 10. Telegrams of protest poured into Johnson's Chicago office. Johnson, in St. Louis, commented that Cobb's offense "in particular is a serious one," inasmuch as he had not only shoved Ormsby but then incited the crowd against the umpire.[7]

After losing three straight at Cleveland with Cobb and Simmons in the stands, the Athletics took a Lake Erie steamer over to Detroit. Waiting to greet Cobb at the boat dock was a delegation led by Major John T. Smith and James O. Murfin, Cobb's attorney in the controversy over Leonard's charges the previous winter. Cobb was escorted to the Masonic Temple for a luncheon in his honor. Connie Mack; Fielding Yost, longtime University of Michigan football coach; and George Moriarty, Cobb's old teammate and his successor as Tiger manager, were among the speakers. Toastmaster Murfin broke into the proceedings with the dramatic announcement that Johnson had just lifted Cobb's suspension, as well as that of Simmons. Ty Cobb Day at Navin Field could go off as planned.

Cobb then rode in a police-escorted motorcade to the ballpark. Despite a threat of rain and uncertainty about whether Cobb would play, 27,410 came out to Navin Field. Besides the inevitable floral horseshoe, Cobb received a new automobile and a silver service from his well-wishers in pre-game ceremonies broadcast by a local radio station. His first time up, with Collins on first, he lifted Earl Whitehill's pitch into the small overflow in right, limped into second, and then limped much faster coming home on Simmons's hit. Many of the same people who the previous summer had hooted him anytime he left the dugout now stood and cheered lustily. When he went out to right field, he walked up and down in front of the temporary bleachers, signing dozens of autographs and holding up the resumption of play. Later he drew a walk, struck out, and hit into a forceout. With the Athletics safely ahead, he retired after seven innings in favor of Bill Lamar. Ty Cobb Day ended with a testimonial dinner given by the Intercollegiate Alumni Asssociation of Detroit.

The next day Cobb and Simmons got word from Johnson that they would have to pay fines of $200 each for their part in the disturbance at Philadelphia. Shrugging off that irritation, Cobb doubled twice in the Athletics' 3–1 victory at Navin Field, doubled again in a losing effort on May 12, and, in the last game at Detroit, beat out a bunt, subsequently stole third, and almost stole home but missed the plate. In the midst of a hitting streak that eventually stretched to twenty-one games, he was batting around .400 and playing as zestfully as ever, albeit not as recklessly.

The Athletics' hopes of overtaking the Yankees were all but ended May 30–June 2, when New York won four of five games before big crowds at Shibe Park and moved six ahead of the locals. Although the White Sox were just back of the Yankees at the time, they soon began to fade into the second division. By the end of June, New York was already so far ahead that the pennant race was virtually over. Philadelphia, Washington, and Detroit were left to jockey for second, third, and fourth.

On June 18 Cobb strained his back and hip running out a ground ball. Except for a few pinch-hitting appearances, he was sidelined for nearly two weeks. In his third game after getting back into the lineup, at Boston against the hapless Red Sox, he executed his tenth theft of the year and his third of home, beating Del Lundgren's pitch and again hooking around Grover Hartley. After slumping badly in June, he began to sting the ball again on a western trip. At Detroit on July 19 he reached another career milestone when he lined one of big Sam Gibson's pitches for a double and thereby collected his four-thousandth hit in the majors. It was a mark that for many decades would look absolutely unattainable by anyone else. In that less record-fixated time, Cobb became aware of his achievement only when he read about it in the late editions of the afternoon Detroit papers.

"This was the Ty Cobb of ten or twelve years ago," marveled Henry P. Edwards after watching an old-fashioned exploit at Cleveland's League Park the following week. Reaching first on an error, Cobb then pulled off a delayed steal—a rarely seen maneuver by 1927—and made it all the way home on Luke Sewell's throw over an unguarded second base and then center fielder Bill Jacobson's wild throw to the plate. When Edwards asked him about that play while they waited through a rainout the next day, Cobb remarked that he couldn't understand why younger ballplayers didn't take more risks. Attributing the lack of daring in today's game to the lively ball, he went on to wonder aloud what the likes of Lajoie or Crawford would have been able to do with it. Baseball was no longer played "scientifically," he lamented, nor was there as much hustle as in the old days. Too many second-division teams let down as soon as they dropped from contention. "How foolish" that was, because the clubowners would reward hard work. "But you can't tell that to every player and have it sink in."[8]

Cobb showed Edwards and other Cleveland onlookers what he meant by hustle when play resumed on July 24. Late in the first game of a double-header (which the Athletics swept), he came all the way in from right field to cover home on a rundown play, and ended up taking Grove's return toss of Dykes's wild throw in a vain attempt to tag a sliding Indian runner.

Yet he got tired, very tired. Besides spending as much time as possible in bed while on the road, he went to a lighter bat—34 to 36 ounces now as opposed to 40 ounces in past years. He also began carrying a portable phono-graph with him on road trips after he found that listening to a half-hour or so of music by the famed concert violinist Fritz Kreisler helped him to relax. After a game he undressed slowly, took a leisurely shower, and usually left the locker room after everybody else.

Carefully conserving his energy and particularly his troublesome legs, Cobb continued to be a pronounced asset to his team. Late in July, Simmons tore a groin muscle and was out for six weeks. Mack moved Cobb to center field and into the cleanup spot in the batting order. Walter French went from left to right; Zack Wheat took over in left and hit well, although he and Cobb had to chase after many drives that went between them. Cobb, after going hitless in twenty at bats, the worst slump of his career, broke out with a homerun and single to drive home two in a win over the White Sox at Shibe. That was the start of a hitting surge that included a 17–25 performance in six games against Chicago and St. Louis in mid-September. In the three games against the White Sox, moreover, he stole four bases.

Despite the loss of Simmons, the Athletics were a hot club in August and September. By winning thirty-six of their last forty-nine games while Wash-ington and Detroit were obligingly having losing streaks, they took firm pos-session of second place. So firm, in fact, that after going 0–6 in a September 21 doubleheader against the Browns and then failing in three times up over five innings against Cleveland the next day, Cobb left the game, showered and dressed, and returned to the dugout to say goodbye to Mack and his teammates. With a wave to some friends sitting in nearby box seats, he left the ballpark with his wife. With Mack's blessings, he had decided to "get away early and attend to some hunting."[9] Again he was going out to the Grand Te-ton country, this time accompanied by Charlie. On their way they intended to stop off in Chicago for the heavyweight championship rematch between Gene Tunney and Jack Dempsey. Along with more than 100,000 others at Soldier Field, they would gasp as Tunney went down and took the fabled "long count" in the seventh round before rising to continue outfighting Dempsey and re-tain his title.

Cobb's baseball future was very much up in the air when he left Philadel-phia. Mack had given him "a cordial invitation to return," he told reporters before his last game, but he wasn't sure what he'd do. As he had been saying for six or seven years, he acknowledged "getting old" and not being able to "step around the way I'd like to." Still, "I've played baseball ever since I was 16 years old and it's pretty hard to break old habits." [10]

Certainly his "campaign of vindication" had been a resounding success. Appearing in 133 of his team's 154 games, he finished with a .357 batting average, fifth best in the league. (Harry Heilmann won the fourth and last of his odd-year titles, hitting .398.) Cobb knocked in ninety-five runs, hit five homers, and stole twenty-two bases. Only Bob Meusel of the Yankees (24) and George Sisler of the Browns (26) had more steals. It had been a solid season for a man of forty years—or any age. Stan Baumgartner, a former Athletic pitcher and now a local sportswriter, quoted Mack as crediting Cobb with the team's second-place finish. Rumors that some of his players were unhappy because they thought Cobb had played for his own statistics were "bunk," said Mack. "I never handled a finer baseball man, one who gave me less trouble than Cobb." [11] Yet because of the Yankee runaway the past season, and of course the continuing absence of Sunday baseball at home, the Philadelphia franchise had not made much money despite the team's excellent performance in the last part of the season. Whether or not Mack actually paid Cobb the $20,000 World Series bonus, as he later said he did, the Athletics were in no shape to carry Cobb at the same salary for 1928.

Cobb and his wife returned from their hunting and camping excursion at the beginning of November. After a couple of weeks in Wyoming, they had decided to try northern Arizona as well. All told, Cobb had shot two brown bear, two elk, two deer, and an antelope—the largest haul he ever made hunting big game. Instead of heading straight for Augusta, they traveled to Philadelphia by way of Detroit, where Cobb told reporters, "I am sound physically, but there is no telling what might happen if I tried to drag on." [12] The word he got from Mack when they met in Philadelphia was that the ball club simply could not afford him. Cobb would remain on the Athletics' reserve list and have to be waived in the usual way, but the club would not interfere in whatever deal Cobb might work out for himself elsewhere.

Back at the Bellevue-Stratford, Cobb invited a group of reporters up to his room. "Well, dearie, I have been released," he greeted his wife. "I'm glad of it," she said. Of course Cobb had not actually been released; that would come only if nobody claimed him on waivers. "One thing, I do not have to worry," he told the newsmen. "Whatever happens, I am going to consider my own wishes and comfort first." [13] The interview was interrupted when seventeen-year-old Ty, Jr., burst into the room, having caught a train down from Princeton to see his parents for the first time since September. Already six-feet tall and weighing about 175 pounds, the Cobbs' first-born played guard on his prep school football team, although tennis was his first love.

Then the Cobbs went home. In fact Mack never asked waivers on Cobb, although he undoubtedly would have if Cobb had wanted to sign with another team. In January, when Cobb was in Washington to straighten out some personal income tax matters, he remarked, "I have been in harness long enough." Asked whether he might consider managing again, he answered sharply: "Being a manager is a lot of grief. You never know when someone is going to chop your feet out from under you." Twelve days later, in Augusta, he confirmed that he had received offers from two other clubs, rumored to be the St. Louis Browns and the Chicago Cubs. Evidently John McGraw was no longer interested in him. No, Cobb said, he wasn't dickering with Mack; he still wasn't sure whether or not he wanted to come back.[14]

Meanwhile Clark Griffith at Washington, also having gone through a disappointing year at the gate, gave Tris Speaker his unconditional release. Like Cobb, "Spoke" had come back in the aftermath of the Leonard furor to have a fine year. Playing all season as the Senators' regular center fielder, he had batted .327 and fielded his position capably, although he no longer covered the vast expanses he once had. Early in February, after talking by telephone with Mack, who was down at Fort Myers golfing and making arrangements for spring training, Speaker signed to play in 1928 with the Athletics. Baseball pundits put his salary at around $30,000, but in all likelihood it was substantially less than that.

Cobb remained unsigned—by Mack or anybody else. The Athletics' manager said repeatedly that he'd like to have Cobb for another year but only if he took a sizable cut. Toward the end of February, Mack let it be known that he had just received a long letter from Cobb and "I really think he is going to be with us again." I don't care how many games he plays," added the dean of baseball field leaders, "just so he is on the team."[15]

On his way to Forida to open spring training, Mack stopped off at Augusta to talk with Cobb and make him a definite offer. Subsequently Thomas Shibe, Athletics president, called to urge him to come into the fold. On March 1, Cobb wired Mack in Fort Myers that he accepted his terms, which he described to the press as "highly satisfactory to me." While he'd had other offers, all along he'd had his mind made up to play for Philadelphia if he played at all. Mack's "kind persistence" had finally persuaded him.[16]

Cobb's willingness to play another season defies rational explanation. Although neither he nor Mack ever disclosed his salary terms, they probably provided for less than half what he had been paid in 1927. Cobb no longer had anything to prove; his play the previous year should have given him as much vindication—as much demonstrated proof of both his dedication to the game and his durable talents—as anybody needed. While his batting eye was still sharp, the legs were about gone. Beating out bunts, going for the extra base, sliding on much-scarred thighs and hips were painful things for a forty-one-year-old man to have to do day after day. Crippling injury was more of a threat now than ever. In recent years, moreover, Cobb had often complained of not having more time for his family and particularly of not being able to take a summertime vacation when they could all be together. Yet again he was ready to take up the disruptive routine of a professional ballplayer. What it all came down to was that after twenty-three major-league seasons, Cobb was just not ready to retire. Coming back in 1928 had nothing to do with money, with setting more records, or with anything else except Cobb's emotional need to stay in uniform.

Instead of making the trip to Fort Myers right away, Cobb decided to work out locally with the New York Giants, who were training in Augusta in 1928. He would join the Athletics later when they came up for a scheduled game with the Giants. At Augusta, Cobb took the field only after the Giants were through for the day, promising to coach anybody willing to pitch batting practice for him. Among those who lingered to get hitting instruction from Cobb was Frank "Lefty" O'Doul, a fun-loving San Franciscan who had failed in the American League as a pitcher and then come back up as an outfielder. Cobb worked with O'Doul mainly on loosening his grip so he could manipulate the bat and line the ball to different fields. O'Doul stuck with the Giants that year and went on to lead the National League in hitting twice (with Philadelphia and Brooklyn) and compile a .349 career average in the majors. Russell "Red" Reeder, a rookie catcher who also sought Cobb's help, remembered him as "a smart, crafty, dynamic and intense batting instructor. . . . Ty Cobb absorbed you. You became *his* pupil. When he talked batting, if you were absorbing the instruction, his eyes glittered."[17]

When the Athletics got into Augusta on March 16, Cobb and Charlie went to the team's hotel to renew acquaintances, especially with Collins, Speaker, and their wives. While they were there, Shirley Cobb, now sixteen, and a friend came in to beg Cobb to pass up the ballgame that afternoon and come watch Shirley perform in a horseshow. Cobb, though, was determined to be in uniform with the team. Three innings into the game with the Giants, he took over for Walter French in right. Playing the rest of the way, he popped up and hit into a forceout.

Cobb returned to Florida on the train with the team. In games against the Giants and the St. Louis Cardinals, he performed spiritedly alongside Speaker in center and Simmons in left. Zack Wheat had been released over the winter, but the Athletics still had Collins, Cobb, Quinn, and now Speaker in the forty-plus range. Including coach William "Kid" Gleason, who had led the White Sox in 1919–23, Mack employed no fewer than four ex-managers. While Collins intended to play only occasionally in 1928, Cobb and Speaker were supposed to be regulars. Those two plus Simmons had hit for a combined average of .358 in 1927. It was apparent to those who watched the Athletics closely that spring, however, that a Cobb-Speaker-Simmons outfield would be the slowest in the league. Wrote the New York *Times*'s Richards Vidmer from Florida, "the Athletic outfield situation simmers down to two important items: Cobb can't come in and Speaker can't go back."[18]

Cobb had been with the ball club less than a week when he received word at Fort Myers that his wife was about to undergo surgery at an Augusta hospital. After assuring Mack that he would rejoin the team in Philadelphia in time for the series with the Phillies, Cobb hurried north in a rented car. Charlie Cobb's surgery, probably undertaken to repair damage done by five childbirths, of which the last two had been quite difficult, lasted about two hours and was termed a complete success. Cobb stayed on in Augusta until April 2, sparring with reporters about how much he had recently made in the stock market, how sound his legs were, and how many games he would play. When he left for Philadelphia, his wife was out of the hospital but still in need of several weeks of convalescence.

So, alone, Cobb arrived to start his twenty-fourth big-league season. After playing every inning of three games against the Phillies and one at Baltimore, he pronounced himself in the best shape in years. Mack put him down to start in right field in the season opener against New York, with Speaker in center and Bing Miller in left in place of Simmons, who was hospitalized with tonsilitis and rheumatoid ankles.

Some 25,000 people gathered in cold, misty rain at Shibe Park to see their favorites open the season against New York. In a close replay of the 1927 opener, the Yankees got to Lefty Grove and his successors for eight runs, while their own pitcher, Herb Pennock, held the Athletics to three. Cobb, hitting second, singled his first time up and waited out Pennock twice. Two days later, after a cancellation because of the cold, the two teams hit three homeruns apiece, Lou Gehrig's winning it 8–7. Cobb had two hits and two runs driven in. On April 16, when the Athletics lost their third straight, to Washington at Shibe, Washington sportswriter Frank Young heard scattered jibes, mostly directed at Cobb, after balls dropped between him and Speaker. The two would have to hit .350 each, thought Young, "to make up for their ground-covering shortcomings."[19]

For a while that spring it seemed as if Mack's middle-aged outfield tandem might do just that. In the Yankees' home opener, played before 55,000, the fans jeered Cobb when he lost a fly ball and was thrown out trying to go from first to third on Speaker's hit, and Speaker as well when he failed to get under a short fly. But with the score 1–1 in the top of the ninth, the pair won it for Grove, Cobb hitting George Pipgras's pitch for a triple over Earle Combs's head, and Speaker following with a sacrifice fly. That was the Athletics' first win after four losses.

Both Cobb and Speaker, particularly Cobb, continued to hit with customary authority for the next several weeks. Each had a bases-loaded triple in a

10–0 shutout pitched by forty-three-year old Jack Quinn at Washington on
April 26. The game ended, moreover, when Cobb fielded a bloop base hit and
threw to second, where Speaker was waiting to put the tag on an over-sliding
Ossie Bluege. Cobb was full of fire during Detroit's first stay at Shibe Park.
Besides razzing Earl Whitehill unmercifully until the Athletics knocked him
out, Cobb singled twice, stretched another hit into a double, and scored from
first on a wild throw. The next day he singled and doubled and scored ahead
of Speaker's homer to provide the winning margin over the Tigers. In the
Monday finale Cobb and Speaker each drove in a run in Grove's 10–0 white-
wash. Against Cleveland the next week, Cobb hit his first (and only) homer of
the year into Twentieth Street beyond Shibe Park's right-field fence. Yet even
though he pulled off double steals with both Speaker and Max Bishop in that
series, to Gordon Cobbledick of the Cleveland *Plain Dealer* he seemed "pathetically slow."[20]

After their poor start, the Athletics won twenty-one of their next twenty-
five games and pulled well in front of everybody except the Yankees, who were
even hotter than the year before. New York remained three-and-a-half games
up after the two teams split a doubleheader on Thursday, May 24, before a
Philadelphia crowd that not only filled every seat but sat in the aisles and on
the steel girders, stood in a roped-off area in left, and swarmed over the fence
in right when the gates were finally locked. On Friday, before a turnout that
merely occupied all the seats, the Yankees took both ends of another doubleheader. They also won on Saturday to leave town leading by six and one-
half. For the second year in a row they had come into Philadelphia relatively
early in the season, taken four out of five, and put the Athletics at a disadvan-
tage they could never make up.

Speaker had to stop playing regularly after he was banged up in an outfield
collision with Bing Miller on May 21. Cobb, suffering from what was described as "nervous indigestion," yielded right field for a three-game series in
Boston to rookie George "Mule" Haas, but he was back in the lineup on June
2 at Chicago. Meanwhile Simmons had finally returned, taking over left field
while Miller moved into center and Speaker accepted his new role as bench-
warmer and occasional pinch hitter.

That was not for Cobb, at least not yet. He was hitting well above .300
and still capable of a trick or two. On June 15, in the eighth inning of a game
at Cleveland, he hit a bad-bounce double by Lou Fonseca at first base to drive
in Grove and took third on Bishop's groundout. With the Athletics safely ahead,
he caught relief pitcher George Grant not paying attention to him and came
in under Luke Sewell's tag for a clean steal of home. That was the thirty-fifth
time in regular-season play he had successfully completed baseball's most difficult offensive maneuver.[21] It was also to be his last.

The trouble was that, for all his cleverness and savvy on the bases and afield, he just could not compensate for his failing legs. In that same Cleveland series he twice hit line drives off the screen atop the fence in right and both times had to stop at first. In New York a few days later he made three hits but also fell on his face going after Ben Paschal's bounding single and let in two runs. Now he regularly grounded into double plays, something that almost never happened ten years ago. It was harder and harder for him to take the extra base; even outfielders with mediocre arms managed to throw him out.

On July 18, in a game against Detroit at Shibe Park, Cobb took a pitch from Sam Gibson on his right wrist and had to leave in the fourth inning. Up to then he had rapped out a single but also got picked off first by Gibson and later played Charley Gehringer's hit off his chest into the right-field corner for a two-base error. After a few days the wrist had healed enough for him to pinch hit and strike out against Washington to end a game that broke an Athletics winning streak at seven. Two days later he played both ends of a doubleheader at Chicago. The day after that, July 27, he singled and doubled to help pile up a lead for Grove before White Sox reliever George "Sarge" Connally hit him in the right side of the chest with a pitch and forced him to give way to French. X-rays, taken when the team got to St. Louis, revealed nothing broken, but Cobb was badly bruised and so sore he could barely lift his right arm.

That game in Chicago—Cobb's eighty-sixth of 1928—was his last as a regular. At that point he was batting .332. His slowness afield, though, was such a drawback that when he was ready to play again, Mack decided to stay with the younger and more mobile outfield of Simmons in left, Miller in center, and Haas in right. Meanwhile Mack had finally made hard-hitting Jimmy Foxx his regular third baseman and was alternating Jimmy Dykes at first against lefthanders with Joe Hauser against righthanders. Playing at a torrid pace, the Athletics had gained so much ground on the injury-riddled Yankees that a pennant had come to seem a real possibility. So Cobb took his place on the bench with Speaker and Collins, three men from another era who had once battled each other fiercely and now sat watching a new generation of ballplayers play a different kind of baseball.

For the first time since the early part of the 1906 season, Cobb found himself a substitute, and an infrequently used one at that. On August 28 he made his first appearance in two weeks, striking out as a pinch hitter in the nightcap of a doubleheader sweep of the White Sox at Shibe Park. When the Athletics played an exhibition game in a minor-league town to try to make up some of the money lost by not having Sunday home dates, not only Cobb but Speaker and Collins as well would appear to fatten the crowd. Stripped of his first basemen when Dykes and Hauser were both injured, Mack turned not to Cobb, who had gained a fair amount of experience at the position in exhibition and spring-training games over the years, but to Ossie Orwoll, a good-hitting rookie pitcher. To Cobb's credit, he understood that Mack was in the midst of a pennant race and could ill afford to play him or anybody else out of sentiment. Besides, going out there everyday had come to be, as he later put it, "hellishly hard."[22]

On September 7 Mack's newly constituted ball club gained a tie for first place by winning two from the Red Sox while New York lost to Washington. The Yankees won the next day, but in sweeping another doubleheader at Boston, the Athletics took a half-game lead—the first time one of Mack's teams had been in first place that late in fourteen years. That set up a climactic four-game series in New York. On Sunday the 10th the largest crowd in baseball history up to then—put at 85,265 by Ed Barrow—jammed Yankee Stadium to see George Pipgras shut out Philadelphia 5–0 in the first game of a doubleheader and the Yankees take the second game as well, 7–3 on Bob Meusel's grandslam homer. Fifty-one thousand were there on Tuesday as Ruth hit a two-run homer, his forty-ninth, in the bottom of the eighth inning to break Lefty Grove's fourteen-game winning streak, 5–3. The Athletics salvaged the fourth game, before some 35,000 on Wednesday, 4–3 on Bishop's ninth-inning homer. Having lost sixteen of twenty-two games with the Yankees that year, Mack and his men left New York with pennant hopes sagging. They pulled to within half a game of first a few days later, but the Yankees just kept winning. At Detroit on September 28 they clinched their third straight pennant.

Cobb's last time at bat in American League competition came on September 11 in the third game of the series in New York. After Ruth's homer put the Yankees up 5–3, Mack sent Cobb up to hit for Dykes at the start of the ninth. He lifted a pitch from Henry Johnson back of third, where shortstop Mark Koenig easily made the catch. Cobb did make two more appearances in an Athletics uniform. On September 13, in an exhibition game at Albany, New York, against the local Eastern League team, he played five innings and hit two singles; and the next day, in still another stop on the circuitous route the Athletics took from New York to Cleveland, Cobb went most of a game at Toronto and again singled twice. Only about two thousand people saw his last outing as a member of a major-league ballclub.

During the Athletics' stay in Cleveland, on September 17, Cobb summoned the baseball writers on hand and announced that he would retire at the end of the season. He assured the skeptics who had listened to him talk retirement for years that this time he meant it. "Never again," he told the writers, "will I be an active player." It would be hard to leave the game that had "paved the road to lift me to a place of prominence and affluence." But the past season had been "hard labor." "I'm just baseball tired and want to quit." "Why, I scarcely know my children," he admitted. The time had come "to get out of the game and play with my kids before they grow up and leave me." Besides, he had promised his wife a trip to Europe. Connie Mack, he went on, was "the squarest man in baseball," a manager for whom it had been a privilege to play.[23]

Ten days later, as soon as they learned that New York had clinched the pennant, both Cobb and Speaker packed their bags in Chicago and said good-bye to Mack and the rest of the team. Speaker was on his way to join a hunting party in Wyoming. When he returned he would sign to manage Newark in the International League. Cobb caught a train for Detroit and a session with his dentist.

In such an unspectacular way Cobb's long, tempestuous, glittering career came to an end. Following his vindication year, the 1928 season had been an anticlimax, one in which he simply extended the numerous career records he already held. Through July it had been a tough but respectable season; after that he had been an onlooker most of the time while the ball club made its pennant bid. In ninety-five games and 353 times at bat, he hit .323. His hits, which included a homer, twenty-seven doubles, and four triples, were good for forty runs batted in. His old legs carried him to only five stolen bases, but at least there was that last satisfying theft of home at Cleveland.

The American League's official records gave Cobb 3,033 games played, 4,191 hits, 2,245 runs scored, 893 stolen bases, and a lifetime batting average of .367. At the time he retired, moreover, he had the most career runs batted in (1,933) and the season record for stolen bases (96 in 1915). He was also second to Speaker in career doubles (725) and to Sam Crawford in triples (294). In 11,429 at bats, Cobb had struck out just 357 times—about once in every thirty-two official plate appearances. As Walter Johnson (and lots of other pitchers) had complained, it had been hard to get a strike past him.

A man who loved figures, whether baseball or financial, Cobb would remain highly cognizant of his own and others' records in the long years that followed his departure from the game. He would often surprise interviewers with his mastery of baseball statistics, which, in highly selective fashion, he liked to quote in his ongoing quarrel with the game as it had developed since 1920. There would be many interviews, many opportunities to press his case against baseball, a lot of time to ruminate on what had been and begrudge what was. Altogether too much time.

XII

"Just Looking In Doesn't Help"

For the very few people who manage to become highly successful professional athletes, the period following retirement from active competition is almost inevitably anticlimactic. That was especially true for Ty Cobb. It was as a baseball player that the public knew him and that he knew himself. As he often freely acknowledged, he had no vocation besides baseball, knew no other way to organize his life. In terms of his own emotional well-being, Cobb would probably have been better off if he had not retired as the first millionaire ballplayer. Needing to work to support himself and his family, he might have been able to bring his day-to-day existence into some kind of focus. As it was, he never really adjusted to a retirement that lasted thirty-three years. Without baseball's exacting but predictable demands, its clearly measurable achievements, its springtime renewal of hopes, its glamor and drama, Cobb found life difficult. Later on Babe Ruth understood Cobb's predicament, because it was his as well. Usually much less articulate than Cobb, Ruth nonetheless said it best: "It's hard to be on the outside of something you love. Just looking in doesn't help."[1]

After the 1928 season Cobb effectively put off coming to terms with his retirement when he went to Japan to appear in a few games with Japanese university teams and to conduct a series of clinics. Since about 1910 various groups of college players from the United States and Japan had exchanged visits, and enthusiasm for baseball was running high in the Asian nation. Herb Hunter, a former outfielder who had failed to stick with various major-league teams, promoted the trip and guaranteed Cobb $15,000 for his services as player and instructor. So early in October, accompanied by his wife and the youngest three Cobb children—Herschel, Beverly, and James Howell—Cobb embarked from Seattle aboard the S. S. President Jefferson. To assist him in demonstrating how the game should be played, Cobb took along Bob Shawkey, onetime Yankee ace, and Fred Hofmann, veteran catcher with the Yankees and Red Sox. Ernie Quigley of the National League staff would demonstrate umpiring.

At least in terms of the public interest it generated, the trip was a big success. Cobb played first base most of the time in Japan but also occasionally relieved Shawkey on the mound. Crowds of up to 20,000 Japanese turned out for the games Cobb played in, and one of his clinics, at Waseda University, drew 4000 would-be ballplayers. The Japanese impressed Cobb with their eagerness to learn, at the same time that they mystified and amused him by playing strictly according to form, always doing the same thing in the same circumstances. Cobb and his teammates, repeatedly pulling the unexpected, ran up football-sized scores on their bewildered opponents.

After stopping off for about a week in Honolulu, Cobb and his party arrived at San Francisco in the first part of December. By mid-month the Cobbs were back in Augusta. That winter brought the customary bird-hunting and a few field trials with his dogs. When spring-training time came around, Cobb "grew a bit restless" but then realized, he said, that he was free to go anywhere and do anything he wanted.[2] What he did was fulfill an old promise to his wife by taking her on an extended European trip. En route through Philadelphia, he stopped off to wish Mack and the Athletics luck and pick up his last year's uniform.[3] In New York they took passage on the S. S. *Roosevelt*.

For months Ty and Charlie Cobb toured the southern and western parts of the Continent in the best guidebook fashion, seeing, Cobb thought, "half the museums in Europe." After that they visited England and finally Scotland. Near Keith, Scotland, he shot grouse and quail with Sir Isaac Sharpe, internationally renowned as a trainer of pointers and setters. For Cobb "it was the big league of upland bird hunting."[4]

The Cobbs arrived in New York harbor on October 1, in plenty of time for the World Series, which began a week later at Chicago between the Athletics and Cubs. Just before his return, the Philadelphia *Bulletin* began serializing a collection of reminiscent pieces he had dictated for the afternoon daily during his stopover in the spring. Again Cobb praised Mack unstintingly. He was "the supreme master of the diamond," "the greatest manager our national game has known." Mack, Cobb said, had made him believe he could help the Athletics when he thought he was through with baseball, and had been willing to pay him more than he was really worth. He'd never have anything but "pleasant recollections" of his two years with the Athletics; his only regret was that he hadn't put in all of his twenty-four years in the majors with Connie Mack.[5]

If Cobb had any regrets about not hanging on for one more year and thereby getting into one more World Series, he kept them to himself. In 1929 Mack's array of talent had finally jelled into one of the game's all-time great teams. In the opening game Howard Ehmke, with whom Cobb had never got along as either player or manager, was Mack's surprise starter. The fourteen-year veteran proceeded to strike out thirteen Cubs, a new Series record, en route to a 4–1 win. Six days later the Athletics wrapped it up, four games to one, at Philadelphia.

Meanwhile Cobb told reporters that he'd had offers from several clubs to become either an executive or a field manager. Although he wasn't ready to rule out managing altogether, "the executive end of the game" had the most appeal because, he joked, an executive "can hide in his office or get under the stands. However, I never thought I was such a bad manager as many people thought." In Europe being out of baseball hadn't really bothered him, "but now that I'm back it's different." He even went so far as to say he thought he'd be in baseball next year.[6]

In fact Cobb would never get back into baseball in any official way. He had long since severed his connections with the Providence and Augusta teams. For a while early in 1928, he had thought about heading up a group to buy the San Francisco Seals in the Pacific Coast League. But then he signed to play another season and had to write George H. Maines, a Detroit public-relations man who was promoting the project, that "I will have my hands full with the Athletics."[7] Just before he left for Europe, according to veteran sportswriter Fred Lieb's recollection, Cobb made an offer of $275,000 for the Cincinnati Reds franchise. Such a deal may still have been cooking when Cobb returned from his trip, which would explain his remark about being in baseball in 1930. Cobb's bid was eventually rejected, Lieb has written. If so, it was a fortuitous outcome for Cobb, at least financially. The coming of the Great Depression sent baseball attendance plummeting and brought big losses for most major-league clubs, including the habitually second-division Reds.

One franchise that continued to thrive in the Depression years was Detroit's. Although the Tigers' home attendance was second only to that of the Yankees in the early thirties, Frank Navin had lost the bulk of his personal fortune in the stock market crash in the fall of 1929. By 1933 he had told co-owner Walter Briggs that he was ready to sell the ball club for two million dollars to a syndicate headed by Cobb's longtime Detroit friend James O. Murfin and including Cobb as a major investor. Briggs vetoed the sale, however, and he and Navin continued to control the Tigers until shortly after the 1934 World Series, which the Tigers lost in seven games to the St. Louis Cardinals. At that time Navin died after suffering a heart attack while horseback riding. Briggs bought Navin's shares in the franchise and went on to operate it for nearly twenty-five years.

So Cobb remained on the outside looking in. In a later period he might have put his supreme knowledge of how to hit to use as a batting instructor. It was not until near the end of his life, however, that ball clubs started to employ such coaching specialists. For that matter, if the designated hitter rule adopted by the American League in 1973 had been in force in 1929, he might have stayed on as a player for a few more years, even with his sore legs. In the circumstances of the 1930s, though, Cobb's baseball options were severely limited. The consensus among big-league owners continued to be that he had demonstrated with the Tigers that he lacked the qualities of a successful manager (whatever those qualities might be). Conceivably he could have managed in the minors, as Speaker was willing to do, or been a minor-league club executive, but that would probably have meant buying some debt-ridden franchise. Ever penny-wise, Cobb was not about to make a losing investment just for the sake of having a new project to occupy himself.

What he ended up doing was spending a small part of his time dealing in stocks and real estate and trying to make his former offseason recreations—hunting, fishing, golfing—fill up the rest of his days. His fortune suffered some from the stock market crash that hit the nation's and the world's economy within two weeks after the 1929 World Series. Yet Cobb's investments proved to be sufficiently distributed in soundly operating businesses so that he came through the panic in good shape. The backbone of his stock holdings, General Motors and Coca-Cola, held up throughout the Depression years. Even in the depths of the economic downturn, in 1932, GM continued to pay a dividend. Coca-Cola turned out to be depression proof. While others sold, Cobb steadily increased his holdings in both GM and Coca-Cola, as well as in the American Can Company, Timken Roller Bearing, and other businesses. At the end of a decade of generally hard times, Cobb had seen his personal wealth at least double. Mainly because of his experience in the Depression years, he came to believe that, as he later phrased it, "What's worth buying is worth holding."[8]

On December 18, 1930, Cobb marked his forty-fourth birthday, the last, as it happened, he would ever spend in the house at 2425 William Street in Augusta. When asked about reports that he would buy or become an executive with this or that ball club, he said that for now his dickerings with everybody in baseball were over. He was content to serve as recreation director for the city of Augusta, a post he had recently agreed to take. Before long, though, he intended to move his family from Georgia to the San Francisco Bay area. He had been in love with that part of the country ever since managing two seasons in the California winter league during the early twenties.

At the beginning of March 1931, Cobb played in his first officially organized golf tournament. After shooting an eighty-three over the eighteen-hole Augusta Country Club course and beating a local businessman for the winner's cup, he left for the West Coast to look for a suitable house for the Cobb family. Early in April he was on hand to take part in ceremonies inaugurating the San Francisco Seals' new million-dollar stadium.

Eight days later he was golfing at Delmonte, near Monterrey, when he was notified that Charlie Cobb had filed for divorce in Augusta. Her suit charged "cruel treatment within the meaning of the law and of such character as to warrant a total divorce." Cobb told newsmen that he was shocked, didn't know what to say "except that I have always loved my wife, my children and my home."[9]

Cobb could hardly have been shocked, nor could intimates of the family. The Cobbs' marriage had been deteriorating for some time, probably even before Cobb left baseball. Just as he had been a hard man to play with and for, so he was a hard man to live with. Possessed of a restless, sensitive, mercurial disposition even in his palmiest baseball days, he was even more given to temperamental behavior now that he found himself with so much time and not enough to fill it with. For years his family had had to put up with his periods of brooding and outbursts of sarcasm and anger. Cobb was a healthy, energetic middle-aged retiree who in almost any other profession would have been at the height of his powers. As a rich ex-ballplayer, though, he lacked much of anything to do with himself. After a quarter-century of relentless driving to become the best and remain the best—of "fighting off Nap Lajoie, Joe Jackson, Eddie Collins, Tris Speaker and Babe Ruth, trying to stay ahead of them," as he once put it[10]—it was just not possible for a man like Cobb to settle comfortably into the roles of paterfamilias, solid citizen, and baseball elder statesman.

Cobb was no ogre. He did not physically abuse his wife and children. Always primarily "a man's man," he appears to have resisted the baseball groupies of his time and remained faithful to his marriage vows. James Howell Cobb, called "Jimmy," the baby of the Cobb family, described his father as a strict disciplinarian who was sparing in his praise, especially of his three sons. He pressured all of his children to do well in school and witheld their privileges whenever their grades fell down. But Jimmy Cobb also remembered his father's tucking him in at night and playing catch with him in the backyard, as well as Cobb's worry that the undersized Jimmy would get hurt playing grade school football or that Beverly, the next-to-youngest Cobb child, would somehow be injured in archery classes.

Cobb's main difficulty as a parent had to do with Ty, Jr., who was a major disappointment to his father. Whereas Herschel (born in 1916) played baseball avidly and well until he suffered an eye injury when he was eleven, Ty, Jr., disliked the game and took up tennis while attending Richmond Academy in Augusta and then the Hun School in New Jersey. At Princeton University he played more tennis, drove flashy cars, had a good time, and flunked out. Subsequently, at Yale, he captained the varsity tennis team and did a little better scholastically but still did not manage to finish his bachelor's degree.

Ty, Jr.'s, checkered collegiate career coincided with Cobb's first few years out of baseball and doubtless contributed to the strain on the Cobb marriage. Eventually Cobb and his son became totally alienated from each other, an outcome for which Cobb came to hold the boy's mother responsible. In obvious ways Cobb's relationship with Ty, Jr., paralleled what his own relationship with W. H. Cobb had been and might have become, despite Cobb's unquestioned success in baseball, if his father had lived.

In April 1931, after Cobb hurried back to Augusta, he and Charlie agreed to try to hold their family together. At the end of the month he announced that his wife had withdrawn her divorce suit. She had done that "on her own initiative and . . . no further comment is to be made on account of the sacredness relating to her decision."[11] At least for the time being, the marriage remained intact. Cobb went back to California to resume his systematic search for a place that would combine roominess, seclusion, and convenience—at a good price.

He found what he was looking for at 48 Spencer Lane in the little town of Atherton, about twenty-two miles south of the San Francisco city limits and three miles or so from Menlo Park (which would be the Cobbs' mailing address). The Atherton home was actually a small estate—a fifteen-room (seven bedrooms) house in the Spanish Mission style, complete with swimming pool, guest house, and servants' quarters, located on several acres with plenty of trees to conceal the house from the street. Into that house Cobb moved his family in 1932. Presumably it was where he intended to live out his days, surrounded by loved ones and friends, enjoying his wealth and leisure.

In California he played golf most of the year at the many courses built in the Bay Area over the past two decades in response to affluent America's discovery of the game. He hunted wildfowl in California and big game in Idaho, Wyoming, and Canada; fished in mountain streams; and even tried his hand at polo. He also continued to make money.

His famous temper was frequently in evidence, in both public and private circumstances. He stormed around golf courses, impatiently demanding to play through other parties of golfers he considered incompetent and too slow. He went at polo with a fierceness that dismayed his gentlemanly teammates and opponents. At the Detroit Athletic Club in 1935 he was dining with Grantland Rice when Nig Clarke, the old Cleveland catcher and now a Detroit resident, came over and joined them. Clarke entertained Cobb and Rice for a while by telling how he had sometimes swiped at sliding runners he couldn't reach and then nonchalantly tossed aside his equipment to fool the umpire into thinking the tag had been made for the third out. But when Clarke laughed and confessed that he'd even gotten Cobb called out a couple of times with that tactic, Cobb bolted from his chair and began cursing and violently shaking Clarke, until Rice pulled him off and the stunned Clarke left the room.

In October of the next year Cobb's mother died in Georgia at the age of sixty-five. She was buried near her husband in the cemetery at Royston. Cobb's sister Florence had been crippled for a long time with arthritis and was unable to look after herself. She ended up living most of her remaining years, until her death at fifty-one in 1944, at her brother Paul's place at Sarasota, Florida. She spent one period, however, with the Cobbs in California. There Cobb often waited on her himself and was usually as kind and considerate as anyone could be. On other occasions, however, even his bedridden sister did not escape his biting sarcasm, especially on the subject of her fondness for radio soap operas.

In the mid-thirties baseball's leaders, most notably Ford C. Frick, a former sportswriter who had become president of the National League, hit upon the twin ideas of establishing an official gallery of the game's "immortals" and making 1939 baseball's centennial. A small baseball museum already existed at Cooperstown, New York, where, according to the folklore that the game's officialdom had long ago accepted as fact, Abner Doubleday had laid out the first baseball diamond in 1839. That museum was to become the basis for a much bigger museum incorporating a Hall of Fame, a place of enshrinement for baseball's greatest names and of pilgrimage for devout fans.

By the end of 1935 Henry P. Edwards, now secretary of the American League Service Bureau, was polling the 226 members of the Base Ball Writers Association of America to select the first group of "immortals." The writers were to choose from a list of thirty-three players, all of whom had made their records primarily or exclusively after 1900. (Later on a BBWAA veterans committee was to pick men from the pre-1900 years.) To be chosen for the projected Hall of Fame, a player had to be named on at least 75 percent of the ballots.

Early in February 1936, Edwards announced that Cobb had received 222 votes, only four shy of unanimity. Babe Ruth (who had just retired the previous year) and Honus Wagner were tied for second with 215. Christy Mathewson (205) and Walter Johnson (189) were the only others named on the necessary three-fourths of the ballots. Interrupted with the news on the golf course, Cobb was gracious: "I am overwhelmed. I'm glad they felt that way about me."[12] If he held any resentment at the perversity of the four writers who had refused to vote for him, he kept quiet about it. Jimmy Cobb believed that his father was prouder of that Hall of Fame vote than of anything else connected with his baseball career.

The completed National Baseball Museum and Hall of Fame was dedicated on June 12, 1939. Some 10,000 visitors jammed Main Street in the little upstate town for the ceremonies. Since 1936 two more BBWAA polls had added Nap Lajoie, Tris Speaker, Cy Young, George Sisler, Eddie Collins, Willie Keeler, and Grover Cleveland Alexander to the first class of Hall of Fame inductees, as well as thirteen pre-1900 figures chosen by the veterans committee. Of the twentieth-century performers, all but Mathewson and Keeler were still living. Nine of them, together with seventy-six-year-old Connie Mack, were

on hand for the ribbon-cutting at the entrance to the museum and then for
the induction ceremonies, with Ruth arriving just as the band was striking up
"Take Me Out to the Ball Game."

Cobb was nowhere to be seen—at the ceremonies, the picture-taking sessions afterward, or the baseball game played by two groups of contemporary
major leaguers that afternoon at the little ballpark the town had built near by
(supposedly on the site of Doubleday's primal act). "Ty's late—just as he always was for spring training," quipped one of the old ballplayers.[13] Complaining of train delays and missed connections, Cobb finally arrived late in
the day, in the company of nineteen-year-old Beverly and Jimmy, now nearly
eighteen. At least he was able to make the Hall of Fame banquet. Twenty
years later he admitted that he had purposely missed the noontime ceremonies to avoid having to be photographed with Commissioner Landis. Cobb would
never forgive Landis for not moving with dispatch to clear his name back in
1926.

At Cooperstown, Cobb renewed acquaintances with Ruth, whom he had
seen from time to time over the past decade and visited in New York on a
few occasions. Cobb had developed a real fondness for this man who was so
different from him in so many ways. Loud-mouthed, gluttonous, and coarse,
Ruth, as Cobb had discovered, was nonetheless ultimately charming and em-
inently likeable. Whereas Cobb had been unable to work out a satisfactory
business deal that would bring him back into baseball, Ruth had waited in
vain for somebody to ask him to manage a major-league team. Thus besides
talking over old times, Ruth and Cobb could commiserate on how tough it
was no longer to be a part of the game that had been their lives for so long.
Still another tie between the two men was Claire Merritt Hodgson Ruth, the
former showgirl whom Ruth had married in 1929 after the death of his long-
estranged first wife. Claire Ruth was the daughter of James M. Merritt, a
prominent Georgia attorney and sometime University of Georgia law professor, who had occasionally handled legal matters for Cobb. "In Georgia," she
later wrote, "I had known Ty Cobb very well."[14]

In the summer of 1941 Cobb and Ruth, both dedicated golfers who usually
shot in the eighties, agreed to play a series of three matches, with all proceeds
to go to charitable causes. Exactly who first challenged whom is a matter of
question, but the press quickly seized on the idea of a showdown on the links
between the two greatest ballplayers and ballyhooed it to the hilt. Arranged
by Fred Corcoran of the Professional Golfers Association, the matches would
supposedly pit the Babe's power versus Cobb's cunning and skill. When Cobb
got to New York on his way to the Boston area for the first match, sportswriters told him that Ruth had been working hard and shooting great golf. If Cobb
needed anything to stimulate his competitive juices, that did it. "I went into
those Ruth matches as determined to win as I ever was on the ball field," he

said later. The rivalry between Cobb and Ruth, John Kieran observed, was real enough. "It sticks out all over the two contenders."[15]

Weighing 212 pounds and described as "a picture of health at the age of 54," Cobb teed off against the forty-six-year-old Ruth on June 25 at the Commonwealth Country Club in West Newton, Massachusetts.[16] Bette Davis, the movie star, was present with a trophy she had donated for the winner. Cobb's superior putting was the difference. His eighteen-hole score was eighty, Ruth's eighty-three. The proceeds from the dollar-per-person admissions went to a farm operated for underprivileged New England children.

Two days later, at the Fresh Meadows course on Long Island, with proceeds targeted for the USO, Ruth and Cobb tied after eighteen holes. Ruth took five strokes to Cobb's six on the playoff nineteenth hole to go even with Cobb in matches. They were to play the third match on June 29 at Grosse Isle Golf and Country Club outside Detroit.

Throughout the series but especially for the deciding match, Cobb later maintained, he used psychology on the ingenuous Babe. In a practice round at Cleveland he deliberately missed shots, bemoaned his poor performance, and generally behaved as if he thought he didn't have a chance at Grosse Isle. On the steamer trip across Lake Erie, Cobb recalled, Ruth was so confident that he downed considerably more scotch than would be good for his game the next day.

Whereas only a couple of hundred spectators had bothered to watch the second match, some 2500 were on hand at Grosse Isle, with the proceeds again to go to the USO. While Ruth sweated out last night's booze and shot poorly in the intense heat, Cobb played his average game. It took him only sixteen holes to clinch the match at fifteen over par. Ruth was nineteen over. Malcolm Bingay, who for many years was on the staff of the Detroit *News,* came out to see "if the years had dimmed the fierce competitive spirit of Cobb."[17] What he saw convinced him otherwise.

That evening Cobb celebrated winning what he termed "The Has Beens' Golf Championship of Nowhere in Particular" by throwing a dinner at the Statler Hotel for such old friends as Bingay, H. G. Salsinger, and William Kuenzel, longtime photographer of Detroit sights, including Cobb's diamond feats. Another of Cobb's guests was Major James Doolittle, Air Reserve Corps, who had been a Cobb fan while growing up in St. Louis. Within a little over nine months Doolittle would be leading a carrier-based strike of sixteen B-25 bombers against Tokyo, doubtless flying over some of the same ballfields on which Cobb had taught the game to young Japanese.

By the time their son Jimmy finished at New Mexico Military Institute and entered the army in 1942, Ty and Charlie Cobb had long since stopped being husband and wife in any but the legal sense. After the family moved to California in 1932, Charlie Cobb had filed for divorce on two more occasions, only to change her mind both times. She and Cobb continued to live together in the Atherton home until August 1939, when she left Cobb and moved into a place of her own in Menlo Park. Their two daughters, who had not yet married, divided their time between their separated parents.

Early in 1942, about two months after the Japanese attack at Pearl Harbor brought the United States into the war, Ward Morehouse, doing a piece for the *Sporting News*, visited Cobb at Atherton. Larry Woodall, Cobb's second-string catcher in the twenties, and Roy Corhan, once a light-hitting shortstop for the White Sox and Cardinals, were there as his golfing guests. Cobb told Morehouse that he had established legal residence in Nevada and kept the Atherton place mainly to entertain people. Recently he had bought a lodge on Lake Tahoe, accessible from U. S. Highway 50 between Stateline and Glenbrook, south of Carson City.

After showing the journalist around the main house, Cobb took him out past the unfilled swimming pool to his "sports house," which was crowded with baseball and hunting trophies and other mementos, including pictures autographed by famous personages. Cobb said he prized most a photo of Woodrow Wilson signed "To my friend, Ty Cobb—1913." Although he had a Filipino house servant, Cobb himself insisted on making sardine sandwiches for his guests' lunch. While he drank bourbon and ate sardines, he talked about the "Asiatic mind" and how "tricky" the Japanese were. In 1928 somebody had stolen his uniform, glove, and baseball shoes from his room at the Imperial Hotel in Tokyo. "I've always thought the things were stolen to be copied by a manufacturer," he said. "That's the way those fellows are."[18]

Although he had the company of his daughters and occasional guests and hunting, fishing, and golfing companions, Cobb was now basically by himself. The Atherton house was far more than he needed, and he spent an increasing amount of his time at the Lake Tahoe place, which over the years he enlarged and improved. He was at dockside in San Francisco to greet Jimmy when his son returned from the Pacific region early in 1946. But Jimmy had to hurry off to Twin Falls, Idaho, to join his wife and baby. At Twin Falls, moreover, his brother Herschel was waiting to make him a partner in the local Coca-Cola bottling plant in which Cobb had helped set up Herschel several years earlier.

In March 1947, at Redwood City, California, Charlie Cobb filed her fourth and last divorce action. Represented by Melvin Belli, a young San Francisco attorney who would later become a celebrated criminal lawyer, she now alleged "extreme cruelty from the date of marriage to the present time." Besides half of Cobb's wealth—a putative $7 million—she asked for $5000 per month in alimony and $60,000 for attorneys' fees and other costs. Cobb acknowledged not being surprised this time around. The estimate of his estate, though, was just "too big."[19] He was probably telling the truth, although the war-triggered economic revival and the postwar continuation of the boom had made him a substantially richer man.

As Belli predicted, the Cobbs' eventually reached agreement out of court. The easiest way out was for them to agree on a property settlement, for her to withdraw her suit in California, for Cobb himself to file suit in Reno under Nevada's liberal divorce laws as a resident of the state, and then for her to sign a waiver giving jurisdiction to the Nevada courts. That was the way it was all done, so that by the fall of 1947 the divorce was final, ending thirty-nine years of marriage. The terms of Cobb's settlement with "that old woman," as he now referred to her, never became public.[20]

It was generally a bad period for Cobb, what with the final breakup of his marriage, the publicity surrounding the divorce, and the continuing antagonism between himself and Ty, Jr. Hearing about the deaths of men he had played with and against reminded him of his own mortality and advancing age. Fat Roy Fothergill had died in 1938. Lou Gehrig succumbed to a rare disease of the nervous system in 1941, two years after taking himself out of the Yankee lineup and ending his incredible consecutive-games-played streak at 2,130. Dan Howley died in 1944, Bobby Veach the next year, Walter Johnson late in 1946. It was also saddening to stop off in Greenville, South Carolina—on the way to New York with Grantland Rice following the Master's Golf Tournament at Augusta—and discover Joe Jackson working behind the counter at a little liquor store and obviously consuming about as much as he sold. At first embarrassed to say anything, he finally brightened up when Cobb started talking about Jackson's beautiful swing and natural hitting ability. A few years later Jackson too would be dead.

Early in 1947 it became known that Babe Ruth had throat cancer. That year and the next the Yankees staged a total of three commemorative occasions for the dying baseball idol. The second was on Sunday, September 28, 1947, the last day of the season, when Yankee president Larry McPhail arranged a two-inning game between old Yankee ballplayers and oldtimers from other American League teams, with all proceeds to be turned over to the Babe Ruth Foundation for boys. Cobb was one of forty or so former players coming to New York to participate in the game and visit with Ruth, who was barely able to whisper his thanks to the crowd of 25,000 during pre-game ceremonies. After renewing acquaintances with such old foes as Tris Speaker, Cy Young, Ed Walsh, Frank Baker, George Sisler, Billy Evans, and even Bill Bradley, his favorite player when he was a kid in Georgia, Cobb led off the contest against Waite Hoyt. Just before stepping into the batter's box, he told Wally Schang, catching for the Yankee oldtimers, that it had been a long time since he'd swung a bat and he was afraid it might slip out of his hands, so maybe Wally should move back a few feet. After Schang obliged, Cobb assumed his familiar stance with hands apart on his bat. Hoyt tossed one in, and

Cobb bunted neatly in front of the plate. His ploy was unsuccessful, though, because before his sixty-year-old legs could get him to first, Schang fielded his bunt and threw him out. At first Cobb winced in disgust, then seemed to remember that it was all for fun and broke into a big grin as he puffed back to the visitors' dugout.

That oldtimers' game was the last time Cobb saw Ruth alive. After a final appearance at Yankee Stadium the next June, the Babe died in New York at fifty-three on August 16, 1948. "I can't honestly say that I appreciate the way in which he changed baseball," Cobb remarked toward the end of his own life, "but he was the most natural and unaffected man I ever knew. . . . I look forward to meeting him some day."[21]

A few years after Ruth's passing, death came to Cobb's immediate family. In April 1951 Herschel Cobb suffered a fatal heart attack at the age of thirty-four, leaving a wife and three children. About a year and a half later Ty, Jr., forty-two, died of a malignant brain tumor at his mother's home in Menlo Park, where, hopelessly ill, he had come to be taken care of.

In the late 1930s Ty, Jr., had finally settled down. Deciding on a career in medicine, he gained admission to the Medical College of South Carolina at Charleston. In 1942 he finished his M.D. with a specialty in gynecology and obstetrics, married Mary Frances Dunn of Daytona Beach, Florida, and set up practice at Dublin, Georgia. There he continued to practice and live with his wife and children until the brain tumor was discovered in 1951. Not long before he died, Ty, Jr., the boy who had not liked baseball, was finally reconciled with his famous father.

In the years that followed Ty, Jr.'s, death, Cobb often lamented that as a ballplayer he'd not had as much involvement with his family as he should have. "When you get older, you wish for companionship," he said. "I was just a loner; I couldn't have that with my children." If he'd gone into medicine and become a surgeon, it might have been different. He'd have been able to "talk over operations" with his physician son. "But I was a ballplayer, and my son had no inclination toward baseball."[22]

In his sixties Cobb's own health remained reasonably good, even though he had about abandoned cigars and now smoked cigarettes steadily. He also tended to drink more as the years passed, one reason his weight crept up to 230 pounds at one time. In June 1946, while he was in Detroit for the golden jubilee of the American automotive industry, he was briefly hospitalized with acute bronchitis. A year and a half later he spent a few days at the Lahey Clinic in Boston being treated for a gall bladder flareup. In June 1949, after a month's hospitalization at Stanford University Hospital for the same condition, he came out relieved to have avoided surgery and weighing a trim 186 pounds.

By then Cobb was involved with a project that was taking up a considerable amount of his time and providing a great deal of personal satisfaction. In 1945 he had decided that, as a memorial to his parents, he would make it possible for his hometown of Royston to have its own modern hospital. Cobb said that he wanted to benefit not only the townspeople but also Stewart D. Brown, M.D., his boyhood friend and teammate on the Royston Reds and "one of Georgia's outstanding country doctors." So he donated $100,000 and began lengthy discussions by mail and telephone with Brown, Charles S. Kennedy, a physician acquaintance in Detroit, and various architects and contractors. Facilitated by a $72,000 grant from the federal government and about $38,000 in contributions from local people, the hospital project went forward at a good pace. In January 1950, Cobb flew across the country to be on hand for the dedication of Cobb Memorial Hospital. It had twenty-five beds and, according to Superintendent Brown, was "filled with the latest equipment." "This hospital belongs to all of you people here where I used to live," Cobb told the crowd of about three thousand, "and it's for you people, whom I've always had in my heart."[23]

Then came the formal opening of the hospital with a gold key turned by Frances Fairburn Cobb, the benefactor's forty-year-old wife of four months. An attractive brunette, Cobb's new mate was the daughter of John Fairburn, a Buffalo, New York, physician whom Cobb had known for some years. The marriage to Cobb, at Buffalo on September 24, 1949, was her third. She had lost one husband in an airplane crash in 1934 and had recently divorced another. He'd not intended to marry again, Cobb told newsmen after the wedding. But then he'd met Frances, a rare woman who liked to golf, hunt, travel, and cook. So at sixty-two he had taken another wife.

Cobb's contacts with baseball remained peripheral. He corresponded regularly with George Weiss, his friend from Weiss's days as owner of the New Haven Colonials, and now general manager of the Yankees. Cobb reported to Weiss about prospects he had seen in his travels, assessed the Yankees' pennant chances, and even suggested trades Weiss should make. For three weeks in the summer of 1951 Cobb was guest instructor at a boys' baseball camp in the Ozarks. The next year, on his way home from fishing in the upper Columbia River region, he came by Sicks Stadium in Seattle, got into the batting cage, and demonstrated that at sixty-five he could still rap line drives. Later that same summer, before a Dodgers-Giants game at Ebbets Field in Brooklyn, he showed a young Dodgers' catcher how to drop a handful of dirt at a batter's feet when the pitch came in, just as Nig Clarke had done it half a century earlier.

In July 1951 the Subcommittee on the Study of Monopoly Power, of the U. S. House of Representatives' Judiciary Committee, held hearings on the old question whether Organized Baseball, through its reserve clause, operated in violation of the antitrust laws. Cobb came all the way from Nevada to be the lead-off witness before the subcommittee, chaired by Representative Emmanuel Celler of New York. Wearing reading glasses and frequently cupping his ear to hear questions from subcommittee members, Cobb testified for about an hour and a half. Mostly he entertained the congressmen with stories from his early baseball years. The players of today, he wanted the congressmen to know, weren't up to those of his time. When asked about the issue at hand, he stoutly defended the basic reserve clause, although he did suggest a plan he had first talked about as early as 1908: After five years under contract to one ball club, a dissatisfied player ought to be able to take his case before a board of arbitration and, if the board ruled in his favor, become a free agent. In general, though, Cobb endorsed the status quo. "Baseball," he declared, "has made it possible for hundreds of young men from small towns, like myself, to improve their lot in life and become useful members of their communities. I revere baseball."[24]

Whether he was testifying before a congressional subcommittee, giving an interview, or just having a casual conversation, Cobb usually could not resist comparing baseball then and now, always to the discredit of the present-day version. Years before his retirement he had started carping about the way the game had changed, particularly about the baneful effects of homerun-oriented baseball. He continued in the same vein as a retiree. Finally, in 1952, *Life* magazine paid him $25,000 to put his complaints down in sustained, systematic form.

In a two-part article he blasted just about everything connected with the game at mid-century. Ted Williams, Joe DiMaggio, and most of the other stars of today, he argued, couldn't have "hit the top" in the old days. The trouble was that they "limped along on one cylinder," swinging for the fences, not using their talents to the fullest, unwilling to pay the price to be as good as they could be. Phil Rizzuto, the Yankees' hard-driving little shortstop, and Stan Musial, the Cardinals' batting star, were the only present-day performers who could stand comparison with the oldtimers. The Red Sox' Williams, though a fine natural hitter, obstinately pulled the ball and thereby lost numerous base hits. DiMaggio of the Yankees let himself get out of shape in the offseason and consequently suffered more injuries than he should. Today's overpaid athletes lolled around during the winter months and otherwise neglected their careers in ways "that make my flesh crawl." As a whole they just weren't as tough as Cobb's contemporaries. "To an oldtimer like me," Cobb grumbled, "today's ballplayers seem like a particularly fragile lot." The men of his day had been "a strange, hard-bitten and ambitious crew—up from the small towns and by no means eager to go back, trained at nothing but that one profession and battling to hang on to it to their last breath."[25]

Cobb also had nothing but contempt for the current practice of giving unproven teenagers huge bonuses, for the inability of most ballplayers to bunt, and (despite his own player-switching when he managed) for the obsessive platooning done by today's managers. Above all he abominated fence-swingers. It seemed to Cobb that "Given the proper physical equipment—which consists solely in the strength to knock a ball 40 feet farther than the average man can do it—anybody can play big league ball today." With everybody trying to hit homeruns, base-stealing was almost a thing of the past and brute power ruled the game. "In other words science is out the window." [26]

The counterarguments of various sportswriters and managers that today's baseball was a basically different game from that of the dead-ball era, and that any evaluation of the sport now had to take into account such new factors as night play and relief-pitching specialists, carried no weight at all with Cobb— if he even bothered to read them. As some of his critics pointed out, he had seen relatively little major-league competition since moving to California. His assault on present-day baseball and ballplayers was patently unfair in a number of ways. But Cobb went to his grave convinced that the game's most glorious years had been his own as a player.

Maybe out of a deep need to maintain as much of a living connection with that time as he still could, Cobb started going back for the Hall of Fame inductions and reunions of old ballplayers. Beginning in 1951, he made the long trip to Cooperstown every two years or so. Sid Keener remembered seeing Cobb, Cy Young, Ed Walsh, and Connie Mack walk arm in arm from the stately Otesaga Hotel to the 1953 ceremonies. Getting Sam Crawford into the Hall of Fame became something of a cause for Cobb. Although Cobb and Crawford had never cared for each other personally, Cobb had always admired his old outfield mate's ability and achievements. He talked up Crawford's qualifications when he was at Cooperstown and regularly wrote letters to the BBWAA veterans committee urging his admission. In 1957 Crawford was finally voted into the Hall of Fame. He arrived from rural California in the company of Davy Jones. When Crawford, Jones, and Cobb sat together and swapped reminiscences at the annual banquet, the rancor that had marked their years as teammates seemed forgotten.

A much bigger cause for Cobb in the 1950s was the Cobb Educational Fund, which he announced at a press conference in Atlanta late in 1953. A three-person board of trustees, chaired by Daniel C. Elkin, M.D., professor of surgery at Emory University Hospital, would administer Cobb's endowment of $100,000. Named for Cobb's father, the fund would provide scholarships for needy Georgia residents wanting to attend college and "definitely would not be athletic." Recipients would have to make it through their freshman years on their own before they could qualify for a CEF scholarship. Cobb's intent was to help only those who showed a determination to succeed, "the Lincolnesque characters, the boys and girls out of the fields and mountains. . . . We want stars—stars in medicine, in law, in teaching and in life. We want to be identified with their success." His motives, he said, were selfish ones. "I feed on the warm feeling that I have inside me."[27]

By all indications the Cobb Educational Fund, like the little hospital Cobb had given to the town of Royston, was a successful venture. Thirty-one students were on CEF scholarships by 1958. When people came to interview him, Cobb would usually oblige them by going over the same baseball yarns he had been telling for decades. Speaking quietly with an accent that was no longer deeply southern, he sometimes seemed to tire and lose interest in talking about the past. But when the subject of his scholarship fund came up, he would become animated and his eyes would glitter as they had when he taught hitting. The work of the students had been "phenomenal," he told a visitor in 1958. Although he had met only about ten of the scholarship recipients, he knew they were all the kind of people he originally had in mind. Pulling out dossiers on each of them, he talked glowingly about their progress and admitted a preference for north Georgia youth. "I mean their faces," he enthused as he showed pictures of several CEF scholars, "they've got *character*."[28]

Besides his organized and public philanthropies, Cobb also did more than his share of individual, mostly private charitable deeds. After leading Detroit to two pennants and a world's championship, Mickey Cochrane had suffered a frightful beaning in 1937. He never fully recovered from his head injury and was thoroughly down on his luck by the 1950s, when Cobb began sending him regular checks. Hearing that Lu Blue was dying in a Washington, D.C., hospital, Cobb helped pay his hospital costs and later gave money to his widow. George Leidy, who had taken Cobb in hand at Augusta in 1905, also received help, as did a number of other old ballplayers.

Yet the same man who was capable of such quiet generosity had always tended to be suspicious, cheap, and cantankerous when dealing with people in service positions. His frequent quarrels with taxi drivers, parking-lot attendants, hotel clerks, and restaurant personnel embarrassed his companions— and anybody else within hearing distance. One of his Georgia kinsmen remembered an especially unpleasant scene in an Atlanta restaurant in the late fifties when Cobb found a three-cent error on a large bill for dinner and drinks. After the waiter and manager finally satisfied him that it had been an honest mistake, Cobb gave the waiter a good tip and then went over to the orchestra, also tipped them handsomely, and left smiling.

He also tended to brood over the past, especially when he was drinking. Early in 1955 he wrote Connie Mack, who four years earlier had finally turned the Athletics over to Jimmy Dykes and was spending his last years in Florida. In an uncharacteristically shaky hand, Cobb again raked through the Cobb-Speaker affair, which practically everybody had long ago forgotten. "I never wagered on a game in my life," Cobb protested, "not even on our own club which before 1919 Black Sox scandal was done openly. . . . Ty Cobb never liked even that, he worshipped the game [,] he was reared different, he never once did wager, he never liked horse races or prize fights on account of the betting angle." His greatest regret, he reassured Mack, was not playing his whole career under him. If only Mack knew "how many times I have reflected and wished I could have come up with you [in 1905] instead of *that Navin. . . . .* I still feel bitter about him."[29]

In the spring of 1955 John D. McCallum, a free-lance sports journalist, came to the Lake Tahoe lodge to conduct extensive interviews for a book on Cobb. Intending to do a combination popular biography and how-to-play book, McCallum had sought Cobb's cooperation, unlike Gene Schoor, whose carelessly done 1952 biography Cobb dismissed as worthless.[30] In the time he spent with Cobb at Lake Tahoe and elsewhere, McCallum got a good idea of how rich Cobb really was. Three or four mornings each week he talked with his stockbrokers in San Francisco and New York. Just before McCallum left, Cobb disclosed that in the few weeks McCallum had been there, he'd made $375,000. On another occasion he told McCallum that his fortune was now somewhere between six and ten million dollars.

McCallum also had ample oportunity to discover just how difficult Cobb could be. "When he was sober," McCallum recalled, "he could be a very charming host; when drinking, there was the devil to pay. Unfortunately he drank most of the time."[31] Sometimes Cobb would refuse to talk if McCallum tried to take notes; at other times he ordered that something be written down exactly as he said it. Cobb had a little notebook wherein he kept a "son of a bitch" list. Among the entries were Ban Johnson, Kenesaw M. Landis, and Dutch Leonard (all long dead), as well as his ex-wife, New York baseball writers in general, Eleanor Roosevelt, and the Democratic party. Cobb was rabid on the subject of what had happened to the country since the Roosevelts and the New Dealers took over what had once been his party and turned it into a leftwing outfit.

Later that summer, after McCallum had returned to New York, Cobb flew in for that year's Hall of Fame festivities. McCallum drove him upstate in an automobile borrowed from a New York GM executive. En route Cobb and McCallum made a detour to reach a service station that gave Green Stamps. There he took his companion to task for buying a 7-Up from the soft-drink machine while Cobb, as always, spent his nickel on a Coke. At Cooperstown, Cobb first apologized for having to sit with the Hall of Famers at the banquet rather than with McCallum, then drank too much during the cocktail hour, bawled McCallum out for not sitting at Cobb's table, and ended up spilling a plate of roast beef in the writer's lap.

Cobb's moods and tempers eventually became too much for Frances Cobb. She confided to McCallum that she feared her husband, especially when he was drunk. A few months before McCallum's arrival, she had filed a divorce suit in Reno but had withdrawn the suit twelve days later. In September 1955 she filed again, charging "extreme cruelty, entirely mental in nature."[32] Cobb counterfiled, also alleging mental cruelty. The divorce was awarded to Cobb in May 1956 at Minden, Nevada, with Frances Cobb receiving the court's permission to resume the name Cass from her previous marriage. As in his first divorce, whatever financial arrangements Cobb agreed to remained private.

Cobb was by himself more than ever now. From time to time he was able to visit his rapidly growing number of grandchildren. That phase of his old age, at least, he seems to have enjoyed. He made several trips to Daytona Beach, Florida, where Ty, Jr.'s, wife Mary lived with her three children, and got to know them for the first time. With his own three surviving children, however, his relations were not good. Jimmy Cobb, now employed at Lockheed Aircraft Corporation down the coast at Santa Maria, and Shirley and Beverly, married but still living near by, found it harder and harder to put up with their father's contemptuous attitude toward their mother and his general contrariness.

"In this house, I'm just a lonesome old man," he told a visitor to his Atherton place in the spring of 1957. "All my interests are on the other side of those mountains," he added, gesturing eastward. "I want to build a house, hunt birds, and just visit."[33] Georgia, he had decided, was where he wanted to live out his last years in a place that would be uniquely his own.

In Georgia, Cobb first looked for a suitable site around Royston. But with his boyhood pals Joe Cunningham and Stewart Brown now both dead, he soon discovered that there was not a great deal left for him there. He also seems to have balked at some of the real-estate quotations he got. So he chose instead Cornelia, a town of about 3800 located some twenty-eight miles northwest of Royston, very close to his birthplace. Cobb came to Cornelia late in the summer of 1957. After staying for a time at the home of his second cousin Harrison Gailey, he ended up at the town's only modern apartment complex. On Chenocetah Mountain just north of town he found a piece of land he liked. His view overlooked a lake in one direction, while across the hills to the south one could barely make out where the little community called The Narrows had once been.

Cobb wanted to live on that mountain and "be by myself while I rest." He had to admit that he was old and tired. Only occasionally did he drive the forty miles down to Athens to the nearest golf course. Mostly he slept late, watched TV quiz shows and Lawrence Welk's program, drove his housekeeper into town for groceries, attended the Christian Church in Cornelia, and dropped in on Kiwanis and Chamber of Commerce luncheons. Once he got settled, he wanted to travel to colleges around the state and meet Cobb Educational Fund scholars. His house, he explained with enthusiasm, would be constructed of local stone and brick and have eight rooms plus a guest house and servants' quarters. When it was finished, he just wanted "to move in and belong. That's all that this fellow Cobb wants here."[34]

For all his good intentions, Cobb as an old man was no better able to relax and remain in one place than he had been as a ballplayer during the offseasons. Since July he had been "on the go," he wrote a friend from California in November 1957, crossing and recrossing the country three times and talking to architects and contractors.[35] After another stay at Cornelia, where he had a partial excavation made for his house site, he was back on the coast in time to attend San Francisco's first major-league baseball game—the home opener between the Giants, newly relocated from New York, and the Los Angeles Dodgers, who had forsaken Brooklyn over the winter. Late in June, Cobb was in Detroit for a Tiger oldtimers' night. Although he declined to don a uniform, he did acknowledge the cheers, take his seat in a box behind the home dugout off third, and patiently sign scorecards for a long procession of kids, probably few of whom had any real notion who he was. After eight innings of such labor, he suddenly unlatched the gate leading from the boxes onto the field and, while the umpires held up the game, went into the Tiger dugout to say goodbye to everybody before leaving the Detroit ballpark for the last time.

If old and tied, Cobb had lost little of his combativeness. In 1958–59 he took on the state of California, which had billed him for nearly $52,000 in unpaid taxes and penalties. Cobb, said the California authorities, had failed to file state income tax returns from 1949 through 1957. The old man admitted as much but argued that since the 1940s his legal residence had been Nevada. Thus California had no business taxing the personal income of a nonresident. With the state having already secured a lien on his Atherton home, Cobb had to post bond in the amount of his tax bill before he could appeal to the state board of equalization. In March 1959 the board ruled that Cobb had to pay. That he did, as he was obliged to under the law. But then, over the advice of his lawyers, he filed suit in superior court seeking the return of the money. When advised that the case would probably take years to come to trial, Cobb insisted that he was ready to stay in the courts as long as it took to obtain justice.

Yet by the time he filed the suit on Christmas Eve 1959, Cobb must have understood that he did not have a great deal of time left for bringing the state of California to heel, for building a house in Georgia, or for doing much of anything else. As he had just recently found out, he had cancer. He would fight that foe with the same unyielding passion to win he had exhibited for a quarter-century on the ballfield. This time, though, not even Cobb's ferocious will could make any difference in the outcome.

The discovery of the cancer dated from the fall of 1959. That September

40

Cobb was hunting birds a few miles from his Lake Tahoe lodge with Pete Buffering, a frequent hunting companion from Reno, when he suddenly experienced terrific pain in his back and legs. "The pain almost paralyzed me and I found myself unable to walk," he said later.[36] For hours Buffering half-carried, half-dragged him through the hills and ravines before he finally got him back to the lodge and into his bed. Cobb would not let Buffering call a physician, insisting that he'd only had a flareup of an old back injury. Buffering left him alone and in agony.

A few days later Frances Cass, having heard about Cobb's illness, arrived at the lodge. Although she still carried plenty of hurts and resentments from their marriage, she offered to take care of him. Cobb protested that because they were no longer married, she ought not to be there, but she stayed for two weeks anyway. By the time she left, she had managed to convince Cobb to enter the Scripps Clinic at La Jolla, California, for a thorough physical examination.

The Scripps diagnosticians reported that Cobb had diabetes, a weak heart, high blood pressure, an enlarged prostate gland, and Bright's disease, a degenerative kidney condition. Cobb went back to Lake Tahoe with a supply of insulin and syringes for self-injections, as well as antibiotics, stimulants, strong pain-killers, and instructions to follow a strict diet. Shortly afterward George H. Maines, an old friend from Detroit who had been chief organizer of the big banquet in February 1921 after Cobb became the Tigers' manager, happened to be in Reno with his wife. Upon hearing about Cobb, they immediately drove out to find him "alone, and a tired out man." Yet Cobb greeted them warmly and even cooked bacon and eggs for their dinner. He was "always the perfect host if he liked you," Maines recalled.[37]

During the three weeks the Maines visited with him, Cobb repeatedly kept them up past midnight talking about his baseball days, his recently successful efforts to get Sam Crawford into the Hall of Fame, his pride in the Cobb Educational Fund youngsters, and numerous other subjects. He knew he was very sick and not getting any better. "My pain is so great I never get a full hour's sleep any night," he told them. "The medicines and pills I take are no longer potent. Nothing kills the pain." So he had taken to consuming about a quart of Jack Daniels bourbon, mixed with a quart of milk, every day. "This has an effect of dulling somewhat my senses and nerves," was the way he rationalized his disregard for the dietary regimen he was supposed to be following.[38]

Dissatisfied with the Scripps Clinic's explanation for his ills, Cobb decided to seek another opinion. Early in December, Maines drove him from Atherton to the San Francisco airport, where he caught a plane for Chicago and a reunion with Ray Schalk, his longtime foe when Schalk was catching for the White Sox but for many years now Cobb's faithful friend. From Chicago Cobb flew to Atlanta to enter Emory University Hospital for examination by a medical staff he knew fairly well and was inclined to trust. At Emory he was found to have not Bright's disease and not just an enlarged prostate but a cancerous growth that had already spread rapidly from the prostate to other parts of his body. He soon underwent surgery for the removal of nearly all of his prostate and then began a series of cobalt radiation treatments. When Maines welcomed him back at the Reno airport later in the month, he was walking well and seemed to feel better. One of the first things he did was file suit against the state of California for recovery of his taxes.

Toward the end of January 1960, Cobb flew east again, to be honored first by B'nai B'rith of New York as one of the "men of the age in sports," then by the New York baseball writers at their annual dinner. He gave every indication of being in good spirits and enjoying himself, even though another round of cobalt treatments awaited him at Emory as soon as he left New York.

After resting at Cornelia for a couple of months, Cobb returned to Lake Tahoe. For some time he had been supposed to start work on an autobiography, under contract to Doubleday and Company and with help from a sportswriter named Al Stumpf. Now he was finally ready for Stumpf to come up from his home at Santa Barbara, California, so they could begin. Stumpf arrived to find Cobb in much worse shape than he had anticipated and in an ugly mood most of the time. He ate very little and drank a great deal, particularly his whiskey-milk concoction. As the Maines had learned and as Stumpf now discovered as well, despite his enfeeblement Cobb had no domestic help, having either fired or driven away a succession of servants. "I had a very sick and difficult man on my hands," Stumpf later said. "Ty's family and ex-friends backed clear away from him." Stumpf came to feel that he was a combination "nurse, keeper and whipping boy. . . . at no time was it easy."[39]

Stumpf's involvement with Cobb on the book project extended over parts of the next year. His published account of his experiences with the old man sometimes reads like a gothic horror tale. Cobb kept huge sums of money at his lodge and with him whenever he went anywhere. He also kept a loaded Luger pistol on or near his person at all times, and on one occasion fired three shots into a darkened motel parking lot to quiet a group of rowdies who had disturbed a rare period of sleep. As Stumpf described his situation, he had little choice but to do Cobb's bidding, not only because he wanted to get the book finished but also because he was often afraid of what Cobb might do if he refused. So, for example, one night they took a terrifying ride down the mountainside in a blizzard so Cobb could hit the casinos in Reno. Sometimes gasping for breath, barely able to stand, Cobb nonetheless stayed around the dice tables for several days, quarreling with stickmen, bartenders, and other people but winning consistently—about $3000 in all. On an earlier trip into Reno, he told Stumpf, he'd won $12,000 in three hours. Obviously his lifelong distaste for gambling had faded in Nevada's free and easy moral atmosphere.

Not long after the Reno excursion, Cobb and Stumpf transferred their fit-ful literary efforts from Lake Tahoe to Atherton. There Stumpf was astounded to find that Cobb had no electricity, his power having been shut off by the Pacific Gas and Electric Company because he had refused to pay a $120 bill. That amount was outrageous, Cobb protested; the house hadn't even been oc-cupied during the billing period. He'd already had his lawyers file suit against the utility, he assured Stumpf. Working by a single electric bulb hooked up with two-hundred feet of extension cord that was plugged into a neighbor's outlet, Stumpf managed to make some progress with Cobb on the book. But Cobb grew so weak he had to enter Stanford University Hospital for more bombardments of cobalt. There he managed to record a lot of his reminis-cences by using a microphone suspended over his bed. In the strange night-time quiet of the hospital, Cobb spoke to himself about his triumphs and heartaches in baseball a half-century earlier, when it seemed that the game and life generally had been better.

With his cancer's spread slowed by the radiation treatments, Cobb left Stumpf on the West Coast and returned to Georgia. Nothing more had been done on his homesite on Chenocetah Mountain, nor was Cobb any longer willing to pursue the project. The lush undergrowth soon covered over the excava-tion, covered all signs that a man had once started to have something built there. Cobb's ambitions had become short term: to stifle the pain enough so he could get through a day, a week; to do something now that would take mind off his deadly predicament.

Late in June he went to the Hall of Fame reunion. This would be his last visit to Cooperstown, he told Sid Keener, director of the Hall of Fame. "I'm a sick man and I know it." That night after the banquet Cobb, using a cane and moving with considerable effort, walked with Keener from the Otesaga Hotel back to the exhibits building. They entered the Hall of Fame Gallery, where Cobb stood looking at his plaque near the gallery front. Seeing that he was wiping away tears, Keener tried to comfort him. Cobb pulled away, said only "Goodbye," and moved unsteadily through the exhibits and out the front door of the building. That was the last time Keener saw him alive.[40]

Later that summer Cobb decided that he wanted to take in the 1960 Olympic Games in Rome, and that he was strong enough to make the long trip. After talking with Harrison Gailey and various others about going with him, he fi-nally persuaded Stewart Brown, Jr., who had followed his father into medi-cine and assumed directorship at Cobb Memorial Hospital following the elder Brown's death. Cobb and Brown flew from New York to Rome during the third week in August. Unaccountably, Cobb arrived with only twenty dollars in his possession, and for their first couple of days in Rome, Brown had to run around to banks getting drafts cashed on Cobb's Reno bank. But they managed to make it to the opening Olympic ceremonies on August 24. Although Brown was prepared to give Cobb medical attention at any time, his strength held out well in the heat and pressing crowds. He even felt well enough to stay on by himself for the remainder of the Games when Brown had to return to the States after about ten days. Cobb's fourth trip outside the North American continent (including the 1910 Cuban excursion) ended when his Boeing 707 landed at New York on September 10.

Then it was back to California and Nevada and more sporadic work with Stumpf on the book that seemed less and less likely ever to see print. Late in the fall he returned to Georgia, bringing Stumpf with him. After four weeks of cobalt treatments at Emory Hospital, Cobb again went to Cornelia to recuperate.

On Christmas Eve 1960, Stumpf drove him down to Royston so Cobb could see the gray marble mausoleum he had recently had installed at the local cemetery. The mausoleum contained the remains of Cobb's parents, disinterred from gravesites near by, and of his sister Florence, moved from Sarasota, Florida. On the steps of the crypt Cobb asked Stumpf to pray with him. When they entered, Cobb pointed out his father's tomb and talked for a while about his character and achievements. "My father was the greatest man I ever knew," Cobb said. "He was the only man who ever made me do his bidding." Then he added slowly, "My father had his head blown off with a shotgun when I was eighteen years old—*by a member of my own family.* I didn't get over that. I've never gotten over it."[41] It was possibly the first time in his life that Cobb had been able to say that much about how W. H. Cobb had died. Even then he could not name his mother as the one who had pulled the trigger.

At the insistence of his physicians at Emory, Cobb had taken a full-time nurse with him to Cornelia. She was supposed to make sure that he got his insulin injections and medications on schedule and followed a correct diet. But Cobb quickly rebelled against having his life managed and particularly not being able to consume his daily quart-plus of bourbon or scotch. By the time George Maines and his wife arrived at Cobb's apartment late in February 1961, he had discharged his nurse. Meanwhile Stumpf had flown back to California.

The dying old man was desperately lonely. He put up a good front, telling the Maines about his house plans and gesturing out the window in the direction of "my mountain." But what he really wanted to talk about was getting the elderly couple to stay on, live with him on a permanent basis for $200–$300 a month plus all expenses. Maines had to answer that he and his wife were just too old to give him the kind of care he needed. "That was one of the hardest decisions I ever made," said Maines later.[42]

After a few days with Ray Schalk, who flew down from Chicago, Cobb had another round of treatment at Emory before returning to California. In a letter to Maines he alluded to the recent death from cancer of the movie star

Gary Cooper: "Mine is a slow type, Cooper's fast." He had taken on a ghastly look, the skin hanging from his once-jowly face and his weight now down to about 175 pounds from the 210 or so he had carried before the onset of his illness. Yet he seemed to feel better, in fact well enough to travel with Stumpf to Phoenix and Scottsdale, Arizona, where the Indians, Giants, Cubs, and Red Sox were all conducting spring training. In a suite at the Ramada Inn, Stumpf recalled, "Cobb held court. He didn't go to see anybody."[43] Instead such luminaries as Ford Frick, now baseball's commissioner; American League president Joe Cronin; and Ted Williams, who had just finished his mighty career with the Red Sox, came by at various times to listen to Cobb's preachments about the superiority of the old game and the old ballplayers.

Cobb and Stumpf left Scottsdale early in April, Cobb clutching the brown paper bag in which, for years now, he had carried around more than a million dollars worth of negotiable securities. Starting to fail fast, he stayed at Stumpf's Santa Barbara beach house. There two physicians examined him and found that the cancer had moved up his back and into his skull. Refusing strong medications, Cobb wondered aloud whether Max Fleischmann, heir to the Fleischmann's Yeast fortune and once his friend, hadn't done the right thing in committing suicide instead of suffering hopelessly with cancer. "Where's anybody who cares about me?" he burst out on another occasion. "Where are they? The world's lousy . . . no good."[44]

On April 27 Cobb somehow gathered his strength to make it to Wrigley Field in Los Angeles for the home opener of the new Los Angeles Angels, one of two expansion teams added to the American League over the winter. He thereby kept a promise he had made during spring training in Arizona to Fred Haney, his old utility infielder and now general manager of the Angels. "I told you I'd make it," he greeted Haney.[45] After throwing out the first ball and sitting through two innings of the Angels-Minnesota Twins game, he left leaning on his cane and on a park attendant's arm. He had seen his last baseball game.

Confident that he finally had plenty of material to put together Cobb's autobiography, Stumpf drove Cobb back up to his Atherton place, which still had no electricity, and said goodbye. One of the last to see Cobb at the house where he had entertained so many people over the past thirty years was the aging movie comedian Joe E. Brown. A longtime acquaintance, Brown spent the better part of a week with Cobb and was surprised to hear him say that if he had his life to do over, he'd "do things a little different." Maybe, he mused, he'd been "too aggressive, maybe I went too far. I always had to be right in any argument I was in, and wanted to be first in everything." A day or so later he added, "Joe, I do indeed think I would have done things different. And if I had, I would have had more friends."[46]

In mid-May he flew to Georgia for what he must have known would be his last stay in Cornelia. During the two-and-a-half weeks he was there, Gailey checked on him nearly every day. Sometimes he seemed fairly strong and in reasonably good spirits, at other times pathetically weak and depressed. Gailey, who had never really known Cobb before he moved to Cornelia in 1957, had come to care deeply about the old man. "I loved him, that's how I felt," was the way Gailey put it later on.[47]

It was Gailey who got Cobb to Emory Hospital on June 5, when he could no longer bear the pain. As always Cobb had his brown paper sack of securities with him, as well as his Luger. When he occupied his room, he placed the sack on top of the table by his bed and put the Luger on top of that. He then lay back finally to accept the injections of drugs that would ease his suffering. For the next month he drifted in semi-consciousness most of the time. Early in July his life signs began to fail. Charlie Cobb, accompanied by Jimmy Cobb, Shirley Cobb Beckwith, and Beverly Cobb McLaren, arrived from the West Coast. Whether Cobb recognized any of them during his last days is doubtful. At 1:18 on the afternoon of Monday, July 17, 1961, Cobb died. Physicians officially attributed his death to cancer complicated by a cardiac condition and diabetes. He had lived just short of seventy-four years and seven months.

Gailey made the funeral arrangements. The services were held on the 19th in Cornelia at the Christian Church, with the Reverend E. A. Miller, the local minister, and Dr. James R. Richardson of Westminster Presbyterian in Atlanta officiating. "His influence will continue to bring the best out of youth," Miller told the 150 or so people in the church. "Ty Cobb was never satisfied with second best."[48] Then a hearse carrying his bronze casket led the automobile procession slowly through the red clay hills over the twenty-eight miles to Royston. Uniformed members of local Little League teams lined the way from the Royston cemetery gate to the Cobb mausoleum. In all about four hundred people had gathered to watch Cobb's casket borne into the mausoleum and placed above his sister's tomb and directly across from those of his parents. Besides Charlie Cobb, his two daughters, and his one surviving son, his two sons-in-law and his daughter-in-law had also come, as well as Mary Dunn Cobb and her three children. Sid Keener was there representing the Hall of Fame. Ray Schalk and Mickey Cochrane had flown down together from Chicago, and Nap Rucker, Cobb's old Sally League roommate, had driven over from Alpharetta, north of Atlanta. Otherwise the world of baseball had no visible presence at the funeral of the man who had been possibly its greatest performer, certainly its most fiercely competitive spirit.

Epílogue

Cobb had waited until May 22 to have a will drawn up. Signed and witnessed at Cornelia and filed at Clarksville, the Habersham County seat, it left a quarter of his estate to the Cobb Educational Fund. The remainder—three-quarters of his holdings in stocks and bonds, his two houses, and assorted other properties—he bequeathed to his three children and, in a trust, to his grandchildren, who now numbered fifteen. Cobb's will relieved the executor, the Trust Company of Georgia, from filing an inventory of the estate, and his family would give out no details. Thus how much Cobb was actually worth at his death remained something of a mystery. The *Sporting News* estimated his fortune as being at least $11,780,000. According to what the baseball paper had learned, Cobb had held approximately $10 million in General Motors stock and $1,780,000 in Coca-Cola. Harrison Gailey, however, thought his total worth was about $6 million. Whatever the true figure, Cobb remained the richest man up to that time who had made his name as a professional athlete.

Two months after Cobb's death, Doubleday and Company brought out *My Life in Baseball: The True Record*, the autobiographical book on which he and Al Stumpf had worked intermittently for a year. Stumpf had put Cobb's recollections into book form in a matter of a month or so, and Doubleday had rushed its publication to take advantage of the publicity surrounding Cobb's death. At first the book sold "furiously," Stumpf reported to Sid Keener.[1] Ultimately Doubleday recorded sales of 12,000 to 15,000 copies, quite respectable though not spectacular. *My Life in Baseball* remained in print until 1965.

It was possibly the best book of its kind ever published. Like most autobiographies, memoirs, and reminiscences, Cobb's account was self-serving and self-justifying. Yet it was also remarkably candid, revealing, and faithful to its subject. The basic Ty Cobb—sensitive, distrustful, courageous, often arrogant, and sometimes mean—came through clearly. The book amounted to a heroic feat of memory inasmuch as Cobb worked much of the time without notes, clippings, or other referential material. It was not, of course, "the true record." Factual mistakes abounded, as did distortions and half-truths. Like John McCallum and numerous others who had written about Cobb, Stumpf made little effort to check details of Cobb's recollections against contemporary press reports. Yet as first-hand accounts by sports figures go, *My Life in Baseball* would prove exceptionally valuable for understanding a complex man and his time in baseball.

Baseball people who read the book failed to question the accuracy of Cobb's memory or interpretation of past events. He did raise a fair number of hackles, though, by his assault on the contemporary game and contemporary players. What he had to say on that score was basically a reprise of his 1952 *Life* pieces and sections of McCallum's 1955 book.

Cobb's all-time all-star team, for example, consisted wholly of men who had broken into the majors before 1920—with the exception of Mickey Cochrane as one of his catchers, Lefty Grove as one of his pitchers, and Harold "Pie" Traynor at third base. Even those three had been at the height of their careers when Cobb retired. For all his regard for the heroes of the dead-ball era and his regret over what Ruth's slugging ways had done to the game, Cobb had to put the Babe in his all-time outfield, along with Tris Speaker and Joe Jackson. George Sisler, Eddie Collins, and Honus Wagner were the rest of his infield, Ray Schalk his other catcher, Ed Walsh, Walter Johnson, Christy Mathewson, Grover Cleveland Alexander, and Eddie Plank his pitchers along with Grove. It was a formidable group, so formidable that Cobb was convinced such mid-century stars as Bob Feller, Joe DiMaggio, Stan Musial, Ted Williams, Duke Snider, Mickey Mantle, and Willie Mays "would stand little show with the men of my era."[2]

In Cobb's view baseball had reached "a perilous moment" in its history. "Wild things are happening. The fabric of baseball is crumbling." Other sports, promoted better than baseball, were steadily encroaching on its season and eroding its once-dominant place in the American sports scene. Baseball had also undermined itself in various ways. Its recent shifts and additions of franchises had weakened old club loyalties and identities. The virtual abandonment of the waiver system and the introduction of interleague trading had broken down the traditional integrity of the two major leagues. Television and the majors' "wild-eyed, desperate expansion" had largely destroyed the minor leagues. With their bonuses and big salaries, players lacked the fiery competitiveness of the oldtimers. "I'd want players less interested in a bonus, a business manager, and a bowling alley than in fighting to win," declared Cobb.[3]

But most of all it was the lively ball and fence-swinging that threatened the survival of the game's popularity. Heady play afield and on the bases and scientific hitting had long since gone out the window. Before long, Cobb predicted, the .300 hitter would become extinct. Games were overly long and dull, plagued by ho-hum homeruns and a parade of pitchers. The excitement, the unpredictability, the daring and hustle and fight of Cobb's day had largely disappeared. The game had lost its fire and was in danger of losing its place in the hearts of the American sports public.

Cobb's jeremiad, commonly dismissed as the rantings of an old man long out of touch with the realities of a changing sport and business, nevertheless hit the mark in several ways. Franchise-hopping, which had started in 1953 and continued through the 1960s, discouraged the kind of fierce attachments to ball clubs that had been one feature of baseball in the old days. The creation of ten new franchises between 1961 and 1977 spread the talent thinly and brought into being a collection of chronically weak ball clubs, major league in name only. Cobb's prediction about the extinction of .300 hitters almost came true, at least in the American League. In 1968 Carl Yastrzemski, at .301, was that circuit's one and only .300 batsman. (The National League that year had a total of five .300-plus regulars.)

Yet ironically, just when Cobb died, baseball was entering upon still another phase in the evolution of its playing style. With the elimination of racial barriers in the 1940s and 1950s, brilliantly talented American black and Hispanic-American players began to make it to the majors. The combination of speed and power so many of them possessed added an exciting new dimension to the game.

The very next year after Cobb's death, Maury Wills did what just a few years earlier had seemed absolutely impossible: He broke Cobb's single-season stolen base record and went on to steal an astonishing 104 bases during a 162-game season. In 1965, moreover, Wills stole ninety-four; five times he stole at least fifty bases in a major-league career that did not begin until he was twenty-six. In 1974 Lou Brock, another black player, stole 118 bases one year and later smashed Cobb's record for career steals, amassing 938 by the time he retired after the 1979 season. Three years after that Rickey Henderson, still another black performer who would have been barred from Organized Baseball in Cobb's day, reached 130 steals in a single season and seemed quite capable of averaging a steal a game.

An overall renaissance in team base-stealing accompanied those stunning individual achievements. While homerun-hitting on a per-club basis tended to level off toward the end of the fifties, the average number of steals per club increased dramatically—from 43 in 1955 to 127 in 1976. If Cobb had lived another decade or so, he would have continued to find much in contemporary baseball to grumble about, and he would have been justified in much of what he had to say. A lack of base-stealing, however, would no longer have been a legitimate complaint.

For those who revered Cobb's prowess on the diamond and for his kins-people who wanted to remember his good qualities and let his faults be entombed with his body, Al Stumpf's recapitulation of his "wild" year as Cobb's book collaborator was a most unhappy event.[4] It did not help that the piece was published in *True* magazine, which aimed at a predominantly male readership interested less in factual accuracy than in robustly told, often mildly risqué tales of adventure and exploit. Yet if overdrawn in places—as it no doubt was—Stumpf's account had a basic ring of authenticity. The most questionable aspect of what he wrote had to do with his willingness to repeat unverified gossip about events in Cobb's life that took place before Stumpf knew him. And of course the timing of the piece, which appeared only six months after Cobb's death, was in dubious taste.

In Royston, Georgia, people who had known and liked Cobb and appreciated what he had done for the town had already undertaken a project to commemorate the life of the man they understood to have been basically generous and warm hearted. Shortly before Cobb died, a group of prominent Royston citizens led by Stewart Brown, Jr., had started raising money to build a Ty Cobb museum in the town. After Cobb's death, Brown and his associates secured the passage of a bill in the Georgia legislature creating a Ty Cobb Baseball Memorial Commission. Brown was the commission's chairman. Such notables as Governor Carl Sanders, former Governor Ernest Vandiver, Mayor Ivan Allen of Atlanta, George Weiss, now president of the New York Mets, and J. G. Taylor Spink, publisher of the *Sporting News*, agreed to serve as honorary members of the commission. Each biennium the legislature was supposed to make an appropriation for the project. Meanwhile private contributions were supposed to supply more than $500,000. The site chosen for the memorial was two acres fronting U. S. Highway 29 on the western outskirts of the town, just down the road from Cobb Memorial Hospital.

It was an ambitious scheme, intended not only to memorialize "the greatest and smartest player baseball has ever known" but to attract tourists to the little town as well.[5] It never really worked out. By 1970 the legislature had appropriated $175,000, but Brown now said the commission needed at least $75,000 more from the state. Private contributions had been woefully disappointing. Only about $20,000 had been collected, of which the largest single contribution, $2500, had come from John E. Fetzer, president of the Detroit Tigers. The commission did have enough to build a structure—a rather handsome one, too. Made of brick, it had two wings and an open courtyard with a reflecting pool. A lack of money had forced cancellation of the original plan for a big bronze statue of Cobb to stand in the courtyard area.

Apart from insufficient funds, the project's promoters soon discovered that almost no Cobb baseball artifacts were available, inasmuch as nearly all of them had long ago gone to the National Baseball Hall of Fame and Museum. There simply was very little to put inside a Cobb shrine at Royston. Another problem was Royston's location, too far off the interstate routes to encourage much tourism. So after fifteen years of trying to provide a lasting monument to the most famous person ever to live in Royston, Georgia, Brown and his associates finally had to give up. In the mid-1970s the commission deeded the building to the town, which made it into a new city hall. The small collection of Cobb memorabilia the commission had put together over the years was moved over to the hospital. A billboard outside town advertising the shrine and featuring a reproduction of a famous photograph of Cobb tearing around third was painted over, producing the strange effect of a blank white rectangle with the silhouette of a baseball player protruding from one corner.

Thus the principal memorial to Ty Cobb would have to be found in the record books and in the first-hand accounts of people who had seen him play. In the 1980s Cobb's name was again frequently in the baseball news, as Pete Rose continued his steady climb toward Cobb's total career base-hits record. Rose, who was a rookie two years after Cobb died, was often described as the one contemporary ballplayer who came closest to playing the game the way Cobb had. Both Rose and Cobb were exceptionally durable, hard-driving men with a passion for winning. There, though, the similarity ended. Cobb was a much faster, more daring, more clever baserunner and a far better hitter according to many people, including Waite Hoyt, who pitched against Cobb and then for years, as a broadcaster for the Cincinnati Reds, watched Rose in action. "As far as skills are concerned," commented Hoyt, "there is no comparison. . . . Cobb was so brilliant with his bat manipulation that it would be impossible to describe the things he could do."[6] And unlike Cobb, Rose consistently exhibited an affable, even-tempered nature, was able to take criticism, and had no trouble laughing at himself.

Cobb's career base-hits mark might go the way of his base-stealing records. But his greatness was vastly more than statistics. It was something that only those who saw him in person could really understand, and even they usually had a hard time putting their feelings into words. "It was like he was superhuman," Casey Stengel, a National League contemporary, finally summed up his memory of Cobb.[7] A man who set the highest standards for himself and consistently met them, Cobb was never able to understand why most other people failed to share his passion for excellence and refusal to settle for second best. He was never an easy man to know, never easy to get along with in or out of uniform, never really at peace with himself or the world around him. Ty Cobb was the most volatile, the most fear-inspiring presence ever to appear on a baseball field. His equal is not likely to come along again.

Notes

PROLOGUE

1. Or .366, depending on whether one accepts the 1981 revisions made by the *Sporting News* in Cobb's basehit and at-bat totals for the years 1906 and 1910.
2. Sisler quoted in David Holland, "The One and Only Cobb," *American Mercury*, LXXXIII (Sept. 1956), 104; New York *World* editorial quoted in "Why Ty Cobb Is Tired—and Retired," *Literary Digest*, XCI (Nov. 20, 1926), 56.
3. Lawrence Ritter. *The Glory of Their Times* (New York: Macmillan, 1966), 197.
4. New York *Times* editorial, quoted in "Why Cobb Is Tired—and Retired," 56.
5. Tristram Coffin, *The Old Ball Game: Baseball in Folklore and Fiction* (New York: Herder and Herder, 1971), 80, 90–91, 93.
6. Ty Cobb, with Al Stumpf, *My Life in Baseball: The True Record* (Garden City: Doubleday, 1961), 280.
7. Ritter, *Glory of Their Times*, 42, 62, 81; Fred Lieb, *Baseball as I Have Known It* (New York: Tempo/Grosset and Dunlap, 1977), 63; Donald Honig and Lawrence Ritter, *Baseball: When the Grass Was Real* (New York: Coward, McCann, and Geohegan, 1975), 42; Ritter and Honig, *The Image of Their Greatness* (New York: Crown Publishers, 1979), 28.

CHAPTER I: "DON'T COME HOME A FAILURE"

1. Detroit *Free Press*, Oct. 11, 1906, p. 1.
2. C. Vann Woodward, *The Strange Career of Jim Crow* (Rev. ed., New York: Oxford University Press, 1964), 49–95; Charles Reagan Wilson, *Baptized in Blood: The Religion of the Lost Cause, 1865–1920* (Athens: University of Georgia Press, 1980), 30 and passim.
3. Quoted in James McCallum, *Ty Cobb* (New York: Praeger, 1975), 4.
4. Ty Cobb, with Al Stumpf, *My Life in Baseball: The True Record* (Garden City: Doubleday, 1961), 280.
5. Ibid., 42.
6. W. H. Cobb to Tyrus Cobb, Jan. 5, 1902, Personal folder, Ty Cobb Collection, National Baseball Library, Cooperstown, New York.
7. Cobb, *My Life in Baseball*, 37.
8. Quoted in Furman Bisher, "A Visit with Ty Cobb," *Saturday Evening Post*, CCXXX (June 14, 1958), 53.

9. Cobb, *My Life in Baseball*, 43.

10. Ibid.

11. Quoted in Jack Sher, "Greatest Player of Them All," *Reader's Digest*, LVI (May 1950), 101.

12. Cobb, *My Life in Baseball*, 44. The Methodist minister at Royston in 1904, the Reverend John F. Yarborough, later promoted the story that he had managed the Royston Reds when Cobb played for the team and was personally responsible for W. H. Cobb's willingness to let his son go to Augusta for a tryout. In his old age Ty Cobb scoffed at the story, maintaining that Yarborough was "more or less of a joke among us boys." Besides, "he was a Methodist and we were Baptists. My father wouldn't have listened to him." Taped interview, Cobb with William A. Emerson, Jr., Cornelia, Ga. [early 1958], Cobb Collection, NBL.

13. Cobb. *My Life in Baseball*, 45.

14. Typescript of boxscore, Columbia at Augusta, April 26, 1904, with accompanying typescript comments by Ernest J. Lanigan, Records/Statistics folder, Cobb Collection, NBL. Cobb's account in *My Life in Baseball* has him hitting an inside-the-park homerun in his first game and getting a hit and stealing a base in his second. Many others have given erroneous accounts of Cobb's performance in the two games.

15. Cobb, *My Life in Baseball*, 47; Dayton Stoddart, "What Baseball Has Taught Ty Cobb," *Collier's*, LXXIV (July 19, 1924), 7.

16. Quoted in Cobb, *My Life in Baseball*, 48.

17. Quoted in *Sporting News*, Feb. 24, 1927, p. 8.

18. Cobb, *My Life in Baseball*, 50.

19. In his autobiography Cobb termed his father's death "a gun accident" and treated the whole affair cursorily. Ibid., 52.

20. Interview with Susie Cunningham Bond, Royston, Ga., July 7, 1982.

21. Cobb, *My Life in Baseball*, 52. Earlier that season Edward Grant Barrow, former Tigers manager and currently managing Indianapolis in the American Association, had had a chance to buy either Engle or Cobb for $500 or both for a total of $800. "Thinking Cobb the less desirable of the two," Barrow lamented in his memoirs, "I offered $300, which Augusta turned down. So I lost this great player for $200." Ed Barrow, *My Fifty Years in Baseball* (New York: Coward-McCann, 1951), 61. The $700 price the Tigers paid for Cobb was not the pittance it would later seem. At the time top-flight Class A (highest minor classification) ballplayers regularly sold for $2000 to $3000. The purchase of pitcher Rube Marquard from Indianapolis for an unprecedented $11,000 in 1908 startled the baseball world. The purchase price on Cobb actually was $700, not $750 as it has usually been given. See W. R. Armour to Cobb, % Augusta Baseball Club, Aug. 25, 1905, Detroit Baseball Club letterbooks, III, Ernie Harwell Collection, Detroit Public Library, Detroit.

22. Philadelphia *Bulletin*, Sept. 23, 1929, p. 30B, in Connie Mack clippings, Historical Society of Pennsylvania, Philadelphia.

23. Detroit *Free Press*, Aug. 30, 1905, p. 9.

CHAPTER II: THE WORLD HE ENTERED

1. In fairness it should be noted that the veteran umpires generally preferred to work alone, and that a quick changeover to a multiple-umpire system would have necessitated forced retraining for them. It took more than four additional decades, until the 1950s, for the two leagues to arrive at a four-umpire arrangement for every regular-season game.

2. William J. Klem and William J. Slocum, "Umpire Bill Klem's Own Story," *Collier's* CCXXVIII (April 14, 1951), 31. When in 1914 Klem used twenty-eight balls in a game in Boston, owner James Gaffney of the Boston Braves protested to National League President John Heydler that Klem would bankrupt him.

3. New York *Times*, April 12, 1907, p. 10.

4. Detroit *Free Press*, July 14, 1905, p. 10; *Sporting News*, June 26, 1905, p. 4. In 1905 the Chicago White Sox drew 696,853 to lead the American League.

5. Frank J. Navin to Sam Crawford, Feb. 23, 1905; Navin to Robert Lowe, same date; Navin to Frank Van Dusen, April 28, 1912; W. R. Armour to Matty McIntyre, Feb. 24, 1905, Detroit Baseball Club letterbooks, II, XII, Ernie Harwell Collection, Detroit Public Library, Detroit.

6. Taped interview, Cobb with William A. Emerson, Jr., Cornelia, Ga. [early 1958], Ty Cobb Collection, National Baseball Library, Cooperstown, N. Y.

7. Chesbro's 41 wins in 1904, when the Highlanders narrowly missed edging Boston for the American League pennant, are a record for the twentieth century.

8. Ty Cobb, with Al Stumpf, *My Life in Baseball: The True Record* (Garden City: Doubleday, 1961), 18.

9. Washington *Post*, Sept. 22, 1905, p. 8.

10. *Sporting Life*, Sept. 30, 1905, p. 7; *Sporting News*, Sept. 23, 1905, p. 3.

11. Detroit *Free Press*, Jan. 22, 1912, p. 8.

CHAPTER III: "THE MOST MISERABLE AND HUMILIATING EXPERIENCE"

1. *Sporting Life*, Jan. 27, 1906, p. 7.

2. W. R. Armour to Tyrus R. Cobb, Jan. 6, 1906, Detroit Baseball Club letterbooks, IV, Ernie Harwell Collection, Detroit Public Library, Detroit. Like most field managers early in the century, Armour also acted pretty much as the Detroit club's general manager.

3. Armour to Cobb, Jan. 20, Feb. 19, 1906; Frank Navin to Edward Barrow, March 24, 1906, ibid.

4. Detroit *Free Press*, March 10, 1906, p. 10. Grantland Rice is usually credited with coining the nickname "Georgia Peach" for Cobb after Rice came to the New York newspaper scene from Atlanta a few years later. It appears, though, that Jackson, as early as 1906, was the actual originator.

5. Ty Cobb, with Al Stumpf, *My Life in Baseball: The True Record* (Garden City: Doubleday, 1961), 20.

6. Lawrence Ritter, *The Glory of Their Times* (New York: Macmillan, 1966), 62.

7. Quoted in Joseph Durso, *The Days of Mr. McGraw* (Englewood Cliffs: Prentice-Hall, 1969), 69.

8. *Sporting News*, May 19, 1906, p. 3; *Sporting Life*, same date, p. 7; Detroit *Free Press*, May 23, 1906, p. 12.

9. *Sporting Life*, July 7, 1906, p. 7, July 21, 1906, p. 7; *Sporting News*, July 7, 1906, p. 4.

10. Cobb, *My Life in Baseball*, 24. If Willett drank his share of beer in the majors, he also won his share of games—101 in ten years with Detroit and St. Louis in the Federal League.

11. *Sporting Life*, July 28, 1906, p. 7, Sept. 9, 1906, p. 6; Detroit *Free Press*, July 7, 1906, p. 15, July 27, 1906, p. 15, Aug. 1, 1906, p. 9.

12. Cobb, *My Life in Baseball*, 25.

13. In his autobiography Cobb was at pains to deny that he had kicked Siever. Ibid., 26–27.

14. Ibid., 26.

15. Cobb actually hit .316 in 1906, in 98 games. For some reason his records in the first two games he played that year were never recorded at Johnson's office. He was one for eight in those games, thus giving him 113 hits in 358 at bats for the season.

16. Cobb, *My Life in Baseball*, 31.

CHAPTER IV: A PENNANT FOR DETROIT

1. *Sporting Life*, Oct. 17, 1906, p. 5; Frank Navin to Tyrus Cobb, Feb. 11, 1907, Detroit Baseball Club letterbooks, IV, Ernie Harwell Collection, Detroit Public Library, Detroit.

2. *Sporting News*, June 14, 1950, p. 8; Detroit *Free Press*, Jan. 22, 1912, p. 8.

3. Augusta *Chronicle*, March 17, 1907, p. 12.

4. Detroit *Free Press*, March 17, 1907, p. 17.

5. *Sporting News*, April 8, 1907, p. 12; Detroit *Free Press*, March 30, 1907, p. 8, April 2, 1907, p. 8, April 13, 1907, p. 11.

6. Detroit *Free Press*, May 17, 1907, p. 9.

7. Ty Cobb, with Al Stumpf, *My Life in Baseball: The True Record* (Garden City: Doubleday, 1961), 65.

8. *Sporting News*, Sept. 9, 1907, p. 3, Sept. 26, 1907, p. 1; Detroit *Free Press*, Sept. 21, 1907, p. 15.

9. New York *Times*, Sept. 30, 1907, p. 5.

10. Ibid., Oct. 1, 1907, p. 13.

11. Until 1955, when Al Kaline, another Tiger, led the league. Kaline was exactly one day younger than Cobb had been when he won the hitting title in 1907.

12. *Sporting Life*, Oct. 5, 1907, p. 7.

13. Quoted in Fred Lieb, *The Detroit Tigers* (New York: G. P. Putnam's Sons, 1946), 104.

14. *Sporting News*, Oct. 10, 1917, p. 1.

CHAPTER V: TWO MORE PENNANTS AND OCTOBER DISAPPOINTMENTS

1. New York *American*, quoted in *Sporting Life*, Nov. 30, 1907, p. 3.

2. *Sporting Life*, Dec. 14, 1907, p. 3.

3. Frank J. Navin to Tyrus Cobb, Jan. 9, 1908, Detroit Baseball Club letterbooks, VI, Ernie Harwell Collection, Detroit Public Library, Detroit; *Sporting Life*, Feb. 15, 1908, p. 6.

4. Ibid., March 7, 1908, pp. 7, 10.

5. Augusta *Chronicle*, March 18, 1908, p. 12.

6. *Sporting Life*, March 28, 1908, p. 10.

7. Ibid., April 4, 1908, p. 16.

8. Ibid., April 25, 1908, p. 10.

9. Ty Cobb, with Al Stumpf, *My Life in Baseball: The True Record* (Garden City: Doubleday, 1961), 88.

10. *Sporting Life*, July 7, 1908, p. 6.

11. Ibid., Aug. 8, 1908, p. 11.

12. Augusta *Chronicle*, Aug. 7, 1908, p. 8.

13. New York *Times*, Oct. 8, 1908, p. 7.

14. *Sporting Life*, July 25, 1908, p. 4.

15. Frank J. Navin to Tyrus Cobb, Dec. 15, 1908, Detroit Baseball Club letter-books, VII.

16. Detroit *Free Press*, April 6, 1909, p. 9.

17. St. Louis *Post-Dispatch*, May 9, 1909, pt. IV, p. 1.

18. Ibid.

19. Detroit *Free Press*, June 15, 1909, p. 10; New York *Times*, June 16, 1909, p. 3.

20. Summers was 19-9 in 1909 but slumped to 12-12 and 12-11 the next two years before the Tigers released him early in 1912.

21. Taped interview. Ty Cobb with William J. Emerson, Jr., Cornelia, Ga. [early 1958], Ty Cobb Collection, National Baseball Library, Cooperstown, N.Y.

22. Detroit *Free Press*, Aug. 26, 1909, p. 8.

23. Ibid., Aug. 31, 1909, p. 8; *Sporting Life*, Sept. 4, 1909, p. 6. In the third game of the 1911 World Series, Fred Snodgrass of the New York Giants spiked Baker on the thigh, prompting another outcry from Mack and the reply from John McGraw that Cobb's defenders had been right two years earlier in maintaining that Baker covered third awkwardly and left himself open for spikings.

24. New York *Age*, Sept. 16, 1909, p. 6.

25. Cleveland *Plain Dealer*, Sept. 10, 1909, p. 9.

26. Ibid.

27. It was in the fourth game that, at Billy Evans's suggestion, the National Commission first put four umpires on the field at once in a World Series. Bill Klem worked the plate, Evans the bases, and Jimmy Johnstone (NL) and Silk O'Loughlin (AL) the foul lines.

CHAPTER VI: "THE GREATEST PLAYER OF ALL TIME"

1. St. Louis *Post-Dispatch*, May 9, 1909, pt. IV, p. 1. As indeed there would be; the investment would amortize itself in a little more than a year.

2. Detroit *Free Press*, Feb. 1, 1910, p. 9.

3. Frank J. Navin to Tyrus R. Cobb, Feb. 24, 1910, Detroit Baseball Club letter-books, IX, Ernie Harwell Collection, Detroit Public Library, Detroit; Detroit *Free Press*, March 30, 1910, p. 11.

4. Detroit *Free Press*, March 29, 1910, p. 8; *Sporting Life*, April 9, 1910, p. 2; Frank J. Navin to Tyrus Cobb, March 29, 1910, Detroit Baseball Club letterbooks, IX.

5. *Sporting Life*, Oct. 23, 1909, p. 8; New York *Times*, April 4, 1910, pt. IV, p. 2, April 14, 1910, pt. IV, p. 2.

6. Quoted in Edward Lyell Fox, "Baseball's Heavy Artillery," *Illustrated Sunday Magazine*, April 6, 1913, p. 6.

7. In 1915 a researcher named Arthur MacDonald found that during the previous season 20 percent of the more than 10,000 safely batted balls he had recorded had been bunts, and that 45 percent of all bunts had gone for safe hits.

8. Ty Cobb, *Busting 'Em and Other Stories* (New York: Edward J. Clode, Publishers, 1914), 81.

9. Quoted in "Why Cobb Is Tired—and Retired," *Literary Digest*, XCI (Nov. 20, 1926), 62.

10. Ibid.; "Ty Cobb on the Batting Art," *Literary Digest*, XLVIII (June 27, 1914), p. 1563; Schalk quoted in James T. Farrell, *My Baseball Diary* (New York: Viking Press, 1959), 220.

11. Quoted in Prosper Buranelli, "Ty Cobb Talks Baseball," *Detroit Free Press Magazine Section*, Sept. 25, 1921, p. 1.

12. Ibid.

13. Dayton Stoddart, "What Baseball Has Taught Ty Cobb," *Collier's*, LXXIV (July 19, 1924), 56.

14. Until 1931, balls that bounced into the outfield stands or through openings in the outfield fences were ruled homeruns.

15. *Sporting Life*, Aug. 15, 1910, p. 16.

16. Detroit *Free Press*, Aug. 7, 1910, p. 26.

17. Cleveland *Plain Dealer*, Oct. 9, 1910, pt. 3, p. 2.

18. New York *Times*, Oct. 11, 1910, p. 9; Cleveland *Plain Dealer*, Oct. 12, 1910, p. 8.

19. New York *Times*, Oct. 16, 1910, p. 4, p. 7; *Detroit Free*, same date, p. 15.

20. St. Louis *Post-Dispatch*, Oct. 17, 1910, p. 12. So it remained for seventy years, even though for many people Johnson's verdict never made much sense arithmetically. Finally researchers for the *Sporting News* as well as the Society for American Baseball Research dug back into the controversy and found that whereas McRoy had corrected his figures for the rest of the Tigers, he had let stand an extra two-for-three game for Cobb, erroneously recorded for September 24 as the second game of a doubleheader, when the Tigers actually played only one game. Remedying that mistake, plus minor corrections in Cobb's and Lajoie's statistics otherwise, produced an average of .383 for Lajoie and .382 for Cobb. (See Paul MacFarlane, "After 70 Years, Researchers Prove Lajoie Really Did Win," *Sporting News*, April 18, 1981, pp. 3ff; MacFarlane, ed., *Daguerreotypes of Great Stars of Baseball* [St. Louis: The Sporting News Publishing Co., 1981], 56.) Neither the baseball commissioner's office nor the National Baseball Hall of Fame, however, has seen fit to revise the historical record in favor of Lajoie. In baseball's official statistics Cobb remains the 1910 batting champion.

21. *Sporting News*, Oct. 13, 1910, p. 5; *Sporting Life*, Oct. 8, 1910, p. 18, Oct. 22, 1910, p. 7.

22. Detroit *Free Press*, Oct. 28, 1910, p. 10.

23. *Sporting Life*, Dec. 3, 1910, p. 9.

24. The world's champion Philadelphia Athletics followed the Tigers into Havana and played ten games against the same two Cuban teams, ending with a 4–6 record. In 1911 the Cubans won another series, from the Philadelphia National Leaguers, before John McGraw's Giants became the first major-league team to beat the Cubans convincingly, winning nine of twelve games from Havana and Almendares.

25. Frank J. Navin to Tyrus R. Cobb, Feb. 23, 1911, Detroit Baseball Club letterbooks, X.

26. Where, away from what he no doubt considered the baneful influence of Cobb, McIntyre had his finest year ever in the majors, hitting .323 and scoring 102 runs.

27. Frank J. Navin to Paul Bruske, March 24, 1911, Detroit Baseball Club letterbooks, X.

28. *Sporting Life*, Aug. 5, 1911, p. 15.

29. Review quoted in Detroit *Free Press*, Nov. 1, 1911, p. 6; Cowan quoted in Toronto *Daily Star*, July 19, 1961, p. 16, clipping in Personal folder, Ty Cobb Collection, National Baseball Library, Cooperstown, N.Y.

30. New York *Times*, June 13, 1915, sec. III, p. 3.

31. *Sporting News*, Dec. 28, 1911, p. 5; Detroit *Free Press*, Dec. 18, 1911, pp. 4, 7, Dec. 24, 1911, p. 14.

32. Ibid., Jan. 6, 1912, p. 7.

33. *Sporting Life*, Jan. 20, 1912, p. 7.

34. Hughey Jennings denounced Johnson's order, arguing that it loosened the control over his players that a manager had when he could assemble them all at one time to depart for and return from the ballpark. Left to themselves, Jennings feared, players would be late getting to games and would straggle back to their hotel by way of saloons.

35. *Sporting News*, Dec. 7, 1916, p. 4; *Sporting Life*, May 25, 1912, p. 1.

36. New York *Times*, May 19, 1912, p. 2.

37. *Sporting Life*, May 25, 1912, p. 4; Detroit *Free Press*, May 16, 1912, p. 10.

38. *Sporting Life*, May 25, 1912, p. 6.

39. *Sporting News*, May 23, 1912, p. 4.

40. New York *Times*, May 19, 1912, p. 2; Detroit *Free Press*, May 20, 1912, p. 8.

CHAPTER VII: "TY COBB'S MOST GLORIOUS YEARS ARE BEHIND HIM"

1. *Sporting Life*, Jan. 4, 1913, p. 6, Feb. 1, 1913, p. 3.

2. Detroit *Free Press*, April 17, 1913, p. 6, April 18, 1913, p. 12, March 24, 1913, p. 8; New York *Times*, April 17, 1913, p. 9.

3. Detroit *Free Press*, April 20, 1913, p. 13; New York *Times*, same date, p. 1.

4. New York *Times*, April 26, 1913, p. 12.

5. U. S. Congress, House of Representatives, *Organized Baseball: Report of the Subcommittee on the Study of Monopoly Power of the Committee of the Judiciary*, 82nd Cong., 2nd sess. (1952), 217; *Sporting News*, May 1, 1913, p. 1.

6. Detroit *Free Press*, July 13, 1913, pp. 18, 20.

7. Ibid., Aug. 4, 1913, p. 8.

8. *Sporting News*, Oct. 2, 1913, p. 2.

9. Detroit *Free Press*, Nov. 11, 1913, p. 12; New York *Times*, same date, p. 11; *Sporting News*, Nov. 27, 1913, p. 2.

10. *Sporting News*, June 11, 1914, p. 3.

11. *Sporting Life*, June 27, 1914, p. 10.

12. *Sporting News*, June 23, 1914, p. 9.

13. *Sporting Life*, Oct. 3, 1914, p. 14.

14. Athletics third baseman Frank Baker, dubbed "Home Run" after he hit two round-trippers in the 1911 Series, was so unhappy with his 1915 contract that he held out all that year.

15. *Sporting Life*, Oct. 24, 1914, p. 16.

16. Ibid., Nov. 7, 1914, p. 9.

17. New York *Times*, April 4, 1915, p. 10; Ring W. Lardner, "Tyrus, the Greatest of All," *American Magazine*, LXXIX (June 1915), 19.

18. "Why Ty Cobb is Tired—and Retired," *Literary Digest*, XCI (Nov. 20, 1926), 62; Ty Cobb, with Al Stumpf, *My Life in Baseball: The True Record* (Garden City: Doubleday, 1961), 125. Cobb maintained that Leonard was one of only two men he ever deliberately tried to spike, the other being catcher Harry Bemis of Cleveland, whom he also missed cutting.

19. *Sporting News*, Aug. 5, 1915, p. 3.

20. Detroit *Free Press*, July 20, 1915, p. 12, July 25, 1915, p. 17.

21. New York *Times*, Aug. 25, 1915, p. 8; Detroit *Free Press*, same date, pp. 10–11; Cleveland *Plain Dealer*, Jan. 5, 1927, p. 19.

22. Detroit *Free Press*, Aug. 27, 1915, p. 13.

23. Ibid., Sept. 17, 1915, p. 10.

24. *Sporting Life*, March 4, 1916, p. 17.
25. *Sporting News*, Sept. 28, 1916, p. 3.
26. Ibid., Nov. 30, 1916, p. 3.

CHAPTER VIII: A WORLD WAR AND A NEW ERA

1. Detroit *Free Press*, March 28, 1917, p. 11.
2. Ibid., April 1, 1917, pp. 21–22.
3. Ibid., April 2, 1917, p. 11.
4. Quoted in Ty Cobb, with Al Stumpf, *My Life in Baseball: The True Record* (Garden City: Doubleday, 1961), 130; Frank Graham, *McGraw of the Giants* (New York: G. P. Putnam's Sons, 1944), 98.
5. St. Louis *Post-Dispatch*, July 1, 1917, pt. 4, p. 1, July 2, 1917, p. 6.
6. Crawford was far from through as a ballplayer. For four seasons he played regularly with Los Angeles in the Pacific Coast League, hitting above .300 three of those years and peaking at .360 in 1919, with fourteen homers.
7. Cobb, *My Life in Baseball*, 188.
8. *Sporting News*, Nov. 22, 1917, p. 6, Jan. 24, 1918, p. 5; New York *Times*, Feb. 16, 1918, p. 13.
9. New York *Times*, Feb. 17, 1918, p. 16.
10. Detroit *Free Press*, Jan. 19, 1918, p. 9, Jan. 24, 1918, p. 11.
11. Manly F. Miner, [*Jack Miner*], booklet (no pl., no pub., n.d.) in Ty Cobb Collection, General and Miscellaneous folder, National Baseball Library, Cooperstown, N.Y.
12. St. Louis *Post-Dispatch*, Sept. 2, 1918, p. 6.
13. *Sporting News*, Nov. 14, 1918, p. 2.
14. Cobb, *My Life in Baseball*, 189.
15. New York *Times*, Dec. 17, 1918, p. 14.
16. Ibid., March 18, 1919, p. 12.
17. *Sporting News*, Aug. 21, 1919, p. 1.
18. Ibid., Sept. 11, 1919, p. 3.
19. Cobb, *My Life in Baseball*, 192.
20. New York *Times*, Jan. 6, 1920, p. 16.
21. Cobb, *My Life in Baseball*, 193.
22. New York *Times*, May 25, 1920, p. 16, May 27, 1920, p. 12.
23. Ibid., Aug. 8, 1920, p. 20.
24. *Sporting News*, Aug. 12, 1920, pp. 3, 5.
25. New York *Times*, Aug. 21, 1920, p. 8.
26. In his autobiography Cobb, intentionally or not, heightened the dramatic effect of the New York episode by making the *first* game of the series the occasion for his 5-6 performance. See Cobb, *My Life in Baseball*, 136–39.
27. *Sporting News*, Nov. 11, 1920, p. 3.
28. Ibid., Oct. 21, 1920, p. 2.
29. Detroit *Free Press*, Dec. 19, 1920, p. 11.
30. Ibid., Jan. 6, 1912, p. 11; Cobb, *My Life in Baseball*, 196.

CHAPTER IX: BOSS OF THE TIGERS

1. *Sporting News*, Jan. 27, 1921, p. 1, Feb. 3, 1921, p. 2.
2. Quoted in John D. McCallum, *Ty Cobb* (New York: Praeger, 1975), 105.

3. Ty Cobb, with Al Stumpf, *My Life in Baseball: The True Record* (Garden City: Doubleday, 1961), 198.

4. Detroit *Free Press*, March 9, 1921, p. 11, March 14, 1921, p. 10; *Sporting News*, March 17, 1921, p. 3.

5. Detroit *Free Press*, April 22, 1921, p. 12, April 23, 1921, p. 12.

6. *Sporting News*, Sept. 8, 1921, p. 3.

7. Barnes's account is in Birmingham *News*, Feb. 25, 1973, clipping in Ty Cobb Collection, Personal folder, National Baseball Library, Cooperstown, N. Y.

8. *Sporting News*, April 13, 1922, p. 1, April 20, 1922, p. 1.

9. Because of some oversight, Cobb never received word from Commissioner Landis's office that the suspension imposed at the end of the previous season had been lifted. Thus technically he remained in suspension when he stepped to the plate at Cleveland on April 12, 1922. He was never officially notified to the contrary.

10. New York *Times*, May 14, 1922, p. 27, May 17, 1922, p. 16.

11. Ibid., Dec. 10, 1922, sec. I, pt. 2, p. 1, Dec. 15, 1922, p. 23.

12. Ibid., Dec. 9, 1922, p. 16; Detroit *Free Press*, Dec. 14, 1922, p. 20.

13. Cobb, *My Life in Baseball*, 184.

14. Ibid., 208.

15. *Sporting News*, April 12, 1923, p. 1.

16. St. Louis *Post-Dispatch*, April 19, 1923, p. 32, April 30, 1922, p. 18; Cleveland *Plain Dealer*, May 2, 1923, p. 18.

17. New York *Times*, June 21, 1923, p. 14.

18. Donald Honig and Lawrence Ritter, *Baseball: When the Grass Was Real* (New York: Coward, McCann, and Geohegan, 1975), 40–41.

19. Dayton Stoddart, "What Baseball Has Taught Ty Cobb," *Collier's*, LXXIV (July 19, 1924), pp. 7, 21.

20. *Sporting News*, May 22, 1924, p. 7.

21. Atlanta *Constitution*, Feb. 28, 1925, p. 1, March 1, 1925, p. 11; New York *Times*, Feb. 28, 1925, p. 2.

22. *Sporting News*, Dec. 27, 1961, pp. 11–12.

23. New York *Times*, May 17, 1925, sec. X, pp. 1–2; Washington *Post*, May 27, 1925, p. 15. Some Detroit fans were also unkind enough to remind Cobb that in the two seasons since he traded Howard Ehmke, the tall righthander had won twenty and nineteen games for the Red Sox and had pitched a no-hitter (against the Tigers) in 1923.

24. Washington *Post*, August 4, 1925, pp. 13, 16.

25. New York *Times*, Aug. 31, 1925, p. 12; Detroit *Free Press*, Aug. 30, 1925, pp. 1–2; Cobb, *My Life in Baseball*, 241–42.

26. "Spanking Baseball's Baby and Petting Its Paragon," *Literary Digest*, LXXXVI (Sept. 19, 1925), pp. 58, 67; New York *Times*, Aug. 31, 1925, p. 14.

27. Detroit *Free Press*, Oct. 10, 1925, p. 16.

28. Cobb, *My Life in Baseball*, 201.

29. Ibid., 204.

30. *Sporting News*, April 15, 1926, p. 1.

31. Honig and Ritter, *Baseball*, 43.

32. Cobb taped interview with William A. Emerson, Jr., Cornelia, Ga. [early 1958], Cobb Collection, NBL; Cobb, *My Life in Baseball*, 240; Honig and Ritter, *Baseball*, 42.

33. Cleveland *Plain Dealer*, June 27, 1926, p. 1B; Detroit *Free Press*, July 17, 1926, p. 12.

34. Washington *Post*, Aug. 18, 1926, p. 13; Detroit *Free Press*, Aug. 19, 1926, p. 15; *Sporting News*, Aug. 26, 1926, p. 1.

35. *Sporting News*, Sept. 2, 1926, p. 5.

36. New York *Times*, Nov. 4, 1926, p. 30; Atlanta *Constitution*, Nov. 11, 1926, pp. 1, 3; Detroit *Free Press*, Nov. 4, 1926, pp. 20–21.

37. New York *Times*, Nov. 8, 1926, p. 17; Batchelor quoted in Norman Beasley and George W. Stark, *Made in Detroit* (New York: G. P. Putnam's Sons, 1957), 272–73.

38. *Sporting News*, Nov. 11, 1926, pp. 1, 3; Detroit *Free Press*, Nov. 4, 1926, p. 21; Honig and Ritter, *Baseball*, 41.

CHAPTER X: "IS THERE ANY DECENCY LEFT ON EARTH?"

1. Cleveland *Plain Dealer*, Nov. 30, 1926, p. 1.

2. On December 20, 1926, Rogers Hornsby, who had just led the Cardinals to a world's championship, joined the ranks of the onetime-player-managers when he was traded to the New York Giants.

3. The full text of the letters and of Cobb's, Speaker's, and Wood's testimony before Landis was fully reported by the Associated Press and widely published across the United States. For coverage of the whole affair as well as the roughly parallel controversy over the Swede Risberg accusations, I have relied on Cleveland *Plain Dealer*, New York *Times*, and Detroit *Free Press*, Dec. 21, 1926–Jan. 28, 1927, and *Sporting News*, Dec. 30, 1926–Feb. 3, 1927. All quotations are from those sources unless otherwise indicated.

4. Quoted in Ty Cobb, with Al Stumpf, *My Life in Baseball: The True Record* (Garden City: Doubleday, 1961), 244.

5. Quoted, ibid., 243.

6. Ibid., 246; Ty Cobb to Connie Mack, Feb. 22, 1955, Cobb Letters folder, Ty Cobb Collection, National Baseball Library, Cooperstown, N. Y. Italics in the original.

7. New York *Times*, Dec. 22, 1926, p. 18, Jan. 29, 1927, p. 11; Cobb, *My Life in Baseball*, p. 248; Cleveland *Plain Dealer*, Jan. 30, 1927, p. 27.

8. But only by a little, because Babe Ruth soon signed a three-year contract at $70,000 per year.

9. Cobb to Mack, Feb. 22, 1955.

CHAPTER XI: VINDICATION

1. Philadelphia *Inquirer*, Feb. 9, 1927, p. 16; New York *Times*, Feb. 9, 1927, p. 21; Ty Cobb, with Al Stumpf, *My Life in Baseball: The True Record* (Garden City: Doubleday, 1961), 250.

2. Connie Mack, *My 66 Years in the Big Leagues* (New York: Winston, 1950), 55–56; *Sporting News*, March 31, 1927, p. 7.

3. New York *Times*, March 18, 1927, p. 19; Philadelphia *Inquirer*, March 18, 1927, p. 22.

4. Philadelphia *Inquirer*, April 9, 1927, p. 25.

5. New York *Times*, April 14, 1927, p. 21.

6. Washington *Post*, April 20, 1927, p. 15.

7. New York *Times*, May 9, 1927, p. 16; Cleveland *Plain Dealer*, May 9, 1927, p. 21.

8. Cleveland *Plain Dealer*, July 22, 1927, p. 17; July 24, 1927, pt. 2, p. 1.

9. *Sporting News*, Sept. 29, 1927, p. 7.

10. Philadelphia *Inquirer*, Sept. 22, 1927, p. 20; *Sporting News*, Sept. 29, 1927, p. 7.

11. Philadelphia *Inquirer*, Nov. 1, 1927, p. 27.

12. New York *Times*, Nov. 1, 1927, p. 23.

13. Philadelphia *Inquirer*, Nov. 3, 1927, p. 24.

14. New York *Times*, Jan. 7, 1928, p. 9, Jan. 19, 1928, p. 19.

15. Ibid., Feb. 24, 1928, p. 16.

16. Ibid., March 3, 1928, p. 31.

17. Russell P. Reeder, Jr., to Ken Smith, Nov. 8, 1971, Cobb Letters folder, Ty Cobb Collection, National Baseball Library, Cooperstown, N.Y. Italics in original.

18. New York *Times*, March 20, 1928, p. 22.

19. Washington *Post*, April 18, 1928, p. 13.

20. Cleveland *Plain Dealer*, May 15, 1928, p. 23.

21. Of course Cobb also had one theft of home in World Series play—against the Pirates in 1909.

22. Cobb, *My Life in Baseball*, 259.

23. Philadelphia *Inquirer*, Sept. 18, 1928, p. 24; Cleveland *Plain Dealer*, Sept. 18, 1928, p. 16; New York *Times*, Sept. 18, 1928, p. 24.

CHAPTER XII: "JUST LOOKING IN DOESN'T HELP"

1. Babe Ruth, with Bob Considine, *The Babe Ruth Story* (New York: Dutton, 1948), 218.

2. Ty Cobb, with Al Stumpf, *My Life in Baseball: The True Record* (Garden City: Doubleday), 259.

3. Which now hangs in the Cobb showcase in the National Baseball Museum, its once-bright royal blue trim having faded to purple.

4. Cobb, *My Life in Baseball*, 259–260.

5. Philadelphia *Bulletin*, Sept. 24, 27, Oct. 3, 1929, in Connie Mack clippings, Historical Society of Pennsylvania, Philadelphia.

6. New York *Times*, Oct. 3, 1929, p. 36.

7. Tyrus R. Cobb to George H. Maines, March 7, 1928, Cobb Letters folder, Ty Cobb Collection, National Baseball Library, Cooperstown, N. Y.

8. Cobb taped interview with William A. Emerson, Jr., Cornelia, Ga. [early 1958], Cobb Collection, NBL.

9. New York *Times*, April 16, 1931, p. 34.

10. Furman Bisher, "A Visit with Ty Cobb," *Saturday Evening Post*, CCXXX (June 14, 1958), 42.

11. New York *Times*, April 30, 1931, p. 11.

12. Ibid., Feb. 2, 1936, p. 23.

13. Quoted in Connie Mack, *My 66 Years in the Big Leagues* (New York: Winston, 1950), 116.

14. Mrs. Babe Ruth, with Bill Slocum, *The Babe and I* (Englewood Cliffs: Prentice-Hall, 1959), 17.

15. Cobb, *My Life in Baseball*, 220; New York *Times*, June 25, 1941, p. 27.

16. New York *Times*, June 24, 1941, p. 23.

17. Malcolm W. Bingay, *Detroit Is My Own Home Town* (New York: Bobbs-Merrill, 1946), 259.

18. *Sporting News*, Feb. 26, 1942, p. 4.

19. New York *Times*, March 8, 1947, p. 2.

20. Harrison Gailey interview with CCA, Cornelia, Ga., July 10, 1982.

21. Cobb, *My Life in Baseball*, 222.

22. Cobb taped interview with Emerson; Bisher, "Visit with Ty Cobb," 53.

23. New York *Times*, Feb. 2, 1948, p. 36; *Life*, XXVII (Feb. 26, 1950), 44; *Sporting News*, Feb. 1, 1950, p. 16.

24. U. S. Congress. House of Representatives, *Hearings before the Subcommittee on the Study of Monopoly Power of the Committee of the Judiciary*, 82nd Cong., 1st sess. (1951), pt. 6: *Organized Baseball*, 4–23; New York *Times*, July 31, 1951, pp. 1, 24.

25. Ty Cobb, "They Don't Play Baseball Any More," *Life*, XXXII (March 17, 1952), 137, 141, 147.

26. Ibid., 137, 153.

27. New York *Times*, Nov. 28, 1953, p. 10; Bisher, "Visit with Ty Cobb," 5.

28. Cobb taped interview with Emerson.

29. Ty Cobb to Connie Mack, Feb. 22, 1955, Cobb Letters folder, Cobb Collection.

30. McCallum's book, done after interviews with Cobb, was published as *The Tiger Wore Spikes* (New York: A. S. Barnes, 1956). Schoor's book was *The Story of Ty Cobb* (New York: Messner, 1952).

31. John D. McCallum, *Ty Cobb* (New York: Praeger, 1975), 156.

32. New York *Times*, Sept. 8, 1955, p. 64.

33. *Sporting News*, April 3, 1957, pp. 3–4.

34. Cobb taped interview with Emerson; Bisher, "Visit with Ty Cobb," 52–54.

35. Ty Cobb to Jack McGrath, Nov. 7, 1957, Cobb Letters folder, Cobb Collection.

36. George H. Maines to R. D. Spraker, Aug. 5, 1961, ibid.

37. Ibid.

38. Ibid.

39. Al J. Stumpf to Sid Keener, Oct. 21, 1961, Cobb Letters folder, Cobb Collection.

40. *Sporting News*, Oct. 27, 1961, pp. 12, 14.

41. Al Stumpf, "Ty Cobb's Wild Ten-Month Fight To Live," *True*, XIV (Dec. 1961), 106. Italics in the original.

42. Maines to Spraker.

43. Ibid.; Stumpf, "Ty Cobb's Wild . . . Fight To Live," 112.

44. Ibid., 114.

45. Fred Haney, "My Most Unforgettable Character," *Reader's Digest*, LXXXIV (June 1964), 102.

46. Quoted in Fred Lieb, *Baseball as I Have Known It* (New York: Tempo/Grosset and Dunlap, 1977), 64–65.

47. Gailey interview.

48. Unidentified clipping, Cobb Personal folder, Cobb Collection.

EPILOGUE

1. Al J. Stumpf to Sid Keener, Oct. 21, 1961, Cobb Letters folder, Ty Cobb Collection, National Baseball Library, Cooperstown, N. Y.

2. Ty Cobb, with Al Stumpf, *My Life in Baseball: The True Record* (Garden City: Doubleday, 1961), 269–70.

3. Ibid., 273, 276.

4. Al Stumpf, "Ty Cobb's Wild Ten-Month Fight To Live," *True*, XIV (Dec. 1961), 38–41ff.

5. New York *Times*, Nov. 8, 1970, sec. V, p. 2; *The Ty Cobb Memorial Shrine* (n. p., n. pub., n.d.), brochure in Cobb Memorial Commission folder, Cobb Collection, NBL.

6. Houston *Post*, Aug. 18, 1982, p. 28.

7. Quoted in Stumpf, "Ty Cobb's Wild . . . Fight To Live," 115.

Bibliography

Archival resources:
Connie Mack Clippings. Historical Society of Pennsylvania, Philadelphia.
Ty Cobb Collection. National Baseball Library, Cooperstown, New York.
Sam Crawford Collection. National Baseball Library, Cooperstown, New York.
Detroit Baseball Club Letterbooks. 12 vols. (1900–1912), Ernie Harwell Collection, Detroit Public Library, Detroit.

Government Documents:
U. S. Congress. House of Representatives. *Hearings before the Subcommittee on the Study of Monopoly Power of the Committee of the Judiciary*, 82nd Cong., 1st sess. (1951), Pt. 6: *Organized Baseball.*
U. S. Congress. House of Representatives. *Organized Baseball: Report of the Subcommittee on the Study of Monopoly Power of the Committee of the Judiciary Pursuant to H. Res. 95.* 82nd Cong., 2nd sess. (1952).

Newspapers:
Atlanta *Constitution*, 1904–25.
Augusta *Chronicle*, 1904–05, 1908.
Cleveland *Gazette*, 1909.
Cleveland *Plain Dealer*, 1905–28.
Detroit *Free Press*, 1905–26.
Houston *Post*, 1982.
New York *Age*, 1908–10.
New York *Times*, 1905–75.
Philadelphia *Inquirer*, 1927–28.
St. Louis *Post-Dispatch*, 1905–28.
Sporting Life, 1904–17.
Sporting News, 1904–81.
Washington *Post*, 1905–28.

Personal Communications:
Interview, Susie Cunningham Bond, Royston, Georgia, July 7, 1982.
Interview, Margaret Wolfe Broome, Augusta, Georgia, July 9, 1982, and telephone conversation, February 4, 1983.

Telephone conversation, Roberta M. Brown (Mrs. Stewart Brown, Jr.), February 17, 1983.

Letter, Mary Frances Dunn Cobb to C.C.A., August 8, 1982.

Interview, Sandra Fitzpatrick, Shady Grove, Georgia, July 8, 1982.

Interview, Harrison Gailey, Cornelia, Georgia, July 10, 1983.

Telephone conversation, James Grundell (Doubleday and Company), February 4, 1983.

Interview, Collette Ginn Johnson, Royston, Georgia, July 7, 1982.

Books:

Allen, Lee. *The American League Story* (New York: Hill and Wang, 1962).

Asinof, Elliott. *Eight Men Out: The Black Sox and the 1919 World Series* (New York: Holt, Rinehart and Winston, 1963).

Barrow, Edward Grant. *My 50 Years in Baseball* (New York: Coward-McCann, 1951).

Beasley, Norman, and George W. Stark. *Made in Detroit* (New York: G. P. Putnam's Sons, 1957).

Bingay, Malcolm W. *Detroit Is My Own Home Town* (New York: Bobbs-Merrill, 1946).

Braathen, Sverre O. *Ty Cobb: The Idol of Fandom* (New York: Avondale Press, 1928).

Brown, Warren. *The Chicago Cubs* (New York: G. P. Putnam's Sons, 1946).

—————. *The Chicago White Sox* (New York: G. P. Putnam's Sons, 1952).

Cobb, Ty. *Busting 'Em and Other Stories* (New York: Edward J. Clode, Publishers, 1914).

Cobb, Ty, with Al Stumpf. *My Life in Baseball: The True Record* (Garden City: Doubleday, 1961).

Coffin, Tristram. *The Old Ball Game* (New York: Herder and Herder, 1972).

Creamer, Robert. *Babe: The Legend Comes to Life* (New York: Simon and Schuster, 1974).

Crepeau, Richard C. *Baseball: America's Diamond Mind, 1919–1941* (Orlando: University Presses of Florida, 1981).

Dunbar, William Frederick. *Michigan: A History of the Wolverine State* (Grand Rapids: William B. Eerdmans, 1970).

Durso, Joseph. *The Days of Mr. McGraw* (Englewood Cliffs: Prentice-Hall, 1969).

Einstein, Charles, ed. *The Baseball Reader* (New York: Lippincott and Crowell, 1980).

Farrell, James T. *My Baseball Diary* (New York: Vanguard Press, 1959).

Graham, Frank. *Lou Gehrig: A Quiet Hero* (New York: G. P. Putnam's Sons, 1942).

—————. *McGraw of the Giants* (New York: G. P. Putnam's Sons, 1944).

—————. *The New York Yankees: An Informal History* (New York: G. P. Putnam's Sons, 1943).

Honig, Donald, and Lawrence Ritter. *Baseball: When the Grass Was Real* (New York: Coward, McCann and Geohegan, 1975).

Kahn, James M. *The Umpire Story* (New York: G. P. Putnam's Sons, 1953).

Leitner, Irving. *Baseball: Diamond in the Rough* (New York: Abelard-Schuman, 1972).

Lewis, Franklin. *The Cleveland Indians* (New York: G. P. Putnam's Sons, 1949).

Lieb, Fred. *Baseball as I Have Known It* (New York: Tempo/Grosset and Dunlap, 1977).

—————. *The Boston Red Sox* (New York: G. P. Putnam's Sons, 1947).

—————. *The Detroit Tigers* (New York: G. P. Putnam's Sons, 1946).

Lowenfish, Lee, and Tony Lupien. *The Imperfect Diamond: The Story of Baseball's Reserve Clause and the Men Who Fought To Change It* (New York: Stein and Day, 1980).

McCallum, John D. *The Tiger Wore Spikes* (New York: A. S. Barnes Company, 1956).

—————. *Ty Cobb* (New York: Praeger, 1975).

MacFarlane, Paul, ed. *Daguerreotypes of Great Baseball Stars* (St. Louis: Sporting News Publishing Company, 1981).
Mack, Connie. *My 66 Years in the Big Leagues* (New York: Winston, 1950).
Murdock, Eugene C. *Ban Johnson: Czar of Baseball* (Westport: Greenwood Press, 1982).
Obojski, Robert. *Bush League: A History of Minor League Baseball* (New York: Macmillan, 1975).
Peterson, Robert. *Only the Ball Was White* (Englewood Cliffs: Prentice-Hall, 1970).
Reichler, Joseph L., ed. *The Baseball Encyclopedia* (4th ed., rev., New York: Macmillan, 1979).
Riess, Steven. *Touching Base: Professional Baseball and American Culture in the Progressive Era* (Westport: Greenwood Press, 1980).
Ritter, Lawrence. *The Glory of Their Times* (New York: Macmillan, 1966).
————, and Donald Honig. *The Image of Their Greatness* (New York: Crown Publishers, 1979).
Ruth, Claire Hodgson, and Bill Slocum. *The Babe and I* (Englewood Cliffs: Prentice-Hall, 1959).
Ruth, George Herman (Babe), and Bob Considine. *The Babe Ruth Story* (New York: E. P. Dutton and Company, 1948).
Schoor, Gene. *The Story of Ty Cobb* (New York: Julian Messner, 1952).
Seymour, Harold. *Baseball* (2 vols. to date, New York: Oxford University Press, 1960–).
Shannon, Bill, and George Kaminsky. *The Ballparks* (New York: Hawthorne Books, 1975).
Smelser, Marshall. *The Life That Ruth Built: A Biography* (New York: Quadrangle/New York Times Book Company, 1975).
Smith, Robert. *Babe Ruth's America* (New York: Thomas Y. Crowell Company, 1974).
Sobol, Ken. *Babe Ruth and the American Dream* (New York: Ballantine Books, 1974).
Spalding, Albert G. *America's National Game* (New York: American Sports, 1911).
Spink, J. G. Taylor. *Judge Landis and 25 Years of Baseball* (Reprint ed., St. Louis: Sporting News Publishing Company, 1974).
Treat, Roger L. *Walter Johnson* (New York: Julian Messner, 1948).
Voight, David Quentin. *American Baseball* (2 vols., Norman: University of Oklahoma Press, 1966–70).
————. *America Through Baseball* (Chicago: Nelson-Hall, 1976).
Wallop, Douglas. *Baseball: An Informal History* (New York: W. W. Norton and Company, 1969).
Wilson, Charles Reagan. *Baptized in Blood: The Religion of the Lost Cause, 1865–1920* (Athens: University of Georgia Press, 1980).
Woodward, C. Vann. *The Strange Career of Jim Crow* (Rev. ed., New York: Oxford University Press, 1964).

Articles:
"Base Stealing's Sensational Decline," *Literary Digest,* LXXIII (April 29, 1922), 41–42.
Bisher, Furman. "A Visit with Ty Cobb," *Saturday Evening Post,* CCXXX (June 14, 1958), 42–43f.
Blaisdell, Lowell. "The O'Connell-Dolan Scandal," *Baseball Research Journal* (1982), 44–48.
Bodayla, Stephen D. "Cochrane, Gordon Stanley ('Mickey')," in John A. Garraty, ed.,

Dictionary of American Biography: Supplement Seven: 1961–1965 (New York: Charles Scribner's Sons, 1981), 139–40.

Buranelli, Prosper. "Ty Cobb Talks about Baseball," *Detroit Free Press Magazine Section*, Sept. 25, 1921, pp. 1, 10.

Catton, Bruce. "The Great American Game," *American Heritage*, XII (April 1959), 16–25.

Chipp, Mil. "Inside-the-Park Home Runs," *Baseball Research Journal* (1980), 59–65.

Cobb, Ty. "Batting Out Better Boys," *Rotarian*, LXXI (July 1947), 10–12.

——————. "They Don't Play Baseball Any More," *Life*, XXXII (March 17, 1952), 136–38f.

——————. "Tricks That Won Me Ball Games," *Life*, XXXII (March 24, 1952), 63–64f.

"Cobb, Ty(rus Raymond)," *Current Biography: Who's News and Why, 1951* (New York: H. W. Wilson Company, 1952), 111–113.

Creamer, Richard D. "Average Batting Skill," *Baseball Research Journal* (1980), 167–172.

David, L. Robert. "Modern Base Stealing Proficiency," *Baseball Research Journal* (1981), 173–78.

Fullerton, Hugh. "Baseball: The Business and the Sport," *Review of Reviews*, LXIII (April 1921), 417–20.

——————. "Between Games: How the Ball Players of the Big Leagues Live and Act When off the Diamond," *American Magazine*, LXXII (July 1911), 321–31.

"Fortunes Made in Base Ball," *Literary Digest*, XLV (July 20, 1912), 119.

Fox, Edward Lyell. "Baseball's Heavy Artillery," *Illustrated Sunday Magazine*, April 6, 1913, pp. 6f.

Graff, Henry F. "Cobb, Tyrus Raymond ('Ty')," in John A. Garraty, ed., *Dictionary of American Biography: Supplement Seven: 1961–1965* (New York: Charles Scribner's Sons, 1981), 127–29.

Greenwell, Paul. "The 1922 Browns-Yankees Pennant Race," *Baseball Research Journal* (1979), 68–72.

"Guileful Magician," *Time*, LXXVIII (July 28, 1961), 62.

Haney, Fred. "My Most Unforgettable Character," *Reader's Digest*, LXXXIV (June 1964), 98–102.

Harwell, Ernie. "Cobb's Progress," *Reader's Digest*, LXIV (May 1954), 125.

Holland, David. "The One and Only Cobb," *American Mercury*, LXXXIII (Sept. 1956), 103–107.

Holway, John B. "Cuba's Black Diamond," *Baseball Research Journal*, X (1981), 139–145.

"How to Dominate the Diamond," *Newsweek*, LVIII (July 31, 1961), 54.

Kahn, E. J., Jr. "Profiles: The Story of Coca-Cola," *New Yorker*, XXXIV, XXXV (February 14–March 7, 1959), 37f., 39f., 35f., 39f.

Klem, William J., and William J. Slocum. "Umpire Bill Klem's Own Story," *Collier's*, CXXVII, CXXVIII (March 31–April 21, 1951), 30–31f., 30–31f., 30–31f., 30–31f.

Lardner, John. "Remember the Black Sox?" *Saturday Evening Post*, CCX (April 30, 1938), 14–15f.

——————. "That Was Baseball: The Crime of Shufflin' Phil Douglas," *New Yorker*, XXXII (May 12, 1956), 136f.

Lardner, Ring W. "Tyrus, the Greatest of 'Em All," *American Magazine*, LXXIX (June 1915), 18–23.

"Last Inning of an Angry Man," *Sports Illustrated*, XV (Aug. 21, 1961), 50–56.

Liebman, Ronald G. "Consecutive-Game Hitting Streaks," *Baseball Research Journal* (1979), 24–31.

Leventhal, B. F., and Joseph A. Sexton. "Two Glimpses of Ty Cobb," *American Magazine*, LXXVII (Feb. 1914), 78.

Lucas, John A. "The Unholy Experiment: Professional Baseball's Struggle against Pennsylvania's Sunday Blue Laws, 1926–1934," *Pennsylvania History*, XXXVIII (April 1971), 163–175.

Masin, Herman L. "Cobb vs. Ruth," *Scholastic*, LII (April 5, 1948), 34.

Mouch, Warren W. "Ty Cobb Steals Home," *Baseball Historical Review* (1981), 48–51.

"Picking an All-Time Emperor of the Diamond," *Literary Digest*, CX (Aug. 1, 1931), 30–31.

Reynolds, Quentin. "Ty Cobb's Dream Team," *Collier's*, CIII (June 17, 1939), 19f.

Rice, Grantland. "The Durable Cobb," *Collier's*, LXXVII (April 3, 1926), 24f.

——————. "Fighting Mad," *Collier's*, LXXXIX (May 21, 1932), 24f.

——————. "Four Aces," *Collier's*, LXXXIX (April 9, 1932), 10f.

——————. "Getting A Head," *Collier's*, LXXXV (May 31, 1930), 17f.

——————. "The Grand Old Batting Eye," *McClure's Magazine* XLV (June 19, 1915), 19f.

Rice, Grantland. "The Winner's Way," *Collier's*, LXXVIII (July 10, 1926), 10f.

Riess, Steven. "Professional Sunday Baseball: A Study in Social Reform, 1892–1934," *Maryland Historian*, IV (Fall 1973), 95–108.

Rothe, Emil H. "Was the Federal League a Major League?" *Baseball Research Journal* (1981), 1–10.

Rubinstein, William D. "Average Batting Skill through Major League History: A Commentary," *Baseball Research Journal* (1981), 166–72.

Sher, Jack. "Greatest Player of Them All," *Reader's Digest*, LVI (May 1950), 99–102.

Shoebotham, David. "Relative Batting Averages," *Baseball Research Journal* (1976), 37–41.

Smith, David. "Maury Wills and the Stolen Base," *Baseball Research Journal* (1980), 120–27.

"Spanking Baseball's Baby and Petting Its Paragon," *Literary Digest*, LXXXVI (Sept. 19, 1925), 58–67.

Stoddart, Dayton. "What Baseball Has Taught Ty Cobb," *Collier's*, LXXIV (July 19, 1924), 7f.

Stumpf, Al. "Ty Cobb's Wild Ten-Month Fight To Live," *True*, XIV (Dec. 1961), 38–41f; reprinted in Charles Einstein, ed., *The Baseball Reader* (New York: Lippincott and Crowell, 1980), 282–300.

Thompson, C. S. "$15,000,000 a Year for Baseball," *Collier's*, XLV (July 16, 1910), 17f.

Thompson, Lewis, and Charles Boswell. "Say It Ain't So, Joe," *American Heritage*, XI (June 1960), 24–27f.

"Ty Cobb," *Life*, XXVIII (Feb. 6, 1950), 41.

"Ty Cobb on the Batting Art," *Literary Digest*, XLVIII (June 27, 1914), 1558f.

"Ty Cobb Remains King of All Batsmen," *Literary Digest*, LXIV (Jan. 17, 1920), 118.

Voight, David Quentin. "Johnson, Walter Perry," in John A. Garraty and Edward T. James, eds., *Dictionary of American Biography: Supplement Four: 1946–1950* (New York: Charles Scribner's Sons, 1974), 435–37.

——————. "Ruth, George Herman (Babe)," ibid., 709–12.

Wallace, Francis. "College Men in the Big Leagues," *Scribner's Magazine*, LXXXII
     (Oct. 1927), 490–95.
"Why Ty Cobb Is Tired—and Retired," *Literary Digest*, XCI (Nov. 20, 1926), 54–62.
Woolf, S. J. "Tyrus Cobb, Then and Now," *New York Times Magazine*, (Sept. 19, 1948,
     p. 17.

Index